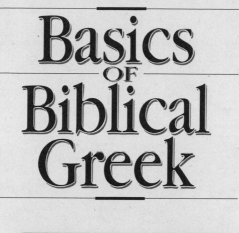

Basics OF Biblical Greek

GRAMMAR

Includes an interactive study aid CD-ROM

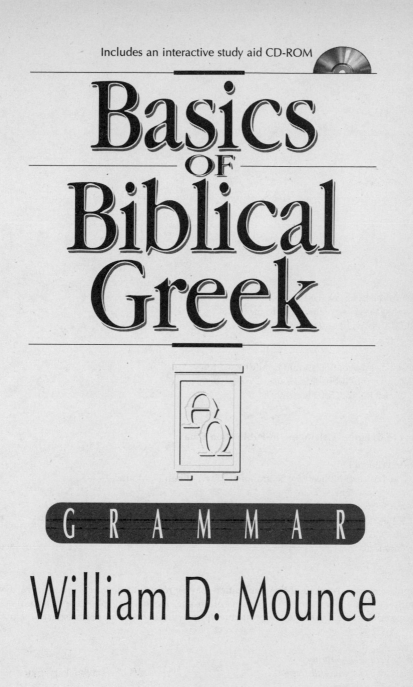

Basics
OF
Biblical
Greek

GRAMMAR

William D. Mounce

ZondervanPublishingHouse
Grand Rapids, Michigan

A Division of HarperCollinsPublishers

T 27036

Basics of Biblical Greek: Grammar
Copyright © 1993 by William D. Mounce
CD-ROM Copyright © 1999 by Teknia Software, Inc.

Requests for information should be addressed to:
  Zondervan Publishing House
  Grand Rapids, Michigan 49530

Library of Congress Cataloging-in-Publication Data

Mounce, William D.
    The basics of biblical Greek: grammar / by William D. Mounce
        p.   cm.
    ISBN 0-310-23211-2
    1. Greek language, Biblical–Grammar   2. Bible. N.T.–Language, style   1. Title
    PA817.M63   1993
    487'.4–dc20   93-19238
                                                                            CIP

Edited by Verlyn D. Verbrugge
Cover design by Dennis Hill Design
Typeset by Teknia Software, Inc.

Printed in the United States of America

08 07 06 05 04 03 02 01 00   / DC / 10 9 8 7 6 5

This edition is printed on acid-free paper.

This text is affectionately dedicated to my parents,

Bob and Jean Mounce.

It is my wish that a study of biblical Greek will help to produce
in you the same qualities that have always been exhibited in
both their lives: a love for their Lord and His Word; an informed
ministry based on His Word; a sense of urgency to share the
good news of Jesus Christ with those they meet.

ὁ νόμος τοῦ κυρίου ἄμωμος,
ἐπιστρέφων ψυχάς·

ἡ μαρτυρία κυρίου πιστή,
σοφίζουσα νήπια·

τὰ δικαιώματα κυρίου εὐθεῖα,
εὐφραίνοντα καρδίαν·

ἡ ἐντολὴ κυρίου τηλαυγής,
φωτίζουσα ὀφθαλμούς·

ὁ φόβος κυρίου ἁγνός,
διαμένων εἰς αἰῶνα αἰῶνος·

τὰ κρίματα κυρίου ἀληθινά,
δεδικαιωμένα ἐπὶ τὸ αὐτό.

καὶ ἔσονται εἰς εὐδοκίαν τὰ λόγια
τοῦ στόματός μου καὶ ἡ μελέτη τῆς
καρδίας μου ἐνώπιόν σου διὰ
παντός, κύριε βοηθέ μου καὶ
λυτρωτά μου.

ΨΑΛΜΟΙ ΙΗ 8-10,15

Table of Contents

Preface

A publisher once told me that the ratio of Greek grammars to Greek professors is ten to nine. It is reasonable to ask, therefore, why this one should be written. There are several good reasons. Most existing grammars fall into one of two camps, deductive or inductive. Deductive grammars emphasize charts and rote memorization, while inductive grammars get the student into the text as soon as possible and try to imitate the natural learning process. Both methods have advantages and disadvantages. The deductive method helps the student to organize the material better, but is totally unlike the process by which we learn languages naturally. The inductive method suffers from a lack of structure that for many is confusing. Our method attempts to teach Greek using the best of both approaches. It is deductive in how it initially teaches the material, but inductive in how it fine tunes the learning process. (See the following "Rationale Statement" for more details.)

Most grammars approach learning Greek primarily as an academic discipline; we make every effort to view learning Greek as a tool for ministry. You are learning biblical Greek so you can better understand the word of God and share that understanding with those around you. If some aspect of language study does not serve this purpose, it is ignored.

There are many practical ways in which teaching methodologies can be improved. For example, anything that encourages students to continue learning should be included. This may not be the normal way textbooks are written, but our purpose is not to write another normal textbook. It is to teach you the language of the New Testament. Learning language can be fun and meaningful.

Probably the greatest obstacle to learning, and continuing to use, biblical Greek is the problem of rote memorization. So many would-be exegetes lose their ability to use language study because they are not able to work in the language on a continuing basis. But there is an interesting observation here. When I was first learning Greek, I used to ask my father what a certain form meant. He would tell me and when I asked how he knew he would respond, "I'm not sure, but that's what it is." What was frustrating for me then is true of me now. How many people who have worked in Greek for years are able to recite obscure paradigms, or perhaps all the tense forms of the sixty main verbs? Very few I suspect. Rather, we have learned what indicators to look for when we parse. Wouldn't it be nice if all students of the language could get to this point of understanding the forms of the language without going through the excruciating process of rote memory? This is the primary distinctive of this textbook. Reduce the nonessentials to a minimum so the language can be learned and retained as easily as possible, so that the Word of God can be preached in all its power and conviction.

The writing style of the text is somewhat different from what you might expect. It is not overly concerned with brevity. Rather, we discuss the concepts in some depth and in a "friendly" tone. The goal is to help students enjoy the text and come to class knowing the information. While brevity has its advantages, we felt that it hindered the self-motivated student who wants to learn outside the classroom. For teachers who prefer a more succinct style, we have included overview and summary sections, and have placed some instruction in the footnotes and the *Advanced Information* sections. The section numbers also make it easy for teachers to remove information that they feel is unnecessary for their students. For example: "Don't read §13.4-5 and §13.7."

It is possible to ignore all the footnotes in this text, except for the footnotes to the vocabulary, and still learn Koine Greek. The information in the footnotes is interesting tidbits for both the teacher and the exceptional student. They will most likely confuse the marginal student. However, the footnotes to the vocabulary, and the footnotes in the workbook, are very important and should be read carefully.

Two typographical notes. When we refer to one Greek letter, we call it by its Greek name (e.g., ο is referred to as "omicron"). This is to avoid confusion with, e.g., citing "ο" and not being clear whether this is an English "o" or a Greek omicron. The symbol ‣ means that the preceding form develops into the following (e.g., the root *αγαπα ‣ ἀγαπάω). On the other hand, ‹ means that the preceding form develops from the following.

There are many people I wish to thank, and although the list is long the people mentioned in it are well deserving. Without my students' constant questioning and their unfailing patience with all my experiments in teaching methods, this grammar could never have been written. While running the risk of forgetting some names, I would like to thank especially Brad Rigney, Ian and Kathy Lopez, Mike De Vries, Bob Ramsey, Jenny (Davis) Riley, Handjarawatano, Dan Newman, Tim Pack, Jason Zahariades, Tim and Jennifer Brown, Lynnette Whitworth, Bob Shisler, Jamie Donahue, Tom Bedford, Carol Romeo, Darren Penny, Annie Carlson, Jonathan Finley, Debbie Fischer, David Keehn, Mike Lee, Neil Price, Todd Radarmel, Matt Valencia, Bill Nishioka, Hiko Ohara, Andy Adams, Steve Armendariz, Flynn Ayers, Steven Braun, Todd Faulkner, Leslieanne French, Clint Gertenrich, Suzanne King, Todd Reid, David Riggs, Rick Roberts, Sean Lumsden, Eric Simpson, Bryant Swenson, Greg Walker, Eric Smith, Steve Jung, Mark Molenar, Jacob Hill, Kristine Harvey, David Sexauer, Robert Dixon, Nemma Estrada, Lemel Firestone, Reed Jaboro, Naomi Johnston, Becki Lawrence, Sue Morzov, Gerald Priest, Kim Redfearn, Dave Sadler, Laci Sarmiento, Chori Seraiah, Jim Shapiro, Scott Simmerok, Jason Smith, Miles Van Pelt, Dan Wolley, Paul Ward, Eric Weaver, Walter Twiddy, Richard Kempton, Randy Coblentz, and the unnamed student who failed the class twice until I totally separated the nouns (chapters 1-14) from the verbs (chapters 15-35), and then received a "B."

I want to thank those professors who were willing to try out the grammar in its earlier stages, and for those upon whom I have relied heavily for help: Robert H. Mounce, William S. LaSor, Daniel B. Wallace, Thomas Schreiner, Jon Hunt, Nancy Vyhmeister, Keith Reeves, Ron Rushing, George Gunn, Chip Hard, Verlyn Verbrugge, and Craig Keener. A very special thank you must go to Walter W.

Wessel, who used the text beginning with its earliest form and who was constant and loving in his corrections, criticisms, and praise. When I thought the text was basically done, my excellent editor, Verlyn Verbrugge, continued to fine-tune my work, not just by finding typos and grammatical errors, but by adding substantially to the content and flow of the chapters. (As always, any errors are my fault, and I would appreciate notification of any errors or suggestions. Correspondence may be sent to me at the addresses on p. xvii.) And if it were not for the diligent efforts of Ed van der Maas and Jack Kragt, this grammar may never have been published and marketed as well as it was. I must also mention my marvelous Greek teachers who first planted the seed of love for this language and nurtured it to growth: E. Margaret Howe, Walter W. Wessel, Robert H. Mounce, William Sanford LaSor, George E. Ladd.

Much of the work, especially in the exercises, could not have been done without the aid of two computer programs, *Gramcord*, built by Paul Miller of the *Gramcord Institute*, and *acCordance* by Roy Brown. *The Creative Educational Project Grant* from Azusa Pacific University funded the purchase of a computer and the help of Brad Rigney for the original writing of the text for use in my classes.

A special thank you to my wife Robin, for her unfailing patience and encouragement through the past ten years, and for believing in the goals we both set for this grammar. Thanks also to my friends at Garland Avenue Alliance Church who have so graciously aided me in my research, Richard Porter, Steve Yoell, Scotte Meredith, and my good friends Tyler, Kiersten, Hayden, Ryan, Regan, Reid, Rance, Nikki, Layton, Trent, Derek, Sean, Chris, Julia, Grace, Jonathan, David, Julie, and Lindsay.

And finally I wish to thank the scholars who in spite of crowded schedules agreed to write the exegetical insights for each chapter. As you see how a knowledge of the biblical languages has aided them in their studies, I trust you will be encouraged in your own pursuit of learning and using Greek. However, just because it is written does not make it true. A warning to the wise.

Thank you.

William D. Mounce

Preface to Subsequent Printings

Thank you to those who have contacted me with corrections. There were substantial corrections and minor changes made for the sixth and seventh printings. There will be no more major changes until the second edition. However, in the June 1999 printing Zondervan changed the text's ISBN and included a CD-ROM. See pages 457-59 of this text for instructions.

Rationale Statement

With so many introductory Greek grammars on the market, it seems appropriate to begin with a rationale for yet another. *The Basics of Biblical Greek* is not just new to be different, but approaches the instruction of the language from a totally different perspective that we hope makes learning Greek as easy as possible, as rewarding as possible, and, yes, even enjoyable.

The following explains our approach, why it is different, and why we think it is better.

Goals

1. To approach learning Greek, not as an intellectual exercise, but as a tool for ministry.

2. To provide constant encouragement for the students, showing them not only what they should learn but why.

3. To teach only what is necessary at the moment, deferring the more complicated concepts until later.

4. To utilize current advances in linguistics, not for the purpose of teaching linguistics but to make learning Greek easier.

1. A tool for ministry

Biblical Greek should not be taught simply for the sake of learning Greek. Although there is nothing necessarily wrong with that approach, it is inappropriate for a great number of students in colleges and seminaries. Too often they are taught Greek and told that eventually they will see why it is important to know the material. In our opinion, they should be shown, in the process of learning, why they are learning Greek and why a working knowledge of Greek is essential for their ministry.

2. Encouragement

Most students come to Greek with varying degrees of apprehension. Their enthusiasm often wears down as the semester progresses. This text, therefore, has built into it different ways of encouraging them.

a. All exercises are from the Bible. From day one, the students are translating the biblical text. If a passage has a word that is taught in a later chapter, it is translated. This gives students the satisfaction of actually having translated a portion of the Bible. Whenever the Greek in the exercises clarifies an exegetical or theological point, we have also tried to point it out.

The disadvantage of using the biblical text is that the student may already know the verse in English. But with a little discipline on the student's part, this disadvantage is far outweighed by the advantages.

b.   After every vocabulary word, its frequency is given. It is one thing to learn that καί means "and," but to see that it occurs 9,164 times in the New Testament will motivate students to memorize it.

c.   There are some 5,437 different words in the New Testament that occur a total of 138,162 times. Therefore, after every section of vocabulary the students will be told what percentage of the total word count they now know. By the eighth chapter the student will know more than one out of every two word occurrences.

3. Teaching only what is necessary

Students only learn what is necessary in order to begin reading the text. After they have mastered the basics and have gained some experience in reading, they are taught more of the details. In order to encourage the better student and make the text more usable for more teachers, this additional detailed material is put in footnotes or in a section at the end of the chapter called "Advanced Information."

For example, notes on accents are included in the "Advanced Information" so it is up to the student or teacher as to whether or not they should be learned. The adverbial participle provides another example. Students are taught to use the "-ing" form of the verb, prefaced by the temporal adverbs "while" for the present participle and "after" for the aorist. In the "Advanced Information" section, advanced students read that they may include a personal pronoun identifying the doer of the participle, and that the time of the finite verb used to translate the participle must be relative to the main verb.

4. Modern linguistics

Modern studies in linguistics have much to offer language learning. The beginning student should not learn linguistics for its own sake, but the basic principles can be taught and applied generally.

For example, the "Square of Stops" is mastered since it explains many of the morphological changes of the verb. Also, a basic set of case endings are learned, and then students are shown how they are modified, only so slightly, in the different declensions. Once it is seen that the same basic endings are used in all three declensions, memorization is greatly simplified. In the lexicon, all words are keyed to the author's *The Morphology of Biblical Greek* (see bibliography at the end of this discussion). As the students' knowledge and interest progresses, they will be able to pursue in-depth morphological work in this text.

5. Innovative

This text seeks to approach the joyful task of learning Greek from new and innovative angles, not merely for the sake of newness but from the desire to make learning Greek as rewarding as possible. The easier it is to learn the language, the more the language will be used by pastors and others involved in ministry.

a. All definitions are derived from Prof. Bruce Metzger's *Lexical Aids for Students of New Testament Greek* and Warren Trenchard's *The Student's Complete Guide to the Greek New Testament*. This way, when students move into second year Greek and use one of these two excellent study aids for increasing vocabulary, they will not have to relearn the definitions.

b. A lexicon is provided which lists all words occurring ten times or more with the principal parts for all simple verbs. (Any word in the exercises that occurs less than fifty times will be identified in the exercise itself.) This will be needed for the review exercises. There also is a full set of noun and verbal charts.

c. Instead of switching students back and forth between nouns and verbs, this text teaches nouns first and then verbs. The continuous occurrence of nouns in the exercises for verbs helps students remember what they have learned. Because verbs are so important, some have questioned the wisdom of not starting them until chapter 15. Here are our reasons.

- It makes learning both nouns and verbs much easier because the student does not have to switch back and forth.

- Nouns are learned so quickly that you get to chapter 15 much sooner than you might expect.

- We are committed to using biblical verses as illustrations. Even if we were to introduce just the present active indicative early, this would limit the number of verses we could use because we would not want to use verses with other verbal forms.

- If you listen to a child learn to speak, you can see that it is more natural to learn nouns first and later move on to the verbal system.

d. At the beginning of every chapter is an exegetical insight based on a biblical text. These are written by New Testament scholars and demonstrate the significance of the grammar in the chapter.

e. Following the insight is an in-depth discussion of English grammar. In the summary of Greek grammar that follows, as many comparisons as possible are made between English and Greek, with heavy emphasis on the similarities of the two languages.

f. Greek grammar is initially taught with English illustrations. When illustrations for new grammatical constructions are given in Greek, students spend much of their concentration on identifying the Greek forms, and often do not fully understand the grammar itself. In this text the grammar is made explicit in English, and only when it is grasped is it illustrated in Greek. For example,

> An adjectival participle agrees with the noun it modifies
> in case, number, and gender. For example, "The fat man,

sitting by the window, is my Greek professor." If this sentence were in Greek, "fat" would be in the same case, number, and gender as the noun "man" because it is an adjective.

Since a participle is a "verbal adjective," it too must agree with the noun it modifies. In this sentence, "sitting" is a participle and would be in the same case, number, and gender as the noun "man."

g. There is a Teacher's Packet available from Teknia's web site. (If you do not have access to the web and are *teaching in an accredited school*, you can receive the Teacher's Packet directly from Zondervan). The Teacher's Packet contains the following, and more.

- Answers for the Workbook (not including the review exercises).

- Sample quizzes for each chapter (no answers).

- Software.

FlashWorks™ is a flash card program that tags each vocabulary word as to its chapter, category (noun, verb, adjective, preposition, other), and its degree of difficulty (1-5). Students can, for example, call up all the verbs in chapters 6-10 with a personal degree of difficulty 3 through 4. The words are then randomly mixed, and the fun begins. As they learn the words, they can change the difficulty rating to a lower number, or *FlashWorks* can change it for them as they get the word right. *FlashWorks* has databases for Hebrew, Greek, French, German, and Spanish.

ParseWorks™ is an interactive parsing program. It includes all the parsing exercises in the Workbook, and we are enlarging it to include unlimited parsing based on the actual biblical text and other databases. It functions as a tutor, watching the student's work and giving specific help when needed.

Teknia Language Tools™ combines *FlashWorks* and *ParseWorks* and will over time add many additional features for helping you learn and use Greek. Watch Teknia's web site for progress.

h. *BBG* now includes a CD-ROM packed full of goodies, including *Teknia Language Tools* for Windows and *Learning the Basics of Biblical Greek* (Macintosh and Windows), which will make vocabulary acquisition much easier. See pages 457-59 of this text for instructions.

All software is being updated. Please watch Teknia's web site for information (see next page).

i. *Audio tapes*. Are you learning Greek on your own? Do your students need a little extra help? Ever wonder how the author teaches his own textbook? Now you can know! Teknia is making an entire Greek course by Bill Mounce available on audio tape (see next page).

j.   Internet. Every teacher has at least a few great ideas on how to teach Greek; but because there is no medium for exchange, the rest of us rarely hear the ideas. We are using the Teknia's web site on the Internet as a repository of ideas and tools. I encourage you to share your ideas there.

The Teacher's Packet, the software, and other helps are available on the web at,

www.teknia.com

See there for the latest versions. You may contact the author through email at lbbg@teknia.com.

You can also write to Zondervan, Academic Editorial, 5300 Patterson Ave., Grand Rapids, Michigan 49530. You can visit Zondervan's web site at,

www.zondervan.com/academic

Greek Class on Audio Tape

If you are interested in the audio tape series by Bill Mounce, please see Teknia's web site for details. One of the lectures is on line so you can check it out.

www.teknia.com

If you do not have access to the web, you may contact Teknia at,

Teknia
PO Box 337
Wenham, MA 01984

Abbreviations

acCordance Roy Brown, *The Gramcord Institute.*

BAGD *A Greek-English Lexicon of the New Testament and Other Early Christian Literature,* eds. W. Bauer, W.F. Arndt, F.W. Gingrich, F.E. Danker, second edition (University of Chicago Press, 1979).

Bl-D *A Greek Grammar of the New Testament and Other Early Christian Literature,* eds. F. Blass, A. Debrunner, trans. R. Funk (University of Chicago Press, 1961).

EDNT *Exegetical Dictionary of the New Testament,* eds. Horst Balz, Gerhard Schneider (Eerdmans, 1990 - 93).

Fanning *Verbal Aspect in New Testament Greek,* Buist M. Fanning (Clarendon Press, 1990).

Gramcord Paul Miller, *The Gramcord Institute.*

Klein *A Comprehensive Etymological Dictionary of the English Language,* Ernest Klein (Elsevier Publishing Co., NY, 1971), from which I drew heavily for cognates and definitions in the vocabulary sections.

LaSor *Handbook of New Testament Greek,* William Sanford LaSor (Eerdmans, 1973).

Machen *New Testament Greek for Beginners* (Macmillan, 1951).

MBG *The Morphology of Biblical Greek,* William D. Mounce (Zondervan, 1994).

Metzger *Lexical Aids for Students of New Testament Greek,* Bruce M. Metzger (Theological Book Agency, 1973).

Smyth *Greek Grammar,* Herbert Weir Smyth (Harvard University Press, 1980).

Wallace *Greek Grammar Beyond the Basics. An Exegetical Syntax of the New Testament,* Daniel B. Wallace (Zondervan, 1995).

Wenham *The Elements of New Testament Greek,* J.W. Wenham (Cambridge University Press, 1965).

Chapter 1

The Greek Language

The Greek language has a long and rich history stretching all the way from the thirteenth century B.C. to the present. The earliest form of the language is called "Linear B" (13th century B.C.). The form of Greek used by writers from Homer (8th century B.C.) through Plato (4th century B.C.) is called "Classical Greek." It was a marvelous form of the language, capable of exact expression and subtle nuances. Its alphabet was derived from the Phoenician's as was Hebrew's. Classical Greek existed in three major families of dialects: Doric, Aeolic, and Ionic (of which Attic was a branch).

Athens was conquered in the fourth century B.C. by King Philip of Macedonia. Alexander the Great, Philip's son, who was tutored by the Greek philosopher Aristotle, set out to conquer the world and spread Greek culture and language. Because Alexander spoke Attic Greek, it was this dialect that was spread. It was also the dialect spoken by the famous Athenian writers. This was the beginning of the Hellenistic Age.

As the Greek language spread across the world and met other languages, it was altered (which is true of any language). The dialects also interacted with each other. Eventually this adaptation resulted in what today we call Koine Greek. "Koine" (κοινή) means "common" and describes the common, everyday form of the language, used by everyday people. It was not considered a polished literary form of the language, and in fact some writers of this era purposefully imitated the older style of Greek (which is like someone today writing in King James English). Koine was a simplified form of classical Greek and unfortunately many of the subtleties of classical Greek were lost. For example, in classical Greek ἄλλος meant "other" of the same kind while ἕτερος meant "other" of a different kind. If you had an apple and you asked for ἄλλος, you would receive another apple. But if you asked for ἕτερος, you would be given perhaps an orange. Some of these subtleties come through in Scripture but not often. It is this common, Koine Greek that is used in the Septuagint, the New Testament, and the writings of the Apostolic Fathers.

For a long time Koine Greek confused many scholars. It was significantly different from Classical Greek. Some hypothesized that it was a combination of Greek, Hebrew, and Aramaic. Others attempted to explain it as a "Holy Ghost language," meaning that God created a special language just for the Bible. But discoveries of Egyptian papyri in the last 100 years have shown that this language was the language of the everyday people used in the writings of wills, private letters, receipts, shopping lists, etc.

There are two lessons we can learn from this. As Paul says, "In the fullness of time God sent his son" (Gal 4:4), and part of that fullness was a universal language. No matter where Paul traveled he could be understood.

But there is another lesson here that is perhaps a little closer to the pastor's heart. God used the common language to communicate the Gospel. The gospel does not belong to the erudite alone; it belongs to all people. It now becomes our task to learn this marvelous language to help us make the grace of God known to all people.

Chapter 2

Learning Greek

Before we start learning the language, we need to talk about how to learn. If you have developed any bad study habits they are going to be magnified as you set out to learn Greek. Let's talk about a few of the essentials.

Goal

The main purpose of writing this book is to help you to understand better and to communicate more clearly the word of God. This must be kept in mind at all times. It should motivate you, encourage you when you are frustrated, and give you perspective when you think you are going to crack. Remember the goal: a clearer, more exact, and more persuasive presentation of God's saving message.

But is knowing Greek essential in reaching this goal? If you are not fully convinced that this is so, you will have difficulty reaching the goal. In other words, is the language worth the effort? We have been blessed with a wealth of good and varied translations. A careful and critical use of these goes a long way in helping the preacher understand the word of God better. It would be unfair to claim that the only way to be a good preacher is to know Greek.

However, allow me a little parable and the point will become clear. You need to overhaul your car engine. What tools will you select? I would surmise that with a screw driver, hammer, a pair of pliers, and perhaps a crow bar, you could make some progress. But look at the chances you are taking. Without a socket wrench you could ruin many of the bolts. Without a torque wrench you cannot get the head seated properly. The point is, without the proper tools you run the risk of doing a minimal job, and perhaps actually hurting the engine.

The same is true with preaching, teaching, preparing personal Bible studies, and learning Greek. Without the proper tools you are limited in your ability to deal with the text. When Jesus says of communion, "Drink ye all of it" (Matt 26:27; KJV), what does the "all" refer to? All the drink, or all the people?[1] When Paul writes to the Ephesians that it is "by grace you have been saved through faith, and this is not of yourselves; it is a gift from God" (Eph 2:8), what does "it" refer to?[2] When Paul asks, "Do all speak in tongues" (1 Cor 12:30), is he implying that

---

[1]   The people.

[2]   The whole process of salvation, which includes our faith.

the answer is "Yes"?[3]

But there is more. Almost all the best commentaries and biblical studies require a knowledge of Greek. Without it, you will not have access to the lifelong labors of scholars who should be heard. I have seen a rather interesting pattern develop. The only people I have heard say that Greek is not important are those who do not themselves know Greek. Strange. Can you imagine someone who knows nothing about tennis say that it is unnecessary ever to take tennis lessons? Sounds ridiculous, doesn't it?

The point of all this is to emphasize that you must think through why you want to learn Greek, and then you must keep your goal in sight at all times. John Wesley, perhaps one of the most effective ministers ever to mount a horse, is said to have been able to quote Scripture in Greek better than in English. How far do you want your ministry to go? The tools you collect, Greek being one of them, will to a significant degree determine your success from a human point of view. Set your goals high and keep them in sight.

Memorization

In order to learn Greek (or any language, as far as that goes) memorization is vital. For Greek you will have to memorize vocabulary words, endings, and various other things. In Greek the only way to determine, for example, whether a noun is singular or plural, or if a word is the subject or object of the verb, is by the ending of the word. So if you have not memorized the endings, you will be in big trouble.

Along with grammar is the importance of knowing vocabulary. There is very little joy in translating if you have to look up every other word in the lexicon. Rote memory will be more difficult for some than others, so here are some suggestions.

1. Make flash cards for vocabulary words and word endings. You can put them in your pocket and take them anywhere. Use them while waiting in lines, during work breaks, before classes, etc. They will become your life saver. 3 x 5 index cards cut in thirds are a nice size.

2. Use the computer flash card system that is available for this text. You can tell it which words you have difficulty in remembering, and it can quiz you just on those.

3. When memorizing words use mnemonic devices. For example, the Greek word for "face" is transliterated as "prosopon," so it could be remembered by the phrase, "pour soap on my face." It seems that the sillier these devices are the better, so don't be ashamed.

4. You must pronounce Greek consistently and write it neatly. If your

---

[3]   He is stating that the answer is "No."

pronunciation varies it is difficult to remember the words.

5. Say the words and endings out loud. The more senses involved in the learning process the better. So pronounce the words, listen to them, and write them out so you can see them.

Exercises

The greatest motivation for learning Greek comes during the homework assignments. Because the exercises are all drawn from the New Testament, you are constantly reminded why you are learning the language. We have pointed out in the footnotes whenever a knowledge of the Greek helps you exegetically or devotionally to better understand the verse's meaning.

We will also be introducing you to intermediate grammar through the footnotes to the exercises. Whereas the footnotes in the grammar are not essential, they are very important in the exercises.

Be sure to treat the exercises as tests. Learn the chapter, do as many of the exercises as you can, work back through the chapter, and then do the exercises again. The more you treat the exercises as a test, the better you will learn the material and the better you will do on actual tests.

Time and Consistency

Very few people can "pick up" a language. For most of us it takes time, lots of it. Plan for that; remind yourself what you are trying to do, and spend the necessary time. But along with the amount of time is the matter of consistency. You cannot cram for tests; Greek will not stick, and in the long run you will forget it. Spend time every day; getting to know the language of the New Testament deserves at least that. Remember, "Those who cram, perish."

Partners

Few people can learn a language on their own. For sake of illustration, let me quote the story of John Brown as told by the great Greek grammarian A.T. Robertson.

> At the age of sixteen John Brown, of Haddington, startled a bookseller by asking for a copy of the Greek Testament. He was barefooted and clad in ragged homespun clothes. He was a shepherd boy from the hills of Scotland. "What would *you* do with that book?" a professor scornfully asked. "I'll try to read it," the lad replied, and proceeded to read off a passage in the Gospel of John. He went off in triumph with the coveted prize, but the story spread that he was a wizard and had learned Greek by the black art. He was actually arraigned for witchcraft, but in

1746 the elders and deacons at Abernethy gave him a vote of acquittal, although the minister would not sign it. His letter of defence, Sir W. Robertson Nicoll says (*The British Weekly*, Oct. 3, 1918), "deserves to be reckoned among the memorable letters of the world." John Brown became a divinity student and finally professor of divinity. In the chapel at Mansfield College, Oxford, Brown's figure ranks with those of Doddridge, Fry, Chalmers, Vinet, Schleiermacher. He had taught himself Greek while herding his sheep, and he did it without a grammar. Surely young John Brown of Haddington should forever put to shame those theological students and busy pastors who neglect the Greek Testament, though teacher, grammar, lexicon are at their disposal.[4]

This story points out how unusual it is for someone to learn Greek without the communal help of the class. Find a partner, someone who will test and quiz you, encourage and support you, and vice versa.

Discipline

Discipline is the bottom line. There are no magical solutions to learning Greek. It is achievable if you want it. It comes at a cost, but the rewards are tremendous. So get ready for the journey of your life as we travel through the pages of the New Testament. Enjoy the excitement of discovery and await the day when it will all bloom into fruition.

---

[4]   *A Grammar of the Greek New Testament in the Light of Historical Research* (Broadman, 1934) 4th edition, xix.

Chapter 3

The Alphabet and Pronunciation

Overview

We start each chapter with an overview of what you will be learning. This will give you a feel for what is to come, and should also be an encouragement when you see that there is not too much information in each chapter.

In this chapter we will learn:

- to write and pronounce the alphabet (consonants, vowels, diphthongs);
- that "breathing marks" are on every word beginning with a vowel.

The Greek Alphabet

3.1 Footnotes in this volume are not necessary to remember (although they are often interesting), except in the vocabulary section where they are significant. (The footnotes in the exercises, volume 2, contain essential information and must be studied.)

3.2 The Greek alphabet has twenty-four letters.[1] At first it is only important to learn the English name, small letters, and pronunciation. The transliterations[2] will help. In our texts today, capitals are used only for proper names, the first word in a quotation, and the first word in the paragraph.[3] There is some disagreement as to the correct pronunciation of a few of the letters; these are marked in the footnotes. We have chosen the

---

[1] There were several more, but they dropped out of use before the classical period. In some cases their influence can still be felt, especially in verbs.

[2] A transliteration is the equivalent of a letter in another language. For example, the Greek "beta" (β) is transliterated with the English "b." This does not mean that a similar combination of letters in one language has the same meaning as the same combination in another. κατ does not mean "cat." But the Greek "β" and the English "b" have the same sounds and often similar functions, and therefore it is said that the English "b" is the transliteration of the Greek "beta."

[3] Originally the Bible was written in all capital letters with no punctuation, accent marks, or spaces between the words. For example, John 1:1 began, ΕΝΑΡΧΗΗΝΟ ΛΟΓΟΣ. Capital letters, or "majuscules," were used until the later centuries A.D. when cursive script was adopted. Cursive script is like our handwriting where the letters are joined together. In Greek texts today, John 1:1 begins, Ἐν ἀρχῇ ἦν ὁ λόγος.

standard pronunciations that will help you learn the language the easiest.

Notice the many similarities among the Greek and English letters, not
only in shape and sound but also in their respective order in the alphabet. The Greek alphabet can be broken down into sections. It will parallel
the English for a while, differ, and then begin to parallel again. Try to
find these natural divisions.

The name of a consonant is formed with the help of a vowel, but the
sound of the consonant does not include that vowel. For example, μ is
the letter "mu," but when mu appears in the word, there is no "u"
sound.

The following chart shows the name of the letter (in English and Greek),
the English transliteration, the letter written as a capital and as a small
letter, and its pronunciation.

Alpha	ἄλφα	a	A	α	a as in f<u>a</u>ther
Beta	βῆτα	b	B	β	b as in <u>B</u>ible
Gamma	γάμμα	g	Γ	γ	g as in gone
Delta	δέλτα	d	Δ	δ	d as in <u>d</u>og
Epsilon	ἒ ψιλόν	e	E	ε	e as in m<u>e</u>t
Zeta	ζῆτα	z	Z	ζ	z as in da<u>z</u>e[4]
Eta	ῆτα	ē	H	η	e as in ob<u>e</u>y
Theta	θῆτα	th	Θ	θ	th as in <u>th</u>ing
Iota	ἰῶτα	i	I	ι	i as in <u>i</u>ntrigue[5]
Kappa	κάππα	k	K	κ	k as in <u>k</u>itchen
Lambda	λάμβδα	l	Λ	λ	l as in <u>l</u>aw
Mu	μῦ	m	M	μ	m as in <u>m</u>other
Nu	νῦ	n	N	ν	n as in <u>n</u>ew
Xsi (xi)	ξῖ	xs	Ξ	ξ	x as in a<u>x</u>iom[6]
Omicron	ὂ μικρόν	o	O	o	o as in n<u>o</u>t[7]
Pi	πῖ	p	Π	π	p as in <u>p</u>each
Rho	ῥῶ	r	P	ρ	r as in <u>r</u>od[8]

---

[4] Some pronounce the zeta as the "dz" combination. This helps to differentiate it from
the sigma. Wenham (19) says that it is pronounced "dz" unless it is the first letter in
the word and then is pronounced "z."

[5] The iota can be either long ("intr<u>i</u>gue") or short ("<u>i</u>ntrigue"). Listen to how your
teacher pronounces the words and you will pick up the differences.

[6] Some prefer a simple "x" sound for the xsi and not the double "xs" as in the word
"axiom." We feel that the "xs" combination helps to differentiate xsi from chi. However, your teacher may prefer that you spell the letter "xi" and not "xsi."

Sigma	σίγμα	s	Σ	σ/ς	s as in <u>s</u>tudy
Tau	ταῦ	t	T	τ	t as in <u>t</u>alk
Upsilon	ῦ ψιλόν	u/y	Y	υ	u as the German <u>ü</u>[9]
Phi	φῖ	ph	Φ	φ	ph as in <u>ph</u>one
Chi	χῖ	ch	X	χ	ch as in lo<u>ch</u>[10]
Psi	ψῖ	ps	Ψ	ψ	ps as in li<u>ps</u>
Omega	ὦ μέγα	ō	Ω	ω	o as in t<u>o</u>ne

3.3   Writing the letters

1. Notice how α β δ ε ι κ ο ς τ and υ look like their English counterparts.

2. In Greek there are five letters that are transliterated by two letters. θ is th; ξ is xs; φ is ph; χ is ch; ψ is ps. These are called **double consonants**.

3. It is important that you do not confuse the η (eta) with the English "n," the ν (nu) with the "v," the ρ (rho) with the "p," the χ (chi) with the "x," or the ω (omega) with the "w."

4. There are two sigmas in Greek. ς occurs only at the end of the word and σ occurs elsewhere: ἀπόστολος.

5. You will learn the alphabet best by pronouncing the letters out loud as you write them, over and over.

3.4   Pronouncing the letters

1. In pronouncing the Greek letters, use the first sound of the name of the letter. Alpha is an "a" sound (there is no "pha" sound); lambda is an "l" sound (there is no "ambda" sound).

2. The following letters sound just like their English counterparts: α β γ δ ε ι κ λ μ ν ο π ρ σ/ς τ.

3. The vowels in Greek are α, ε, η, ι, ο, υ, ω.

4. Gamma (γ) usually has a hard "g" sound, as in "get." However, when it is immediately followed by γ, κ, χ, or ξ, it is pronounced as a "n."

   For example, the word ἄγγελος is pronounced "angelos," from

---

[7]   The omicron is pronounced by some with a long "o" sound as in the word "obey." It is pronounced by others with a short "o" sound as in the word "lot." There is a question as to what the actual pronunciation of this letter was in the Koine period. In modern Greek it is long as in omega. We have chosen to use a short pronunciation in order to differentiate the omicron from the omega.

[8]   Some prefer the "rh" sound.

[9]   Other suggestions are the u in "universe" and the oo in "book."

[10]   Pronounced with a decided Scottish accent.

which we get our word "angel." The gamma pronounced like a "n" is called a **gamma nasal**.[11]

5. Alpha and iota can be either long or short. Iota may have changed its sound (cf. "intr<u>i</u>gue", "<u>i</u>ntrigue"); alpha may not have.[12] Epsilon and omicron are always short while eta and omega are always long.

"Long" and "short" refer to the relative length of time it requires to pronounce the vowel.

6. Greek also has two **breathing marks**. Every word beginning with a vowel and all words beginning with a rho have a breathing mark.

The **rough** breathing is a ῾ placed over the first vowel and adds an "h" sound to the word. ὑπέρ is pronounced "huper." Every word that begins with a rho or upsilon takes a rough breathing.

The **smooth** breathing is a ᾽ placed over the first vowel and is not pronounced. ὐπέρ (which is not a real Greek word) would be pronounced "uper." ἀπόστολος is pronounced "a pó sto los."

3.5   Pronouncing diphthongs

1. A **diphthong** consists of two vowels that produce but one sound. The second vowel is always an ι or an υ. The final three diphthongs in the following chart are less common than the others. Their pronunciations are as follows.[13]

αι	as in <u>ai</u>sle	αἴρω
ει	as in <u>ei</u>ght	εἰ
οι	as in <u>oi</u>l	οἰκία
αυ	as in s<u>au</u>erkraut	αὐτός
ου	as in s<u>ou</u>p	οὐδέ
υι	as in s<u>ui</u>te	υἱός
ευ, ηυ	as in f<u>eu</u>d[14]	εὐθύς / ηὔξανεν

2. An **improper diphthong** is made up of a vowel and an **iota subscript**. An iota subscript is a small iota written under the vowels α, η, or ω (ᾳ, ῃ, ῳ) and normally is the last letter in a word. This iota has no effect on the pronunciation but is essential for translation, so pay

---

11 Most gamma nasals are formed from the γγ combination.

12 There is much discussion on this type of issue among scholars. The long alpha (e.g., "father") would have taken longer to say than the short alpha. (e.g., "cat").

13 The diphthong ωυ is used in classical Greek, but occurs in the N.T. only in the name Μωϋσῆς where there is always a diaeresis indicating that it is not a diphthong.

14 Some suggest that the pronunciation of ηυ is the same as saying "hey you" if you run the words together.

close attention to it.

α   ὥρα

η   γραφῇ

ῳ   λόγῳ

3. Words that begin with a diphthong must have breathing marks. The breathing mark is placed over the second vowel of the diphthong (αἰτέω).

    If the capitalized word begins with a diphthong, the breathing mark is still over the second vowel (Αἰτέω). But if the word begins with two vowels that do not form a diphthong, the breathing mark stands in front of the capital (Ἰησοῦς).

4. In some words we find two vowels that normally form a diphthong, but in this case do not. To show that these two vowels are pronounced as two separate sounds, a **diaeresis** (¨) is placed over the second vowel (Ἡσαΐας). The αι normally forms a diphthong, but in this word the diaeresis indicates that it forms two separate sounds: Ἡ σα ι ας. Cf. naïve in English.

Summary

1. It is essential that you learn the Greek alphabet right away. You cannot learn anything else until you do.

2. Learn the English name, how to write the letter, and how to pronounce the letter.

3. The vowels in Greek are α, ε, η, ι, ο, υ, and ω.

4. Every word beginning with a vowel must have either a rough or smooth breathing mark. If the word begins with a diphthong, the breathing mark is over the second vowel. If the word is capitalized, the breathing mark goes either before the first vowel or over the second vowel, depending on whether the two vowels form a diphthong.

5. A diphthong consists of two vowels pronounced as a single sound. The second vowel is always an iota or upsilon.

6. An improper diphthong is a diphthong with an iota subscript under the vowel. The iota subscript does not affect pronunciation but is important in translation.

Advanced Information

In most of the chapters there is information that some teachers consider essential, but others do not. We have included that kind of information in the "Advanced Information" section of each chapter.

3.6   **Capital letters**. If you want to learn capitals, notice that there are very few unexpected forms. The unusual ones are in bold print and underlined.

capital	small	comments
A	α	
B	β	
Γ	γ	
Δ	δ	
E	ε	
Z	ζ	
H	η	
Θ	θ	
I	ι	
K	κ	
Λ	λ	
M	μ	
N	ν	
Ξ	ξ	Not be be confused with the capital theta (Θ).
O	o	
Π	π	
P	ρ	Not to be confused with a capital English "P".
Σ	σ/ς	Not to be confused with the capital epsilon (E)
T	τ	
Y	υ	
Φ	φ	
X	χ	
Ψ	ψ	
Ω	ω	

The capitals may be familiar to some because of their use in designating fraternities and sororities.

Chapter 4

Punctuation and Syllabification

Exegetical Insight

When the New Testament was first written there were no punctuation marks. In fact, the words were run together one after another without any separation. Punctuation and versification entered the text of manuscripts at a much later period.

Obviously this has created some difficulties for contemporary scholars since the way a verse is punctuated can have a significant effect on the interpretation of the verse. One outstanding example is Romans 9:5. If a major stop is placed after κατὰ σάρκα ("according to the flesh"), then the final section of the verse is a statement about God the Father (the *NEB* has "May God, supreme above all, be blessed for ever! Amen"). However, if a minor stop is placed at that point, the final words of the sentence speak of Christ (the *NIV* has "Christ, who is God over all, forever praised! Amen").

Does it make any difference? Most scholars believe it does. If the latter punctuation brings out what Paul intended, then we have in this verse a clear-cut statement affirming the deity of Jesus Christ. He is, in fact, God. The way a translation handles an ambiguous verse such as this reveals the theological leanings of the translator.

Robert H. Mounce

Overview

In this chapter we will learn:

- four Greek punctuation marks and three accents;
- how to break a Greek word into parts so we can pronounce it ("syllabification").

Greek Punctuation

4.1   Punctuation

Character	English		Greek
θεός,	comma		comma

13

θεός.	period	period
θεός·	period above the line	semicolon
θεός;	semicolon	question mark[1]

4.2   Diacritical marks

1. **Diaeresis**. This has already been explained in §3.5.

2. **Apostrophe**. When a preposition[2] ends with a vowel and the next word begins with a vowel, the final vowel of the first word drops out. This is called **elision**. It is marked by an apostrophe, which is placed where the vowel was dropped (e.g., ἀπὸ ἐμοῦ becomes ἀπ᾽ ἐμοῦ). This is similar to the English contraction (e.g., "can't").

3. **Accents**. Almost every Greek word has an accent mark.[3] It is placed over a vowel and shows which syllable receives the accent. Originally the accent was a pitch accent: the voice rose, dropped, or rose and dropped on the accented syllable. Eventually it became a stress accent as we have in English.[4]

    The **acute** accent shows that the pitch originally went up a little on the accented syllable (αἰτέω).

    The **grave** accent shows that the voice originally dropped a little on the accented syllable (καὶ θεὸς ἦν ὁ λόγος).

---

[1]   The form of a Greek question is not necessarily different from a statement; the punctuation and context are your main clues.

[2]   Prepositions will be discussed in chapter 8. They are little words such as "in" and "over" that describe the spatial relationship between two items.

[3]   Some words appear to have two accents. There are certain words that lose their accent to the following word ("proclitic") or the preceding word ("enclitic"), and you end up with a double accent on one word and no accent on the other.

[4]   In English we use "stress" accents. This means that when we come to the syllable that receives the accent, we put a little more stress on the pronunciation of that syllable. But in Classical Greek, the accent originally was pitch, not stress. The voice rises or falls a little when the accented syllable is pronounced. Most teachers allow their students to use a stress accent when pronouncing Greek because the music pitch accent is difficult. By the time of Koine Greek, the accent may have been stress.

There is an interesting story about a cannibal tribe that killed the first two missionary couples who came to them. They had tried to learn their language, but could not. The third brave couple started experiencing the same problems with the language as had the two previous couples until the wife, who had been a music major in college, recognized that the tribe had a very developed set of pitch accents that were essential in understanding the language. When they recognized that the accents were pitch and not stress, they were able to see the significance these accents played in that language and finally translated the Bible into that musically-minded language. Luckily for us, while Greek accents were pitch, they are not that important.

The **circumflex** accent shows that the voice rose and then dropped a little on the accented syllable (ἁγνῶς).

Notice how the shape of the accent gives a clue as to the direction of the pitch. Most teachers are satisfied with students simply placing stress on the accented syllable.

The question then becomes, when do you use which accent? Opinions vary from viewing the rules of accent placement as essential to being totally unnecessary. Since the biblical manuscripts never had them originally, and since in our opinion they unnecessarily burden the beginning student, this text relegates the rules of accent placement to the Advanced Information section, so they can be ignored by the student if preferred.

However, this does not mean that accents are worthless and should be ignored. Far from it. Accents serve us very well in three areas.

- **Pronunciation**. If all the students in the class accent any syllable they wish, it can become very difficult to talk to each other. Consistently placing the stress on the accented syllable creates a desirable and necessary uniformity.

- **Memorization**. If you do not force yourself to say a word the same way every time, vocabulary memorization becomes very difficult. Imagine trying to memorize the word κοινωνία if you could not decide which syllable to accent. Try pronouncing "koi no ni a" four times, each time accenting a different syllable. See why consistency at this point is desirable?

- **Identification**. There are a few words that are identical except for their accents. Knowing the accents for these few words can be a great help. There are also a few verbal forms where knowing the accent is helpful. We will point out these words and forms as we meet them. However, just remember that accents were not part of the original text and are open to interpretation.

Syllabification

4.3   How to divide the words

Just as it is important to learn how to pronounce the letters correctly, it is also important to pronounce the words correctly. But in order to pronounce a Greek word you must be able to break it down into its syllables. This is called "syllabification," and there are two ways you can learn it.

The first is to recognize that Greek words syllabify in basically the same manner as English words do. Therefore, if you "go with your feelings," you will syllabify Greek words almost automatically. If you practice reading 1 John 1, included in the exercises of this chapter, syllabification should not be a problem. Your teacher may be willing to record the chapter on audio tape so you can listen to it repeatedly.

The second way is to learn some basic syllabification rules. It is essential that you master the process of syllabification, otherwise you will never be able to pronounce the words consistently, and you will have trouble memorizing them and communicating with your class mates.

1.   *There is one vowel (or diphthong) per syllable.*

     (Therefore, there are as many syllables as there are vowels/ diphthongs.)

     ἀ κη κό α μεν   μαρ τυ ροῦ μεν

2.   *A single consonant by itself (not a cluster[5]) goes with the following vowel.*

     (If the consonant is the final letter in the word, it will go with the preceding vowel.)

     ἐ ω ρά κα μεν   ἐ θε α σά με θα

3.   *Two consecutive vowels, which do NOT form a diphthong, are divided.*

     ἐ θε α σά με θα   Ἡ σα ΐ ας

4.   *A consonant cluster that can NOT begin a word[6] is divided, and the first consonant goes with the preceding vowel.*

     ἔμ προ σθεν   ἀρ χῆς

5.   *A consonant cluster that can begin a word goes with the following vowel.*

     Χρι στός   γρα φή

6.   *Double consonants[7] are divided.*

     ἀ παγ γέλ λο μεν   παρ ρη σί α

7.   *Any consonant plus a μ or ν goes with the following vowel.*

     ἔ θνε σιν   πνεῦ μα

---

5   A consonant cluster is two or more consonants in a row.
6   You can tell if a cluster can begin a word by looking up the cluster in a lexicon. For example, you know that the cluster στ can start a word because there is a word σταυ-ρόω. Although the lexicon may not show all the possible clusters it will show you most of them.
7   A "double consonant" is when the same consonant occurs twice in a row.

8.   *Compound words[8] are divided where joined.*

ἀντι χριστός   ἐκ βάλλω

Summary

1.   A period above the line is a Greek semi-colon (literally, half a colon), and an English semi-colon is a Greek question mark.

2.   There are three accents. You do not have to know why they occur where they do, but be sure to pay close attention to them as you pronounce the word.

3.   Greek syllabification basically follows English syllabification. Listen to your teacher pronounce the words and it will become automatic very quickly.

Vocabulary

One of the most frustrating parts of learning language is memorization, especially memorizing vocabulary. And yet, memorizing vocabulary is one of the essential elements if you are going to enjoy the language. If you have to look up every other word the language loses its charm. Because we are learning biblical Greek only, we have a set number of words, and statistically there are a few significant facts.

There are 5,437 different words in the New Testament. They occur a total of 138,162 times.[9] But there are only 313 words (5.8% of the total number) that occur 50 times or more. In addition, for special reasons you will be asked to learn six more words that occur less than fifty times. These 319 words account for 110,425 word occurrences, or 79.92% of the total word count, almost four out of five.[10] For example, καί (the word for "and") occurs 9,153 times. Learn that one word and you know 6.7% of the total word count.

The point is that if you learn these 319 words well, you can read the bulk of the New Testament. We feel it is counterproductive to learn more, unless you really like doing things like that. Your time is better spent reading the Bible or learning grammar. And 319 words are not very many. Most introductory textbooks for other languages have about 2,000 words.

For encouragement we have included in parentheses how many times each vocabulary word occurs, and at the end of every chapter we will tell you what percent of the 138,162 word occurrences you now know.[11]

---

[8]   Compound words are words made up of two distinct words. Of course, right now you cannot tell what is a compound word because you do not know any of the words.

[9]   This number comes from the computer program *Gramcord*.

[10]   There are also a few special forms of words you are given in the vocabulary. If a vocabulary word does not have its frequency listed after it, that word is not included in the frequency counting.

In this chapter we have listed some Greek words that have come over directly into English ("cognates").[12] Seeing the similarities between languages can often be helpful. Some of the cognates are not part of many peoples' vocabulary, but we have found that it is still helpful to know that the cognates exist. Most of the cognates and their definitions were drawn from Ernest Klein's masterful study, *Etymological Dictionary*, with good suggestions from Bruce Metzger's *Lexical Aids*.

But remember: never define a Greek word on the basis of its English cognate! English was not a language until much later, so it had no impact on the meaning of Greek. Think of as many cognates as you can for the following words. We will list cognates in the footnotes.

ἄγγελος	messenger, angel (175)
ἀμήν	verily, truly, amen, so let it be (129)
ἄνθρωπος	man, mankind, person, people, humankind, human being (550)[13]
ἀπόστολος	apostle, envoy, messenger (80)
Γαλιλαία	Galilee (61)[14]
γραφή	writing, Scripture (50)[15]
δόξα	glory, majesty, fame (166)[16]
ἐγώ	I (1725)[17]
ἔσχατος	last (52)[18]
ζωή	life (135)[19]
θεός	God, god (1317)[20]

---

[11] Vocabulary frequencies are drawn from Warren Trenchard's *The Student's Complete Guide to the Greek New Testament*. Other statistics are from *Gramcord*.

[12] As you will see, kappa came over into English as a "c." Remember also that when upsilon is not in a diphthong, it is transliterated and comes into English as "y."

[13] *Anthropology*, the study of humans.

[14] Most names are easily recognized.

[15] An *autograph* is a writing of one's own (αὐτός) name.

[16] The *doxology* is a "word" (λόγος, see below) of "praise."

[17] *Ego*, the "I" or "self" of a person.

[18] *Eschatology* is the study of last things.

[19] *Zoology* is the study of animal life.

[20] *Theology* is the study of God.

καί	and, even, also, namely (9153)[21]
καρδία	heart, inner self (156)[22]
κόσμος	world, universe, humankind (186)[23]
λόγος	word, Word, statement, message (330)[24]
πνεῦμα	spirit, Spirit, wind, breath, inner life (379)[25]
προφήτης	prophet (144)
σάββατον	Sabbath, week (68)[26]
φωνή	sound, noise, voice (139)[27]
Χριστός	Christ, Messiah, Anointed One (529)[28]

Proper names are especially easy to learn.

Ἀβραάμ	Abraham (73)
Δαυίδ	David (59)
Παῦλος	Paul (158)
Πέτρος	Peter (156)
Πιλᾶτος	Pilate (55)

---

[21] We are unaware of any cognates for καί, but it is so common and easy to learn that we included it in this chapter.

[22] *Cardiology* is the study of the heart. Notice how the kappa came over into English as a "c."

[23] *Cosmology* is the philosophical study of the universe.

[24] This word has a wide range of meaning, both in Greek and in English. It can refer to what is spoken, or it can be used philosophically/theologically for the "Word" (John 1:1-18). As you can see from examples above, λόγος (or the feminine λογία) is often used in compounds to denote the "study" of something.

[25] By "Spirit" we mean the Holy Spirit. Remember, in Greek there are no silent consonants, so the pi is pronounced; unlike in English where, for example, the "p" is not pronounced in the word, "pneumatic." *Pneumatology* is the study of spiritual beings.

[26] σάββατον often occurs in the plural, but can be translated as a singular.

[27] The double meaning of "sound" and "voice," along with the double meaning of πνεῦμα as "wind" and "spirit," creates the pun in John 3:8. τὸ πνεῦμα ὅπου θέλει πνεῖ, καὶ τὴν φωνὴν αὐτοῦ ἀκούεις, ἀλλ᾽ οὐκ οἶδας πόθεν ἔρχεται καὶ ποῦ ὑπάγει· οὕτως ἐστὶν πᾶς ὁ γεγεννημένος ἐκ τοῦ πνεύματος. A *phonograph* is literally a "writer of sounds."

[28] In the Old Testament and the earlier parts of the New Testament "χριστός" was a title, but as you move through Acts and it becomes so closely associated with Jesus that it becomes a personal name like "Jesus" and should be capitalized (Χριστός).

Σίμων   Simon (75)

There are many other words that we could show you, but as you can see, learning vocabulary does not have to be that difficult. Learn these vocabulary words now.

Total word count in the New Testament: 138,162
Number of words learned to date: 26
Number of word occurrences in this chapter: 16,100
Number of word occurrences to date: 16,100
Percent of total word count in the New Testament: 11.65%

Remember that 11.65% translates into knowing more than one out of every ten word occurrences. One out of ten! Encouraged?

Advanced Information

4.4   **Basic rules for accents**. If you want to know the basics about accents, here they are.

1. The **acute** (´) can occur on any of the last three syllables.

2. The **circumflex** (ˆ) can occur only on one of the last two syllables and will always be over a long vowel. η and ω are always long vowels. α , ι, and υ can be either long or short. ᾳ is always long.

3. The **grave** (`) is formed when a word is normally accented with an acute on the final syllable. When the word is not followed by a punctuation mark, then the acute becomes a grave. In other words, if the word is accented on the final syllable, the Greeks always dropped their voices at the end of a word, but raised it when the word was at the end of a clause or sentence.

4. Accents on nouns try to stay on the same syllable. Accents on verbs try to move as far back toward the beginning of the verb as possible. This is called *recessive accent*.

4.5   Here are some more Greek words. What are their English cognates? You do not need to learn the Greek words now.

word	*definition*
ἀγάπη	love
ἀδελφός	brother
ἅγιος	holy
αἷμα	blood

ἁμαρτία	sin
γλῶσσα	tongue, language
ἐκκλησία	church, Church, assembly, congregation
ἔργον	work
εὐαγγέλιον	good news, Gospel
θάνατος	death
θρόνος	throne
Ἰησοῦς	Jesus
Ἰσραήλ	Israel
λίθος	stone
μέγας	large, great
μήτηρ	mother
Μωϋσῆς	Moses
νόμος	law
παραβολή	parable
πατήρ	father
πρεσβύτερος	elder
πῦρ	fire
ὕδωρ	water
Φαρισαῖος	Pharisee
ψυχή	soul, life, self

Chapter 5

Introduction to English Nouns

Overview

In this chapter we will learn the following:

- terms used in English grammar (inflection, case, number, gender, lexical form);
- other terms such as definite article, predicate nominative, and declension;
- parts of speech (noun, adjective, preposition, subject/predicate);
- a brief introduction to verbs.

Introduction

5.1   As strange as it may seem, the first major obstacle many of you must overcome is your lack of knowledge of English grammar. For whatever reasons, many do not know enough English grammar to learn Greek grammar. We cannot teach about the Greek nominative case until you know what a case is. You must learn to crawl before walking.

For this reason we begin our discussion of Greek nouns with a short introduction to the English grammar relevant for studying nouns. (A similar discussion is included before we start talking about verbs.) At the beginning of every chapter we will introduce some of the finer points of English grammar that are relevant for that chapter.

There is a lot of information in this chapter. The purpose is not to overwhelm you, but to introduce you to nouns and provide a central location for reference. As you have questions in the later chapters, refer back to this chapter.

Terms

5.2   **Inflection.** Sometimes the form of a word changes when it performs different functions in a sentence or when the word changes its meaning. This is called "inflection." For example, the personal pronoun is "he" if it refers to a male, and "she" if it refers to a female. It is "she" when it is the subject of the sentence (e.g., "She is my wife."), but changes to "her" when it is the direct object (e.g., "The teacher flunked her.") If the king and queen have one son, he is the "prince," but if they have two they are "princes." If their child is a girl she is called a "princess." All these changes are examples of inflection.

Compared with most languages, English is not highly inflected. Greek, on the other hand, is highly inflected. Almost every word is altered depending upon its use in the sentence and its meaning.

The following grammatical concepts can affect the form of a word in both languages.

5.3   **Case**. Words perform different functions in a sentence. These different functions are called "cases." In English there are three cases: subjective, objective, and possessive. Some English words change their form when they switch functions, while other words stay basically the same. (In the following examples, the personal pronoun "he" will change depending upon its case.)

If a word is the **subject** of the sentence, it is in the **subjective** case. ("*He* is my brother.") The subject is that which does the action of the verb. The subject is usually the first noun (or pronoun) before the verb in a sentence. For example: "*Bill* ran to the store." "The *ball* broke the window." Word order shows that both *Bill* and *ball* are the subjects of their verbs. However, sometimes it is hard to determine what is the subject. You can usually find out by asking the question "who?" or "what?" For example, "Who ran to the store?" "Bill." "What broke the window?" "The ball."

If a word shows possession, it is in the **possessive** case. ("*His* Greek Bible is always by *his* bed.")

If a word is the **direct object**, it is in the **objective** case. The direct object is the person or thing that is directly affected by the action of the verb. This means that whatever the verb does, it does to the direct object. ("The teacher will flunk *him* if he does not take Greek seriously.") It usually follows the verb in word order. For example: "Robin passed her *test*." "The waiter insulted *Brian*." *Test* and *Brian* are the direct objects. You can usually determine the direct object by asking yourself the question "what?" or "whom?" Robin passed what? Her test. The waiter insulted whom? Brian.

case	function	example
Subjective	subject	"*He* borrowed my computer."
Possessive	possession	"He borrowed *my* computer."
Objective	direct object	"He borrowed my *computer*."

We chose the pronoun "he" for the illustrations above because it changes its form quite readily. Most words will not, except for the possessive case. For example, the word "teacher" stays the same whether it is the subject ("The *teacher* likes you.") or the direct object ("You like the *teacher*."). However, to form the possessive it will change by the addition of an apostrophe s. ("She is the *teacher's* pet.")

5.4   **Number**. Words can be either **singular** or **plural**, depending upon whether they refer to one, or more than one. For example, "*Students* (plural) should learn to study like this *student*" (singular).

5.5   **Gender**. Some words, mostly pronouns, change their form depending upon whether they are referring to a **masculine, feminine**, or **neuter** object. For example, "*He* (masculine gender) gave *it* (neuter gender) to *her* (feminine gender)." (*He*, *it*, and *her* are all forms of the same pronoun, the third person singular personal pronoun.)

Another example is the word "prince." If the heir to the throne is male, then he is the "prince." But if the child is female, she is the "princess." Most English words do not change to indicate gender. "Teacher" refers to either a woman or a man. If a word refers to neither a masculine or feminine thing, then it is neuter.

Natural gender means that a word takes on the gender of the object it represents. We refer to a rock as an "it" because we do not regard the rock as having gender. But we refer to a man as "he" and a woman as "she."

In Greek, pronouns follow natural gender but nouns for the most part do not. ἁμαρτία is a feminine noun meaning "sin," although "sin" is not a female concept; ἁμαρτωλός can be a masculine noun meaning "sinner," although "sinner" is not a masculine concept.

5.6   **Lexical form**. Whereas most people call them "dictionaries," scholars call them **lexicons**. The form of the word found in the lexicon is called the "lexical form." Your vocabulary words are given in their lexical forms. Whenever you are asked to explain the form of an inflected Greek word, you must be able to indicate its lexical form. Otherwise, you will not be able to look a word up in the lexicon and find its meaning.

For example, if you were declining the inflected form "him," you would say it comes from "he." Lexical forms in English are subjective singular.

5.7   **Indefinite article**. In English, the indefinite article is the word "a." In the sentence, "A good student works every day on her Greek," the article is indefinite because it does not identify any one particular student. It is indefinite about the person of whom it is speaking. Greek does not have an indefinite article, although in certain circumstances you will be able to add "a" to your translation. We will see this in the next chapter.

If the word following the indefinite article begins with a vowel, the indefinite article will be "an."

5.8   **Definite article**. In English, the definite article is the word "the." In the sentence, "The student is going to pass," the definite article is identifying one student in particular (even though context is required to know which one it is).

The difference between the definite and the indefinite article is that the definite article is specific. Not just any student is going to pass; *the* student will pass.

5.9   **Predicate nominative**. The verb "to be" gives rise to a special situation. (The verb "to be" has many different forms: "am"; "are"; "was"; "were"; etc.) If you say, "It is I," the pronoun "I" is not receiving the action of the verb. Rather, it is telling you something about the subject. In grammarians' terminology, the pronoun "I" is "predicating" something about the subject. Because it is not receiving the action of the verb the pronoun cannot be a direct object. Rather, it is called a "predicate nominative" and is put in the subjective case. It is incorrect English to say, "It is me," regardless of current usage, because "me" is objective while "I" is subjective.

The verb "to be" is followed by a predicate nominative, never a direct object.

5.10   **Declension.** In English, there are different ways to form the plural. For example, to form the plural of most words you add an "s" ("books"). However, other words form their plurals by changing a vowel in the word ("man" becomes "men"). Although these two words form their plurals differently, both plurals perform the same function. They indicate more than one item.

Notice that it does not matter how a word forms its plural as far as meaning is concerned. "Children" and "childs," if the latter were a word, would mean the same thing.

In Greek there are three basic inflectional patterns that a word can follow. Each of these patterns is called a "declension." Like the example above in English, which pattern a word follows has no effect on its meaning, only its form.

Some words in Greek are indeclinable, such as personal names and words borrowed from other languages. Their form, therefore, does not change regardless of their meaning or function in the sentence.

Parts of Speech

5.11   **Noun.** A noun is a word that stands for someone or something. In the sentence, "Bill threw his big black book at the strange teacher," the words "Bill," "book," and "teacher" are nouns.

5.12   **Adjective**. An adjective is a word that modifies a noun (or another adjective). In the sentence above, "big," "black," and "strange" are adjectives that modify nouns. In the sentence, "The dark brown Bible costs too much," "dark" is an adjective modifying another adjective "brown."

5.13   **Preposition**. A preposition is a word that shows the relationship between two other words. For example, the relationship can be spatial ("The Greek text is *under* the bed.") or temporal ("The student always studies *after* the ball game.").

The word or phrase following the preposition is the **object** of the preposition ("bed" in the first example, "the ball game" in the second).

5.14   **Subject** and **predicate**. A sentence can be broken down into two parts. The term **subject** describes the subject of the verb and what modifies it. **Predicate** describes the rest of the sentence, including verb, direct object, etc.

Introduction to Verbs

5.15   The formal study of verbs has been deferred until chapter 15. For now, you are to concentrate on nouns and learn them well. Later we will tackle verbs. However, there are a few highly repetitive verbs that we meet early on in the exercises, and they are easy to learn; so they have been included in the vocabulary in the next several chapters.

There is one important grammatical note you need to learn in order to make sense of the exercises. *The ending of the verb indicates person and number.* For example, the εις ending on γράφεις tells you that the subject is "you." The ει ending on γράφει tells you that the subject is "he," "she," or "it." γράφεις means "you write," while γράφει means "he writes." You will see how this works out in the exercises.

5.16   An important consequence of this is that a Greek sentence does not need to have an expressed subject; the subject can be implied by the verb. So, σὺ γράφεις and γράφεις both mean, "You write." The "you" comes from both the pronoun σύ as well as the ending on the verb.

In the exercises, we will always include the pronoun (e.g., "he," "they," "we") in the translation of the verb. If there is an expressed subject, the pronoun would not be used.

> ἄνθρωπος γράφει (he/she/it writes) τὸ βιβλίον.
> A man writes the book.

In this sentence, you would not translate, "A man he writes the book."

You would simply say, "A man writes the book." However, if the subject were not expressed, i.e., if ἄνθρωπος were not present, then you would translate, "He writes the book."

5.17 One more point. γράφει can mean "he writes," "she writes," or "it writes." The ει ending is used with all three genders. Only context will help you decide which gender is correct. We will always translate verbs in the exercises up to chapter 15 with all three pronouns, and it is up to you to decide which is the more appropriate translation.

> ἄνθρωπος γράφει (he/she/it writes) τὴν γραφήν.
> A man writes the book.

Chapter 6

Nominative and Accusative
Definite Article

(First and Second Declension Nouns)

Exegetical Insight

The nominative case is the case that the subject is in. When the subject takes an equative verb like "is" (i.e., a verb that equates the subject with something else), then another noun also appears in the nominative case–the predicate nominative. In the sentence, "John is a man," "John" is the subject and "man" is the predicate nominative. In English the subject and predicate nominative are distinguished by word order (the subject comes first). Not so in Greek. Since word order in Greek is quite flexible and is used for emphasis rather than for strict grammatical function, other means are used to determine subject from predicate nominative. For example, if one of the two nouns has the definite article, it is the subject.

As we have said, word order is employed especially for the sake of emphasis. Generally speaking, when a word is thrown to the front of the clause it is done so for emphasis. When a predicate nominative is thrown in front of the verb, by virtue of word order it takes on emphasis. A good illustration of this is John 1:1c. The English versions typically have, "and the Word was God." But in Greek, the word order has been reversed. It reads,

καὶ θεὸς ἦν ὁ λόγος
and God was the Word.

We know that "the Word" is the subject because it has the definite article, and we translate it accordingly: "and the Word was God." Two questions, both of theological import, should come to mind: (1) why was θεός thrown forward? and (2) why does it lack the article? In brief,[1] its emphatic position stresses its essence or quality: "What God was, the Word was" is how one translation brings out this force. Its lack of a definite article keeps us from identifying the *person* of the Word (Jesus Christ) with the *person* of "God" (the Father). That is to say, the word order tells us that Jesus Christ has all the divine attributes that the Father has; lack of

---

[1] This verse is dealt with in much more detail by Wallace in *GGBB*.

the article tells us that Jesus Christ is not the Father. John's wording here is beautifully compact! It is, in fact, one of the most elegantly terse theological statements one could ever find. As Martin Luther said, the lack of an article is against Sabellianism; the word order is against Arianism.

To state this another way, look at how the different Greek constructions would be rendered:

καὶ ὁ λόγος ἦν ὁ θεός	"and the Word was the God" (i.e., the Father; Sabellianism)
καὶ ὁ λόγος ἦν θεός	"and the Word was a god" (Arianism)
καὶ θεὸς ἦν ὁ λόγος	"and the Word was God" (Orthodoxy).

Jesus Christ is God and has all the attributes that the Father has. But he is not the first person of the Trinity. All this is concisely affirmed in καὶ θεὸς ἦν ὁ λόγος.

Daniel B. Wallace

Overview

In this chapter we will learn:

- to identify whether a noun is first or second declension;
- two cases and their endings:
  - the nominative (used when the noun is the subject);
  - the accusative (used when the noun is the direct object);
- the forms of the word "the" and how they "agree" with the noun they are modifying;
- two hints for effective translation;
- the first three of eight noun rules.

Introduction

6.1 This is by far the longest chapter in this text. We are meeting some very important ideas for the first time, and we want to cover them adequately. Most of it is grammar and not much is memory work, so take heart. There is a review part way through and a summary at the end.

The chapters in this text are laid out consistently. Each one starts with an exegetical insight designed to illustrate some point you will be learning in the chapter, an overview, and a discussion of relevant English grammar. Then you will learn the Greek grammar, and finish with a summary of the entire discussion, a vocabulary section, and sometimes an advanced section.

English

6.2   Everything you need to know about English grammar in this chapter has been covered in chapter 5.

Greek

6.3   Do not memorize the endings in the following illustrations. All we want you to see is how inflection works.

Case endings. The case of a word in Greek is indicated by the "case ending." This is a suffix added to the end of the word. For example, the basic word for "apostle" is ἀπόστολο. If it is functioning as the subject of the verb, it takes a case ending that is equivalent to the "subjective" case in English: ς (ἀπόστολος). If it is functioning as the direct object of the sentence, it takes a case ending that is equivalent to the "objective" case in English: ν (ἀπόστολον).

> ὁ ἀπόστολος πέμπει τὸν ἀπόστολον.
> The apostle sends the apostle.

Since the case endings, *not the word order*, are the key to knowing the function and number of a word, it is extremely important that you learn them well.

There are five cases in Greek. We will learn two of them in this chapter, two in the next, and the fifth later on.

6.4   **Stem**. If you take the case ending off a noun you are left with the stem. The stem of λόγος is λογο. It is the stem of a noun that actually carries the meaning of the word.

It is essential that you be able to identify the stem of a word.

6.5   **Gender**. A noun is either masculine, feminine, or neuter. A noun has only one gender and it never varies.[2]

A word is not always the gender you might expect (cf. "natural gender," §5.5). ἁμαρτωλός means "sinner" and is masculine, but it does not mean that a sinner is male. ἁμαρτία means "sin" and is a feminine noun, but it does not mean that sin is a feminine trait.

However, there are certain patterns that will help you remember the gender of a word. Words listed in the vocabulary section that end in ος are usually masculine, words ending with ον are usually neuter, and words ending in eta or alpha are mostly feminine.

---

[2]   There are a few words that are both masculine and feminine, but we will not meet them for some time.

6.6   **Number.** Instead of adding an "s" to a word, Greek indicates singular or plural by using different case endings. ἀπόστολος means "apostle" and ἀπόστολοι means "apostles." The difference between the singular and plural is indicated by the case endings ς and ι.

6.7   **Declensions**. We discussed above how there are different patterns that English nouns follow in forming their plural. Some add "s," others add "es," while others change the vowel in the stem of the word (e.g., "men"). The pattern a word follows does not affect its meaning, only its form. "Children" and "childs" would mean the same thing, if the latter were actually a word.

In Greek there are basically three inflectional patterns used to create the different case endings. Each of these patterns is called a "declension." What declension a particular noun follows has no bearing on the meaning of the word. *The different declensions affect only the form of the case ending.*

- Nouns that have a stem ending in an alpha or eta are **first declension**, take first declension endings, and are primarily feminine (e.g., γραφή).

- Nouns that have a stem ending in an omicron are **second declension**, take second declension endings, and are mostly masculine or neuter (ἀπόστολος; ἔργον).

- If the stem of a word ends in a consonant it is **third declension**. We will deal with the third declension in chapter 10.

For example, a first declension case ending for the subject of the verb is nothing; the stem stands by itself (γραφή; ὥρα).

> ἡ ὥρα ἐστιν νῦν.
> The hour is now.

A second declension case ending for the subject of the verb is ς (ἀπόστολος).[3]

> ὁ ἀπόστολος λέγει τὸν λόγον.
> The apostle speaks the word.

Declension only affects the case ending used; it does not affect meaning.

Since the stem of a noun determines its declension, *a noun can belong to only one declension.*

6.8   **Nominative.** In this chapter we will learn two of the five cases. The first is the nominative case. There are two functions of the nominative case.

---

[3]   If ἀπόστολος (masc) and ἀποστόλη (fem) were both words, they would have the same meaning (except ἀπόστολος would designate a man and ἀποστόλη a woman).

The first is to indicate the **subject** of the sentence. In other words, if a word is the subject of the verb it will have a nominative case ending.

As we have seen above, one of the nominative singular case endings is sigma. In the following sentence, which word is the subject? (ἀγαπᾷ means "he loves" and τόν means "the.")

θεὸς ἀγαπᾷ τὸν κόσμον.

The second function of the nominative case is the **predicate**[4] **nominative**. Just as it is in English, a noun that follows the Greek verb "to be" is not receiving any action from the verb but rather is telling you something about the subject. Therefore the word is in the nominative case. (ἐστιν means "he is," and κύριος means "Lord.")

θεὸς ἐστιν κύριος.

Notice that in this sentence both the first and last words are in the nominative case. Context should make clear which is the subject and which is the predicate.

6.9 **Accusative**. If a word is the **direct object** of the verb it will be in the accusative case. This means that it will have an accusative case ending.

One of the accusative singular case endings is ν. In the following sentence, which word is the direct object?

θεὸς ἀγαπᾷ Χριστόν.

6.10 **Word order**. Notice in the example above that you do not determine whether a word is the subject or the object by its order in the sentence as you do in English. *The only way to determine the subject or direct object of a Greek sentence is by the case endings.*

This cannot be stressed too much. Your natural inclination will be to ignore the case endings and assume that the word before the verb is the subject and the word after the verb is the direct object. Fight this tendency!

In Greek, the ending ς shows you that this word is in the nominative and therefore is the subject. The ending ν shows you that this word is the accusative and therefore is the direct object.[5] In the following examples locate the subjects and direct objects. Note that although each example has the same meaning ("God loves the world"), the order of the words is different.

---

[4]   Grammatically, the "predicate" is the verb and everything that follows it. It is what is left when you remove the subject and anything modifying it.

[5]   As we will see, these letters are also endings for other cases, but for the sake of this illustration we make the simplification.

Θεὸς ἀγαπᾷ τὸν κόσμον.

ἀγαπᾷ τὸν κόσμον Θεός.

τὸν κόσμον Θεὸς ἀγαπᾷ.

ἀγαπᾷ Θεὸς τὸν κόσμον.

As a general rule, try to maintain the same order of the Greek words in your translation if possible. While word placement does not determine function, it does help in some situations to understand the author's intention. For example, Ephesians 2:8 starts, "For by grace you have been saved through faith." Paul wanted to emphasize, above all else, that salvation is due to God's grace, and therefore he places that fact first for emphasis. Your translation should retain that emphasis, as long as it is acceptable English.

6.11 **Lexical form**. The lexical form of a noun is its nominative singular form. ἀπόστολοι, which is nominative plural, would be listed in the lexicon as ἀπόστολος.

The definite article and adjectives (chapter 9) can be in more than one gender. Their lexical form is the masculine nominative singular.

Review

6.12 We are halfway through this lesson, so let's stop and review what we have learned so far.

a. Greek uses different case endings to indicate the case (nominative; accusative), gender (masculine; feminine; neuter), and number (singular; plural).

b. The stem of the word is the basic form of the word that carries its meaning. It is discovered by removing the nominative singular case ending.

c. Stems ending in an alpha or eta are in the first declension; stems ending in omicron are in the second declension.

d. If a word is the subject of a verb, it is in the nominative case and uses nominative case endings.

e. If a word is the direct object of a verb, it is in the accusative case and uses accusative case endings.

f. Word order does not determine the function of a word, but it can show the emphasis the author intends.

g. The lexical form of a noun is the nominative singular.

Case Endings

6.13   **Form**. The following chart is called a "paradigm." All the paradigms in this book have the same basic structure. Here are some important hints.

- *The singular forms are on top, and the plural below.*

- *The order left to right is masculine, feminine, neuter.*

    The "2 - 1 - 2" along the top means that the masculine follows the second declension, the feminine follows the first declension, and the neuter follows the second. As we will see, the first declension is usually feminine, and the second declension is usually masculine or neuter.

- Learn these endings! Without them, you will never be able to translate anything.

- Be sure to memorize the endings by themselves, not what a noun looks like with the endings. Otherwise you will not easily be able to identify the endings on other nouns.

- The key to learning these paradigms is to realize that *translation does not require you to repeat paradigms; it requires you to recognize the endings when you see them.*

- Older methods of learning Greek required you to memorize paradigm after paradigm, fifty-two in all. You can still do that if you wish, but that means that for the rest of your life you will have to review paradigm after paradigm. You get the picture. We offer you a different approach. Memorize the definite article, one other paradigm, and eight rules. That's all there is to it. Which way would you like to go?

- We suggest that you read the paradigms left to right, not top to bottom. When you are translating a verse, you will be looking for a word in the nominative to be the subject, and at first you do not care about its gender.

- Use flash cards. Put each ending on a different card, carry them with you wherever you go, mix them up, and review them over and over again.

- Always say the endings out loud, and always pronounce them the same way. The more senses you employ in memorization the better. Pronounce the word out loud; listen to yourself speak; write the word; look at what you have written.

This is the paradigm of the case endings used by the first and second declensions, nominative and accusative.[6] A dash (-) means that no case ending is used and the stem of the noun stands by itself. The underline (α) means that the case ending joins with the final stem vowel.[7] These endings must be learned perfectly.[8]

	2 *masc*	1 *fem*	2 *neut*
nom sg	ς	-	ν
acc sg	ν	ν	ν
nom pl	ι	ι	α
acc pl	υς	ς	α

6.14 Hints

- The masculine and feminine case endings are often identical. In the nominative and accusative, the neuter is usually distinct from the masculine.

- In the neuter, the nominative and accusative singular are always the same, and the nominative and accusative plural are always the same. Context will usually show you whether the word is the subject or direct object.

Nouns

6.15 **Paradigm of the word and case endings**. Now let's add the case endings to the nouns. Be sure to differentiate between the stem and the case ending.

---

[6] If you have studied Greek before, you will notice a few differences. Just about every grammar teaches that the final stem vowel is part of the case ending, ος and not ς. Not only is this incorrect, but in our opinion it makes learning Greek much more difficult. If you learn the true case endings, you will find that memorization is kept to an absolute minimum!

[7] This is called "contraction," and we will discuss it in detail later. For example, the stem of the noun ἔργον is ἔργο. When it is in the neuter plural its form is ἔργα. The omicron and alpha have "contracted" to alpha.

[8] If you really want to be technical, the ending for the masculine accusative plural is νς. But because of the nature of the nu, it drops out. In order to compensate for the loss of the letter, the omicron of the stem lengthens to ου (*λογο + νς ▸ λογος ▸ λόγους). It is easier just to memorize the ending as υς.

	2	1	2
	masc	*fem*	*neut*
nom sg	λόγος	γραφή	ἔργον
		ὥρα	
acc sg	λόγον	γραφήν	ἔργον
		ὥραν	
nom pl	λόγοι	γραφαί	ἔργα
		ὧραι	
acc pl	λόγους	γραφάς	ἔργα
		ὥρας	

6.16   **Feminine.** In the paradigm there are two feminine nouns, γραφή and ὥρα. The only difference between the forms of these two words is the stem vowel. γραφή ends in eta, and ὥρα ends in alpha. If you think of the alpha and eta as being related vowels, then you will not have to learn two different patterns for feminine nouns. They are identical except for the stem vowel.

However, notice also that in the plural the stem of γραφή ends in an alpha and not an eta. All first and second declension feminine nouns that have eta in the singular shift to alpha in the plural.

6.17   **Hint**

- Notice which endings are going to give you trouble. The nu occurs in several places. You will also discover that the alpha is used in many places.

6.18   **Parse.** When asked to "parse" a noun, you are to tell the teacher five things about the word.

1. case   (nominative, accusative)
2. number   (singular, plural)
3. gender   (masculine, feminine, neuter)
4. lexical form   (nominative singular)
5. inflected meaning

For example, λόγους is accusative plural masculine, from λόγος, meaning "words."

This is only a suggestion. Teachers will vary on their preferred order of parsing.

6.19 **Parsing neuter nouns**. When parsing a neuter word that is either nominative or accusative, our suggestion is to list both possibilities.

When you are translating a sentence and come across one of these forms, it is important that you have trained yourself to realize that the word can be either the subject or direct object. If you make an assumption that it is the subject when in fact it is the direct object, you may never be able to translate the sentence. But if you are accustomed to parsing it as "nominative/accusative," you will be less likely to make this mistake.

For example, ἔργον is nominative or accusative singular neuter, from ἔργον, meaning "work."

The First Three Noun Rules

6.20 These are the first three of the famous eight noun rules. Learn them exactly!

1. *Stems ending in alpha or eta are in the first declension, stems ending in omicron are in the second, and consonantal stems are in the third.*

2. *Every neuter word has the same form in the nominative and accusative.*

   ἔργον could be either nominative or accusative. Context makes it clear whether it is the subject or the direct object.

3. *Almost all neuter words end in alpha in the nominative and accusative plural.*

   Context makes it clear whether one of these forms is the subject or the direct object.

   All of the eight noun rules are listed in the Appendix.

Definite Article

6.21 **Summary**. The definite article is the only article in Greek. There is no indefinite article ("a"). For this reason you can refer to the Greek definite article simply as the "article."

6.22 **Agreement**. The article has case, number, and gender. *The article always agrees with the noun that it modifies in case, number, and gender.* In other words, if a noun is nominative, singular, masculine (ἄνθρωπος), the article that modifies it will be nominative, singular, masculine (ὁ).

The lexical form of the article is always the nominative, singular, masculine (ὁ).

6.23   **Form**. Here is the paradigm of the article. Compare the forms to the case endings to see all the similarities. The feminine follows the first declension, the masculine and neuter the second.

	2 *masc*	1 *fem*	2 *neut*
nom sg	ὁ	ἡ	τό
acc sg	τόν	τήν	τό
nom pl	οἱ	αἱ	τά
acc pl	τούς	τάς	τά

6.24   **Hints**.

- The article does not care about the declension of the word it is modifying. ἡ will modify a feminine noun whether it is first or second declension. This makes the article consistent, easy to learn, and very important.

- The article begins with either a rough breathing or a tau. Then you have the characteristic vowel of that declension and the case ending. The only exception is neuter singular.[9]

---

[9] Here are some more hints.

- The vowel in the feminine article is always eta in the singular, never alpha as can be the case with nouns.

- The nominative singular is really quite easy to memorize. In the feminine and masculine there is no case ending and no tau. The vowel stands alone, and since you have already associated the eta with the first declension and omicron with the second you already know these forms. But note the breathing.

  The neuter could not follow suit, otherwise it would have been identical to the masculine. Therefore you have the characteristic tau followed by the omicron that you associate with the second declension.

- What are the similarities in the nominative plural? In both the feminine and masculine, the endings are a vowel followed by an iota. Again you see the characteristic alpha and omicron. If you learn that the vowel-iota combination indicates nominative plural, then if it is αι the word is feminine and if it is οι the word is masculine. Of course, it is more important that you recognize the vowel-iota pattern as the nominative plural, and the gender is secondary.

- What are the similarities in the accusative singular? τήν and τόν are exactly alike except that the feminine has an eta and the masculine has an omicron.

- What are the similarities in the accusative plural? You have the characteristic alpha and omicron. You will discover that the vowel-sigma combination is typical for the accusative plural, and the alpha is common in neuter plural words (rule 3).

6.25 *Knowing the forms of the article is the key to understanding the forms of nouns in Greek.* If you learn the forms of the Greek article well, you will not have much more to learn for nouns. Almost all nouns are preceded by the article. If you cannot decline a noun you can look at the article and will know what the noun is. Very few people, even those who have known Greek for many years, can recite all the noun paradigms. They use hints like the article.

A second reason why the article is important is that most of the case endings found on nouns are similar to the definite article. Therefore, if you know the article, you know many of the noun endings.

Translation Procedure

6.26 When students start learning Greek, one of their most serious problems is that when they try to translate a sentence, it looks like a collection of unrelated words. As you learn more about this marvelous language, this problem becomes even more pronounced.

The keys to this problem are your case endings and the article. At this point, all you can do is find the subject and the direct object. It is helpful to split the sentence into its parts.

θεός σώσει ψυχάς.
God will save souls.

The subject is θεός and the direct object is ψυχάς. You could divide the sentence like this:

θεὸς / σώσει / ψυχάς.

If there is an article, keep it with the noun.

ὁ λόγος / σώσει / ψυχάς.
The word will save souls.

6.27 **Article.** As in English, the Greek article is translated "the." The general rule is to translate according to the presence or absence of the article. If an article is present, translate it. If there is no article, do not use "the." If there is no article you may insert "a" before the noun if it makes better sense in English. For example, "ὁ ἄνθρωπος" means "the man" and "ἄνθρωπος" means "man" or "a man."

6.28 You will soon discover that the Greeks do not use the article the same way we do. They use it when we never would, and they omit it when English demands it. Languages are not codes, and there is not an exact word for word correspondence. Therefore, we must be a little flexible at this point. As we work through the following chapters we will note some of the differences. You will meet these two in this chapter:

Names. Greek often uses the definite article before a proper name. For example, you will often find ὁ θεός (the God) or ὁ Ἰησοῦς (the Jesus). You may omit the article in your translation of proper names.

Abstract nouns. Greek often includes the article with abstract nouns such as "The Truth" (ἡ ἀλήθεία), although English does not normally use the article.

Summary

1. **The fog**. You are now entering the fog. You will have read this chapter and think you understand it–and perhaps you do–but it will seem foggy. That is okay. That's what we call "the fog." If this gets discouraging, just look two chapters back and you should understand that chapter clearly. And in two more chapters, this chapter will be clear, assuming of course you keep studying.

2. Greek uses case endings to show the function being performed by a noun. Different case endings are used to designate gender (masculine, feminine, neuter), number (singular, plural), and case (nominative, accusative).

3. The stem of a noun is what is left after removing the case ending.

4. Greek has three different declensions.

    -   Stems ending in alpha and eta are first declension and are usually feminine.

    -   Stems ending in omicron are second declension and usually masculine or neuter.

    The declension of a noun affects only its form, not its meaning.

5. The subject of a verb uses nominative case endings, while the direct object uses accusative case endings.

6. Memorize the paradigm of the case endings and the article.

7. The article agrees with the noun that it modifies in case, number, and gender.

8. Always be able to identify the subject and direct object in a sentence.

9. Learn the endings by themselves. Then learn the full paradigm that lists the article, noun stem, and case endings.

	2 masc	1 fem	2 neut
nom sg	ς	-	ν
acc sg	ν	ν	ν
nom pl	ι	ι	α
acc pl	υς	ς	α

	2 masc	1 fem	2 neut
nom sg	ὁ λόγος	ἡ γραφή ἡ ὥρα	τὸ ἔργον
acc sg	τὸν λόγον	τὴν γραφήν τὴν ὥραν	τὸ ἔργον
nom pl	οἱ λόγοι	αἱ γραφαί αἱ ὧραι	τὰ ἔργα
acc pl	τοὺς λόγους	τὰς γραφάς τὰς ὥρας	τὰ ἔργα

10. The first three noun rules.

    1. Stems ending in alpha or eta are in the first declension, stems in omicron are in the second, and consonantal stems are in the third.

    2. Every neuter word has the same form in the nominative and accusative.

    3. Almost all neuter words end in alpha in the nominative and accusative plural.

11. Divide the sentence you are translating into its parts: subject; verb; direct object. If the subject or direct object has an article, keep the article with the noun.

Vocabulary

All nouns are listed with their article (e.g., ἀγάπη, ἡ). Be sure to memorize the article with the word so you can remember its gender. The stem of the word will be listed, preceded with an asterisk.

Remember: footnotes on vocabulary sections are important and should be learned. Be sure to read the footnote on δέ about **postpositives**.

ἀγάπη, ἡ	love (116; *ἀγαπη)[10]
ἄλλος	other, another (155; *αλλο)[11]
αὐτός	singular: he, she, it (him, her) (5595; *αὐτο)[12]
	plural: they (them)
βασιλεία, ἡ	kingdom (162; *βασιλεια)[13]
δέ	but, and (2792)[14]
εἰμί[15]	I am, exist, live, am present (2460)
ἐν	in, on, among (2752)
ἔργον, τό	work, deed, action (169; *ἐργο)[16]
ἐστίν[15]	he/she/it is[17]
ἦν[15]	he/she/it was
καιρός, ὁ	(appointed) time, season (85; *καιρο)

---

[10] The *agape* was the love feast of early Christians.

[11] An *allegory* is a description of one thing using the image of *another*.

[12] An *autocrat* (αὐτοκρατής) is a ruling by *oneself*. We will see in chapter 12 that αὐτός can also mean "self" and "same," which is reflected in most English cognates and derivatives.

[13] A *basilica* (βασιλική) is a royal palace. Originally it meant "royal colonnade." In Latin its cognate means "a public hall with double colonnades," and came to be used of early Christian and medieval churches of a certain architectural type.

[14] δέ is a **postpositive**. This means that it cannot be the first word in a sentence or clause, even though in your translation it is the first word. It usually is the second word and sometimes the third, e.g., ὁ δε εἶπον ... ("But he said ..."). There are only a few other postpositives.

δέ is written as δ᾽ when it is followed by a word beginning with a vowel (e.g., δ᾽ ἄν...).

[15] εἰμί, ἐστίν, and ἦν are all forms of the same verb. A peculiarity of this word is that it does not take a direct object. It takes a "predicate nominative," which means the word following it is in the nominative. Two other common verbs in Greek that take a predicate nominative are γίνομαι and ὑπάρχω.

[16] *Ergonomics* is the science that coordinates the design of machines to the requirements of the worker to aid in the work.

[17] Because this is a third person singular verb, its subject can be masculine ("he"), feminine ("she"), or neuter ("it"). Context will show you which one to use. The same holds true for ἦν.

νῦν	adverb: now (147; adverb)
	noun: the present
ὁ, ἡ, τό	the (19,870)
ὅτι	that, since, because (1,296)[18]
οὐ, οὐκ, οὐχ	not[19] (1,606)
ὥρα, ἡ	hour, occasion, moment (106; *ὥρα)[20]

Total word count in the New Testament:	138,162
Number of words learned to date:	40
Number of word occurrences in this chapter:	37,311
Number of word occurrences to date:	53,411
Percent of total word count in the New Testament:	38.66%

Previous Words

As we learn more grammar, it will be necessary from time to time to go back to words we have already learned and fine tune our understanding of that word. When that happens, the words in question are listed in this section.

You need to learn the article with the nouns in chapter 4, and their stems.

Ἀβραάμ, ὁ	* Ἀβρααμ
ἄγγελος, ὁ	*ἀγγελο
ἄνθρωπος, ὁ	*ἀνθρωπο
ἀπόστολος, ὁ	*ἀποστολο
Γαλιλαία, ἡ	*Γαλιλαια
γραφή, ἡ	*γραφη
Δαυίδ, ὁ	*Δαυίδ
δόξα, ἡ	*δοξα
ζωή, ἡ	*ζωη
θεός, ὁ	*θεο

---

[18] ὅτι can also act as quotation marks. Our text capitalizes the first word in what the editors feel is a quotation; in these cases they are expecting you to view ὅτι as quotation marks.

[19] οὐκ and οὐχ are different forms of οὐ. οὐ is used when the following word begins with a consonant. οὐκ is used when the next word begins with a vowel and smooth breathing, while οὐχ is used when the next word begins with a vowel and rough breathing. All forms mean "not."

[20] An *hour* is a time period of the day.

κόσμος, ὁ   *κοσμο

λόγος, ὁ   *λογο

Παῦλος, ὁ   *Παυλο

Πέτρος, ὁ   *Πετρο

Πιλᾶτος, ὁ   *Πιλατο

πνεῦμα, τό[21]   *πνευματ

προφήτης, ὁ[21]   *προφητη

σάββατον, τό   *σαββατο

Σίμων, ὁ   *Σιμων

φωνή, ἡ   *φωνη

Χριστός, ὁ   *Χριστο

---

[21] This word does not follow the declension patterns you have learned so far. We will introduce it later.

Chapter 7

Genitive and Dative

First and Second Declension Nouns

Exegetical Insight

"Peace on earth, good will toward men" (Luke 2:14. KJV). You have probably all received Christmas cards containing this part of the angels' song to the shepherds on the fields of Bethlehem. But most modern translations read differently: "on earth peace to men on whom his [God's] favor rests" (NIV); "and on earth peace among those whom he [God] favors" (NRSV). The difference between the KJV and the others is the difference between the nominative and the genitive.

The Greek manuscripts used to translate the KJV contain εὐδοκία (nominative), whereas the older manuscripts used to translate the modern versions contain εὐδοκίας (genitive)–literally translated, "of good will" or "characterized by [God's] good pleasure." In other words, the peace that the angels sang that belonged to the earth as a result of the birth of Christ is not a generic, worldwide peace for all humankind, but a peace limited to those who obtain favor with God by believing in his Son Jesus (see Romans 5:1). What a difference a single letter can make in the meaning of the text!

Verlyn Verbrugge

Overview

In this chapter we will learn:

- the final two major cases, the genitive (when the noun is showing possession) and the dative (when the noun is used as the indirect object);
- the concept of key words;
- nouns rules #4, #5, and #6.

English

7.1   The **possessive case** in English is used to indicate possession. You can either put "of" in front of the word ("The Word *of God* is true."), an "apostrophe s" after the word ("*God's* Word is true."), or just apostrophe if the word ends in "s" ("The *apostles'* word was ignored.").

7.2   The **indirect object**, technically, is the person/thing that is "indirectly" affected by the action of the verb. This means that the indirect object is somehow involved in the action described by the verb, but not directly.

For example, "Karin threw Brad a ball." The direct object is "ball," since it is directly related to the action of the verb. It is what was thrown. But "Brad" is also related to the action of the verb, since the ball was thrown to him. "Brad" is therefore the indirect object. If Karin threw Brad, then "Brad" would be the direct object.

One way to find the indirect object is to put the word "to" in front of the word and see if it makes sense. "Karin threw Brad a ball." "Karin threw to Brad a ball." To whom did Karin throw the ball? To Brad. "Brad" is the indirect object.[1]

English does not have a separate case for the indirect object. It uses the same form as the direct object (objective case).

Greek

7.3   The **genitive** case in Greek is the same as the possessive case in English. Instead of adding an "apostrophe s" or using "of," the genitive case endings are added to the word. For example, if the sentence "Everyone breaks the laws of God" were in Greek, "God" would be in the genitive case and have a genitive case ending.

In English the possessive case can be indicated by the apostrophe. "Everyone breaks God's laws" Greek, however, does not have the apostrophe, and so all Greek constructions are in the form "of ...." "Laws of God" (νόμοι τοῦ θεοῦ) would never be τοῦ θεοῦ's νόμοι. Therefore, in translating you should think with the "of" construction.[2]

The word in the genitive usually follows the word it is modifying (νόμοι τοῦ θεοῦ).

υ is a genitive singular ending, and ων is the genitive plural ending.[3] If you were to see the word λόγου you would know it is singular and is showing possession. If you were to see the word λόγων you would know it is plural and also is showing possession.

---

[1]   In English when the word "to" is used, it would go after the direct object. "Karin threw the ball to Brad." But now "to Brad" is not the indirect object but a prepositional phrase.

[2]   Follow this practice for now. Once you are comfortable with the genitive case, your teacher may allow you to shift to the "'s" construction in your translation.

[3]   The final stem vowel is absorbed by the omega, just like the alpha does in the nominative and accusative plural neuter (λογο + ων ‣ λόγων).

7.4   We now meet an important technique that is helpful in learning Greek. It is the use of what we call **key words**. Key words are words that are associated with a particular case that you should put in front of the translation of the actual word. Doing this will help you understand the function of the case.

The key word for the genitive is "**of**."

ἡ δόξα ἀνθρώπου
The glory *of* mankind.

7.5   The indirect object functions the same in Greek as it does in English. In Greek, the indirect object is put in the **dative** case, which means it uses the dative case endings. For example, if the sentence "God gave the world his Son" were in Greek, "the world" would be in the dative case since it is the indirect object.

The key word for the dative is "**to**." Always place the word "to" in front of any word in the dative case.[4]

Iota is the dative singular case ending and ις is the dative plural. In the singular, the final stem vowel lengthens and the iota subscripts. Because alpha lengthens to long alpha, and eta is already long, you do not see the lengthening in the first declension; but it is visible in the second declension because omicron lengthens to omega.

αι	›	ᾳ	*βασιλεια	+ ι	› βασιλείᾳ		
ηι	›	ῃ	*ἀγαπη	+ ι	› ἀγάπῃ		
οι	›	ῳ	*λογο	+ ι	› λογοι › λογωι › λόγῳ		

If you were to see the word λογῳ you would know it is singular and is functioning as the indirect object. If you were to see the word λόγοις you would know it is plural and also is functioning as the indirect object.

Genitive and Dative Case Endings

7.6   Here is the full paradigm for the first and second declension. Notice that the genitive and dative are placed between the nominative and accusative.[5]

---

[4]   As we have said, in English when the preposition "to" is before the noun it becomes a prepositional phrase and not an indirect object. For the time being though, we want you to learn to recognize the function of the case, so use the key word "to" in your translations.

[5]   A much more logical arrangement, in our opinion, would be to order the cases as nominative, accusative, dative, and genitive. It seems smoother to move from subject to object to indirect object. In the neuter the nominative and accusative are the same, and this arrangement would keep them together. But we gave in to conventional usage and listed the cases in the standard format, even though it is awkward.

	2 *masc*	1 *fem*	2 *neut*
nom sg	ς	-	ν
gen sg	υ[6]	ς	υ[7]
dat sg[8]	ι	ι	ι
acc sg	ν	ν	ν
nom pl	ι	ι	<u>α</u>[9]
gen pl	<u>ων</u>	<u>ων</u>	<u>ων</u>
dat pl	ις	ις	ις
acc pl	υς	ς	<u>α</u>

The Article

7.7   Because the article is the key to learning the noun system, you should commit it to memory. There are no more forms of the article, no more possibilities; this is all you need to know. Learn them well. The feminine follows the first declension, the masculine and neuter the second.

	2 *masc*	1 *fem*	2 *neut*
nom sg	ὁ	ἡ	τό
gen sg	τοῦ	τῆς	τοῦ
dat sg	τῷ	τῇ	τῷ
acc sg	τόν	τήν	τό

---

6   As is the case with the masculine accusative plural case ending υς, the genitive singular ending actually is not upsilon. It is omicron which, when combined with final stem vowel contracts to ου. (This is a slight simplification. See Smyth §230 D1 for details.) But we have found it easier to memorize it as υ.

7   As is the case with the masculine singular, the genitive singular neuter ending is omicron which, when combined with final stem vowel, contracts to ου.

8   In the singular (first and second declensions), the iota will always subscript. This is the only place in the noun system where the iota subscripts.

9   The underlined characters show that the case ending has contracted with the vowel of the stem (ἐργο + α ‣ ἔργα).

nom pl	οἱ	αἱ	τά
gen pl	τῶν	τῶν	τῶν
dat pl	τοῖς	ταῖς	τοῖς
acc pl	τούς	τάς	τά

The Full Paradigm

7.8   Following is the full paradigm of first and second declension nouns with the article. Be sure to identify the true endings.

	2 *masc*	1 *fem*	2 *neut*
nom sg	ὁ λόγος	ἡ γραφή ἡ ὥρα	τὸ ἔργον
gen sg	τοῦ λόγου	τῆς γραφῆς τῆς ὥρας	τοῦ ἔργου
dat sg	τῷ λόγῳ	τῇ γραφῇ τῇ ὥρᾳ	τῷ ἔργῳ
acc sg	τὸν λόγον	τὴν γραφήν τὴν ὥραν	τὸ ἔργον
nom pl	οἱ λόγοι	αἱ γραφαί	τὰ ἔργα
gen pl	τῶν λόγων	τῶν γραφῶν	τῶν ἔργων
dat pl	τοῖς λόγοις	ταῖς γραφαῖς	τοῖς ἔργοις
acc pl	τοὺς λόγους	τὰς γραφάς	τὰ ἔργα

Characteristics of Dative and Genitive Nouns

7.9   **Hints**

a.   Both the masculine and neuter have the same case endings in the genitive and dative. This is *always* true.

b.   In the dative an iota is *always* present for all three genders. In the singular it is subscripted.

c. For the dative singular there is an iota subscript, and the plural has
    ις. The dative plural also has a longer ending (two letters) than the
    singular (one letter); you can associate "longer" with the plural.

d. All three genders have the ending "ων" in the genitive plural. This
    is *always* true.

e. Feminine nouns ending in ας can be either genitive singular or accu-
    sative plural. Look either at the definite article (τῆς/τάς) or the con-
    text to decide.

7.10   **Rules**. We have already learned the first three of the eight noun rules. We
        now need to learn the next three. Be sure to memorize them exactly.

    4. *In the dative singular, the iota subscripts if possible.*

        This rule explains what happens to the dative singular case endings
        in the first and second declension. A vowel can subscript only under
        a long vowel.

    5. *Vowels often change their length ("ablaut").*

        "Ablaut" is the technical term for this. By "change their length" we
        mean that they can shorten (omega to omicron), lengthen (omicron
        to omega), or disappear entirely. We see this in the dative singular
        (where the stem vowel lengthens).[10]

    6. *In the genitive and dative, the masculine and neuter will always be identi-
        cal.*

        This may lead you to think that the masculine and neuter forms are
        more closely aligned than the masculine and feminine. As we will
        see later on, the masculine and feminine are actually more similar.

    There are only two more rules to learn, and we will see them in chapter
    10 on third declension nouns.

Translation

7.11   Hints for translating genitive and dative forms.

    a. Be sure to use your key words when you translate a word in the
        dative or genitive.

    b. Whenever you see a noun, do not stop but look further to see if there
        is a word in the genitive following it.

---

[10] The accusative plural case ending is actually νς. When the nu drops out the stem vowel
      omicron lengthens to ου to "compensate" for the loss. This is called "compensatory
      lengthening" and is very common (λογο + νς ‣ λογος ‣ λόγους).

c. Now that you know all four cases, you should really be concentrating on breaking your exercise verses into their different parts. Be sure to locate the subject and direct object. If there is an indirect object, locate that as well.

d. But there is something new that you have to watch for: the genitive. When you are dividing the sentence, a word in the genitive that is showing possession should be kept with the word it is modifying.

> ὁ λόγος τοῦ θεοῦ σώσει ψυχάς.
>
> The word of God will save souls.

In this sentence, the subject is λόγος and the direct object is ψυχάς. As you divide the sentence, you already know to keep the article with the noun it modifies. Now you must also keep the genitive (and its article) with the noun it modifies.

> ὁ λόγος τοῦ θεοῦ / σώσει / ψυχάς.

Summary

1. There is a chart in the Appendix that covers all the Greek cases and their different uses. Use it for reference.

2. The possessive case indicates possession. It uses genitive case endings, and its key word is "of."

3. The indirect object "indirectly" receives the action of the verb. If you can put the word "to" in front of it, it is the indirect object. It answers the question "to whom?" or "to what?" It uses the key word "to" and dative case endings.

4. Memorize all the case endings and the twenty-four forms of the definite article. When you study the full paradigm, be sure to identify the true case endings.

5. Rule 4: In the dative singular, the iota subscripts if possible.

6. Rule 5: Vowels often change their length ("ablaut"). (This includes "contraction" and "compensatory lengthening.")

7. Rule 6: In the genitive and dative, the masculine and neuter will always be identical.

8. When dividing a sentence into its parts, be sure to keep the article and a word in the genitive with the words they modify.

You now know the four main cases and most of the case endings. Congratulations!

Vocabulary

Now that you know the genitive case, we can explain the full form of the lexical listing. A noun is listed followed by sufficient letters to show you its form in the genitive, and then by its article. ἁμαρτία is a feminine noun (ἡ) with the genitive ἁμαρτίας. Always memorize the genitive form with the nominative. This habit will become especially important later on.

ἁμαρτία, -ας, ἡ	sin (173; *ἁμαρτια)[11]
ἀρχή, -ῆς, ἡ	beginning, ruler (55; *ἀρχη)[12]
γάρ	for, then (1041). Postpositive.
εἶ	you are[13]
εἶπεν	he/she/it said[14]
εἰς	into, in, among (1768)[15]
εἰσίν	they are[16]
ἐξουσία, -ας, ἡ	authority, power (102; *ἐξουσια)
εὐαγγέλιον, -ου, τό	good news, Gospel (76; *εὐαγγελιο)[17]
Ἰησοῦς, -οῦ, ὁ	Jesus, Joshua (917; *Ἰησου)[18]
κύριος, -ου, ὁ	Lord, lord, master, sir (717; *κυριο)[19]
μή	not, lest (1042)[20]
οὐρανός, -οῦ, ὁ	heaven, sky (273; *οὐρανο)[21]

---

[11] This word describes both a specific act of sin ("a sin") as well as the concept itself ("sin," "sinfulness"). *Hamartiology* is the study of sin.

[12] The *archbishop* is the *chief* bishop over the archbishopric.

[13] This is another form of εἰμί, which means it will be followed by a predicate nominative.

[14] This verb form is third person singular. This means that it can be one of the three genders, "he," "she," or "it." Let context determine which is appropriate.

[15] In classical Greek there was no overlap in meaning between εἰς ("into") and ἐν ("in"), but in Koine Greek there is. *Eisegesis* is poor hermeneutical practice because it reads a meaning into the text instead of drawing it out of (*exegesis*) the text.

[16] This is another form of εἰμί, which means it will be followed by a predicate nominative. The nu is actually not part of the verb (cf. "movable nu," §8.10), but in our texts the nu is always present (i.e., the form εἰσί never occurs).

[17] An *evangelist* preaches the good news of the gospel.

οὗτος	singular: this (one) (1,388; *οὗτο)[22] plural: these
σύ	you (singular) (1069)[23]
υἱός, -οῦ, ὁ	son, descendant (377; *υἱο)[24]
ὥστε	therefore, so that (83)

Total word count in the New Testament:	138,162
Number of words learned to date:	54
Number of word occurrences in this chapter:	9,081
Number of word occurrences to date:	62,492
Percent of total word count in the New Testament:	45.23%

Previous words

You need to learn the genitives for all the nouns in chapters 4 and 6. This will be the last time you have to alter your vocabulary cards. You will notice that several of the nouns have no expressed genitive form. This is because they are indeclinable. They can function in any of the cases and will never change their form.

Do not worry about the genitive of πνεῦμα and Σίμων until chapter 10.

---

[18] Certain words are not fully declined, or follow rare patterns. This is especially true of proper nouns. Instead of listing all of these separate paradigms, you will be told about the differences as you meet the words. The pattern for the name of Jesus is,

nom sg	ὁ Ἰησοῦς
gen sg	τοῦ Ἰησοῦ
dat sg	τῷ Ἰησοῦ
acc sg	τὸν Ἰησοῦν

How can you tell the difference between the dative and genitive? Correct! The definite article that precedes his name will tell you.

[19] *Kurie eleison* is a petitionary prayer that is used by some Eastern and Roman churches.

[20] Has the same basic meaning as οὐ but is used in different situations that we will discuss later.

[21] *Uranus* is the Greek god of heaven. You will often find οὐρανός in the plural. This is the result of a Jewish way of speaking, and you can translate the plural as a singular if it fits the context.

[22] There is much more to this word than we are presenting here. Its form changes considerably in its different genders. οὗτος is covered in detail in chapter 13. As an adjective it means "this" (singular) and "these" (plural), and as a noun it means "this one."

[23] In English, "you" can be either singular or plural. σύ is always singular. Greek has a different form for the plural.

[24] Can be used generically to mean *child*.

Ἀβραάμ, ὁ   θεός, -οῦ, ὁ

ἀγάπη, -ης, ἡ   καιρός, -οῦ, ὁ

ἄγγελος, -ου, ὁ   καρδία, -ας, ἡ

ἄνθρωπος, -ου, ὁ   κόσμος, ου, ὁ

ἀπόστολος, -ου, ὁ   λόγος, -ου, ὁ

αὐτός, -οῦ   Παῦλος, -ου, ὁ

βασιλεία, -ας, ἡ   Πέτρος, -ου, ὁ

Γαλιλαία, -ας, ἡ   Πιλᾶτος, -ου, ὁ

γραφή, -ῆς, ἡ   προφήτης, ου, ὁ[25]

Δαυίδ, ὁ   σάββατον, -ου, τό

δόξα, -ης, ἡ   φωνή, -ῆς, ἡ

ἐν   Χριστός, -οῦ, ὁ

ἔργον, -ου, τό   ὥρα, -ας, ἡ

ζωή, -ῆς, ἡ[26]

---

[25] Did you notice that this word is different from what you are used to? The ης ending looks like a genitive singular but actually is nominative singular. Also, it is a first declension word but is masculine. Remember we said that most–not all–first declension nouns are feminine.

The genitive singular of this word is προφήτου. In essence, it borrowed the second declension genitive singular case ending so it could be different from the nominative singular. The rest of the paradigm follows the regular first declension pattern. See paradigm n-1f in the *Appendix* for the full paradigm.

[26] ζωή never occurs in the Bible in the genitive plural, but it would be ζωῶν. The two omegas would not simplify to a single omega.

Chapter 8

Prepositions

Exegetical Insight

"Hand this man over to Satan, so that the sinful nature may be destroyed and his spirit saved on the day of the Lord" (1 Cor 5:5, *NIV*). So reads Paul's command to the Christians about the man who was having an affair with his stepmother. The *NIV* margin notes that "sinful nature" (literally, "flesh") could also be translated "body." Commentators are divided as to whether Paul envisions simple excommunication or actual death here, though the former seems more probable. But either way, this command seems harsh by modern standards, particularly in the majority of our congregations that exercise little or no formal church discipline of any kind.

An understanding of the preposition εἰς can shed some light on this verse. The *NIV* reads as if there were two equally balanced purposes behind Paul's command: one punitive and one remedial. But the Greek prefaces the first with an εἰς and the second with the adverb ἵνα. Εἰς can denote either result or purpose; ἵνα far more commonly denotes purpose. Paul's change of language is likely deliberate–to point out that his *purpose* in discipline is entirely rehabilitative, even if one of the *results* of his action is temporary exclusion and ostracism of the persistently rebellious sinner. Or in Gordon Fee's words, "What the grammar suggests, then, is that the 'destruction of the flesh' is the anticipated result of the man's being put back out into Satan's domain, while the express purpose of the action is his redemption."

Not every scholar agrees with this interpretation. But being able to read only a translation like the *NIV* would never alert us to this as an option. Growing exposure to the Greek of the New Testament brings us into frequent contact with numerous prepositions and other connective words that are often left untranslated in English versions, for the sake of literary style and fluency. But in reading only the English, we may miss altogether the originally intended relationship between sentences and clauses, and we may import motives to writers they never held. Whatever the final solution to 1 Cor 5:5 turns out to be, it is certainly true that in every other New Testament instance of church discipline, the purpose was exclusively remedial or rehabilitative and never punitive or vengeful. "The Lord disciplines those he loves" (Heb 12:6), and so should we.

Craig L. Blomberg

Overview

In this chapter we will not learn as much as in the previous two chapters, but we will learn the following:

- prepositions are little words like "over," "under," and "through" that define the relationship between two words;

- the word following the preposition is called the *object* of the preposition;

- how the meaning of a preposition is changed;

- dependent clauses.

English

8.1   **Prepositions**. A preposition is a word that indicates the relationship between two words. In the sentence, "The book is *under* the table," the preposition "under" describes the relationship between "book" and "table," which in this case is a spatial relationship. What are some other prepositions in English?

The word that follows the preposition is called the **object of the preposition**. In the example above, the object of the preposition "under" is "table."

The object of the preposition is always in the **objective** case. You would not say, "The book is under he." You would say, "The book is under him." "He" is subjective and "him" is objective.

Greek

8.2   The function of a preposition in Greek is the same as English. There is one very important fact, however, you need to understand about Greek prepositions. *In Greek, the meaning of a preposition depends upon the case of its object.* For example, the preposition διά means "through" if its object is in the genitive, but "on account of" if its object is in the accusative.[1] The object almost always immediately follows the preposition.

Some prepositions are always followed by the same case, so they only have one set of meanings. For example, the preposition ἐν always takes an object in the dative and has the basic meaning "in." But other prepositions can be followed by two cases, and a few can even be followed by three cases. The object will never be in the nominative.

---

[1]   Technically, this is not accurate. The object does not govern the preposition, but the preposition governs the object. In other words, when a preposition has a specific meaning, it requires that the object be in a certain case. But from our point of view it is easier to look at the case of the object, and from that determine the meaning of the preposition.

8.3 For the purpose of memorization, you should make a separate flash card for each case. In other words, one flash card should say, "διά with the genitive," while another should say, "διά with the accusative."

8.4 Earlier we learned to use the key word "of" with the genitive and "to" with the dative. *However, if a word is in the genitive or dative because it is the object of a preposition, do not use the key word.*

For example, ὁ λόγος τοῦ θεοῦ means, "the word of God." The key word "of" is used since θεοῦ is showing possession. However, the phrase ὁ λόγος ἀπὸ θεοῦ (ἀπό is a preposition meaning "from" and takes its object in the genitive) is translated "the word from God." You would not say "the word from of God," since θεοῦ is genitive due to the preposition and is not showing possession.

8.5 The form of a preposition does not vary depending on the case of its object. It is not inflected. παρά will be παρά whether its object is in the genitive, dative, or accusative.

The only time the preposition changes its form has nothing to do with inflection but with the word that follows. When a preposition ends in a vowel and the following word begins with a vowel, the final vowel of the preposition may be dropped and marked with an apostrophe. This is called "elision" (cf. §4.2).

μετὰ αὐτόν   ‣   μετ᾽ αὐτόν

When a preposition ends in a vowel and the following word begins with a vowel and rough breathing, the consonant before the vowel in the preposition often changes as well. These changes were necessary in order to pronounce the combination of sounds more easily.

μετὰ ἡμῶν   ‣   μετ᾽ ἡμῶν ‣ μεθ᾽ ἡμῶν

You may want to make separate vocabulary cards for each of these altered forms. Each will be specified in the vocabulary section.

8.6 When memorizing the definition of a preposition, we suggest you use this formula:

_____ with the _____ means _____ .

"ἐν" with the "dative" means "in."

8.7 When asked to explain why the object of the preposition is in a given case, we suggest you respond with the complete formula:

_____ *is in the* _____ *because it is the object of the preposition* _____ *that takes the* _____ .

αὐτῷ is in the dative because it is the object of the preposition ἐν that takes the dative.

8.8   **Prepositional phrase.** The preposition together with its object and modifiers is called a "prepositional phrase."

εἰμί

8.9   We have seen most of the forms of εἰμί. Memorize the paradigm. "1st" means "first person," etc. "Sg" means "singular," and "pl" means "plural."

	present tense	*translation*
1st sg	εἰμί	I am
2nd sg	εἶ	You are
3rd sg	ἐστί(ν)	He/she/it is
1st pl	ἐσμέν	We are
2nd pl	ἐστέ	You[2] are
3rd pl	εἰσί(ν)	They are

See §8.10 for an explanation of the "(ν)" at the end of ἐστίν and εἰσίν.

Movable Nu

8.10   A movable nu is a nu occurring at the end of a word that ends with a vowel when that word is followed by a word beginning with a vowel (e.g., εἰσὶν αὐτοί). The purpose of adding the nu was to avoid pronouncing two successive vowels. By adding a nu, a pause is made and the two vowel sounds can be distinguished. This is like changing the English "a" to "an" when the next word begins with a vowel.

Sometimes in Koine Greek, the movable nu is used even when the following word begins with a consonant, especially in the dative plural. Since we are learning only to read Greek and not to write it, this presents no problem. We simply have to recognize it.

---

[2]   In English we use the same word ("you") for the second person pronoun, both singular and plural. Various ways have been suggested to distinguish them in your translation (e.g., "thou" and "ye," "you" and "y'all"). We will use "you" for both, but your teacher may prefer another method.

Dependent Clauses

8.11   In this vocabulary we will learn the word ἵνα meaning "in order that." ἵνα is always the first word in what is called a "dependent clause."

A dependent clause is a collection of words that cannot stand alone. It has meaning only when it is part of a complete sentence; it is dependent upon that sentence.

For example, in English the clause "if I go home" is not a sentence. It is incomplete when standing on its own. It is therefore dependent on the main sentence. "If I go home, I will eat dinner."

Here is the important point: *as you are looking for the main subject and verb in a sentence, you will never find them in the dependent clause.* There will be a subject and verb in the dependent clause, but they will not be the main subject and verb of the sentence.

In chapter six we learned the word ὅτι. It also introduces a dependent clause. You will never find the subject of the sentence in the ὅτι clause.

Translation

8.12   When you are dividing your sentences into sections, make sure to separate the prepositional phrase as a distinct group and see what word the preposition modifies. It usually will be a verb.

ὁ λόγος / ἔρχεται / εἰς τὸν κόσμον.

The word / goes / into the world.

8.13   Greek regularly drops the article in a prepositional phrase. If it fits the context, you may put it back in.

ὁ λόγος ἔρχεται εἰς κόσμον.

The word goes into *the* world.

Summary

1. The word following the preposition is called the object of the preposition.

2. The meaning of a preposition is determined by the case of its object. Always memorize the prepositions with their case(s).

3. The article is usually dropped from prepositional phrases. You can supply it if the context requires it.

4. A dependent clause cannot contain the main subject and verb in a sentence.

Vocabulary

In this chapter you will learn seven prepositions, two-thirds of all major prepositions. Be sure to read the footnote to θάλασσα.

Many students find a graphic representation easier than relying on rote memory. The following chart illustrates the spatial relationship of the prepositions learned in this chapter. Notice that only some of the meanings can be spatially mapped. Try to identify the correct definitions with the correct arrow or line. Notice that prepositions followed by an object in the accusative are those that normally can be graphed.

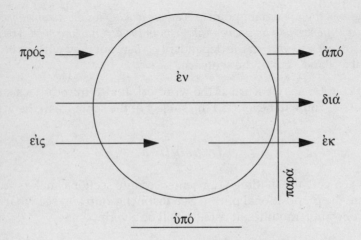

ἀλλά[3]	but, yet, except (638)
ἀπό (ἀπ᾽, ἀφ᾽)[4]	gen: (away) from (646)[5]
διά (δι᾽)	gen: through (667)[6] acc: on account of
ἐκ, ἐξ[7]	gen: from, out of (914)[8]
ἡμέρα, -ας, ἡ	day (389; *ἡμερα)[9]
θάλασσα, -ης, ἡ[10]	sea, lake (91; *θαλασσα)[11]

---

[3] When the word following ἀλλά begins with a vowel, the final alpha elides (ἀλλα Ἰησοῦς ▸ ἀλλ᾽ Ἰησοῦς).

[4] When ἀπό is followed by a word beginning with a vowel, the omicron drops out (ἀπ᾽). If the following word begins with a vowel and rough breathing, it becomes ἀφ᾽.

[5] *Apostasy* (ἀποστασία) is when a person stands off from the truth.

[6] The *diameter* (διάμετρος) measures through the middle of an object.

θάνατος, -ου, ὁ	death (120; *θανατο)[12]
ἵνα	in order that, that (663)
Ἰωάννης, -ου, ὁ[13]	John (135; *Ἰωαννη)
λέγω	I say, speak (2354)
μετά (μετ᾽, μεθ᾽)[14]	gen: with (469)[15]
	acc: after
οἰκία, -ας, ἡ	house, home (93; *οἰκια)
οἶκος, -ου, ὁ	house, home (114; *οἰκο)

---

7   When ἐκ is followed by a word beginning with a vowel, it is written ἐξ.

    If you are really curious, the preposition proper is ἐξ. When it is followed by a word beginning with a consonant, the "sigma" in the "xsi" drops out (think of ξ as "xs") because it is an "interconsonantal sigma," i.e., the sigma occurs between two consonants (exs + consonant ▸ ex ▸ ἐκ).

8   *Ecstasy* (ἔκστασις) is to stand outside of oneself.

9   *Ephemeral* (ἐφήμερος) means that it lasts only one day, is short-lived.

10   Notice anything unusual about this word? Right. The final stem vowel changes to eta in the genitive and the dative singular. Here is the paradigm.

nom sg	θάλασσα	*nom pl*	θάλασσαι
gen sg	θαλάσσης	*gen pl*	θαλασσῶν
dat sg	θαλάσσῃ	*dat pl*	θαλάσσαις
acc sg	θάλασσαν	*acc pl*	θαλάσσας

    There are 36 words in the New Testament that switch their final stem vowel, and of those only four occur with any frequency. See *MBG*, n-1c.

    Here is the rule for the alpha to eta shift. It is important. *If a first declension word has a stem ending in alpha where the preceding letter is epsilon, iota, or rho, it will form the genitive and dative with alpha. Otherwise, the alpha will shift to eta.*

    All feminine plural stems end in alpha, regardless of their form in the singular.

11   *Thalassian* (θαλάσσιος) means "pertaining to the sea."

12   *Euthanasia* ("easy death") refers to a painless death, or allowing or putting to death by withholding medical treatment. *Thanatophobia* is an abnormal fear of death. *Thanatopsis* is a contemplation of death, and the name of a poem by William Cullen Bryant, a good poem but unorthodox theology. "When thoughts of the last bitter hour come like a blight over thy spirit, and sad images of the stern agony, and shroud, and pall, and breathless darkness, and the narrow house, make thee to shudder, and grow sick at heart; – go forth, under the open sky, and list to nature's teachings...."

13   This word follows the same pattern as προφήτης (n-1f). See the Appendix if necessary.

14   When μετά is followed by a word beginning with a vowel, the alpha drops out (μετ᾽). If the following word begins with a vowel and rough breathing, it becomes μεθ᾽.

15   The object of μετά with the genitive will usually be a person or a personal concept. Another preposition (σύν) is used when the object is impersonal. *Metaphysics* is the discussion in Aristotle that comes after his discussion of physics (τὰ μετὰ τὰ φυσικά).

ὄχλος, -ου, ὁ   crowd, multitude (175; *ὀχλο)[16]

παρά (παρ᾽)   gen: from (194)[17]
                                  dat: beside, in the presence of
                                  acc: alongside of

παραβολή, -ῆς, ἡ   parable (50; *παραβολη)[18]

πρός   acc: to, towards, with (700)[19]

ὑπό (ὑπ᾽, ὑφ᾽)[20]   gen: by (220)[21]
                                  acc: under

Total word count in the New Testament:	138,162
Number of words learned to date:	72
Number of word occurrences in this chapter:	8,632
Number of word occurrences to date:	71,124
Percent of total word count in the New Testament:	51.48%

You now know more than one out of every two word occurrences in the New Testament. Congratulations!

Previous Words

εἰς   into, in. εἰς always is followed by the accusative.

ἐν   in. ἐν is always followed by the dative.

---

[16] *Ochlocracy* is mob rule.

[17] A *paragraph* (παράγραφος) was originally a line in the margin beside the writing that marked a division.

[18] A *parable* is a story "thrown beside" (παρά + βάλλω) life.

[19] A *proselyte* (προσήλυτος) is a person who has come over to another religion.

[20] When ὑπό is followed by a word beginning with a vowel, the omicron drops out (ὑπ᾽). If the following word begins with a vowel and rough breathing, it becomes ὑφ᾽.

[21] The object of ὑπό will usually be a person or a personal concept. An *hypothesis* (ὑπόθεσις) is a foundational supposition, which is placed (*θε, forming the Greek word, "I place") under other arguments. A *hypodermic* needle is one that goes under the skin (δέρμα).

Chapter 9

Adjectives

Exegetical Insight

Adjectives have a theological importance that is hard to rival. They can modify a noun (attributive), assert something about a noun (predicate), or stand in the place of a noun (substantival). Sometimes it is difficult to tell exactly which role a particular adjective is in.

Take the adjective πονηροῦ ("evil") in Matthew 6:13, for example. The King James Version (as well as more than one modern translation) translates this as "but deliver us from *evil*." But the adjective has an article modifying it (τοῦ), indicating that it is to be taken substantivally: "the evil one."

And there is no little theological difference between the two. The Father does not always keep his children out of danger, disasters, or the ugliness of the world. In short, he does not always deliver us from evil. But he does deliver us from the evil *one*. The text is not teaching that God will make our life a rose garden, but that he will protect us from the evil one, the devil himself (cf. John 10:28-30; 17:15).

Daniel B. Wallace

Overview

In this chapter you will learn that adjectives:

* can function like an adjective or like a noun;
* can be in three positions;
* agree with the nouns they modify, just like the article;
* can be in any of the three genders, just like the article.

English

9.1   Functions of an adjective

An **adjective** is a word that modifies a noun or pronoun.

Adjectives can function **adjectivally** (i.e., like a regular adjective). "He is a *good* student."

Adjectives can also function **substantivally** (i.e., as if it were a noun). "The *Good*, the *Bad*, and the *Ugly* are all welcome here." "Out with the *old* and in with the *new*." In this case the adjective does not modify anything.

9.2   **Positions of an adjective**. Adjectives can be in one of three positions.

- An adjective in the **attributive** position gives a quality–an attribute–to the word it is modifying (e.g., "The *tall* man plays basketball"). All attributive adjectives function adjectivally; an attributive adjective cannot function substantivally.

- An adjective in the **predicate** position tells us–predicates–something about the word (e.g., "The Bible is *black*." "That idea is *good*."). We have discussed the predicate in chapter 5. A predicate adjective can function either adjectivally or substantivally.

- When an adjective is functioning as a noun, it does not modify another word, and we say it is in the **independent** position.[1]

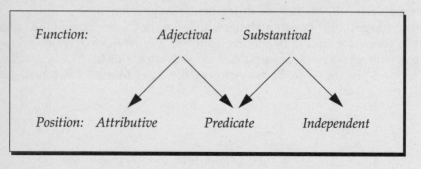

Function: *Adjectival*   *Substantival*

Position: *Attributive*   *Predicate*   *Independent*

Greek

9.3   The adjective in Greek functions both adjectivally and substantivally. The adjectives in this chapter all use the same case endings we have learned so far for nouns.

When an adjective functions **adjectivally**, the *adjective agrees with the noun it modifies in case, number, and gender*. (ἀγαθός is an adjective and means "good.")

ὁ ἀγαθὸς λόγος ἐστίν ...
The good word is ...

When an adjective functions **substantivally**, its *case is determined by its function* as is true of any adjective. Its *gender and number are determined by*

---

1   "Position" may not be the best word, since "independent" is not really a position, but it works.

what it stands for. For example, if it stands for one thing, and that thing is masculine, then the adjective would be masculine singular.

ὁ ἀγαθὸς ἐστίν ...
The good (person) is ...

9.4 To tell the difference between the two functions, ask yourself the question, "Is the adjective modifying something?" If it is, then the adjective is functioning adjectivally. If it is not, if there is no noun for it to modify, then it must be functioning substantivally.

9.5 Because nouns can be in three different genders, and because an adjective must agree with the noun it modifies in case and number as well as gender, an adjective must be able to be masculine, feminine, or neuter.

This is why it is essential that you memorize the gender of all nouns. It will help you determine which noun the adjective is modifying. For example, the adjective ἀγαθή could not be modifying the noun ἄνθρωπος, because ἀγαθή is feminine and ἄνθρωπος is masculine.

9.6 **Forms**

	2	1	2
	masc	*fem*	*neut*
nom sg	ἀγαθός	ἀγαθή	ἀγαθόν
gen sg	ἀγαθοῦ	ἀγαθῆς	ἀγαθοῦ
dat sg	ἀγαθῷ	ἀγαθῇ	ἀγαθῷ
acc sg	ἀγαθόν	ἀγαθήν	ἀγαθόν
nom pl	ἀγαθοί	ἀγαθαί	ἀγαθά
gen pl	ἀγαθῶν	ἀγαθῶν	ἀγαθῶν
dat pl	ἀγαθοῖς	ἀγαθαῖς	ἀγαθοῖς
acc pl	ἀγαθούς	ἀγαθάς	ἀγαθά

Notice the many similarities among these endings and those already learned for nouns and the article.

9.7 **Lexical form.** The lexical form of any word that can appear in more than one gender is the nominative singular masculine.

General Characteristics of the Adjective

9.8   An adjective has case, number, and gender, and will always have the same case, number, and gender as the noun it modifies.

The case endings for adjectives are the same as the case endings for nouns. The feminine follows the first declension and the masculine and neuter follow the second declension.

9.9   Just like nouns, adjectives in the feminine can have an alpha or an eta as the stem vowel. If an adjective has an alpha and not an eta, as in the paradigm above, its singular forms would be as follows.

nom sg	ἁγία	*nom pl*	ἅγιαι
gen sg	ἁγίας	*gen pl*	ἁγιῶν
dat sg	ἁγίᾳ	*dat pl*	ἁγίαις
acc sg	ἁγίαν	*acc pl*	ἁγίας

The final stem vowel in the plural will be alpha, since in the plural all feminine nouns have alpha as the final stem vowel.

9.10   *If the next to the last letter in the stem of an adjective is a rho or a vowel, the feminine stem ends in alpha (νεκρά). All other first and second declension feminine adjectives end in eta (ἀγαθή).*

This is an important rule because it will help determine whether an adjective ending in ας could be genitive or not. For example, the form νεκράς could be either genitive singular or accusative plural, but the form ἀγαθάς can only be accusative plural since its genitive singular must be ἀγαθῆς due to the theta in the stem.

Whether an adjective has an ending in eta or alpha is determined not by the noun but by the adjective. All that an adjective must do is agree in case, number, and gender. How it does it, and what form it uses, is a function of the adjective. Thus the adjective may have an -ης in the genitive even though the noun that it modifies has -ας (e.g., τῆς ἀγαθῆς ὥρας).

Adjectival Use of the Adjective

9.11   *An adjective in the **attributive** position is immediately preceded by the article.* The noun can also be modified by the article. The attributive adjective can appear in two different positions; both are translated in exactly the same way.

First attributive position: ὁ ἀγαθὸς ἄνθρωπος
                                 The good man.

Second attributive position: ὁ ἄνθρωπος ὁ ἀγαθός
The good man.

You will never find ὁ ἀγαθὸς ὁ ἄνθρωπος.[2]

9.12   *An adjective in the **predicate** position is not immediately preceded by the article. The noun is modified by the article. In this case you must use the verb "is" to show the "predicating" nature of the adjective.*

ὁ ἄνθρωπος ἀγαθός
The man is good.

ἀγαθὸς ὁ ἄνθρωπος
The man is good.

9.13   When there is **no article** before the noun or adjective ("independent position"), check the context to determine your translation. Be sure not to supply the article in your translation unless English demands it.

ἀγαθὸς ἄνθρωπος
"A good man" or "A man is good."

ἄνθρωπος ἀγαθός
"A good man" or "A man is good."

Substantival Use of the Adjective

9.14   If there is no noun for the adjective to modify, the adjective must be functioning substantivally. Adjectives used substantivally are regularly (but not always) preceded by the article.

In this case you must use your common sense to translate properly. Ask these questions of the text in order to translate the adjective.

*   What case is it?

    Case is determined by its function in the sentence. If, for example, the adjective is in the nominative case, it must be either the subject or the predicate nominative.

*   What gender and number is it?

    Gender and number are determined by the noun it is replacing. Often you can follow natural gender in deciding how to translate. Notice how you can add an extra word ("man," "woman," "thing," "person," "one") to make sense of the construction in English.

---

[2]   There is a third attributive position. See *Advanced Information.*

ἀγαθός would be translated "a good man" (masculine singular), ἀγαθαί as "good women" (feminine plural), and ἀγαθόν as "a good thing" (neuter singular).

The masculine gender also is used generically; οἱ ἀγαθοί could be "the good ones" or "the good people."

Translation Procedure

9.15   As you divide your sentences into the different parts, be sure to keep the adjective with the noun it is modifying. They form a unit together.

ὁ ἀγαθὸς ἄνθρωπος / γράφει / τὸ βιβλίον.
The good man writes the book.

Summary

1.   Adjectives can function adjectivally (like an adjective) or substantivally (like a noun).

2.   When an adjective functions adjectivally, it can either be in the attributive position (immediately preceded by the article) or in the predicate position (not immediately preceded by the article), in which case you may need to supply the verb "is."

3.   If the next to last letter in the stem of an adjective is a rho or a vowel, the feminine stem ends in alpha (νεκρά). All other first and second declension feminine adjectives end in eta (ἀγαθή).

4.   Attributive adjectives agree with the noun they modify in case, number, and gender.

5.   Substantival adjectives have their case determined by their function, while their gender and number are determined by what they stand for.

Are you getting frustrated with all there is to learn? Go back to chapters 6 and 7, reread them, and see how easy they are now. But remember how difficult they may have been when you first learned them? The fog has just moved from chapter 6 to chapter 9. Keep working, and the fog will continue to move. Ask your teacher to remind you again *why* you are learning biblical Greek.

Vocabulary

Like the article, any word that can occur in all three genders (such as an adjective) uses the masculine form as its lexical form. That is why the word for "good" is listed as "ἀγαθός." What follows ("-ή, -όν") shows the feminine and neuter forms of the word. The feminine of ἀγαθός is ἀγαθή and its neuter is ἀγαθόν. The roots of adjectives are listed with the final stem vowels for both the masculine and the feminine (e.g., *ἀγαθο/η).

Be especially sure to read the footnotes on αἰώνιος.

ἀγαθός, -ή, -όν	good, useful (102; *ἀγαθο/η)[3]
ἀγαπητός, -ή, -όν	beloved (61; *ἀγαπητο/η)[4]
αἰώνιος, -ον[5]	eternal (71; *αἰωνιο)[6]
ἀλλήλων[7]	one another (100; *ἀλληλο)[8]
ἀπεκρίθη	he/she/it answered[9]
δοῦλος, -ου, ὁ	slave, servant (124; *δουλο)
ἐάν	if, when (351), introduces a dependent clause[10]
ἐμός, ἐμή, ἐμόν	my, mine (76; *ἐμο/η)[11]
ἐντολή, -ῆς, ἡ	commandment (67; *ἐντολη)
καθώς	as, even as (182)
κακός, -ή, -όν	bad, evil (50; *κακο/η)[12]

---

[3] *Agatha* is a woman's name.

[4] This is the cognate adjective of the noun ἀγάπη.

[5] αἰώνιος illustrates another kind of adjective. αἰώνιος can be either masculine or feminine. Context will show if a specific form is masculine or feminine. αἰώνιον is neuter.

It is a "2 - 2" pattern because the masculine and feminine follow the second declension; the neuter also follows the second declension but with some variation. In our nomenclature, these adjectives are classified as "a-3," specifically a-3b(1). See *MBG* for the full paradigm.

[6] *Aeonian* means, "eternal."

[7] This is an unusual word because it never occurs in the nominative or in the singular. Its lexical form is therefore genitive plural.

[8] *Parallel* lines (παράλληλος) are lines that are beside (παρά) one another.

[9] This is a common form of a common verb, occurring 82 times in the New Testament. It takes its direct object in the dative, and therefore you do not use the key word with its direct object. ἀπεκρίθη αὐτῷ means, "He answered him," not "He answered to him."

[10] ἐάν is a crasis of εἰ and ἄν. "Crasis" occurs when two words are "pushed together" to make one.

When ἐάν appears after a relative pronoun (ὅς), it has the effect of appending "-ever" to the end of the pronoun, just like ἄν. ὅς ἐάν ... means "whoever ..."

[11] This adjective always means "my" regardless of its case. If it is used substantivally, it always means "mine."

[12] "Caco" is a very common combining form. A *cacophony* is a harsh or bad sound. *Cacoepy* is poor pronunciation. *Cacography* is poor writing skill.

μου (ἐμοῦ)	my[13]
νεκρός, -ά, -όν	adjective: dead (128; *νεκρο/α)[14] noun: dead body, corpse
πιστός, -ή, -όν	faithful, believing (67; *πιστο/η)
πονηρός, -ά, -όν	evil, bad (78; *πονηρο/α)[15]
πρῶτος, -η, -ον	first, earlier (155; *πρωτο/η)[16]
τρίτος, -η, -ον	third (56; *τριτο/η)[17]

Total word count in the New Testament:	138,162
Number of words learned to date:	87
Number of word occurrences in this chapter:	1,668
Number of word occurrences to date:	72,792
Percent of total word count in the New Testament:	52.69%

Previous Words

These are adjectives and other words that can occur in more than one gender. You need to learn their feminine and neuter forms.

ἄλλος, -η, -ο[18]	other, another
αὐτός, -ή, -ό	he/she/it, they
ἔσχατος, -η, -ον	last
οὗτος, αὕτη, τοῦτο[19]	this; these

Advanced Information

9.16   **Third attributive position.** There is a third attributive position: ἄνθρωπος ὁ ἀγαθός. It is rare in the New Testament when the modifier is an adjective, but quite common when the modifier is a phrase.

---

[13] This is the genitive singular of ἐγώ. Unlike ἐμός, μου only means "my" when it is in the genitive case. It can also be written with an initial epsilon and an accent: ἐμοῦ. This word is discussed in detail in chapter 11.

[14] *Necrophobia* is an abnormal fear of death.

[15] *Ponera* is a genus of stinging ants.

[16] A *prototype* is the first of its kind, a model, a pattern.

[17] A *triangle* has three sides.

[18] There are a few words that do not use a case ending for the nominative and accusative singular neuter, and therefore the bare stem stands alone (cf. the article, αὐτός, etc.). They are a-1a(2b) adjectives; their full paradigm is in the Appendix.

[19] The stem of this word changes quite significantly. It is fully explained in chapter 13. It is an a-1a(2b) adjective; its full paradigm is in the *Appendix*.

Chapter 10

Third Declension Nouns

Exegetical Insight

A casual first-century reader of the Fourth Gospel's prologue (John 1:1-18) would have little difficulty understanding John's description of the λόγος. As a concept it was simple enough. Λόγος was the intelligible law of things. ὁ λόγος τοῦ θεοῦ was God's transcendent rationality that gave the universe order and purpose. A Hellenized Jew would quickly reach for a volume of wisdom literature explaining that God's wisdom, his word (or λόγος), provided the universe with its form and coherence. As such, ὁ λόγος τοῦ θεοῦ was foreign to human ways, above us and distant from us, guiding us from afar.

John 1:14, on the other hand, would make any such reader pause in stunned silence. "And the word became flesh (σάρξ) and dwelt among us." Σάρξ is the earthly sphere, the arena of human decisions and emotions, human history, and human sinfulness (cf. John 1:13; 3:6; 17:2, etc.). John 1:14 contains the risk, the scandal, and the gospel of the Christian faith: ὁ λόγος became σάρξ. The center of God's life and thought entered the depths of our world and took up its form, its σάρξ, its flesh, in order to be known by us and to save us.

This affirmation about λόγος and σάρξ is the very heart of our faith. *God has not abandoned us.* No lowliness, no misery, no sinfulness is beyond God's comprehension and reach. He came among us, embraced our world of σάρξ in his incarnation, and loved us. It is easy enough to say that God loves the world (John 3:16). But to say that God loves me, in my frailty and my faithlessness–that he loves σάρξ–this is another matter. This is the mystery and the power of what God has done for us in Jesus Christ.

Gary M. Burge

Overview

In this chapter we will learn:

- the third (and final) declension (i.e., stems ending in a consonant);
- the Master Case Ending Paradigm;
- noun rule 7, the "Square of stops," and the effect of a sigma on it;
- noun rule 8.

Introduction

10.1   What is the difference between the first and second declension? Right. First declension words have stems ending in an alpha or eta. Second declension nouns have stems ending in omicron. And what declension a noun falls into has no effect on its meaning. Regardless of whether ἀπόστολος is first or second declension, it still means "apostle."

The same is true of third declension nouns. Third declension nouns have stems ending in a consonant, but this fact affects only their form, not their meaning.

10.2   *Nouns with stems ending in a consonant follow the third declension pattern.*

The third declension does use a few case endings that are different from those used in the first and second declensions, but not that many. If you have been memorizing the noun with the case endings rather than the actual case endings, you had better go back and relearn your first and second declension case endings now.

10.3   When you first look at a paradigm of a third declension noun, you may think that it is totally different from a first or second declension paradigm. It is not! Because the stem of a third declension noun ends in a consonant, when you add a case ending that begins with a sigma, the final stem consonant and the sigma often change to some other letter, or the consonant drops out, thus hiding the true stem and the true case ending.

For example, the stem of the second declension noun λόγος is *λογο. The omicron joins with the nominative masculine case ending sigma to form λόγος (*λογο + ς ‣ λόγος). No problem. But the stem of the third declension word σάρξ is *σαρκ. The kappa is united with the same nominative singular case ending, and the combination of κσ forms ξ (*σαρκ + ς ‣ σάρξ).

10.4   If you can remember just a few things, these changes will not be a problem.

1.   Because of the changes that take place in the nominative singular, it is often difficult to determine the stem of a third declension noun.

     The solution to this problem is always to memorize the genitive singular form with the lexical form. If you drop the genitive singular case ending, you will always have the word's stem.

2.   Whatever happens in the nominative singular also happens in the dative plural. This is because the dative plural case ending also begins with a sigma.

This is a slight simplification of the situation, but if you can remember these points, the rest is easy to learn.

Since Greek only has three declensions, once you understand these you will be familiar with all the basic forms of nouns in the New Testament. So work on these and you are well on your way toward success.

A Walk Through

10.5 Rather than simply showing you a third declension paradigm, let's walk through one so you can see how easy it is. We will use the stem *σαρκ.

nom sg: The normal nominative singular case ending is sigma. When you add it to this stem, the κσ combination is rewritten as a xsi (σαρκ + σ ▸ σάρξ).

gen sg: The genitive singular case ending for first declension nouns is sigma, and for second declension nouns it actually is omicron (which contracts with the final stem vowel to form ου, *λογο + ο ▸ λόγου). Put those two case endings together, and you have the case ending for the third declension: ος (σαρκ + ος ▸ σαρκός).

dat sg: The dative singular case ending is the same as for the other declensions: iota. But because a third declension stem ends in a consonant and not a long vowel, the iota cannot subscript (σαρκ + ι ▸ σαρκί).

acc sg: The accusative singular case ending is different for the third declension: alpha (σαρκ + α ▸ σάρκα).

nom pl: The nominative plural case ending is different for the third declension: ες (σαρκ + ες ▸ σάρκες).

gen pl: As always, the genitive plural case ending is beautifully consistent: ων (σαρκ + ων ▸ σαρκῶν).

dat pl: The dative plural case ending for a third declension noun is the exact opposite of the first and second declension: σι(ν). Because it begins with a sigma, whatever change we see in the nominative singular will also appear here (σαρκ + σι(ν) ▸ σαρξί [ν]).

acc pl: The accusative plural case ending is different for the third declension: ας (σαρκ + ας ▸ σάρκας). Do not confuse this with a first declension word where the alpha is part of the stem.

There! That was not very difficult, was it?

Forms

10.6   Third declension words are categorized according to the last consonant
of the word's stem. Below you will find four paradigms of the most frequently used classes of third declension words: stems ending in a kappa
(17 words in the New Testament); stems ending in a tau or delta (45)[1];
stems ending with ματ (149); words that have a stem that ends with a
consonantal iota (written as ι)[2] (173). We separated the case ending from
the stem to emphasize the similarities with the first and second declensions.

Do not try to memorize the paradigms. Read through the footnotes so
you can see why the forms do what they do, and then be sure you can
recognize the same endings and changes on other words.

---

[1]   In the following paradigm we have not listed a stem ending in delta. These words follow the same pattern as those ending in tau.

nom sg	ἐλπίς	*nom pl*	ἐλπίδες
gen sg	ἐλπίδος	*gen pl*	ἐλπίδων
dat sg	ἐλπίδι	*dat pl*	ἐλπίσι(ν)
acc sg	ἐλπίδα	*acc pl*	ἐλπίδας

[2]   A consonantal iota looks just like an iota. However, before New Testament times it
was a different character in the alphabet. It dropped out and the vowel iota took over
some of its functions. This is worth noting because iotas will not always behave in a
regular fashion. Down the line knowing this will be a great help. It is called a consonantal iota because the old character shared the characteristics of both a vowel and a
consonant. It is written in the grammars as "ι." It is discussed in more detail in chapter
20.

10.7

	κ *stem*	τ/δ *stem*	ματ *stem*	ι̯ *stem*[3]
	*σαρκ	*χαριτ	*ονοματ	*πιστι
nom sg:	σάρξ[4]	χάρι ς[5]	ὄνομα[6]	πίστι ς
gen sg:	σαρκ ός[7]	χάριτ ος	ὀνόματ ος	πίστε ως[8]
dat sg:[9]	σαρκ ί	χάριτ ι	ὀνόματ ι	πίστε ι
acc sg:	σάρκ α	χάριτ α[10]	ὄνομα[11]	πίστι ν[12]

---

[3] "Consonantal iota." This type of third declension noun is very easy to decline if you realize that the stem vowel is changing between iota and epsilon, but the case endings themselves are consistent.

Because you only have to recognize the forms and not be able to tell when it will be an iota or an epsilon, the rule governing their change is not significant. But if you really want to know, here it is. If the case ending begins with a vowel, the final stem vowel is an epsilon; if the case ending begins with a consonant, then the final stem vowel is an iota. But in the dative plural an epsilon precedes a sigma.

[4] The case ending is sigma, and kappa plus sigma forms xsi (κ + σ ▸ ξ, §10.16).

[5] A tau of the stem drops out when followed by a sigma (χαριτ + ς ▸ χάρις). The same is true of the delta (§10.16).

[6] No ending is used and the final consonant of the stem, which is a tau, drops out because a tau cannot stand at the end of a word (§10.18).

[7] In the first declension, the genitive singular case ending is sigma (γραφῆς). In the second declension it is omicron, and when that omicron contracts with the omicron of the stem ending they form ου (*λογο + ο ▸ λόγου). This is a slight simplification; see *MBG*.

Therefore, the case ending in the third declension should not come as a surprise. It is ος. The trick here is not to confuse this with the second declension final stem vowel and nominative singular case ending (e.g., λόγος).

[8] Think of the ως as a lengthened ος.

[9] Note that the iota does not subscript in the third declension as it does in the first and second. This is because iota can subscript only under a vowel.

[10] In a few cases this word (and others like it) can have an accusative singular in nu (χάριν).

[11] All nouns ending in -μα are neuter. This is one of the few consistent patterns in the third declension. And like all neuter nouns, the nominative and accusative forms are always the same.

[12] This particular pattern of third declension nouns uses nu as the accusative singular case ending.

nom pl:	σάρκ ες	χάριτ ες	ὀνόματ α[13]	πίστε ις[14]
gen pl:	σαρκ ῶν	χαρίτ ων	ὀνομάτ ων	πίστε ων[15]
dat pl:[16]	σαρξ ί(ν)	χάρι σι(ν)	ὀνόμα σι(ν)	πίστε σι(ν)
acc pl:	σάρκ ας	χάριτ ας	ὀνόματ α	πίστε ις[14]

10.8   You now know all the case endings. Congratulations! See the *Master Case Ending Chart* on the next page.

Note that in the first and second declensions, the masculine and feminine are separated. Although they are similar, there are a few significant differences. In the third declension, however, they are almost always identical. There is, in fact, more similarity between masculine and feminine than there is between masculine and neuter, since in the nominative and accusative, the masculine and neuter are always different.

If you learn this paradigm well, you can account for almost every noun form in biblical Greek.

Characteristics of Third Declension Nouns

10.9   **Function**. It is vital that you remember that all Greek nouns function the same. Therefore, whether it is a first, second, or third declension noun, it functions the same. Only the form is somewhat different.

10.10   **Recognition of case endings**. Do not try to memorize the paradigms in §10.7. Memorize the case endings in the *Master Case Ending Chart* and see how the case endings appear when attached to a noun(§10.7). Study them carefully, note what they have in common with each other, and especially what they have in common with the first and second declensions. There are other patterns within the third declension, but if you know these the rest are relatively easy to recognize. Try to list all the similarities.

---

[13]   The way to tell the difference between this form and the nominative singular is to see if the whole stem is present (e.g., *ονοματ). If it is (ὀνόματα), then you are in the plural; if not, the singular (e.g., ὄνομα).

[14]   The nominative case ending is the same as χάριτες (πιστε + ες ‣ πίστεις). The accusative plural uses the same case ending as the nominative plural, as if the word were neuter.

[15]   Notice that the ων case ending does not swallow up the final stem vowel as it does in the first and second declensions. This is evidence that the epsilon has replaced the consonantal iota.

[16]   Whatever change is seen in the nominative singular is also present in the dative plural because both case endings begin with sigma. The case ending is σι, the reverse of the first and second declension ending. The nu in parentheses after every form is a "movable nu" (§8.10).

Master Case Ending Chart

	first/second declension			*third declension*	
	masc	*fem*	*neut*	*masc/fem*	*neut*
nom sg	ς	-	ν	ς -	$-^1$
gen sg	v^2	ς	υ	ος	ος
dat sg	$ι^3$	ι	ι	$ι^4$	ι
acc sg	ν	ν	ν	$α/ν^5$	-

	masc	*fem*	*neut*	*masc/fem*	*neut*
nom pl	ι	ι	<u>α</u>	ες	$α^6$
gen pl	<u>ω</u>ν	<u>ω</u>ν	<u>ω</u>ν	ων	ων
dat pl	ις	ις	ις	$σι(ν)^7$	σι(ν)
acc pl	$υς^8$	ς	<u>α</u>	$ας^9$	α

1. Be prepared for the final stem letter to undergo changes (rule 8).
2. The ending is actually omicron, which contracts with the final stem vowel and forms ου (rule 5).
3. The vowel lengthens (rule 5) and the iota subscripts (rule 4).
4. Because third declension stems end in a consonant, the iota cannot subscript as iota does in the first and second declensions; so it remains on the line.
5. The case ending alternates between alpha and nu.
6. As opposed to the first and second declensions, this alpha is an actual case ending and not a changed stem vowel. This is also true of the accusative plural.
7. The nu is a movable nu. Notice that the ending σι is a flipped version of ις found in the first and second declensions.
8. The actual case ending for the first and second declension is νς, but the nu drops out because of the following sigma. In the first declension the alpha simply joins with the sigma (*ωρα + νς ‣ ὥρας), but in the second declension the final stem omicron lengthens to ου (rule 5; λογονς ‣ λογος ‣ λόγους).
9. As opposed to the first declension (e.g., ὥρα), the alpha here is part of the case ending.

10.11 **Gender.** Like the first and second declension nouns, third declension nouns have gender. But their gender can often be difficult to determine because the inflectional patterns are not as distinct as those of the first and second declensions. There are, however, a few patterns.

- All nouns with stems ending in ματ are neuter (e.g., ὄνομα).

- All nouns with stems that end in consonantal iota are feminine (e.g., πίστις).

It is important to memorize the gender of nouns, especially if they are neuter, because of their specific characteristics.

10.12   **The article**. The article becomes especially important in the third declension. Even though a noun itself changes its form, the article always remains the same. τῷ will always be τῷ whether the noun it modifies is first, second, or third declension.

Do not forget that most nouns are modified by the article, and that makes it easy to determine the noun's gender.

Square of Stops

10.13   *Rule 7: Square of Stops*

The seventh of the eight noun rules is this chart. Be sure to memorize it exactly. Not only should you be able to repeat it left to right but also top to bottom.[17]

Labial	π	β	φ
Velar	κ	γ	χ
Dental	τ	δ	θ

The chart is important because the stops behave in the same way. Whatever happens to a stem ending in tau also happens to a stem ending in delta, because tau and delta are both dentals. If you will learn the pattern, you will be able to predict what is going to happen. This is much easier than memorizing charts of specific changes. This same Square of Stops will also be important when we study verbs, so a little time spent here saves hours of frustration later.

---

[17]   There are also titles for the columns. π, κ, and τ are "unvoiced" because the voice box is not used in their pronunciation. β, γ, and δ are "voiced" because the voice box is used. (Place your fingers on your voice box and pronounce these letters. You will feel it vibrate when you say the voiced stops.) φ, χ, and θ are "aspirates." (The rough breathing is also an aspirate.)

10.14   A **stop** is a consonant whose sound is formed by slowing down or completely stopping the flow of air through the mouth.[18].

10.15   "Stops" are broken down into three classifications.

- **Labial.** π, β, and φ are formed by using the lips to impede the air flow momentarily, which is essential in creating the sound. Try to say π without letting your lips touch.

- **Velar.** κ, γ, and χ are formed by pushing up the middle of the tongue against the soft part of the roof of the mouth.[19]

- **Dental.** τ, δ, and θ are formed by clicking the tongue against the back of the teeth.[20]

10.16   **Stops plus a "σ."** Whenever a stop and a sigma come into contact the results are very predictable. Learn these changes well because you will encounter them often.

Labial	+ σ	‣	ψ
Velar	+ σ	‣	ξ
Dental	+ σ	‣	σ

*σκολοπ   + σ ‣ σκόλοψ[21]
*σαρκ   + σι ‣ σάρξι
*χαριτ   + σ ‣ χάρις[22]

10.17   **ν plus "σ."** Nu drops out when followed by a sigma.

λογο + νς ‣ λογος ‣ λόγους[23]

---

[18] The final column of stops, φ, χ, and θ, technically are not stops but "aspirates" because the air flow is not stopped but only slowed down. However, because they fit into the pattern so well it is easier to view them as stops.

[19] Some people use the term "palatals" to describe these three consonants because the soft part of the mouth's roof is the "palate."

[20] Actually, it is not the teeth but the "alveolar ridge" behind the teeth that is used, but the word "teeth" is easier for most to associate with "dental."

[21] There are only seven nouns in the New Testament whose stems end in a pi, but many stems end in a kappa or tau.

[22] Actually, the dental forms a sigma and the double sigma simplifies to a single sigma (χαριτ + σ ‣ χαρισσ ‣ χάρις).

[23] In second declension nouns, the final omicron lengthens to ου to compensate for the loss of the nu.

Because a dental also drops out when followed by a sigma (§10.16), the combination ντσ will also become sigma.

παντ + ς ‣ πᾶς

10.18 *Rule 8: A tau cannot stand at the end of a word and will drop off.* For example, the stem of the word for "name" is *ὀνοματ. No case ending is used in the nominative singular and tau drops off (*ονοματ + - ‣ ὄνομα).

This is the final rule for case endings. You know all eight. All eight are listed in the Appendix.

πᾶς

10.19 πᾶς is a 3-1-3[24] type adjective and is often used as the paradigmatic word for the third declension. The root of the word is *παντ, which in the feminine is altered to πασα.[25] Armed with this knowledge and the rules in this chapter, you should be able to write out the whole paradigm for this word without looking below. Try it. If you can you are doing well.

	3	*1*	*3*
	masc	*fem*	*neut*
nom sg	πᾶς[26]	πᾶσα	πᾶν[27]
gen sg	παντός	πάσης	παντός
dat sg	παντί	πάσῃ	παντί
acc sg	πάντα	πᾶσαν	πᾶν
nom pl	πάντες	πᾶσαι	πάντα
gen pl	πάντων	πασῶν	πάντων
dat pl	πᾶσι(ν)[28]	πάσαις	πᾶσι(ν)
acc pl	πάντας	πάσας	πάντα

---

[24] "3-1-3" means the masculine and neuter follow the third declension while the feminine follows the first declension. See §10.20.

[25] For you who are interested in advanced morphology, it is altered because consonantal iota was added to form the feminine stem, and ντ + consonantal iota form σα (see *MBG* on πᾶς).

[26] The ντ drops out before sigma (§10.17).

[27] No case ending is used, and a tau cannot stand at the end of a word, so it drops off (§10.18).

[28] The ντ drops out before sigma (§10.17). This is also true in the dative plural neuter.

You may not have expected to see the alpha to eta shift in the feminine singular, genitive and dative. Remember this rule: *If a first declension word has a stem ending in alpha where the preceding letter is epsilon, iota, or rho, it will form the genitive and dative with alpha. Otherwise, the alpha will shift to eta* (see page 61, footnote 10).

εα	▸	ας
ια	▸	ας
ρα	▸	ας

Because πᾶς is an adjective, it can function substantivally. When it does, it may require the use of an additional word like "people" or "things." But unlike other adjectives, πᾶς usually is in the predicate position when modifying a noun.

Categories

10.20   Adjectives fall into four basic categories, depending on which declension they follow and whether the feminine and masculine forms are the same or different. The masculine and neuter always follow the same declension. We met two of these categories earlier: here are all four.

category	masculine	feminine	neuter
2-1-2	2 declension	1 declension	2 declension
3-1-3	3 declension	1 declension	3 declension
2-2	2 declension	2 declension	2 declension
3-3	3 declension	3 declension	3 declension

Article

10.21   There are times when the meaning of the article seems to shift. When you find the phrase ὁ δέ, the article is translated as a personal pronoun, "but he."[29]

---

[29] The Greek article actually is a weakened form of the demonstrative pronoun, and so we will see it used with several different meanings. But this is more second year intermediate grammar than first year. Something to look forward to.

Summary

1. Nouns whose stems end in a consonant use third declension case endings.

2. To find the stem of a third declension noun, find the genitive singular form and drop off the case ending.

3. To memorize the gender of a third declension noun, memorize its lexical form with the article. This is especially important for a neuter noun.

4. Memorize the *Master Case Ending Chart* perfectly.

5. Rule 7: The Square of Stops.

Labial	π	β	φ
Velar	κ	γ	χ
Dental	τ	δ	θ

6. Labial + σ forms ψ. Velar + σ forms ξ. Dental + σ forms σ.

7. Nu and ντ drop out before sigma.

8. Rule 8: A tau cannot stand at the end of a word and will drop off.

9. ὁ δέ can be translated "But he."

Be encouraged! You now know all three declensions and almost all noun forms.

Vocabulary

Be sure to memorize the nominative, genitive, and article for each third declension noun. Normally a lexicon gives just the final letters of the genitive form of a third declension, but we will spell it out for you in this chapter. Be sure to read the footnote for εἷς and ὕδωρ.

ἅγιος, -ία, -ιον	adjective: holy (233; *ἁγιο/α; 2-1-2)[30]
	plural noun: saints
ἀνήρ, ἀνδρός, ὁ[31]	man, male, husband (216; *ἀνδρ)[32]

---

[30] The *Hagiographa* (ἁγιόγραφα) are the holy writings, the third and final part of the Jewish canon. *Hagiolatry* is the worship of saints.

[31] See the Appendix for the full paradigm of this word (n-3f[2c]). It is similar to the pattern of πατήρ. "n-3f[2c]" is an example of the coding system we use for establishing the classes of nouns. It is explained in the introduction to the lexicon.

εἰ | if (503)[33]

εἷς, μία, ἕν[34] | one (344; *εν/*μια; 3-1-3)[35]

ἤδη | now, already (61)

ὄνομα, ὀνόματος, τό | name, reputation (231; *ονοματ)[36]

πᾶς, πᾶσα, πᾶν | singular: each, every (1244; *παντ/πασα; 3-1-3)[37]
| plural: all

πατήρ, πατρός, ὁ[38] | father (413; *πατρ)[39]

περί | gen: concerning, about (333)[40]
| acc: around

πίστις, πίστεως, ἡ | faith, belief (243; *πιστι)[41]

---

[32] *Androgynous* (ἀνδρόγυνη) is being both male and female (i.e., hermaphroditic).

[33] This is not the same as εἶ that means "you are." Watch the accents here carefully, because εἰ does not have its own accent.

Like ἐάν, εἰ always introduces a dependent clause, and therefore you will not find the main subject or verb of the sentence in the εἰ clause.

[34] Notice that this word has a rough breathing in the masculine and neuter. This will help differentiate it from the prepositions εἰς and ἐν. This adjective follows the 3-1-3 pattern, the masculine and neuter following the third declension and the feminine the first. The stem is ἑν and is a third declension stem.

nom sg	εἷς	μία	ἕν
gen sg	ἑνός	μιᾶς	ἑνός
dat sg	ἑνί	μιᾷ	ἑνί
acc sg	ἕνα	μίαν	ἕν

In the nominative masculine, when the nu of the stem drops out because of the sigma, the epsilon lengthens to ει to compensate for the loss (εν + ς ‣ ες ‣ εἷς). Why is there no plural to this word?

[35] A *hendiadys* is a figure of speech in which two nouns describe one thing. It is from the phrase ἓν διὰ δυοῖν, meaning "one thing by means of two." *Henotheism* is the belief in one God while allowing for the existence of other gods.

[36] *Onomatopoeia* (ὀνοματοποιία) is when the name of a word sounds like its meaning, such as "bang" and "whisper."

[37] *Pantheism* is the belief that God is in all things.

[38] See the declension pattern of this word in the Appendix.

[39] The *patriarch* (πατριάρχης) is the father and head of a family or tribe.

[40] The final iota elides only when the following word begins with an iota. The *perimeter* (περίμετρος) is the boundary around an object or area.

[41] *Pistology* is the study of faith.

σάρξ, σαρκός, ἡ   flesh, body (147; *σαρκ)[42]

σύν   dat: with (128)[43]

σῶμα, -ματος, τό   body (142; *σωματ)[44]

τέκνον, -ου, τό   child, descendant (99; *τεκνο)[45]

τις, τι[46]   someone/thing (525; *τιν; 3-3)
                               certain one/thing,
                               anyone/thing

τίς, τί   who? what? which? why? (555; *τιν; 3-3)[47]

ὕδωρ, ὕδατος, τό[48]   water (76; *ὑδατ)[49]

φῶς, φωτός, τό   light (73; *φωτ)[50]

χάρις, χάριτος, ἡ   grace, favor, kindness (155; *χαριτ)

---

[42] A *sarcophagus* (σαρκοφάγος) is a stone coffin. In Greece they were made of limestone, which was believed would consume, or "eat" (φαγέω), the flesh.

[43] "Syn" is a common prefix. A *synagogue* (συναγωγή) is a place where people come together. *Synaeresis* (συναίρεσις) is the contraction of two sounds into one.

[44] A *psychosomatic* disorder is a physical disorder caused by the psychic/emotional processes. *Somatology* is the study of the body.

[45] *Teknonymy* is the custom of naming the parent from the child.

[46] This word and the following are identical in form except for the accent. See their full paradigm in the *Appendix*. This is one situation in which knowing accents is helpful. See the *Appendix* for others.

τις is either not accented or it is accented on its last syllable ("ultima"). It is the indefinite pronoun.

τίς is always accented on its first syllable. It is the interrogative pronoun.

Both are 3-3 adjectives, using the same third declension pattern for the masculine and feminine (τίς), and the third declension for the neuter (τί).

[47] When this word means "why?" it will usually be in the neuter (τί).

[48] This is a different class of third declension noun. Because it is neuter it has the same form in the nominative and accusative singular. All the other forms are built regularly from the stem *ὑδατ (see n-3c[6c] in the Appendix).

nom sg	ὕδωρ	*nom pl*	ὕδατα
gen sg	ὕδατος	*gen pl*	ὑδάτων
dat sg	ὕδατι	*dat pl*	ὕδασι(ν)
acc sg	ὕδωρ	*acc pl*	ὕδατα

[49] *Hydrology* is the study of water. *Hydraulic* (ὕδραυλις) refers to something operated by water.

[50] A *photograph* is a picture drawn by light.

Total word count in the New Testament: 138,162
Number of words learned to date: 106
Number of word occurrences in this chapter: 5,721
Number of word occurrences to date: 78,513
Percent of total word count in the New Testament: 56.83%

Previous words

πνεῦμα, -ματος, τό   spirit, Spirit

Σίμων, -ωνος, ὁ   Simon

10.22 **Hint**. It is common for students to stop memorizing vocabulary because there is so much grammar to learn. Even if you are struggling with grammar, be sure to stay up with your vocabulary, and be sure you are reviewing. How well you know the grammar serves little purpose (or has little value) if you do not know what the words mean. You will not be able to translate the passage.

Chapter 11

First and Second Person Personal Pronouns

Exegetical Insight

Small words sometimes carry a big punch, especially when combined with other features of the Greek language. Pronouns can be those kind of small words. They, like moving vans, can carry a big load. I am thinking of a particularly sinister example of this in Jesus' temptations in Luke 4:6. The devil has taken Jesus on a cosmic ride so he can see all the kingdoms of the world. Then he says to Jesus, "To *you* I will give all of this authority and their glory; for *it* has been delivered to *me* and *I* give *it* to whom *I* will. If *you*, then, will worship *me*, *it* shall be *yours*."

Here is a great (but deceitful) offer, and all the freight is carried in the various exchanges of personal pronouns throughout the passage. To read through the verse one must follow the bouncing ball through various pronoun changes. The devil (*I, me*) offers authority over all the earth (*it*), if Jesus (*you, yours*) will but worship the devil.

But there is one other touch to this verse. To sweeten the offer the pronoun "to you" (σοι) is put at the front of the Greek sentence for emphasis in verse 6. Though some translations suggest this emphasis (*RSV*), a knowledge of Greek reveals its significance. The devil makes the personal and unique nature of the offer clear. The devil is saying, "This offer is just for you!" He tries to present the offer in as attractive a way as possible to Jesus. It is a good thing the devil is not a used car salesman! Fortunately, loyalty to God was more important to Jesus than seizing power. He did not let the devil's use (and abuse) of pronouns trip him up.

Darrell L. Bock

Overview

In this chapter we will learn:

- the first ("I") and second ("you") person personal pronouns;
- that a pronoun's case is determined by its function in the sentence, just like a noun;
- that a pronoun's number and gender are determined by its antecedent.

English

11.1 A **pronoun** is a word that replaces a noun. "It is red." "It" is a pronoun referring back to something.

A **personal pronoun** is a pronoun that replaces a noun referring to a person. "My name is Bill. I will learn Greek as well as possible." "I" is a personal pronoun referring to me, Bill.

The word that a pronoun refers back to, "Bill," is the **antecedent**.

11.2 **Person**. Pronouns can be first person, second person, or third person.

- First person refers to the person speaking ("I", "we").

- Second person refers to the person being spoken to ("you").

- Third person refers to all others ("he," "she," "it," "they").

Notice how highly inflected the English pronoun is. Pronouns are radically changed, depending upon their function.

There is no easy way to distinguish between second person singular and plural. Some grammars retain the old "thou" (singular) and "ye" (plural).[1]

11.3 **Case, Number, and Person**

The case of a pronoun is determined by its function in the sentence, its number and person by its antecedent.

1. The **case** of a pronoun is determined by its function in the sentence. For example, if the pronoun is the subject of the sentence, you would use "I" and not "me," since "I" is in the subjective case. You would not say, "Me would like to eat now," because "me" is objective.

   This is different from an adjective, which determines its case by the word it is modifying. A pronoun does not modify a word (except in the genitive).

2. The **number** of the pronoun is determined by the antecedent. Because "Bill" is singular, you would use "I" and not "we."

3. The **person** of the pronoun is determined by the antecedent. If the antecedent was the person speaking (1st person), you use "I," not "you."

---

[1]

	singular	plural
subjective	thou	ye
possessive	thy, thine	your, yours
objective	thee	you, ye

Another option is to use "you" for the singular and "y'all" for the plural.

4. There is no **gender** in the first and second person. "I" or "you" can be either a woman or a man. The third person pronoun has gender, but we will meet it in the next chapter.

11.4 English forms

	first	*second*
subjective sg	I	you
possessive sg[2]	my	your
objective sg	me	you
subjective pl	we	you
possessive pl	our	your
objective pl	us	you

Greek

11.5 The Greek pronoun is similar to the English pronoun.

*   It replaces a noun.

*   Its case is determined by its function in the sentence.

*   Its number is determined by its antecedent.

*   First and second person pronouns do not have gender.

11.6 Greek forms

We have already learned some of these forms and have seen many of them in the exercises. They should be quite familiar and easy to learn. They follow third declension patterns. The alternate forms in parentheses are discussed in §11.8.

	first	*second*	*translation*	
nom sg	ἐγώ	σύ (σύ)	I	you
gen sg	μου (ἐμοῦ)	σου (σοῦ)	my	your
dat sg	μοι (ἐμοί)	σοι (σοί)	to me	to you
acc sg	με (ἐμέ)	σε (σέ)	me	you

---

[2] If the possessive forms are used substantivally, they are translated "mine," "yours," and "ours."

nom pl	ἡμεῖς	ὑμεῖς	we	you
gen pl	ἡμῶν	ὑμῶν	our	your
dat pl	ἡμῖν	ὑμῖν	to us	to you
acc pl	ἡμᾶς	ὑμᾶς	us	you

Characteristics of first and second person pronouns

11.7 **Form.** Notice the many similarities among the case endings of the pronouns and case endings for the nouns you have already learned.

- The nominative (singular and plural) and accusative (singular) are a little different, but the others are virtually identical with other third declension nouns.

- In the plural, the first and second person personal pronouns are identical except for the first letter.[3]

- Although there are many similarities among these forms and those you already know, some students prefer just to memorize this paradigm.

11.8 **Accents.** In the first person singular, the genitive, dative, and accusative cases will sometimes include an epsilon and an accent (ἐμοῦ, ἐμοί, ἐμέ). The second person pronoun will not add an epsilon but it can add an accent (σύ, σοῦ, σοί, σέ). These accented forms are called the **emphatic** forms.

The emphatic and unemphatic forms basically have the same meaning. The emphatic form is used when the author wants to be especially emphatic, usually because he is contrasting one person with another.

> ἐγὼ ἐβάπτισα ὑμᾶς ὕδατι, αὐτὸς δὲ βαπτίσει ὑμᾶς ἐν πνεύματι ἁγίῳ.
> *I* baptized you in water but *he* will baptize you with the Holy Spirit.

(αὐτὸς is the third person personal pronoun meaning *he*.) The contrast is usually difficult to bring into English.

11.9 **Parsing.** When asked to decline a first or second person personal pronoun, we suggest that you list the case, number, person (not gender), lexical form, and inflected meaning.

> σού: genitive singular second person from σύ meaning "of you" (or "your").

---

[3] Since the upsilon with the rough breathing makes a "hoo" sound, you can remember the person of the plural form by associating "hoo" with "σου."

The lexical forms of the first and second person personal pronouns are the nominative. Some teachers view ἐγώ as the lexical form of ἡμεῖς while others see ἡμεῖς as a separate word. The same holds true for ὑμεῖς.

11.10   **Translation procedure**. If the pronoun is the subject or direct object, then treat it as you would any other subject or direct object. If it is in the genitive, treat it like any other possessive.

> ἐγώ / πιστεύω / λόγον σου.
> I believe your word.

The possessive forms of the pronouns (μου, σου) usually follow the word they modify.

> κύριός μου εἶπεν ....
> My Lord said ....

Summary

1.   A personal pronoun is a word replacing a personal noun.

2.   The English personal pronouns are "I, my, me, we, our, us" (first person) and "you, your" (second person).

3.   The case of a pronoun is determined by its function in the sentence, person and number by its antecedent.

4.   Most of the forms of these two pronouns are similar to the case endings. Concentrate on those similarities.

Vocabulary

ἀδελφός, -οῦ, ὁ   brother (343; *ἀδελφο)[4]

ἄν   an untranslatable, uninflected particle, used to make a definite statement contingent upon something, e.g., changing "who" to "whoever" (167). You usually cannot translate it.

εἰ μή   These two words together can form an idiom[5] meaning "except." Other times they are best translated, "if not." It often introduces a dependent clause.

---

[4]   *Philadelphia* is the city of brotherly love.

[5]   An "idiom" is a phrase that does not have the same meaning as the sum of its parts. When looking at the meaning of each word in the idiom, you can seldom find the meaning of the idiomatic phrase.

This idiom occurs 86 times in the New Testament.

ἐκκλησία, -ας, ἡ	a church, (the) Church, assembly, congregation (114; *ἐκκλησια)[6]
ἔξω	adverb: without (63) preposition (gen): outside
ἐπί (ἐπ᾽, ἐφ᾽)[7]	gen: on, over, when (890)[8] dat: on the basis of, at acc: on, to, against
ἡμεῖς	we (864)
θέλημα, θελήματος, τό	will, desire (62; *θελημaτ)[9]
ἰδέ	See! Behold! (34; interjection)[10]
ἰδού	See! Behold! (200; interjection)[11]
καλός, -ή, -όν	beautiful, good (100; *καλο/η)[12]
μήτηρ, μητρός, ἡ[13]	mother (83; *μητρ)[14]
οὐδέ	and not, not even, neither, nor (143)
οὐδείς, οὐδεμία, οὐδέν[15]	no one, none, nothing (234; οὐ[δε] + *εν/*μια)
ὑμεῖς	you (plural) (1,840)
ὧδε	here (61)

---

[6] *Ecclesiology* is the study of the church. *Ecclesiastical* means "relating to the organization of the church."

[7] When ἐπί is followed by a word beginning with a vowel and smooth breathing, the iota elides (ἐπ᾽). If the following word begins with a rough breathing, the iota elides and the pi aspirates to a phi (ἐφ᾽).

[8] The *epidermis* (ἐπιδερμίς) is the outer layer of skin, "that which is on the skin."

[9] *Monothelitism* is a seventh century heresy that stated Jesus had only one nature and therefore only one will.

[10] Originally ἰδέ was an aorist active imperative of εἶδον, but came to be used as a particle. It only occurs 34 times but because of its similarity with the following ἰδού, we thought it best that you learn it. It is used with the same basic meaning as the following ἰδού.

[11] This form of the verb occurs 200 times. It is actually the aorist middle imperative form of εἶδον, but it is used so many times in this particular form that we thought it best to view it as a separate word.

[12] *Calligraphy* (καλλιγραφία) is "beautiful handwriting."

[13] Follows the same declension pattern as πατήρ, losing the eta elsewhere and adding an alpha in the dative plural. See n-3f(2c) in the Appendix.

[14] A *matriarchal* society is one in which the mother is the dominant figure.

[15] The second half of this word declines just like εἷς.

Total word count in the New Testament: 138,162
Number of words learned to date: 121
Number of word occurrences in this chapter: 5,198
Number of word occurrences to date: 83,711
Percent of total word count in the New Testament: 60.66%

Chapter 12

αὐτός

Exegetical Insight

Pronouns have many different uses in Greek. One of the most common pronouns is αὐτός. Its ordinary use is to "stand in" for a noun to avoid repetition. "James loved Mary, but Mary couldn't stand James" reduces to "James loved Mary, but she couldn't stand him." But sometimes the pronoun is used with a noun to add some kind of stress to it. This is a construction that Peter uses in 1 Peter 5:10, where he writes "And the God of all grace, who called you to his eternal glory in Christ, after you have suffered a little while, will *himself* restore you and make you strong, firm and steadfast." Here Peter reinforces the subject of the sentence by adding the pronoun αὐτός, and the force of the addition is to indicate that God is personally involved in caring for his people.

In his comment on the verse P.H. Davids says, "Our author is emphatic, indicating that God is not removed from their situation, but personally involved." Such a verse would thus have come as all-the-more powerful comfort to Christians who faced hostility from the people round about them. They were being told to recognize in their activity the malevolent working of Satan and to resist him firmly, lest they succumb to the temptation to give up their faith because the going was too tough. In such a situation they needed to be convinced that, just as Satan was at work in their opponents, so God himself was not far away, leaving them to struggle on their own, but was personally concerned for each one of them, to strengthen and sustain them, and eventually to summon them to their eternal reward with him.

I. Howard Marshall

Overview

In this chapter we will learn:

- the three different ways αὐτός is used;

- that since αὐτός is a 2-1-2 adjective, we already know all its forms.

93

English

12.1   **Third person personal pronoun**

	masc	*fem*	*neut*
subjective sg	he	she	it
possessive sg	his	her	its
objective sg	him	her	it

	all genders
subjective pl	they
possessive pl	their
objective pl	them

12.2   The only significant difference between the third person pronouns and the first and second is that third person singular pronouns have gender. The gender and number of pronouns are determined by the gender and number of the antecedent, and their case is determined by their function in the sentence.

For example, if "Robin" is the antecedent, you would say, "I would like to talk to her." You would not say, "I would like to talk to it," because Robin is not an "it." You would not say "them" because Robin is only one, and you would not say, "I would like to talk to she," since the pronoun is the object of the preposition that takes the objective case ("her").

Greek

12.3   You have already met αὐτός meaning "he." It is the third person personal pronoun. Unlike ἐγώ and σύ, αὐτός uses the normal case endings. αὐτός also has gender.

	2	1	2			
	masc	*fem*	*neut*	*translation*		
nom sg	αὐτός	αὐτή	αὐτό	he	she	it
gen sg	αὐτοῦ	αὐτῆς	αὐτοῦ	his	her	its
dat sg	αὐτῷ	αὐτῇ	αὐτῷ	to him	to her	to it
acc sg	αὐτόν	αὐτήν	αὐτό	him	her	it
nom pl	αὐτοί	αὐταί	αὐτά	they		
gen pl	αὐτῶν	αὐτῶν	αὐτῶν	their		
dat pl	αὐτοῖς	αὐταῖς	αὐτοῖς	to them		
acc pl	αὐτούς	αὐτάς	αὐτά	them		

Characteristics of αὐτός

12.4 **Form.** αὐτός uses case endings just like nouns.

- The feminine follows the first declension (which always has eta as the final stem vowel) and the masculine and neuter follow the second declension.

- In the neuter nominative and accusative singular, αὐτός does not use a case ending, so the word ends with the final stem vowel (see a-1a[2b] in the Appendix).

- αὐτός always has a smooth breathing.[1]

12.5 **Declining.** αὐτός is declined just like a regular adjective (i.e., case, number, gender, lexical form, and inflected meaning). Its lexical form is αὐτός.

αὐτοῖς: dative plural masculine or neuter from αὐτός meaning "to them."

12.6 **Gender.** Do not be confused by the difference between Greek and English in the plural. Although in English we do not designate gender, they did in Greek. But regardless of the gender of the Greek pronoun, it will be translated the same in English. αὐταῖς (feminine) and αὐτοῖς (masculine) both are translated "to them."

---

[1] This is important to remember. In chapter 13 we will meet a word whose form is very similar; the only consistent difference between the two is that αὐτός always has a smooth breathing.

The Three Uses of *αὐτός*

12.7   **Summary.** It is wrong to think of αὐτός only as the third person pronoun. The word αὐτός actually performs three distinct functions.

12.8   **Use 1: Pronoun.** αὐτός can function as the third person **personal pronoun**. This is by far its most common use.[2] Translate it as you have become accustomed to.

αὐτός	he	αὐτοί	they
αὐτή	she	αὐταί	they
αὐτό	it	αὐτά	they

In this use, the case of the pronoun is determined by its function, its gender and number by its antecedent. This raises a potentially confusing point. The gender of the Greek pronoun is determined not by natural gender but by the gender of the antecedent. For example, if the antecedent is "world" (κόσμος), you would use the masculine form of the pronoun (αὐτός). However, you would not translate αὐτός as "he" but as "it." We think of the world not as a "he" but as an "it." Choose the translation of the pronoun based on natural gender.

12.9   **Use 2: Adjectival intensive.** αὐτός can also function intensively when it is used adjectivally.[3] In this case αὐτός normally modifies another word and is usually in the predicate position.[4] Translate αὐτός with the reflexive pronoun (himself, herself, itself, themselves, etc.).[5]

---

[2]   In the oblique cases (genitive, dative, accusative), αὐτός is used 5,203 times in the New Testament out of the total 5,595 times as a personal pronoun .

[3]   "Adjectival intensive" is non-standard terminology but it is helpful. It is the terminology used by *Gramcord*.

 Gramcord lists 143 occurrences in the New Testament of αὐτός as the adjectival intensive pronoun, but it includes the uses of αὐτός as the identical adjective (below). It lists fourteen occurrences as a strictly reflexive pronoun.

[4]   Some beginning Greek grammars such as Machen (§105) say that αὐτός must be in the predicate position to function as an intensive. As you will see from the exercises, this is not always the case. In fact, this chapter makes a significant departure from other grammars. They tend to translate αὐτός on the basis of its position, specifically, whether it is preceded by the article or not. Because there are so many exceptions to this way of looking at αὐτός, and because we feel it is theoretically preferable, we have classified αὐτός on the basis of function rather than position.

[5]   The Greek reflexive pronoun ἐμαυτοῦ was formed through the combination of the personal pronoun ἐγώ and αὐτός. This illustrates the close relationship between αὐτός and the reflexive idea.

αὐτός agrees with the noun it modifies in case, number, and gender. Choose the gender of the reflexive pronoun based on the natural gender of the word αὐτός modifies.

αὐτὸς ὁ ἀπόστολος
the apostle himself

ἡ ἐκκλησία αὐτή
the church itself/herself

αὐτὸ τὸ δῶρον
the gift itself

ἐγὼ αὐτός
I myself

ὁ πέμψας με πατὴρ αὐτός μοι ἐντολὴν δέδωκεν (John 12:49).
The one who sent me, the *father himself*, has given me a command.

Do not confuse this with the predicate position of other adjectives. When an adjective is in the predicate position you must insert the verb "to be." When αὐτός is in the predicate position, it is modifying the noun adjectivally.

12.10   When functioning as an intensive, αὐτός is usually in the nominative case and modifies the subject.[6]

αὐτὸς Δαυὶδ εἶπεν ἐν τῷ πνεύματι τῷ ἁγίῳ (Mark 12.36).
David himself spoke by the Holy Spirit.

Ἰησοῦς αὐτὸς οὐκ ἐβάπτιζεν ἀλλ᾽ οἱ μαθηταὶ αὐτοῦ (John 4:2).
Jesus *himself* was not baptizing but his disciples.

This is the same use of the personal pronoun we saw with ἐγώ and σύ. Remember, because the verb indicates its own subject, the use of αὐτός is unnecessary, and therefore its presence can be emphatic.

Different suggestions have been made on how to translate αὐτός when it occurs in this situation. Some suggest using a reflexive pronoun as in the illustrations above. In this situation, αὐτός gives emphasis to the subject. It is David himself and not someone else who spoke by the Holy Spirit. The pronoun also shows if the subject is masculine, feminine, or neuter.

Others suggest ignoring the personal intensive use of αὐτός in the nominative because this translation does not sound proper to English ears. If

---

6   Some grammarians argue that αὐτός can be used in the nominative without any sense of emphasis, simply as the personal pronoun and not as an intensive pronoun.

Gramcord separates this use from the adjectival intensive, calling it the "personal intensive." For didactic reasons we have put them together. αὐτός is used 243 times in the New Testament as a personal intensive, 239 times in the nominative.

you do ignore it, be sure to remember that it can add an intensifying force.

The subject of the verb does not have to be third person. When used with the first or second person, αὐτός still adds emphasis.

> σὺ αὐτὸς λέγεις τοῖς ἀνθρώποις
> You (yourself) speak to the men.

12.11   **Use 3: Identical adjective.** αὐτός is sometimes used as the identical adjective meaning "same." It is normally in the attributive position when used this way, but not always.[7] Its case, number, and gender are determined by the word it modifies, as is the case with any adjective.

> καὶ πάλιν ἀπελθὼν προσηύξατο τὸν αὐτὸν λόγον (Mark 14:39).
> And again after going away he prayed *the same thing*.

> Ἐν αὐτῇ[8] τῇ ὥρᾳ προσῆλθάν τινες Φαρισαῖοι (Luke 13:31).
> In *the same hour* some Pharisees came.

12.12   **Chart**

use	comment	translation
1. *Pronoun*	Non-intensive.	"he, she , it"
2. *Adj. intensive*	Usually predicate position. Normally in the nominative.	"him/her/itself"
3. *Identical adj.*	Usually attributive position.	"same"

1. αὐτὸς λέγει ...

2. τὸν Ἰησοῦν αὐτόν
   Ἰησοῦς αὐτός ....

3. ὁ αὐτὸς Ἰησοῦς ...

---

[7]   αὐτός is found in the attributive position 60 times in the New Testament.

[8]   Notice that there is no article in this example. This shows that the anarthrous αὐτός can function as the identical adjective, despite what many grammars say.

Translating the Third Person Pronoun

12.13   Most of the time αὐτός functions as the third person personal pronoun. In the nominative, it may be adding emphasis, usually by way of contrast.

Always confirm your translation of the pronoun with its antecedent. Make sure that the word you use to translate the pronoun agrees with its antecedent.

12.14   In chapter 10 we saw how the article can function as a personal pronoun in the expression ὁ δέ. We will see later that other words can as well be translated as a third person personal pronoun. The demonstrative pronouns (chapter 13) are often translated as "he," "she," etc.

Summary

1.   αὐτός uses the normal case endings except for the nominative and accusative neuter singular that drop the nu. This is a common variation.

2.   When αὐτός functions as a pronoun, its case is determined by function, its number and gender by antecedent.

3.   When αὐτός adds emphasis it is usually translated with the reflexive pronoun. It usually will be in the predicate position, in the nominative case.

4.   αὐτός can function as the identical pronoun and be translated "same." In this case it normally is in the attributive position.

Vocabulary

αἰών, -ῶνος, ὁ	age, eternity[9] (122; *αἰων)[10]
διδάσκαλος, -ου, ὁ	teacher (59; *διδασκαλο)[11]
εὐθύς	immediately (51)[12]
ἕως	conj: until (146) gen: as far as
μαθητής, -οῦ, ὁ[13]	disciple (261; *μαθητη)

---

[9]   The idioms εἰς τὸν αἰῶνα and εἰς τοὺς αἰῶνας τῶν αἰώνων both mean "forever."

[10]   Cognate noun of the adjective αἰώνιος.

[11]   Different teachers have different *didactic* (διδακτικός) methods.

[12]   This adverb is different from the adjective εὐθύς, -εῖα, -ύ, meaning "straight" and occurring only nine times in the New Testament.

[13]   μαθητής is declined just like προφήτης. A disciple is a "learner." *Math* is related to μάθημα, meaning "that which is learned." *Mathematics* is from μαθηματική.

μέν	on the one hand, indeed[14] (179)
μηδείς, μηδεμία, μηδέν	no one/thing (90; μη[δε] + *εν/*μια)[15]
μόνος, -η, -ον	alone, only (114; *μονο/η)[16]
ὅπως	how, that, in order that (53)
ὅσος, -η, -ον[17]	as great as, as many as (110; *ὁσο/η)[18]
οὖν	therefore, then, accordingly (499)[19]
ὀφθαλμός, -οῦ, ὁ	eye, sight (100; *ὀφθαλμο)[20]
πάλιν	again (141)[21]
πούς, ποδός, ὁ	foot (93; *ποδ)[22]
ὑπέρ	gen: in behalf of (150)[23] acc: above

Total word count in the New Testament:	138,162
Number of words learned to date:	136
Number of word occurrences in this chapter:	2,168
Number of word occurrences to date:	85,879
Percent of total word count in the New Testament:	62.16%

---

[14] Postpositive. Sometimes this word is untranslatable. It can occur as a correlative conjunction with δέ. In this case you can translate μέν ... δέ as "on the one hand ... but on the other."

[15] Declines just like οὐδείς.

[16] A *monogamous* marriage is a marriage in which a person has only one spouse. All adjectives can function adverbially. This word does so quite often, usually as an accusative neuter (μόνον).

[17] The initial ὁσ retains the same form, but the second half of the word declines like the relative pronoun. For example, the nominative plural masculine is ὅσοι.

[18] This word is idiomatic; rely on context to help with a precise definition.

[19] Postpositive.

[20] *Ophthalmology* is the study of the eye.

[21] A *palimpset* (παλίμψηστος, "scraped again") is a parchment that has had the original writing scraped off so it can be used again. *Palilogy* (παλιλογία) is the repetition of words for emphasis. The *paligenesia* (παλιγγενεσία) is the rebirth, both of the Christian (Titus 3:5) and of the world in Stoic thought.

[22] A *podiatrist* is a doctor dealing with foot disorders. Notice how the word's root came over into English with the "d," even though it is not visible in the nominative πούς. Most cognates are formed from the Greek root and not an inflected form such as the nominative.

[23] "Hyper" is a common prefix designating excess, abundance. An *hyperbole* is an exaggeration for effect.

Chapter 13

Demonstrative Pronouns/Adjectives

οὗτος, ἐκεῖνος

Exegetical Insight

δικαιοσύνη is one of the great words in Christian theology. Basically it means, "the character or quality of being right or just." It is a word used to describe God. He is in the ultimate sense the Just One (Rom 3:5, 25). It is also used to describe the righteous life of the believer, i.e., a life lived in obedience to the will of God (Rom 6:13, 16, 18, 19, 20; Eph 6:14, etc.).

But the most important use of δικαιοσύνη in the New Testament is to describe the gracious gift of God by which through faith in Jesus Christ one is brought into a right relationship to God. Such a relationship is apart from law, i.e., apart from the works of the law–we can do nothing to obtain it. However, the "Law and the Prophets," i.e., the Old Testament Scriptures, testify to it. It was all a part of God's redemptive plan that we should have been put into a right relationship with him through his Son.

Luther was right when he wrote: "For God does not want to save us by our own but by an extraneous righteousness, one that does not originate in ourselves but comes to us from beyond ourselves."

> My hope is built on nothing less
>
> Than Jesus' blood and δικαιοσύνη.

Walter W. Wessel

Overview

In this chapter we will learn:

- the demonstrative pronouns and adjectives "this" and "that";
- that they behave just like pronouns and adjectives except that when functioning as adjectives they are in the predicate position;
- the fifth and final case, the vocative, used when addressing a person directly.

101

English

13.1 Demonstratives in English are "this/these" and "that/those" (singular/plural). For example, "This book is the greatest Greek textbook." "Those students really work hard." They are never inflected except to indicate singular and plural.[1]

13.2 The same word can be either a pronoun ("*That* is mine.") or an adjective ("*That* car is mine.").[2]

Greek

13.3 The demonstratives in Greek are οὗτος (this/these) and ἐκεῖνος (that/those). They function the same way as they do in English, both as pronouns and as adjectives. The difference between the English and Greek demonstratives is that the Greek demonstratives also have case and gender.

- When a demonstrative functions as a pronoun, its case is determined by its function in the sentence. Its number and gender are determined by its antecedent, just like any pronoun.

- When a demonstrative functions as an adjective, its case, number, and gender are determined by the noun it is modifying, just like any adjective.

   In the following paradigms, translate each form as an adjective and then as a pronoun. The feminine follows the first declension, and the masculine and neuter follow the second.

13.4 **The forms of οὗτος**

	masc	fem	neut
nom sg	οὗτος	αὕτη	τοῦτο
gen sg	τούτου	ταύτης	τούτου
dat sg	τούτῳ	ταύτῃ	τούτῳ
acc sg	τοῦτον	ταύτην	τοῦτο

---

[1] A distinction that some find helpful is that between the "near" and "far" demonstratives. The near is "this/these" and the far is "that/those." The idea is that "this/these" refers to something in relative proximity, and "that/those" to something relatively far away.

[2] For the sake of simplicity we will simply call them the demonstratives.

nom pl	οὗτοι	αὗται	ταῦτα
gen pl	τούτων	τούτων	τούτων
dat pl	τούτοις	ταύταις	τούτοις
acc pl	τούτους	ταύτας	ταῦτα

13.5   The forms of ἐκεῖνος

	masc	*fem*	*neut*
nom sg	ἐκεῖνος	ἐκείνη	ἐκεῖνο
gen sg	ἐκείνου	ἐκείνης	ἐκείνου
dat sg	ἐκείνῳ	ἐκείνη	ἐκείνῳ
acc sg	ἐκεῖνον	ἐκείνην	ἐκεῖνο
nom pl	ἐκεῖνοι	ἐκεῖναι	ἐκεῖνα
gen pl	ἐκείνων	ἐκείνων	ἐκείνων
dat pl	ἐκείνοις	ἐκείναις	ἐκείνοις
acc pl	ἐκείνους	ἐκείνας	ἐκεῖνα

Characteristics of Demonstrative Pronouns

13.6   Form. The demonstratives use the regular case endings. There are three peculiarities that need to be learned carefully.

1. The neuter singular nominative and accusative do not use a case ending, so the form ends in the stem omicron rather than ov. This is the same as αὐτός, ἄλλος, and ὁ.

2. οὗτος always begins with a rough breathing or tau. Think of the two as interchangeable. This is important in distinguishing the demonstrative (αὗται) from αὐτός, which always has a smooth breathing (αὐταί).

3. The first stem vowel used in οὗτος depends upon the final stem vowel. If the final vowel is alpha or eta, the demonstrative will have αυ in the stem. If the final vowel is omicron, the stem will have ου. This point is not as significant as the first two since we are only learning to recognize the forms and not memorizing paradigms.

13.7   **Demonstrative pronoun**. Demonstratives can be either pronouns or adjectives. If they are functioning as pronouns, they are in the **isolated** position, which means they have nothing to modify. If they are functioning adjectivally, they must modify a word.

	οὗτος		ἐκεῖνος
οὗτος	this (man/one)	ἐκεῖνος	that (man/one)
αὕτη	this (woman)	ἐκείνη	that (woman)
τοῦτο	this (thing)	ἐκεῖνο	that (thing)
οὗτοι	these (men/ones)	ἐκεῖνοι	those (men/ones)
αὗται	these (women)	ἐκεῖναι	those (women)
ταῦτα	these (things)	ἐκεῖνα	those (things)

The word in parentheses is the meaning of the demonstrative when it is used substantivally. If your translation requires this additional word, pick whatever makes the best sense, following natural gender. For example, ἐκείνη would not be translated "that man."

13.8   **Demonstrative adjectives**. If a demonstrative is functioning as an adjective, it is written in the **predicate** position although it is translated as an attributive adjective.

> οὗτος ὁ ἄνθρωπος
> This man
>
> ὁ ἄνθρωπος οὗτος
> This man
>
> ἐκεῖνοι οἱ ἄνθρωποι
> Those men

This is the opposite of regular adjectives, so do not get them confused.

13.9   Sometimes the demonstrative pronoun weakens in its force and functions as a personal pronoun.

> οὗτος ἔσται μέγας καὶ υἱὸς ὑψίστου κληθήσεται (Luke 1:32).
> *He* will be great and will be called "Son of the Most High."

As you might have guessed, there is substantial overlap among the article, the demonstrative pronoun, and the personal pronoun.

Vocative

13.10   The fifth, and final, case is the vocative, the "case of direct address." A noun uses vocative case endings when it is being directly addressed. In the following example, the person is addressing the "Lord" directly.

> Οὐ πᾶς ὁ λέγων μοι, Κύριε κύριε, εἰσελεύσεται εἰς τὴν βασιλείαν τῶν οὐρανῶν (Matt 7:21).
> Not everyone saying to me, "Lord, Lord," will enter into the kingdom of heaven.

The forms of the vocative, for the most part, are quite simple. It is usually obvious from context when the word is in the vocative.

- In the plural, the vocative is always identical to the nominative plural (ἄνθρωποι).

- In the singular first declension, the vocative is the same as the nominative (ἀδελφή).

- In the singular second declension, the vocative ending is usually epsilon. If you were speaking directly to a man you would say, ἄνθρωπε.

- In the singular third declension, the vocative is usually the bare stem of the word, sometimes with the stem vowel being changed due to ablaut. The vocative of πατήρ is πάτερ.

There are a few other forms of the vocative, but this information is enough for now. Normally context will warn you when a form is in the vocative.

Summary

1.   The demonstrative "this/these" is οὗτος and "that/those" is ἐκεῖνος. οὗτος always begins with either a rough breathing or tau. Neither uses a case ending in the nominative/accusative neuter singular.

2.   When they function as a pronoun their case is determined by their function in the sentence, number and gender by their antecedent. You can supply a helping word if you wish, determined by natural gender.

3.   When they function as an adjective, their case, number, and gender agree with the word they are modifying. They will always be in the predicate position although they are translated as attributive adjectives.

4.   A demonstrative can weaken in force and be used as a personal pronoun.

5.   The vocative is the case of direct address.

- In the plural, it is identical to the nominative regardless of declension.

- In the singular first declension, it is always identical to the nominative.

- In the singular second declension, it usually has the case ending epsilon.

- In the singular third declension, it usually is the bare stem.

Vocabulary

Be sure to read the footnote about "crasis" on κἀγώ.

γυνή, γυναικός, ἡ[3]	woman, wife (215; *γυναικ)[4]
δικαιοσύνη, -ης, ἡ	righteousness (92; *δικαιοσυνη)
δώδεκα	twelve (75). Indeclinable.[5]
ἑαυτοῦ, -ῆς, -οῦ[6]	singular: of himself/herself/itself plural: of themselves[7] (319; *ἑαυτο/η)
ἐκεῖνος, -η, -ο	singular: that man/woman/thing plural: those men/women/things (265; 2-1-2; *ἐκεινο/η)
ἐλπίς, -ίδος, ἡ	hope, expectation (53; *ἐλπιδ)[8]
ἤ[9]	or, than (343)
κἀγώ[10]	and I, but I (84). Indeclinable.
μακάριος, -ια, -ιον	blessed, happy (50; 2-1-2; *μακαριο/α)[11]
μέγας, μεγάλη, μέγα[12]	large, great (243; 2-1-2; *μεγαλο/η)[13]

---

[3]   γυνή is declined like σάρξ (n-3b[1]). The ικ is lost in the nominative singular.

[4]   *Gynecology* is the branch of medicine dealing with women's diseases.

[5]   A *dodecagon* is a plane with twelve sides and twelve angles.

[6]   Because of the word's meaning, it can never occur in the nominative; so for this word the lexical form is the genitive singular. It follows the same inflectional pattern as αὐτός.

[7]   ἑαυτοῦ in the plural can also be translated as first ("ourselves") or second ("yourselves") person.

[8]   The Christian "hope" is not a wondering if something will happen, but the "confident anticipation" of what we know will surely come to pass. This is a great word for a word study. In a less serious vein we might mention that *Elvis* fans hope that he did not really die.

[9]   Do not confuse this with the article ἡ, which always has a rough breathing.

[10]   A crasis of καί and ἐγώ. A "crasis" is when a word is formed by combining two words. See the Appendix for a list of all forms of crasis in the New Testament.

[11]   Metzger, *Lexical Aids*, suggests the cognate "macarism," which is a beatitude.

[12]   See the paradigm of this word in the Appendix (a-1a[2a]).

πόλις, -εως, ἡ   city (162; *πολι)[14]

πολύς, πολλή, πολύ[15]   singular: much (416; 2-1-2; *πολλο/η)[16]
                                   plural: many
                                   adverb: often

πῶς   how? (103)[17]

σημεῖον, -ου, τό   sign, miracle (77; *σημειο)[18]

Total word count in the New Testament:	138,162
Number of words learned to date:	150
Number of word occurrences in this chapter:	2,497
Number of word occurrences to date:	88,376
Percent of total word count in the New Testament:	63.97%

Previous Words

οὗτος, αὕτη, τοῦτο   singular: this; he, she, it (1388; 2-1-2; *τουτο/η)
                                   plural: these

---

[13] *Mega* is a common prefix meaning "large" or "great": *megaphone, megavolt, Megalosaurus*, which is a genus of extremely large dinosaurs (σαῦρος means "lizard").

[14] *Metropolis* ("mother-city") is the parent city of a colony, especially an ancient Greek colony. The word came to be used of any capital or large city. *Neapolis* is the port city of Philippi (Acts 16:11).

[15] For the full paradigm see a-1a(2a) in the Appendix.

[16] *Poly* is a common combining form meaning "many": *polysyllabic, polyandry, polygamy, polyglot, polygon*.

[17] There is another word πώς meaning "at all, somehow, in any way," occurring 15 times. The only difference between the two words is the accent.

[18] In John's gospel especially, miracles are signs as to who Jesus truly is. *Semeio* is a combining form meaning "sign" or "symptom." *Semeiology* is sign language. *Semeiotic* means, "pertaining to symptoms."

Chapter 14

Relative Pronouns

Exegetical Insight

One author refers to the author of the first of our four canonical Gospels as "meticulous Matthew." Matthew regularly displays intentional precision in his account of the Savior's earthly life and ministry in order to accentuate truths that are important for devotion and doctrine. This precision is quite evident in the genealogy Matthew uses to introduce Jesus the Christ at the beginning of his gospel. When he comes to the listing of Jesus he says, "... and Jacob the father of Joseph, the husband of Mary, *of whom* was born Jesus, who is called Christ" (Matt 1:16, *NIV*). To whom do the italicized words "of whom" refer? Joseph as father? Mary as mother? Both Joseph and Mary as parents? It is possible for the English words "of whom" to mean any of these.

However, behind the English words "of whom" stands the Greek relative pronoun ἧς. The feminine gender of the relative pronoun points specifically to Mary as the one from whom Jesus Christ was born. The genealogy regularly emphasizes the male who fathers a child, but here "meticulous Matthew" delivers a precise statement of the relationship of Jesus Christ to Joseph and Mary. While the genealogy establishes that Joseph is the legal father of Jesus, Matthew emphasizes that Mary is the biological parent "of whom" Jesus was born. Further, the passive voice of the verb ἐγεννήθη ("was born")–the only passive among the forty occurrences of γεννάω in the genealogy–prepares for Matthew's emphasis upon divine action in the conception and birth of Jesus (1:18-25).

In his comment on this verse, R.H. Gundry says, "the feminine gender of ἧς prepares for the virgin birth by shifting attention from Joseph to Mary." The Greek relative pronoun is a subtle signature of the relationship of one substantive to another. Here, by the use of the feminine form the author intentionally stresses that Mary is the mother of our Lord, and later he will clarify that the conception is miraculous, brought about by the Spirit of God coming upon her. Jesus Christ is indeed the son of David, the son of Abraham (1:1), but he is also the Son of God, Immanuel, "God with us" (1:23). This is no ordinary king in the line of David. This is our Savior and Lord, born of the virgin Mary.

Michael J. Wilkins

Overview

In this chapter we will learn:

- the relative pronouns "who," "that," and "which";

- that like any pronoun, their gender and number is determined by their antecedent, while their case is determined by their function in the relative clause;

- relative clauses are always dependent clauses, so they cannot contain the main subject and verb of the sentence.

English

14.1 The relative pronouns in English are "who," "whom," "that," "which," and "whose." Usage of these words today differs widely, and therefore the following examples merely reflect general usage.

- "Who" and "whom" are used to refer to humans (e.g., The teacher, whom the students love, won the teacher of the year award.).

- "Who" is used for masculine and feminine concepts and "which" for neuter.

- "That" can refer to either (e.g., The glass that broke was my favorite. I helped the boy that fell off his bike.).

- "Whose" usually refers to humans, but generally speaking it is accepted for non-humans as well (e.g., I sold the car whose color made me ill. I love the girl whose eyes sparkle in the moonlight.).

Notice that the relative pronouns can refer back to a singular ("the student who") or plural ("the students who") antecedent.

14.2 A relative pronoun introduces a clause that usually modifies a noun. In the examples just given,

- "whom" introduced the clause "the students loved" and modified the noun "teacher";

- "that" introduced the clause "broke" and modified the noun "glass."

Note how little the pronoun is inflected.

14.3 It is important to note that relative pronouns do not introduce questions. They always refer to a noun or a noun phrase. For example, a relative pronoun is not used in a question like, "Whose eyes sparkled in the moon light?" The word "whose" in this example is an interrogative pronoun.

14.4   A **relative clause** is the relative pronoun and the clause it introduces. "The teacher *who has a halo around his head* teaches Greek."

14.5   Do not forget that clauses can perform many of the same functions as nouns and adjectives. A relative clause can be the subject (*"Whoever is with me* is not against me."), direct object ("I eat *what is placed before me."*), object of a preposition ("Give the Bible to *whomever asks for it."*). This becomes very important in our translation procedure because the relative clause must be viewed as a unit.

Greek

14.6   The relative pronouns in Greek are basically the same as the English except that they have case, number, and gender. They are ὅς, ἥ, and ὅ for the masculine, feminine, and neuter respectively.

14.7   **The forms of the relative pronoun**

	2	1	2	
	masc	*fem*	*neut*	*translation*
nom sg	ὅς	ἥ	ὅ	who/which/that
gen sg	οὗ	ἧς	οὗ	of whom/which
dat sg	ᾧ	ᾗ	ᾧ	to whom/which
acc sg	ὅν	ἥν	ὅ	whom/which/that
nom pl	οἵ	αἵ	ἅ	who/which/that
gen pl	ὧν	ὧν	ὧν	of whom/which
dat pl	οἷς	αἷς	οἷς	to whom/which
acc pl	οὕς	ἅς	ἅ	whom/which/that

The accent helps distinguish the relative pronoun from the article in the nominative that has no accent in the masculine and feminine (ὁ, ἡ; οἱ, αἱ).

Characteristics of Relative Pronouns

14.8   **Form.** Notice the similarities between the relative pronouns and the noun endings. They are almost identical. The neuter nominative and accusative singular do not have the nu but only the omicron, just like αὐτός and the demonstratives.

The relative pronouns are also similar to the article. The key for distinguishing the two is noting the breathings and accents. The relative pronouns always have a rough breathing mark and an accent. The article always has either a rough breathing mark or a tau, and may be unaccented.

14.9 **Antecedent.** *The number and gender of a relative pronoun are the same as its antecedent*, just like αὐτός. You can see how looking for the antecedent will help check your translations and make them accurate.

Sometimes the antecedent will not be in the same verse as the relative pronoun; you will have to look at the preceding verse(s). Even then sometimes you will find no antecedent. How then do you determine to what the relative pronoun is referring? Context!

14.10 **Case of the relative pronoun.** *The case of the relative pronoun is determined by its function in the relative clause.* Do not confuse the relative pronoun with the adjective whose case is determined by the word it modifies.

ὁ ἄνθρωπος ὃν γινώσκομεν διδάσκει ἡμᾶς.
The man whom we know teaches us.

In this example you can see that even though the antecedent (ἄνθρωπος) is nominative, the relative pronoun (ὅν) is accusative because it is the direct object of the verb γινώσκομεν.

14.11 **Relative clause**. The term "relative clause" refers to the relative pronoun and the words that follow it. If you place a comma before the relative pronoun and after the last word of the clause, the enclosed phrase should make sense. In fact, this kind of partitioning is a good practice when learning to translate.

14.12 A relative pronoun is translated various ways depending upon the function of the relative clause. This is an issue of English grammar and not Greek.

1. If the relative clause modifies a word, then the relative pronoun is translated with the simple "who," "which," or "that."

   The man *who is sitting at the table* is my pastor.

2. Relative clauses can also be the subject, direct object, indirect object, object of a preposition, etc. In other words, they can perform almost any function that a noun can. In these cases, it may be necessary to add a pronoun to the clause to make better sounding English.

   For example, in the sentence *"Who will be first* will be last," the relative clause is the subject of the verb "will be." To make the translation smoother you could add a personal pronoun, *"He* who will be first will be last."

You can also add a demonstrative pronoun ("Give the good grade to *those* who deserve it.")

Use your educated common sense to determine the appropriate pronoun. Gender and number are determined by the context.

Translation Procedure

14.13 As was the case with prepositional phrases, it is important to keep the relative clause together as a unit when you are dividing up the sentence.

> ὁ Ἰησοῦς / ἐλάλησεν / ὅ ἐστιν δίκαιον.
> Jesus spoke what is righteous.

14.14 Relative clauses are always dependent; they may never contain the main subject and verb of the sentence.

Summary

1. Relative pronouns introduce relative clauses that are capable of performing many tasks like nouns, adjectives, and adverbs.

2. The relative pronouns are ὅς, ἥ, and ὅ. They follow the normal 2-1-2 declension patterns (like αὐτός) and always have a rough breathing and an accent.

3. Like other pronouns, the case of a relative pronoun is determined by its use in the relative clause, and its number and gender by its antecedent.

4. You can add a pronoun to your translation of a relative clause; use your educated common sense and context to determine the best pronoun.

5. They always introduce a dependent clause.

Vocabulary

ἀλήθεια, -ας, ἡ	truth (109; *ἀληθεια)[1]
εἰρήνη, -ης, ἡ	peace (92; *εἰρηνη)[2]
ἐνώπιον	gen: before (94)
ἐπαγγελία, -ας, ἡ	promise (52; *ἐπαγγελια)
ἑπτά	seven (88). Indeclinable.[3]
θρόνος, -ου, ὁ	throne (62; *θρονο)[4]

---

[1] The girl's name *Alethea* means "truth." *Alethiology* is the science of the truth.

[2] *Irenic* (εἰρηνικός) means "peaceful."

[3] A *heptagon* has seven sides.

Ἰερουσαλήμ, ἡ	Jerusalem (77)[5]
κατά (καθ')	gen: down from, against (473)[6] acc: according to, throughout, during
κεφαλή, -ῆς, ἡ	head (75; *κεφαλη)[7]
ὁδός, -οῦ, ἡ[8]	way, road, journey, conduct (101; *ὁδο)
ὅς, ἥ, ὅ	who (whom), which (1,365)
ὅτε	when (103)[9]
οὕτως	thus, so, in this manner (208)
πλοῖον, -ου, τό	ship, boat (68; *πλοιο)
ῥῆμα, -ματος, τό	word, saying (68; *ῥηματ)[10]
τε	and (so), so (215)[11]
χείρ, χειρός, ἡ	hand, arm, finger (177; *χειρ)[12]
ψυχή, -ῆς, ἡ	soul, life, self (103; *ψυχη)[13]

Total word count in the New Testament:	138,162
Number of words learned to date:	168
Number of word occurrences in this chapter:	3,530
Number of word occurrences to date:	91,906
Percent of total word count in the New Testament:	66.52%

---

[4] *Throne.*

[5] Ἰερουσαλήμ is indeclinable; it will not change its form regardless of usage. However, the article will be inflected.

[6] *Cata* is a common combining form meaning "down." *Catabasis* is the declining stage of a disease. *Catalogue* (κατάλογος) is a counting down in the sense of creating a list. A *catastrophe* (καταστροφή) is a sudden disaster, a down turn.

[7] *Hydrocephalus* (ὑδροκέφαλον) is the name given to the condition of an increase in the amount of water in the cranium with resulting brain damage.

[8] Notice that although this word appears to be masculine, it is really feminine. It is a second declension feminine noun (n-2b in the Appendix). It looks like λόγος but is feminine. The article that modifies it will always be feminine.

[9] Do not confuse this word with ὅτι.

[10] *Rhetoric* (ῥητορική) is the art of using words effectively.

[11] τε is a postpositive and weaker in force than καί.

[12] *Chirography* is writing. A *chiromancer* is a palmist, a palm reader.

[13] *Psychology* is the study of a person's self.

Previous Words

ἄν   When used in conjunction with a relative pro-
                                noun, ἄν makes the pronoun indefinite (e.g.
                                "who" becomes "whoever").

ἐάν   if, when, -ever[14]

Advanced Information

14.15   **Attraction.** Greek, as is the case with any language, does not always follow the basic rules. All spoken languages are in a constant state of flux,
so nice, neat grammatical rules often break down.

This is the case with the relative pronoun. Its case is supposed to be determined by its function, but in certain situations we see that it is altered
to be the same case as its antecedent, as if it were modifying it. This is
called "attraction."

Attraction occurs when the case of the relative pronoun is attracted to
the case of its antecedent. It happens usually when the relative pronoun
occurs in the immediate proximity to the antecedent, when the antecedent is dative or genitive, and when the relative pronoun normally would
be accusative.

ἤγγιζεν ὁ χρόνος τῆς ἐπαγγελίας ἧς ὡμολόγησεν ὁ θεὸς τῷ Ἀβραάμ.
The time of the promise that God promised to Abraham has drawn
near.

The relative pronoun ἧς *should* have been the accusative ἥν because it is
the direct object of ὡμολόγησεν, but it was attracted to the genitive case
of its antecedent ἐπαγγελίας.

---

[14] We have already learned this word in chapter 9, but now you know to use "-ever" in
your translation when it is associated with a relative pronoun.

Chapter 15

Introduction to Verbs

Exegetical Insight

In some translations of Matthew 18:18, it sounds like Jesus promised his disciples that whatever they bound on earth would be bound in heaven, and whatever they loosed on earth would be loosed in heaven. In other words, they had the power to bind and loose, and Heaven (i.e., God) would simply back up their decrees. But the matter is not quite so simple; the actions described in heaven are future perfect passives–which could be translated "will have already been bound in heaven ... will have already been loosed in heaven." In other words, the heavenly decree confirming the earthly one is based on a prior verdict.

This is the language of the law court. Jewish legal issues were normally decided in Jesus' day by elders in the synagogue community (later by rabbis). Many Jewish people believed that the authority of Heaven stood behind the earthly judges when they decided cases based on a correct understanding of God's law. (This process came to be called "binding and loosing.") Jesus' contemporaries often envisioned God's justice in terms of a heavenly court; by obeying God's law, the earthly court simply ratified the decrees of the heavenly court. In Matthew 18:15-20, Christians who follow the careful procedures of verses 15-17 may be assured that they will act on the authority of God's court when they decide cases.

Just as we struggle to affirm absolutes in a relativist culture, Christians today sometimes wonder how to exercise discipline lovingly against a sinning member of the church. In this text, Jesus provides an answer: when the person refuses to turn from sin after repeated loving confrontation, the church by disciplining the person simply recognizes the spiritual reality that is already true in God's sight.

Craig S. Keener

Overview

In this chapter we will learn:

- the basic grammar relating to verbs;
- the concept of "aspect" and its tremendous significance for a proper understanding of the Greek verb;
- the following terms: agreement, person, number, tense, time, voice, mood;

115

- the main components of the Greek verb (stem; connecting vowel; personal endings; augment; tense formatives).

Introduction

15.1   In chapter five we covered the basic grammar relating to nouns. Now it is time to begin with verbs.

As we have been going through the previous chapters, we have covered bits and pieces of the verbal grammar. This was done so that you would already know some of the basics about verbs before we begin this chapter.

Do not try to learn the Greek forms you see in this chapter. They are given just to expose you to the concepts. We will start learning the actual forms in the next chapter.

Terms

15.2   **Verb.** A verb is a word that describes action or state of being. "I *am studying* Greek." "Greek *is* the heavenly language."

15.3   **Agreement.** A verb must *agree* with its subject in person (first, second, or third) and number (singular or plural). This means that if a subject is singular, the verb must be singular. If the subject is third person, the verb must be third person.

For example, in English you would not say "*Bill say* to the class that there *are* no test." Since "Bill" is singular, you would say, "*Bill says* to the class that there *is* no test." The presence or absence of the "s" at the end of the verb is an example of *agreement* in English.

A Greek verb accomplishes this by using personal endings, which are suffixes added to the end of the verb. For example, ω is a first person singular personal ending, and therefore λέγω means "I say." ουσι is a third person plural personal ending, and therefore λέγουσι means "they say."

Do not try to learn the following paradigm. It is designed merely to show you how the endings function. The verbal stem *ἀκου means "to hear."

ἀκούω	I hear
ἀκούεις	You hear
ἀκούει	He/she/it hears
ἀκούομεν	We hear
ἀκούετε	You hear
ἀκούουσι	They hear

Because the verbal ending agrees with its subject, the ending can help confirm if you found the correct subject. For example, if you think that the word "book" is the subject and yet the verb is first person, then "book" cannot be the subject since "book" is third person. This process of double checking the ending against the subject is an extremely important habit to develop.

Notice that there is no such thing as case or gender in verbs. Case and gender belong to the noun system.

The Greek sentence does not require an expressed subject. A verb by itself may be a complete sentence in Greek. Both ἐγὼ λέγω and λέγω mean "I say."

15.4 **Person.** There are three persons: first, second, and third. This is the same thing we saw with ἐγώ, σύ, and αὐτός.

- First person is the person speaking ("I," "we").

- Second person is the person being spoken to ("you").

- Third person is everything else ("he," "she," "it," "they," "book").

A verb must agree with its subject in person. It does this by using the appropriate personal ending. For example, εις is a normal ending for second person singular. Therefore, if the subject is "you" (σύ) the verb would end in εις. σὺ λέγεις means "You say." If the subject is "we" (ἡμεῖς) the verb would end in ομεν. ἡμεῖς λέγομεν means "We say."

15.5 **Number.** Number refers to whether a word is **singular** (referring to one thing) or **plural** (referring to more than one thing). Because subjects can be singular or plural, and because a verb must agree with its subject in number, Greek must have different personal endings for singular and plural.

If the subject is "I," then the personal ending will be a first person singular (ω). If the subject is "we," then the personal ending is a first person plural (ομεν). If the verb is referring to one boat, then the personal ending is third person singular (ει); but if there are many boats, then the ending is third person plural (ουσι).

15.6   **Aspect**. This is perhaps the most difficult concept to grasp in verbs, and yet it is the most important and most misunderstood. The basic genius of the Greek verb is not its ability to indicate *when* the action of the verb occurs (time), but *what type of action* it describes, or what we call "aspect."

For example, what is the difference between saying "I studied last night" and "I was studying last night"? The first merely says that an event occurred last night; it describes a simple event. It does not give you a clue as to the precise nature of your study time. The second pictures the action of studying as an ongoing action, a process, something that took place over a period of time. This difference between a simple event and a process is what we mean by "aspect."

Another example is Jesus' words to his disciples: "If anyone wishes to come after me, let him deny himself and take up his cross and follow me" (Mark 8:34). "Deny" and "take up" are undefined while "follow" is continuous. The aspect of "deny" and "take up" does not tell us anything about the nature of those actions except that they are to occur. But the aspect of "follow" emphasizes that the commitment to discipleship involves a day to day following.[1]

In Greek there are three aspects.

- The **continuous** aspect means that the action of the verb is thought of as an ongoing *process*.

- The **undefined** aspect means that the action of the verb is thought of as a *simple event*, without commenting on whether or not it is a process.

  It is argued by some that "undefined" is not an aspect, and by "undefined" we simply mean the absence of aspect. This may or may not be technically correct, but if it is helpful for the time being, then think this way. The "undefined aspect" is the absence of any specific aspect.

- The **perfect** aspect describes an action that was brought to completion but has effects carrying into the present. "Jesus *has died* for our sins." "It *is written*, you shall not cram for a test."

In English, you form the continuous by adding a **helping** verb ("I *am* eating; I *was* eating"), while the undefined is the simple form of the verb ("I eat; I ate"). English has no exact equivalent to the perfect.

---

[1]   Another example would be, "How do you do?" versus "How are you doing?"

15.7 **Undefined vs. Punctiliar.** One of the primary areas of confusion in Greek exegesis comes when people confuse the Greek undefined with the English punctiliar aspect. The English punctiliar describes an action as occurring in a single point of time. "The tidal wave *hit* the boat."[2] The Greek undefined is not punctiliar. It tells you nothing about the action of the verb except that it happened.

It is interesting that Luke's version of Jesus' statement we mentioned above is a little different from Mark's. He says, "If anyone wishes to come after me, let him deny himself and *take up his cross daily,* and follow me" (Luke 9:23). He includes "daily" to emphasize that the action of "taking up" occurs every day. Does this contradict the Markan account that simply says, "take up"? No. Both Mark and Luke use the same undefined aspect when saying "take up." The verb does not specify the nature of the action; it merely says that it should occur. But Luke includes the adverb "daily" to clarify that this action is a daily action. He could just have easily used the continuous aspect ("taking up") and arrived at the same meaning.[3]

Part of the misconception surrounding the Greek undefined aspect is due to the fact that it can be used to describe a punctiliar action. However, such a verb is not punctiliar because of the aspect of the Greek verb but because of the context and the meaning of the word. You cannot use the continuous aspect to describe a punctiliar action, so by default you must use the undefined.

15.8 Certain tenses[4] in Greek, such as the present tense, can be either continuous or undefined. The verb λέγω is in the present tense and can mean either "I am saying" (continuous) or "I say" (undefined). The first describes an ongoing process while the second simply describes an event. Which translation you choose is determined by the context of the passage.

However, there are other tenses that are either continuous or undefined. For example, in Greek there are two tenses that indicate past time, the "imperfect" and the "aorist." In the imperfect tense the aspect is continuous, but in the aorist the aspect is undefined.

---

2   The *continuous* version of this sentence would be, "The tidal wave *was hitting* the boat."

3   If you want to get very specific, the Greek undefined aspect does not describe what actually happened. It describes how the writer chooses to tell you about the action. You could describe a waterfall with a continuous verb, emphasizing the continual flow of water. You could also use the undefined aspect to describe the waterfall. This would not mean that you did not know whether the water was continually falling or not. It means that you did not care to emphasize its continual flowing. You just wanted to say that the water started at the top and ended at the bottom.

4   "Tenses" in English are the present, future, past, etc. See §15.10.

15.9   **Perfect** aspect. The third aspect is the perfect. It describes an action that was brought to its full completion but has effects carrying on into the present. For example, on the cross Jesus cried out, "It is finished" (τετέλεσται). His life and sacrifice are the completed action, and the ongoing effects are the story of Pentecost and beyond. We will not deal with the perfect until chapter 25.

15.10   **Tense.** "Tense" in English refers to the **time** when the action of the verb takes place. If you study your Greek right now, then the verb is in the **present tense** ("study"). If you are planning on doing it tomorrow, then the verb is in the **future tense** ("will study"). If you did it last night, then the verb is in the **past tense** ("studied"). In other words, in English the terms "tense" and "time" refer to the same thing, i.e., when the subject performed the action of the verb.

The term "tense" is used differently in Greek grammars; it is quite easy to become confused. It perhaps would be easiest at first simply to use "tense" and "time" interchangeably. But this would build a significantly erroneous misconception into your basic thinking that will constantly get in the way of proper exegesis down the road. So, from the very beginning, we will use exact terminology.

The problem is that in Greek a tense carries two connotations: aspect and time. For example, the aorist tense describes an undefined action (aspect) that normally occurs in the past (time). In this grammar, we use the term "tense" to refer only to the *form* of the verb (e.g., present tense, future tense, aorist tense), and we do not use the term to designate *when* the action of a verb occurs. We always use the term "time" to describe "when" the action of that verb occurs. Do not confuse "tense" and "time."

15.11   **Time.** As we have just said, "time" refers to when the action of the verb takes place. In English the different "times" are past, present, and future.

15.12   **Voice.** "Voice" refers to the relationship between the subject and the verb.

- If the subject *does* the action of the verb, then the verb is in the **active** voice. "Bill hit the ball. "Hit" is in the active voice because the subject, Bill, did the hitting.

- If the subject *receives* the action of the verb, the verb is in the **passive** voice. "Bill was hit by the ball." "Was hit" is the passive voice because the subject "Bill" was hit.

   The passive voice is formed in English by adding a helping verb ("was" in the example above). Greek uses a different set of personal endings to indicate the passive. ἐσθίω means "I eat," while ἐσθίομαι means "I am being eaten."

- Greek has a third voice called the **middle**. Although it has several different nuances, for the time being equate the middle with the active.

15.13 **Mood**. Mood refers to the relationship between the verb and reality. A verb is in the **indicative** if it is describing something that is, as opposed to something that may or might be. This includes statements and questions. For example, "I am rich." "Are you rich?" We will not meet any mood other than the indicative until chapter 31 so we will not confuse you by discussing the other moods now.

15.14 **Parse**. When you parse verbs, we suggest you do it as follows:[5]

person; number; tense; voice; mood; lexical form; definition of inflected form.

first person singular, present active indicative, of ____ meaning ____.

The only mood we will learn for quite a while is the indicative, so just get used to saying "indicative" in your parsing.

15.15 **Lexical form.** The lexical form of verbs is the first person singular, present indicative. Always![6] This grammar always lists words in the vocabulary section in their lexical forms.

The Main Components of the Greek verb

15.16 **Stem**. The stem of a verb is the part of the verb that carries its basic meaning. It is like the stem of a noun. While it is possible for the stem of a verb to undergo some changes, most of the changes are in the ending of the verb, just like the nouns. But there can also be changes at the beginning of the verb and sometimes in the stem itself (like the vowel shift from πατήρ to πατρός).

The form λύομεν means "We destroy." The stem is *λυ.

15.17 **Connecting vowel**. Often Greek adds a vowel between the stem or tense formative of a verb and its personal ending. This is to aid in the pronunciation of the word.

λέγετε means "You say." The stem is *λεγ. The connecting vowel is the second ε.

---

5   Teachers will differ on the parsing order, so this is only a suggestion.

6   Some of the older grammars list the infinitive form (λέγειν, "to say") as the lexical form, but lexicons are consistent now in listing verbs in the first person singular, present (λέγω, "I say").

15.18 **Personal endings**. In nouns, the different functions are indicated by different case endings. We have somewhat the same situation with verbs, although here they are called personal endings. These are suffixes that are added to the end of the verb and indicate person and number.

For example, the stem *λεγ means "say" and the personal ending ω means "I," therefore λέγω means "I say." λέγομεν means "we say," because the personal ending μεν means "we." ("ο" is the connecting vowel.)

15.19 This chapter is not intended to teach you the specifics of Greek verbs. Each of these topics will be covered in detail at the proper time. These examples are intended merely to give you a general idea of the types of things we will be looking at in the next several chapters.

Verbs are the most exciting part of the Greek language. Many times the theology of a passage, or a clearer insight into the nuance of the passage, is hidden in the aspect of the verb. But knowing verbs requires work, and without a good knowledge of verbs you will never enjoy the language. So hang in there, and keep on working.

Incidentally, it will be quite easy to mix nouns and verbs unintentionally. For example, verbs do not have case or gender; but in parsing verbs you might get confused and say that a verb is in the accusative. One of the main reasons why we taught you nouns first and then verbs is to help minimize this natural confusion.

Summary

1. A verb agrees with its subject in person (first; second; third) and number (singular; plural).

2. Agreement is accomplished through the use of personal endings.

3. The true significance of the Greek verb is its ability to describe aspect. A verb can be continuous, which means the process it describes is an ongoing action. It can be perfect, which means the action it describes has been brought to completion, the effects of which reach into the present. Or a Greek verb can be undefined, which means that the author is not giving us a clue as to the true nature of the action other than to say that it occurred.

4. The undefined aspect can be used to describe what in English we call the punctiliar aspect, but the fact that the Greek form is undefined does not mean that it necessarily describes a punctiliar action.

5. "Tense" describes the form of the verb.

6. "Time" describes when the action of the verb occurs.

7. Voice can be active (i.e., the subject does the action), passive (i.e., the subject receives the action of the verb), or middle (which we are equating with the active for the time being).

8. The indicative mood is the dominant mood, used to make a statement of fact or a question.

Advanced Information

15.20 **Augment**. An augment is a prefix that is attached to the beginning of the verb–much like "ed" is added to some English verbs to make them past time–showing that the action of the verb occurred in the past. In most cases it is an epsilon.

For example, λύω means "I destroy"; ἔλυσα means "I destroyed." The initial epsilon is the augment. (As you can see, the ending has changed as well from ω to σα.)

You will not see augments until chapter 21.

15.21 **Tense formatives**. To indicate different tenses in Greek, along with the augment Greek can also add a tense formative to the end of the verbal stem but before the connecting vowel and personal ending. A tense formative is a consonant or collection of letters. They are called the "tense formative" because they form the different tenses for the Greek verb.

For example λύω means "I destroy." The present tense uses no tense formative. *λυ is the stem and ω is the personal ending. However, to say "I will destroy" (future), you add the tense formative "σ" between the stem of the verb and its personal ending. λύσω means "I will destroy." To make it past time you augment the verb and add the past tense formative σα. ἔλυσα means "I destroyed."

There are six tenses in Greek. For the most part, all but the present tense use a tense formative. You will not see tense formatives until chapter 19.

Chapter 16

Present Active Indicative

Exegetical Insight

One of the elements of Greek grammar that you will meet in this lesson is that if a sentence does not contain a word in the nominative, the subject is included in the verb itself; you can tell what pronoun to use as the subject by the ending on the verb. But if the Greek sentence has a pronoun in the nominative, the author is placing emphasis on the subject of the verb.

Numerous times in John's gospel, beginning with John 6:35, Jesus uses the pronoun ἐγώ with the verb "to be" in the expression ἐγώ εἰμι ὁ ... ("*I* am the ..."; see also 6:41; 8:12; 9:5; 10:7,9,11,14; 11:25; 14:6; 15:1,5). In each case, he is emphasizing who *he* is. For example, when Jesus says ἐγώ εἰμι ὁ ἄρτος τῆς ζωῆς (6:35) he is, as it were, pointing a finger towards himself and saying, "If you want spiritual nourishment in your life, then look to me and me only, for *I* am the bread of life." The other ἐγώ εἰμι verses have a similar emphasis. Anything that we want in our spiritual lives we can find by looking to our blessed Savior Jesus Christ.

There is more. Jesus' use of ἐγώ εἰμι harks back to the Old Testament, to the story of Moses when he was approached by God at the burning bush (Exod 3). When Moses challenged the Lord to give his name, God replied by saying (in the Septuagint), ἐγώ εἰμι ὁ ὤν ("I am the one who is"). That is, Yahweh is the great "I AM" (Exod 3:14). Jesus taps into this famous title for God when he says to the Jews, "Before Abraham was, I am (ἐγώ εἰμι)" (John 8:58), ascribing to himself the very same name that Yahweh used in the Old Testament concerning himself. And this same name and expression underlie all of Jesus' ἐγώ εἰμι statements in John's Gospel.

Verlyn Verbrugge

Overview

In this chapter we will learn:

- that the present tense describes an action that usually occurs in the present time;
- that the present tense can describe an ongoing action (continuous aspect), or say nothing about the verb's aspect (undefined);
- the three parts to a present active indicative verb: present tense stem, connecting vowel; personal ending;
- the primary active personal endings.

English

16.1 The present indicative describes an action occurring in the present. The active voice is used when the subject is performing the action of the verb. The indicative mood describes a fact or asks a question.

For example, "I see the tall man." "See" describes an action that is being performed by the subject of the sentence "I" at the present time.

Greek

16.2 The present active indicative verb in Greek is basically the same as in English. It describes an action that usually occurs in the present. It can be either a continuous ("I am studying") or undefined ("I study") action. We recommend using a continuous translation by default, and if it does not fit the context switch to the undefined.

16.3 **Chart**. At the beginning of every chapter that introduces a new verbal form, we will include one of these summary charts.

> *Present tense stem + Connecting vowel +*
>
> *Primary active personal endings*
>
> λυ + ο + μεν ‣ λύομεν

The chart is one of the most important elements of each chapter, so be sure to learn it well. Of course, you first must read through the chapter for it to make sense.

In the present tense, a verb is composed of three parts: the present tense stem; the connecting vowel; a personal ending.

16.4 **Present tense stem.** In chapter 20 we will discuss in detail the concept of the tense stem. For now it is sufficient to say that the tense stem is *the most basic form of the verb in a particular tense*. It is what is left when you remove the connecting vowel and personal endings. For example, the stem of λύετε is λυ. The stem is what carries the basic meaning of the verb.[1]

---

[1] Usually, the stem of a verb stays the same in all tenses. In a past tense, the stem of λύω is still *λυ. However, in many common verbs the stem changes in different tenses. For example, βάλλω is a present tense form and means "I throw." The present tense stem is *βαλλ. But in a past tense, the stem shifts to *βαλ (one lambda). This is why it is important to connect stems with tenses in your thinking. But more about this later.

16.5   **Connecting vowel.**[2] The connecting vowel is the vowel that connects the verbal stem to the personal ending. *In the indicative mood, if the personal ending begins with mu or nu, the connecting vowel is omicron; the connecting vowel in every other case is epsilon. If no personal ending is used, the connecting vowel can be either omicron or epsilon.*

λεγ + ο + μεν ▸ λέγομεν
λεγ + ε + τε ▸ λέγετε

The connecting vowels are the same for all the tenses in the indicative mood. Their purpose is to help with pronunciation. It is easier to pronounce λέγομεν than λέγμεν.[3]

16.6   **Personal ending.** The personal ending is added to the connecting vowel in order to designate person and number. This is necessary because the verb must agree with its subject in person and number.

One of the advantages of a language using personal endings is that you can always tell who is doing the action of the verb because the ending shows person and number. Even if the subject is not stated, you can discover it from the personal ending on the verb. Another advantage is that if the subject is expressed, you can confirm that it is the subject by checking the person and number of the verb against it. This double check should *always* be employed since you are really serious about learning the language.

For example, the verb λέγεις means "you say." If you have the two words σύ and ἄνθρωπος and both look like the subject, the verb tells you that the subject must be σύ because ἄνθρωπος is third person.

The disadvantage of using personal endings is that there is more to memorize, but this is really a small price to pay for the advantages you receive.

16.7   **Primary endings**. There are two sets of personal endings you need to learn. The **primary** personal endings are used in the present tense, and

---

[2]   It is also called a "thematic" vowel.

[3]   Most grammars teach that the connecting vowel is a part of the personal ending, at least in the present tense. This is understandable: when the connecting vowel and true personal ending combine they are often altered. For example, a third person plural form is λέγουσι. It is formed from λεγ + ο + νσι ▸ λέγουσι. The nu drops out and the omicron lengthens to ου.

This teaching technique is fine for a while, but after you have learned a few tenses it becomes *extremely* important to see the difference between the connecting vowel and the personal ending. For this reason we will always list the true connecting vowel and true personal ending to the right of every paradigm. This way you can see the true similarities throughout the whole verbal paradigm as well as the different rules that govern the final form of the word.

in the tenses discussed through chapter 20. We will discuss the **secondary** personal endings in chapter 21 and the differences between the two sets of endings.

16.8 **Voice.** Greek differentiates the present active (this chapter) from the present middle and passive (chapter 18) by using two different sets of personal endings.

Form of the Present Active Indicative

16.9 **Introduction.** The forms in our paradigms are listed first, second, and third person singular, and then first, second, and third person plural. (The personal endings are separated from the stem of the verb to clarify their identity.) From left to right we list the inflected forms, definition, the connecting vowel, and the personal ending. In some paradigms we include a similar paradigm for comparison in the far right column.

Pay special attention to the connecting vowel/personal ending combination and what is happening. This becomes extremely important later on.

16.10 **Form**[4]

Be sure to read the footnotes to the paradigm.

	form	translation	connecting vowel	personal ending
1 sg	λύ ω	I am loosing	ο	_[5]
2 sg	λύ εις	You are loosing	ε	ς[6]
3 sg	λύ ει	He/she/it is loosing	ε	ι[7]

---

[4] λύω has a wide and varied assortment of meanings. It is the word used for "breaking" the Sabbath, or for "destroying" the temple. It is commonly used in paradigms because it is short and regular. "Loose" is a general meaning that basically encompasses all its other meanings. If "loose" sounds strange to you it may be easier to think in terms of "destroy."

[5] No personal ending is used and the connecting vowel omicron lengthens to omega to compensate for the loss (*λυ + ο ‣ λύω).

[6] The personal ending actually is σι. The sigma dropped out and was evidently added back on to the end (λυεσι ‣ λυει ‣ λύεις). This is the explanation in Smyth (§463b). It seems easier to think that the sigma and iota underwent metathesis, i.e., they switched places. Just remember that the ending is sigma and the connecting vowel changes.

[7] The ending actually is τι, but the tau dropped out. The original form can be seen in ἐστί.

1 pl	λύ ομεν	We are loosing	ο	μεν
2 pl	λύ ετε	You are loosing	ε	τε
3 pl	λύ ουσι(ν)	They are loosing	ο	νσι[8]

16.11 You will notice that the personal endings have sometimes been changed when they are actually affixed to the verbs. We are faced here with somewhat the same dilemma we were with nouns: you need to learn what the personal endings actually are, but at times they have been modified.[9] With the primary active endings it is best to learn the endings as ω, εις, ει, ομεν, ετε, ουσι(ν). But always be able to identify the connecting vowel and the true personal ending.

16.12 **First of four.** As we said in the beginning, there are only four paradigms that you need to learn for verbs. The following is the first of those four. We will fill in the other areas of this chart as we learn them. The forms in parentheses (except for the moveable nu) are the real personal endings; be sure to learn them.

In a sense, these four paradigms are like the one noun paradigm. If you know them and a few rules, you can identify almost any verbal form in the New Testament.

---

[8] The third plural ending can take a movable nu.

The nu drops out because of the following sigma (just as it does in the accusative plural of second declension nouns) and the connecting vowel omicron lengthens to ου to compensate for the loss (λυονσι ‣ λυοσι ‣ λύουσι).

It is important to remember that the ending actually is νσι because it will make other forms easier to remember.

[9] For example, the genitive singular case ending for the second declension is omicron, but it contracts with the final stem vowel and we see λόγου (*λογο + ο ‣ λόγου). You should memorize the ending as upsilon but remember that it actually is omicron.

	primary tenses	
	λύω	(-)
	λύεις	(ς)
active voice	λύει	(ι)
	λύομεν	(μεν)
	λύετε	(τε)
	λύουσι(ν)	(νσι)

Characteristics of the Present Active Indicative

16.13 **Aspect**. The present tense indicates either a continuous or undefined action. You can translate either "I am studying" or "I study." Choose the aspect which best fits the context. Remember: aspect always takes precedence over time. More often than not the present tense describes a continuous action.

16.14 **Time.** The present tense form of a verb generally indicates an action occurring in the present time.[10]

Verbs and Personal Pronouns

16.15 **Personal pronouns in the nominative.** Because the personal ending indicates person, it is generally unnecessary to supply the personal pronoun as the subject of the sentence. Greek could say "I love Robin" by

---

[10] This is true only in the indicative mood. When we move into the other moods you will see that they have no time significance, or the time significance is only incidental.

writing ἐγὼ ἀγαπῶ ῾Ρόβιν[11] or simply ἀγαπῶ ῾Ρόβιν. When a personal pronoun does occur, it is for *emphasis* or to clarify the *gender* of the subject.

- *Emphasis*. ἐγὼ ἀγαπῶ ῾Ρόβιν would be saying "**I** love Robin." The combination of the personal pronoun and the "I" in the verb creates an emphatic expression. Often the emphasis is by way of contrast, as the examples below show.

  οὐχ ὡς ἐγὼ θέλω ἀλλ᾽ ὡς σύ (Matt 26:39).
  Not as *I* will but as you (will).

  Ἰησοῦς αὐτὸς οὐκ ἐβάπτιζεν ἀλλ᾽ οἱ μαθηταὶ αὐτοῦ (John 4:2).
  Jesus was not baptizing, but his disciples.

  Some grammars ask you to translate the nominative form of the pronoun with an intensive pronoun: "I myself love Robin." "Jesus himself was not baptizing." Others permit you to avoid the awkward English and simply to recognize that the emphasis is there.

- *Gender*. When we find the third person personal pronoun in the nominative, the pronoun tells us the gender of the subject—something the personal ending cannot. One note of caution. When αὐτός is the subject and the verb is first or second person, you may have a tendency to translate αὐτός as a third person pronoun ("he/she/it"). But since the verb is first or second, αὐτός is "I/we" or "you."

  For example, αὐτὴ λέγεις (second person singular "you speak") ἀνθρώποις might seem to mean, "She speaks to men." This is incorrect. The αὐτή is merely adding emphasis to the subject, which is "You." It should be translated "You (yourself) speak to men."

Summary

1. The present active indicative describes an action that normally occurs in the present time. By default choose a continuous translation, and if it does not fit the context choose an undefined aspect.

2. The present tense verb is composed of three parts: present verbal stem, connecting vowel, and primary personal ending.

3. The tense stem is the most basic form of the verb in a particular tense.

4. In the indicative mood, if the personal ending begins with mu or nu, the connecting vowel is omicron; otherwise the connecting vowel is epsilon. If there is no personal ending, the connecting vowel can be either omicron or epsilon.

5. A verb must agree with its subject in person and number.

---

[11] ῾Ρόβιν is not a real Greek word.

6. The present active tense uses the primary active endings: ω, εις, ει, ομεν, ετε, ουσι(ν). The real personal endings are -, ς, ι, μεν, τε, νσι.

7. A movable nu can be added to the third person plural personal ending.

At the end of the summary section in each chapter, we will include our "Master Verb Chart." It lists the different parts of each verbal form. As we learn new verbal forms, the chart will grow. It is one of the two or three most significant charts to know and is the key to the entire verbal system, so learn it well. The full chart is in the Appendix.

As you can see, there is a column for "Aug/Redup" and another for "Tense form." We will not learn what these mean until later chapters, so ignore them for now. The column entitled "1st sing paradigm" is the form of the paradigm verb in the first person singular.

Master Verb Chart						
Tense	Aug/ Redup	Tense stem	Tense form.	Conn. vowel	Personal endings	1st sing paradigm
Present act		pres		o/ε	prim act	λύω

Vocabulary

Teachers differ on this point, but some would encourage you to start taking your Greek Bible to church with you. You will be amazed at how much you can follow as the English is read.

Following the frequency of each verb, we have listed the word's present tense stem.

ἀκούω	I hear, learn, obey, understand (428; *ακου)[12]
βλέπω	I see, look at (133; *βλεπ)
ἔχω	I have, hold (708; *εχ)
λύω	I loose, untie, destroy (42; *λυ)[13]
νόμος, -ου, ὁ	law, principle (194; *νομο)[14]

---

[12] ἀκούω can take a direct object in either the genitive or accusative. *Acoustics* (ἀκουστικός) is the science of sound.

[13] λύω occurs less than fifty times, but because it is our paradigm verb you will have learned it anyway.

[14] An *autonomous* (αὐτόνομος) person is self-governed.

ὅπου	where (82)
πιστεύω	I believe, have faith (in), trust (241; *πιστευ)[15]
πρόσωπον, -ου, τό	face, appearance (76; *προσωπο)[16]
τότε	then, thereafter (160)
τυφλός, -ή, -όν	blind (50; *τυφλο/η)[17]
χαρά, -ᾶς, ἡ	joy, delight (59; *χαρα)

Total word count in the New Testament:	138,162
Number of words learned to date:	179
Number of word occurrences in this chapter:	2,173
Number of word occurrences to date:	94,079
Percent of total word count in the New Testament:	68.1%

Advanced Information

16.16   You may be wondering why we asked you to learn what the true primary active endings are as well as the altered forms in the present active indicative. The answer is that on down the road it makes things much easier if you know the true endings.

For example, the second person singular ending is ς, and the connecting vowel lengthens (ablaut) to ει (λυ + ε + ς ‣ λύεις). Why not learn the ending as ις? Because the second person singular ending in the *secondary* active is ς and there is no lengthening of the connecting vowel (ε + λυ + ε + ς ‣ ἔλυες). If you learn just ς as the primary ending, you already know the secondary.

You are just going to have to trust me on this one. If you really want to learn Greek well and not have to review paradigms for years to come, then learn what the real endings are.

---

[15] πιστεύω can take a direct object in either the dative or accusative. It is the cognate verb of the noun πίστις and adjective πιστός.

[16] *Prosopography* refers to describing a person's face.

[17] *Typhlosis* is the technical term for blindness.

Chapter 17

Contract Verbs

(Present Active Indicative)

Exegetical Insight

The present active indicative often has an imperfective force; that is, it conveys the idea of ongoing or continuous action. When the Apostle Paul wrote his first letter to the Thessalonian Christians, he wanted to reassure these new believers that they were not forgotten–that he and his companions still cared deeply for them. He tells them, "We always thank God for all of you, mentioning you in our prayers" (1 Thess 1:2).

Paul expresses his constant practice of giving thanks to God by using the present active indicative verb εὐχαριστοῦμεν. The verb could also of course be interpreted as "simple" or "undefined" actions with no overtones of continuous prayer. The adverb "always" (πάντοτε), however, reinforces our impression that Paul is stressing that he prays regularly for the Thessalonians. It is also likely that in using the plural "we," Paul is implying that he met often with Silas and Timothy to pray for these dear people. Certainly Paul also remembered the Thessalonians in his private times of prayer.

Far from being victimized by a group of itinerant moral preachers who sought their money and food, the Thessalonians were evangelized by a trio of men who proclaimed to them the living and true God. These were men whose lives had been touched deeply by the risen Christ and they poured themselves out to the Thessalonians in a loving and caring way. Their abrupt departure did not indicate a lack of concern; on the contrary, they were forced to leave and now they prayed together constantly to the living God for these fledgling and vulnerable believers!

Clinton E. Arnold

Overview

In this chapter you will learn:

- the five basic rules governing the contractions of vowels;
- that contract verbs contract as if the personal endings are those visible in the present active indicative (except the first person singular).

Introduction

17.1   Contract verbs are verbs whose stems end in alpha, epsilon, or omicron.[1]
That final vowel is called the "contract vowel." For example, the verb
ἀγαπάω has a stem ending in alpha (*αγαπα).

Contract verbs follow the standard rules for verbs, but there is one additional point that needs to be emphasized. When that final stem vowel
comes into contact with the connecting vowel, the two vowels **contract**.[2]
The two vowels will join and often form a different vowel or a diphthong.

17.2   Contract verbs are categorized according to their final stem vowel. What
is encouraging about contract verbs is that all alpha contracts behave
similarly, as do all epsilon and all omicron contracts. In other words, all
contract verbs with stems ending in alpha form their different inflected
endings the same way. Once you learn the forms of ἀγαπάω, you know
the inflection pattern of all other alpha contracts.

Contractions

17.3   It is important that you learn §17.4 well. Contract verbs are common,
and you need to be able to "figure out" what vowels led to a certain contraction. If you cannot, then you will not be able to discover the lexical
form of the verb and thus its meaning.

For example, if you find the form ποιεῖτε, the ει is going to cause serious
problems for you unless you recognize that ει can be the result of the
contraction of two epsilons. Then you can see that ποιεῖτε is second person plural of an epsilon contract verb (ποιεῖτε ‹ ποιε + ετε).

Often you will discover that several vowel combinations could have
given rise to the same contracted form. For example, ου is formed from
the contractions of εο, οε, and οο. If you see ποιοῦμεν, the connecting
vowel and personal ending are ομεν, but is its lexical form ποιέω or
ποιόω?

---

[1]   The usual definition for contract verbs is that they have stems ending in a vowel.
While this is true it is also confusing. ἀκούω has a stem ending in what appears to be
a vowel, but it is not a contract verb.

Actually, the final upsilon in ἀκούω is an old letter called "digamma" (Ϝ) that has long
since dropped out of the Greek alphabet. It was replaced in most cases by an upsilon,
but because it was a digamma the upsilon does not contract. Cf. p. 159n3, *MBG*, §27.

[2]   This is the same phenomena that we saw with case endings. The genitive singular case
ending, second declension, is actually omicron. It contracts with the omicron of the
noun stem to form ου (*λογο + ο ‣ λόγου).

We meet contractions only in two tenses, the present and the imperfect (chapter 21). In the other tenses the vowel lengthens and there is no contraction, but more about this later.

17.4 **Rules on contraction.**[3] Following are the rules showing what contractions are caused by what vowel combinations. There are a few other possibilities, but you will be shown them as we come across them. Rules #1 and #2 are by far the most common.

Rule #7 governs contractions of diphthongs, and illustrations of contracting diphthongs are listed throughout the rules.

You may also notice that the vowels listed as contracting in rules #1 through #6 are not the real personal endings but are the altered personal endings we have learned for λύω.[4] Rule #8 explains this.

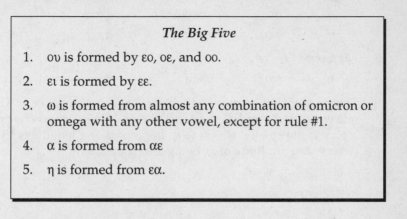

The Big Five

1. ου is formed by εο, οε, and οο.

2. ει is formed by εε.

3. ω is formed from almost any combination of omicron or omega with any other vowel, except for rule #1.

4. α is formed from αε

5. η is formed from εα.

---

1. ου *is formed by* εο, οε, *and* οο.

ου	‹ εο	ποιοῦμεν	‹ ποιεομεν
ου	‹ οε	πληροῦτε	‹ πληροετε

---

[3] We will present the rules governing contractions a little differently. Usually the rules move from the uncontracted form to the contracted. For example, "When epsilon and epsilon contract, they form ει." If you want to learn the rules this way, they are given in the *Advanced Information* section in this chapter.

This approach, however, seems to us to be backwards. When you are reading the text, you start with the contracted form and need to know what formed the contraction. Also, the two most common rules, as they are usually presented, are exceptions (see rules #2 and #4 in the *Advanced Information* section).

Therefore, we will present the rules of contraction moving from the contracted form to the uncontracted.

[4] For example, ποιοῦσιν contracts from *ποιε + ουσι (ποιουυσι ‣ ποιοῦσι).

2. ει *is formed by* εε.

    ει ‹ εε   ποιεῖτε   ‹   ποιεετε

3. ω *is formed from almost any combination of omicron or omega with any
    other vowel, except for rule #1.*

    ω   ‹   αο   ἀγαπῶμεν ‹   ἀγαπαομεν
    ω   ‹   αου   ἀγαπῶσι   ‹   ἀγαπαουσι

    We have a special situation in the lexical form of contract verbs. The
    alpha, epsilon, or omicron of the stem is listed in the lexical form
    because you need to know what that vowel is (e.g., ἀγαπάω). How-
    ever, when the word occurs in the text in the first person singular, it
    will have contracted to the forms in the paradigm (ἀγαπῶ).[5]

4. α *is formed from* αε.

    α   ‹   αε   ἀγαπᾶτε   ‹   ἀγαπαετε
    ᾳ   ‹   αει   ἀγαπᾷ   ‹   ἀγαπαει

5. η *is formed from* εα.

    η   ‹   εαι   ποιῇ   ‹   ποιηι ‹ ποιεαι[6] ‹ ποιεσαι[7]

    The relationship between αε and εα is easy to remember. "The first
    one wins." If the alpha is first (αε), the diphthong lengthens to a long
    alpha. If the epsilon is first (εα), the diphthong lengthens to an eta
    (which you can think of as being a long epsilon).

---

[5] The following is quite advanced information, so you may want to ignore it.

   In the first person singular of epsilon and omicron contracts, there is one extra step in
   the contraction process. No personal ending is used, so the connecting vowel lengthens to compensate, and the ensuing contraction is between the contract vowel and the
   lengthened connecting vowel.

   ποιεο › ποιεω › ποιῶ.

   πληροο › πληροω › πληρῶ.

   If the contraction were with the contract vowel and the unlengthened connecting
   vowel, rule one would change the form of the first person singular of contract verbs.

   ποιεο › ποιουω.

   πληροο › πληρουω.

[6] The sigma drops out because it is between two vowels.

[7] You will meet this form in chapter 18.

6. Miscellaneous

οι ‹ οει[8]　　πληροῖς ‹ πληροεις

　　　　　　　πληροῖ ‹ πληροει

7. The contraction of diphthongs

What happens with a diphthong depends upon whether the contract vowel and the first vowel of the diphthong are the same or different vowels.

a. If the contract vowel and the first vowel of the diphthong are the same, they simplify (i.e., one of the double letters drops out).

ει ‹ εει　　ποιεῖς ‹ ποιεεις

ου ‹ οου　　πληροῦσι ‹ πληροουσι

b. If the contract vowel and the first vowel of the diphthong are different, they contract.[9] If the second vowel of the diphthong is an iota, it subscripts if possible; if it is an upsilon it drops off.

ου ‹ εου　　ποιοῦσιν ‹ ποιεουσι

8. Contract verbs contract as if the true personal endings are those visible in the present active indicative.

1 sg	αω	›	ἀγαπῶ	*1 pl*	αομεν › ἀγαπῶμεν
2 sg	αεις	›	ἀγαπᾷς	*2 pl*	αετε › ἀγαπᾶτε
3 sg	αει	›	ἀγαπᾷ	*3 pl*	αουσι › ἀγαπῶσι(ν)

Be sure to learn these rules exactly. We will be meeting other contracted forms, and if you know the rules you will be able to figure them out.

17.5 **Present active forms of ἀγαπάω** ("I love"), **ποιέω** ("I do"), **πληρόω** ("I fill"). The contracting vowels are listed in parentheses. Work through the paradigm, explaining all the contractions. Pay special attention to any that may cause you difficulty.

The verb endings behave as if the contract vowel of the stem contracts with the personal endings as they appear in the paradigm of λύω (ω, εις, ει, ομεν, ετε, ουσι), and not with the true personal endings (ς, ι, μεν, τε, νσι; cf. §16.10). The only exception is the first person singular.

---

[8]　This combination occurs in the second and third person singular of an omicron contract verb.

[9]　You have seen no examples of this to this point.

-άω		*-έω*		*-όω*	
ἀγαπῶ	(αω)	ποιῶ	(εω)	πληρῶ	(οω)
ἀγαπᾷς	(αεις)	ποιεῖς	(εεις)	πληροῖς	(οεις)
ἀγαπᾷ	(αει)	ποιεῖ	(εει)[10]	πληροῖ	(οει)
ἀγαπῶμεν	(αομεν)	ποιοῦμεν	(εομεν)	πληροῦμεν	(οομεν)
ἀγαπᾶτε	(αετε)	ποιεῖτε	(εετε)	πληροῦτε	(οετε)
ἀγαπῶσι(ν)	(αουσι)	ποιοῦσι(ν)	(εουσι)	πληροῦσι(ν)	(οουσι)

17.6 **Characteristics of contract verbs**

There always will be a circumflex over the contracted vowels in the present active indicative.

Notice that the endings are nearly the same even when a contraction has not taken place. The omega is the first person singular ending. The sigma is still present for the second person singular ending. The plural endings are virtually the same. Concentrate on the similarities.

17.7 **Hint.** Be sure to remember the rules for the connecting vowel. If you see ἀγαπᾶτε, you may recognize that the personal ending is τε, but is the verb ἀγαπάω, ἀγαπέω, or ἀγαπόω?

- Since the personal ending begins with tau (ἀγαπᾶτε), the connecting vowel must be an epsilon.

- Since ει is formed by εε, you know the verb cannot be an epsilon contract.

- Since ου is formed by οε, you know the verb cannot be an omicron contract.

- Therefore, the stem must be an alpha contract: ἀγαπάω.

---

[10] Unlike ἀγαπᾷ, ποιεῖ does not subscript the iota of the original diphthong. Rather, the two iotas simplify to one (ποιεει ‣ ποιειι ‣ ποιεῖ). An iota cannot subscript under a short vowel, and iota here is short.

Summary

1. The Big Five

The Big Five

1. ου is formed by εο, οε, and οο.

2. ει is formed by εε.

3. ω is formed from almost any combination of omicron or omega with any other vowel, except for rule #1.

4. α is formed from αε

5. η is formed from εα.

---

2. οι is formed from οει.

3. If the contract vowel and the first vowel of the diphthong are the same, they simplify.

    If the contract vowel and the first vowel of the diphthong are different, they contract. If the second vowel of the diphthong is an iota, it subscripts if possible; if it is an upsilon it drops off.

4. Contract verbs contract as if the personal endings are those visible in the present active indicative (except the first person singular).

5. The lexical form shows the contract vowel (ἀγαπάω), but if that form actually occurs in the text the contract vowel and omicron will have contracted (ἀγαπῶ, ποιῶ, πληρῶ).

6. In the first person singular, no personal ending is used so the connecting vowel lengthens to omega.

7. The second person singular seems to follow its own rules.

Vocabulary

ἀγαπάω   I love, cherish (143; *ἀγαπα)[11]

δαιμόνιον, -ου, τό   demon (63; *δαιμονιο)[12]

ζητέω   I seek, desire, try to obtain (117; *ζητε)

---

[11] Cognate verb of ἀγάπη and ἀγαπητός.

[12] *Demon* (δαίμων).

καλέω   I call, name, invite (148; *καλεϜ)[13]

λαλέω   I speak, say (296; *λαλε)[14]

οἶδα[15]   I know, understand (318; *οιδα)

ὅταν   whenever (123)[16]

πλείων, πλεῖον[17]   larger, more (55; *πλειο/ο)[18]

πληρόω   I fill, complete, fulfill (86; *πληρο)

ποιέω   I do, make (568; *ποιε)[19]

τηρέω   I keep, guard, observe (70; *τηρε)

Total word count in the New Testament: 138,162
Number of words learned to date: 190
Number of word occurrences in this chapter: 1,987
Number of word occurrences to date: 96,066
Percent of total word count in the New Testament: 69.53%

Of contract verbs occurring fifty times or more in the New Testament, there
is only one omicron contract (πληρόω), four alpha contracts (ἀγαπάω, γεννάω,
ἐρωτάω, ἐπερωτάω), but many epsilon contracts.

---

13 The *Paraclete*, the Holy Spirit, is a Christian's counselor, advocate, one who is called
    (κλητός, "called") alongside (παρά) to aid. On the root see p. 160n16.

14 This word is onomatopoetic. Its meaning corresponds to the sound of the word
    ("lala").

15 οἶδα is a different type of word. It actually is another tense (perfect), but it functions as
    if it were a present. Its paradigm is as follows.

1 sg	οἶδα	1 pl	οἴδαμεν
2 sg	οἶδας	2 pl	οἴδατε
3 sg	οἶδε(ν)	3 pl	οἴδασιν

16 A crasis of ὅτε and ἄν.

17 πλείων is the form for the masculine and feminine, πλεῖον for the neuter. It is a 3-3
    adjective. The genitive of both is πλείονος. Notice the ablaut in the final stem vowel.
    See the Appendix for its full declension pattern.

    Because of the word's meaning, it will often be followed by a word in the genitive. You
    can use the key word "than" with the word in the genitive.

18 A *pleonasm* is a redundancy, using superfluous words.

19 The translation of this word can sometimes be quite idiomatic. It has a wide range of
    meaning. A *poem* (ποίημα) literally means "something done." A *poet* (ποιητής) is "one
    who makes."

Advanced Information

Here are the rules for contraction as they are normally listed.

17.8 **Rules for the contraction for single vowels** (i.e., total of two vowels).

The full form of the rules is given, but only those illustrations that apply to contract verbs are listed.[20] Exceptions #2 and #4 are by far the most frequent.

1. *Two like vowels form their common long vowel.*

   αα ▸ α

2. *Exception: When ε and ε contract they form ει, and when ο and ο contract they form ου.*

   εε ▸ ει   ποιε + ε + τε ▸ ποειτε

   οο ▸ ου   πληρο + ο + μεν ▸ πληρουμεν

3. *An ο or ω will overcome an α, ε, or η regardless of their order, and form ω.*

   οα ▸ ω

   αο ▸ ω   ἀγαπα + ο + μεν ▸ ἀγαπῶμεν

4. *Exception: When an ε and ο contract they form ου, regardless of their order.*

   εο ▸ ου   ποιε + ο + μεν ▸ ποιοῦμεν

   οε ▸ ου   πληρο + ε + τε ▸ πληροῦτε

5. *If an α comes before an ε or an η, they will contract to an α.*
   If an ε or an η comes before an α, they will contract to an η.[21]

   αε ▸ α   ἀγαπα + ε + τε ▸ ἀγαπᾶτε

17.9 **Rules for the contraction of a single vowel and a diphthong**

Diphthongs follow the same rules as single vowels described above. However, because there are three and not two vowels involved, a few extra rules come into play. The only time this takes place in the present active indicative is the third person plural. Even though the personal ending actually is not ουσι(ν), for contraction purposes think that it is. Then the contraction rules all make sense.

---

[20] It is difficult to know who deserves the credit for these rules since they are repeated in so many grammars. I learned them initially from J. Gresham Machen's grammar (143), and he cites White's *Beginner's Greek Book* (1895), pp. 75f.

[21] There is no example of this rule in the present active, but there is in the present passive. λυ + ε + σαι ▸ λυεαι ▸ λυηι ▸ λύῃ.

1. When a single vowel is followed by a diphthong that begins with the
    same vowel as the single, the two similar vowels simplify[22] and the
    second vowel remains the same.

    οου   ›   ου   πληρο + ουσι › πληροῦσι

    αα   ›   ᾳ

2. When a single vowel is followed by a diphthong that begins with a
    different vowel than the single, the single vowel and the first vowel
    of the diphthong contract according to the regular rules. If the third
    vowel is an upsilon it will drop off. If it is an iota it will subscript.

    αου   ›   ωυ › ω   ἀγαπα + ουσι › ἀγαπῶσι

    εου   ›   ουυ › ου   ποιε + ουσι › ποιοῦσι

    ααι   ›   αι › ᾳ

    Exceptions

    εοι   ›   οι

    αει   ›   αι › ᾳ   ἀγαπα + ειν › ἀγαπᾶν[23]

    οει   ›   οι   πληρο + ει › πληροῖ

    οη   ›   οι

17.10   Following is a chart of all possible contractions of single vowels. The
            four most common (and troublesome) are bolded and enlarged. A more
            complete chart is given in the Appendix.

	α	ε	η	ι	υ	ο	ω
α	α	α	α	αι	αυ	ω	ω
ε	η	**ει**	η	ει	ευ	**ου**	ω
ο	ω	**ου**	ω	οι	ου	**ου**	ω

---

[22]   One drops out. This is not an actual contraction, technically speaking.

[23]   This word is an infinitive, and you will not meet these words until chapter 32.

17.11 Chart of contraction of vowels and diphthongs

	αι/ᾳ	ει[24]	ει[25]	η	οι	ου[26]	ῳ
α	ᾳ	ᾳ	α	ᾳ	ῳ	ω	ῳ
ε	η	ει	ει	η	οι	ου	ῳ
ο	ῳ	οι	ου	οι[27]	οι	ου	ῳ

---

[24] This column describes what happens when a vowel is followed by a genuine diphthong. A "genuine" diphthong is a diphthong that was not formed by a contraction.

[25] This column describes what happens when a vowel is followed by a spurious diphthong. A "spurious" diphthong is a diphthong that was formed by a contraction.

[26] This diphthong is spurious.

[27] Can also be ῳ.

Chapter 18

Present Middle/Passive Indicative

Exegetical Insight

ἀρχήγος as a title for Jesus appears only four times in the New Testament, twice each in Acts (3:15; 5:31) and Hebrews (2:10; 12:2). It is notoriously difficult to translate. A survey of the Greek translation of the Old Testament (LXX) and non-biblical use of the term suggests a threefold connotation: (a) path-breaker (pioneer) who opens the way for others, hence, "guide," "hero;" (b) the source or founder, hence, "author," "initiator," "beginning;" (c) the leader-ruler, hence, "captain," "prince," "king."

These ideas are not necessarily exclusive of each other. In fact they probably all combine to speak of someone who explores new territory, opens a trail, and leads others to it. There he builds a city or fortress for those who follow and leads them in defense against attackers. When the peace has been won he remains as their ruler and the city or community bears his name. He is thereafter honored as the founding hero.

The Old Testament speaks of several individuals who held such a position. For at least one our word is actually used. In Judges 11:6 ff., we learn that Jepthah was asked to become "head" over the inhabitants of Gilead in order to deliver them from the Ammonites (v. 6); one version of the Greek translation uses the word ἀρχήγος here. Jepthah agreed on condition that the position would be made permanent. The elders consented and he was made κεφαλὴ καὶ ἀρχήγος even before the battle (vv. 8-11). At the conclusion of his struggles, "Jepthah judged Israel six years" (Judges 12:7).

In Acts 3:15 Peter accuses the Jews of killing the "ἀρχηγός of life," suggesting that Jesus is not only the origin of biological life, but also of "new life" and the guide-protector-provider-ruler-namesake of those identified with him. Later Peter speaks of Jesus as the "ἀρχηγόν and Savior, to give repentance to Israel" (5:31). The word "Savior" was associated with the judges of old. Jesus is the one who meets the emergency situation caused by the sin of God's people. He comes to bring not only deliverance but also the continuing service of ἀρχηγός. The writer to the Hebrews speaks of the suffering "ἀρχηγός of salvation" (2:10) and the ἀρχηγός and Perfecter of our faith" (12:2). In each case Jesus as ἀρχηγός not only initiates and provides the new life for his people, but remains with them through it; they bear his name. He is their hero.

J. Julius Scott, Jr.

Overview

In this chapter we will learn:

- the passive voice in which the subject receives the action of the verb;
- that the present middle/passive is formed by joining the present tense stem, connecting vowel, and primary middle/passive endings;
- about deponent verbs that are middle or passive in form but active in meaning;
- that in the present tense, the middle and passive are identical in form.

English

18.1   When a verb is active, the subject is performing the action of the verb. When a verb is passive, the subject of the sentence is receiving the action. Sometimes there will be a prepositional phrase specifying who or what is doing the action of the verb (e.g., "by the ball"). English forms the present passive by adding the helping verb "am/is/are" for the punctiliar and "am/are being" for the continuous.

Active. "I *hit* the ball." "I" is the subject of the sentence and is the one performing the action of the verb "hit."

Passive. "I *am hit* by the ball." "I" is the subject of this sentence, but "I" is not doing the action of the verb "hit." The action of the verb is being performed by "ball," and it is being done to the subject, "I."

You can often identify a passive verb by placing "by" after the verb and seeing if it makes sense. "I was hit." "I was hit by what?" "I was hit by the ball." "Was hit" is a passive verb.

	continuous	*punctiliar*
present active	I am hitting	I hit
	They are hitting	They hit
present passive	I am being hit	I am hit
	They are being hit	They are hit

A full chart of the English tenses is given in the Appendix. If you are unsure of your English you may want to spend some time studying the chart.

18.2   When you use a helping verb to form the passive voice, the time of the verbal construction is determined by the helping verb, not the main verb. For example, the active construction "I remember" shifts to "I am remembered" in the passive. Because "am" is present, the construction "am remembered" is present, even though "remembered" is a past participle.

Greek

18.3   In the present tense, the middle and passive forms of the verb are identical. Context will tell you whether a form is middle or passive. We will discuss the passive first.

Present Passive Indicative

18.4   **Chart**

> *Present tense stem + Connecting vowel +*
> *Primary passive personal endings*
>
> λυ + ο + μαι ‣ λύομαι

18.5   The present passive indicative verb functions basically the same in Greek as in English. To form the present passive indicative, Greek adds the primary passive endings to the verbal stem. Read the footnote to the second singular form.

	form	translation	conn. vow.	ending	pres. act.
1 sg	λύ ο μαι	I am being loosed	ο	μαι	λύω
2 sg	λύ ῃ[1]	You are being loosed	ε	σαι	λύεις
3 sg	λύ ε ται	He, she, it is being loosed	ε	ται	λύει

---

[1]   The second person singular ending is quite troublesome. Because the sigma occurs between vowels (λυ + ε + σαι), it will usually drop out and the vowels will contract. In this case, they contracted to eta as per the rules, and the iota subscripted (λυ + ε + σαι ‣ λυεαι ‣ λυηι ‣ λύῃ). Be sure to remember that the true ending is σαι; this will become especially important later.

1 pl	λυ ό μεθα	We are being loosed	ο	μεθα	λύομεν
2 pl	λύ ε σθε	You are being loosed	ε	σθε	λύετε
3 pl	λύ ο νται	They are being loosed	ο	νται	λύουσι(ν)

As you can see, the connecting vowels are more visible in the passive than they are in the active.

18.6 This paradigm below shows the second of the four sets of paradigms you must memorize. You are now halfway home. Since the middle and passive forms are identical in the present tense, we can group them together and use the label, "middle/passive."

<table>
<tr><td colspan="3">primary tenses</td></tr>
<tr><td rowspan="6">active voice</td><td>λύω</td><td>(-)</td></tr>
<tr><td>λύεις</td><td>(ς)</td></tr>
<tr><td>λύει</td><td>(ι)</td></tr>
<tr><td>λύομεν</td><td>(μεν)</td></tr>
<tr><td>λύετε</td><td>(τε)</td></tr>
<tr><td>λύουσι(ν)</td><td>(νσι)</td></tr>
<tr><td rowspan="6">middle/passive voice</td><td>λύομαι</td><td>(μαι)</td></tr>
<tr><td>λύῃ</td><td>(σαι)</td></tr>
<tr><td>λύεται</td><td>(ται)</td></tr>
<tr><td>λυόμεθα</td><td>(μεθα)</td></tr>
<tr><td>λύεσθε</td><td>(σθε)</td></tr>
<tr><td>λύονται</td><td>(νται)</td></tr>
</table>

Translation of Present Passive Indicative Verbs

18.7 **Person and time.** There is no difference between the active and passive on these two points.

18.8 It is common to find the equivalent of "by" in a Greek sentence after a passive verb. It will either be ὑπό followed by a noun in the genitive, indicating a personal agent (e.g., "by God"), or the simple dative indicating an impersonal instrument ("by the word of God").

Deponent Verbs

18.9 **Deponent Verb.** This is a verb that is *middle or passive in form but active in meaning*. Its form is always middle or passive, but its meaning is always active. It can never have a passive meaning. We will discuss the middle voice below.

You can tell if a verb is deponent by its lexical form. Deponent verbs are always listed in the vocabulary sections with passive endings. In other words, if the lexical form ends in an omega, it is not deponent (e.g., ἀγα-πάω). If the lexical form ends in -ομαι, the verb is deponent (e.g., ἔρχο-μαι). *You will have to remember that the word is a deponent.*

When parsing a deponent verb, instead of saying "active" or "passive" you should say "deponent." In the translation of the inflected form you should always use an active English verb. For example, ἔρχεται is present deponent indicative, third person singular, of ἔρχομαι, meaning "he/she/it is coming."

In a single tense a verb will be either regular or deponent. It cannot be both. However, a verb can be deponent in one tense and not deponent in another.

Present Middle Indicative

18.10 **Chart**

> *Present tense stem + Connecting vowel +*
> *Primary passive personal endings*
>
> ερχ + ο + μαι ‣ ἔρχομαι

18.11 In the present tense, the forms of verbs in the middle voice are identical to their forms in the passive. For the paradigm we use ἔρχομαι, which is a middle deponent verb meaning "I come."

	form	translation	conn. vow.	ending	pres. act.
1 sg	ἔρχ ο μαι	I come	ο	μαι	λύω
2 sg	ἔρχ η²	You come	ε	σαι	λύεις
3 sg	ἔρχ ε ται	He, she, it comes	ε	ται	λύει

1 pl	ἔρχ ό μεθα	We come		ο μεθα	λύομεν
2 pl	ἔρχ ε σθε	You come		ε σθε	λύετε
3 pl	ἔρχ ο νται	They come		ο νται	λύουσι(ν)

18.12 When we introduced the middle voice in chapter 15, we said that it is roughly equivalent to the active. As we will see in later chapters, there is more here than meets the eye; but for the time being this is sufficient. One of the reasons why we said this is that the vast majority of middle forms in the New Testament, approximately 75%, are deponent and therefore active in meaning.

Present Middle/Passive Forms of Contracts

18.13 Contract verbs follow the same rules in the middle/passive as they do in the active.

	-άω	*-έω*	*-όω*
1 sg	ἀγαπῶμαι	ποιοῦμαι	πληροῦμαι
2 sg	ἀγαπᾷ[3]	ποιῇ[4]	πληροῖ[5]
3 sg	ἀγαπᾶται	ποιεῖται	πληροῦται
1 pl	ἀγαπώμεθα	ποιούμεθα	πληρούμεθα
2 pl	ἀγαπᾶσθε	ποιεῖσθε	πληροῦσθε
3 pl	ἀγαπῶνται	ποιοῦνται	πληροῦνται

Notice the many similarities between the regular present passive endings and their contracted forms. Remember: concentrate on the similarities. You should be able to look at these contracted forms and discover what the original vowels were that formed this particular contraction.

Summary

1. If a verb is in the passive voice, the subject is receiving the action of the verb.

---

[2] The second person singular ending is troublesome. Because the sigma occurs between vowels, it will usually drop out and the vowels contract. In this case they contracted to η as per the rules and the iota subscripted (ερχ + ε + σαι ‣ ἐρχεαι ‣ ἐρχηι ‣ ἔρχῃ).

[3] αεσαι ‣ ασαι ‣ ααι ‣ αι ‣ ᾳ. Do not confuse this with the identical form that is a third person singular active. Context will tell you the difference.

[4] εεσαι ‣ εσαι ‣ εαι ‣ ηι ‣ ῃ.

[5] οεσαι ‣ οεαι ‣ οει ‣ οι (irregular).

2. To form the English passive you add a helping verb. The tense of an English verb that has helping verbs is determined by the tense of the helping verb.

3. The present middle/passive is formed by joining the present tense stem + connecting vowel + primary middle/passive endings. The primary middle/ passive personal endings are μαι, σαι (which changes to η when joined with the connecting vowel), ται, μεθα, σθε, νται.

4. Deponent verbs are middle or passive in form but active in meaning. Their lexical form is always middle or passive, but their meaning is always active. You can tell if a verb is deponent by its lexical form.

5. In the present tense, the middle and passive are identical in form. Almost all middles are deponent and therefore active in meaning.

Master Verb Chart

Tense	Aug/ Redup	Tense stem	Tense form.	Conn. vowel	Personal endings	1st sing paradigm
Present act		pres		ο/ε	prim act	λύω
Present mid/pas		pres		ο/ε	prim mid/pas	λύομαι

Vocabulary

ἀποκρίνομαι	I answer (231; *ἀποκριν)[6]
δεῖ	it is necessary (101)[7]
δύναμαι[8]	I am able, am powerful (210; *δυνα)[9]
ἔρχομαι	I come, go (634; *ἐρχ)
νύξ, νυκτός, ἡ	night (61; *νυκτ)[10]

---

[6] ἀποκρίνομαι can take a direct object in the dative.

[7] This verb is always third person singular, does not change its form, and its subject is always neuter. (It has a different form for the past tense.)

[8] δύναμαι is one of the few exceptions to the rules concerning connecting vowels. δύναμαι uses alpha throughout.

1 sg	δύναμαι	1 pl	δυνάμεθα
2 sg	δύνασαι or δύνῃ	2 pl	δύνασθε
3 sg	δύναται	3 pl	δύνανται

[9] A *dynamo* is a machine that converts mechanical energy into electrical energy. It is used metaphorically of a person with a lot of energy.

[10] *Nocturnal,* "pertaining to night," looks related to the Greek νύξ but according to Klein is actually from the Latin "nocturnus."

ὅστις, ἥτις, ὅτι[11]	whoever, whichever, whatever (153; *ὁ +* τιν)[12]
πορεύομαι	I go, proceed, live (153; *πορευ)
συνάγω	I gather together, invite (59; *συναγ)[13]
τόπος, -ου, ὁ	place, location (94; *τοπο)[14]
ὡς	as, like, when, that, how, about[15] (504)

Total word count in the New Testament:	138,162
Number of words learned to date:	200
Number of word occurrences in this chapter:	2,200
Number of word occurrences to date:	98,266
Percent of total word count in the New Testament:	71.12%

Advanced Information

18.14   **Greek and English passives.** What may have been passive to a Greek is not necessarily passive to the English mind. There is a significant number of Greek verbs that are passive in form but their English translation is active. If you are translating a Greek sentence and the passive translation does not make sense, be sure to look up the Greek verb in a lexicon; it may have a separate definition for the passive that sounds active to you.

For example, φοβέω in the active means, "I frighten" (which does not occur in the New Testament), and in the passive means, "I fear, am afraid."

---

[11]   This word is the combination of the relative and the indefinite pronouns (ὅς + τις). As such, both halves decline. See the Appendix for the full paradigm.

[12]   Because ὅστις is formed with the relative pronoun, it will only occur in a dependent clause; the ὅστις clause cannot contain the main subject and verb.

In Koine Greek, this relative indefinite pronoun was starting to shift so that it could also be used as the relative pronoun. In other words, its indefinite significance can be lost.

[13]   In chapter 21 we will learn the cognate noun, συναγωγή, which is a meeting place where people gather together.

[14]   *Topology* is the science of describing a place. A *toponym* is the name of a place.

[15]   "About" in the sense of "approximately."

Chapter 19

Future Active/Middle Indicative

Exegetical Insight

In English we think of the future tense as the tense of simple prediction. Greek often uses the future that way, too, but in many biblical passages it carries a different sense. Particularly when quoting the Old Testament (under the influence of a parallel Hebrew construction), the future is used to give a command. "Thou shalt not kill, thou shalt not commit adultery," and so on, are not predictions about the behavior of God's people, or we would have repeatedly proven God wrong! Rather they are commands, what grammarians often call the imperatival or volitive use of the future tense. We do this in English occasionally, particularly in casual speech. For example, the student insistently says to her friends about an upcoming party, "You *will* be there!" This is not a prediction but a demand!

An excellent New Testament example appears when both Jesus and Paul quote Genesis 2:24: "For this reason a man will leave his father and mother and be united to his wife, and they will become one flesh." In the context of the story of Adam and Eve, it is natural to take this as God's prediction about how married life will proceed among the offspring of these first two human beings, and there may be a partially predictive element intended here. But when Jesus cites this passage to refute the Pharisees' generally more lenient views on divorce (Matt 19:5), he knows full well that many of God's people have violated and will continue to violate this creation ordinance. The same is true of Paul when he establishes the principles of a Christian marriage in the midst of the highly promiscuous pagan culture of Ephesus (Eph 5:31). Rather, both Jesus and Paul are using the future tense verbs of the Genesis text primarily in their imperatival sense–telling believers that God commands them to be faithful to their spouses for life.

That command remains crucial today, when Christians divorce for so many flimsy reasons that the Bible never condones. As the pastor who married my wife and me told us during premarital counseling, "There may be extreme instances in which divorce is biblically legitimate. But if you go into marriage looking for a way out, you will almost surely find it. Far better to commit to each other that you will never divorce, even if those extreme circumstances were to occur. Then you will have to turn to God, to Christian friends, and to each other to see you through the difficult times. And God will prove faithful." We have heeded this advice for fourteen years now, and will continue to heed it for as long as we live. And in that period of time, while there have been struggles, there certainly has been nothing emerge to seriously threaten our marriage. God does remain faithful when we commit to his *commands*. And some of them come "disguised" in the future tense.

Craig L. Blomberg

Overview

In this chapter we will learn that:

- the future tense indicates an action occurring in the future;

- the future is formed by adding a sigma to the end of the future tense stem (λύσω);

- contract verbs lengthen their contract vowel before the sigma (ἀγαπήσω);

- knowing the Square of Stops is especially useful in identifying the future tense.

English

19.1   The future describes an action that will occur in the future. To form the future you add a helping verb ("will"/"shall") to the present tense stem of the verb.

The basic rule in older English for the future tense is that "shall" is used for the first person and "will" for the second and third. "I shall work hard." "You will work hard." "He will slack off." That distinction has generally fallen into disuse today.

19.2   English grammar seems to be in a constant state of change, and it is therefore difficult to say, "In English ...." But in an attempt to teach Greek we must simplify the issues somewhat. With that as a disclaimer we can say that English verbs are centered on three different tenses, and it is from these three forms that all the variations of the verb are formed.

Present. The present tense is also used to form the future tense, among other things. "I eat." "I shall eat."

Past. The past tense of "eat" is "ate."

Past perfect. The past perfect tense of "eat" is "eaten."

Usually the past tense of verbs is formed by adding "-ed": "kick, kicked, kicked." Other times you change the stem: "swim, swam, swum." Sometimes the past and past perfect are identical: "study, studied, studied." In the Appendix, at the beginning of the discussion of verbs, there is a chart showing all the basic forms of the English verb.

Future Active Indicative

19.3   **Meaning**. The future tense in Greek has the same meaning as in English. It describes an action that will occur in the future.[1] As is true of the other tenses, the time reference of the verb is from the point of view of the writer, not the reader.

19.4   **Chart**

Future active tense stem + Tense formative (σ) +

Connecting vowel + Primary active personal endings

λυ + σ + ο + μεν ‣ λύσομεν

19.5   **Tense stem**. The verbs we will see in this chapter have the same tense stem in the future as they have in the present. In chapter 20, we will see verbs whose future tense stem differs from their present tense stem.

When lexicons list a verb and its different tense forms, they list the future active as the second form.

ἀγαπάω, ἀγαπήσω, ἠγάπησα, ἠγάπηκα, ἠγάπημαι, ἀγαπηθήσομαι

ἀγαπήσω is the future active form of ἀγαπάω.

19.6   **Tense formative**. The future is formed by inserting a sigma between the present tense stem and the connecting vowel. This sigma is called the "tense formative" because it helps form the future tense.

19.7   **Connecting vowel**. The connecting vowel is the same as in the present.

19.8   **Personal endings.** The future active indicative uses the same primary active endings as the present active. They contract with the connecting vowels as they do in the present.

19.9   **Paradigm: Future Active Indicative**

In the following chart, the tense formative has been separated from the verbal stem, but the connecting vowel and personal ending are shown together. As usual, the form is followed by the definition, connecting vowel, personal ending, and the present active indicative paradigm for comparison.

---

[1]   Unlike the other tenses in which the time element is not primary, the future tense always refers to an event in the future.

	form	translation	conn. vow.	ending	pres. act.
1 sg	λύ σ ω	I will loose	ο	-	λύω
2 sg	λύ σ εις	You will loose	ε	ς	λύεις
3 sg	λύ σ ει	He/she/it will loose	ε	ι	λύει
1 pl	λύ σ ομεν	We will loose	ο	μεν	λύομεν
2 pl	λύ σ ετε	You will loose	ε	τε	λύετε
3 pl	λύ σ ουσι(ν)	They will loose	ο	νσι	λύουσι(ν)

Characteristics of Future Active Indicative

19.10 **Translation**. To translate a future verb you add the word "shall" or "will." As a general rule, translate the future with the undefined aspect ("I will eat") rather than the continuous ("I will be eating").

Of all the Greek tenses, the future has the strongest emphasis on time, describing an action occurring in the future.

19.11 **Contract verbs**. So far you have learned what happens when the contract vowel comes into contact with the connecting vowel: they contract. But what happens if the contract vowel does not come into contact with another vowel? Such is the case in the future tense where the contract vowel is immediately followed by the tense formative. In this case, *the contract vowel lengthens before a tense formative*. Alpha and epsilon both lengthen to eta while omicron lengthens to omega.

*ἀγαπα	+	σ	+	ω	▸ ἀγαπήσω
*ποιε	+	σ	+	ω	▸ ποιήσω
*πληρο	+	σ	+	ω	▸ πληρώσω

As we will see, this lengthening before a tense formative occurs whenever there is a tense formative; it is not restricted to just the future tense. Notice that the accent is always over the lengthened contract vowel.

19.12 **Square of stops**. If the stem of a verb ends in a stop, when the sigma is added to form the future we see the same types of changes that we saw in third declension nouns ending in a stop (e.g., *σαρκ + σ ▸ σάρξ). Whenever you see a psi or xsi before the personal ending (e.g., βλέψω, διώξω), it is relatively safe to assume there is a sigma in there.

Labial	πσ	‣	ψ	βλεπ	+	σω	‣	βλέψω
	βσ	‣	ψ					
	φσ	‣	ψ	γραφ	+	σω	‣	γράψω
Velar	κσ	‣	ξ	διωκ	+	σω	‣	διώξω
	γσ	‣	ξ	αγ	+	σω	‣	ἄξω
	χσ	‣	ξ	ἐλεγχ	+	σω	‣	ἐλέγξω
Dental	τσ	‣	σ					
	δσ	‣	σ	βαπτιδ	+	σω	‣	βαπτίσω
	θσ	‣	σ	πειθ	+	σω	‣	πείσω

The following chart shows the Square of Stops, with a fourth column showing what consonant results from joining the stop with a sigma.

labial	π	β	φ	‣	ψ
velar	κ	γ	χ	‣	ξ
dental	τ	δ	θ	‣	σ

Future Middle Indicative

19.13   In the present tense, the middle and passive are the same form. In the future, the form of the middle is distinct from both the active and the passive. (We will learn the future passive in chapter 24.) The future middle is formed from the future active tense stem but uses primary passive endings.

As we said before, there is more to the middle than simply being equivalent to the active; but all the middles that we have seen so far, and will for some time, are deponent and therefore active in meaning. That is why the definitions in the following paradigm are active.

Because λύω is not a deponent future middle, we will use πορεύομαι that does have a deponent future middle.

19.14 Chart

> *Future active tense stem + Tense formative (σ) +*
>
> *Connecting vowel + Primary passive personal endings*
>
> πορευ + σ + ο + μαι › πορεύσομαι

19.15 Paradigm: Future middle indicative

	form	translation	conn. vow.	ending	pres. middle
1 sg	πορεύσομαι	I will go	ο	μαι	λύομαι
2 sg	πορεύσῃ	You will go	ε	σαι	λύῃ
3 sg	πορεύσεται	He/she/it will go	ε	ται	λύεται
1 pl	πορευσόμεθα	We will go	ο	μεθα	λυόμεθα
2 pl	πορεύσεσθε	You will go	ε	σθε	λύεσθε
3 pl	πορεύσονται	They will go	ο	νται	λύονται

19.16 Because a verb is deponent in the present does not mean that it will be deponent in the future (or any other tense). *You can look at the verb in the lexicon, and if the second form listed ends in -ομαι, then it is deponent in the future.*

19.17 Future of εἰμί The future of εἰμί is middle in form. Its root is *εσ. Memorize this paradigm.

1 sg	ἔσομαι	I will be
2 sg	ἔσῃ	You will be
3 sg	ἔσται[2]	He/she/it will be
1 pl	ἐσόμεθα	We will be
2 pl	ἔσεσθε	You will be
3 pl	ἔσονται	They will be

---

[2] Notice that no connecting vowel is visible.

Summary

1. The future tense indicates an action that will occur in the future. It usually carries the undefined aspect.

2. The future tense uses the tense formative sigma. The active uses the primary active endings while the middle uses primary passive. All future middle forms we have seen so far are deponent and therefore active in meaning.

3. Contract verbs lengthen their contract vowel before a tense formative.

4. Knowing the Square of Stop. is especially useful in the future tense.

labial	π	β	φ	‣	ψ
velar	κ	γ	χ	‣	ξ
dental	τ	δ	θ	‣	σ

Master Verb Chart

Tense	Aug/ Redup	Tense stem	Tense form.	Conn. vowel	Personal endings	1st sing paradigm
Present act		pres		o/ε	prim act	λύω
Present mid/pas		pres		o/ε	prim mid/pas	λύομαι
Future act		fut act	σ	o/ε	prim act	λύσω
Future mid		fut act	σ	o/ε	prim mid/pas	πορεύσομαι

Vocabulary

It is important that from the very beginning you do not simply memorize these different tense stems. Learn to apply the rules and concentrate on recognition. This text does not require you to move from English to Greek, only Greek to English.

In the Appendix there is a list entitled, *Tense Stems of Verbs Occurring Fifty Times or More*. It lists all the verbs you will learn in this text with all their different forms in the different tenses. Refer to it regularly.

We list a verb's different tense stems on a second line under the definition. In this chapter we have listed the future active tense.

βασιλεύς, -έως, ὁ   king (115; *βασιλεϝ)[3]

γεννάω	I beget, give birth to, produce (97; *γεννα)[4]
	γεννήσω
ζάω	I live (140; *ζα)[5]
	ζήσω
Ἰουδαία, -ας, ἡ	Judea (43; * Ἰουδαια)[6]
Ἰουδαῖος, -αία, -αῖον	adjective: Jewish (195; * Ἰουδαιο/α)[7]
	noun: Jew
Ἰσραήλ, ὁ[8]	Israel (68; *Ἰσραηλ)
καρπός, -οῦ, ὁ	fruit, crop, result (66; *καρπο)[9]
μείζων, -ον	greater (48; *μειζον)[10]
ὅλος, -η, -ον	adjective: whole, complete (109; *ὁλο/η)[11]
	adverb: entirely
προσκυνέω	I worship (60; *προσκυνε)[12]
	προσκυνήσω

Ignore the future forms of λέγω, οἶδα, and ἔρχομαι until the next chapter.

---

3 A cognate noun of βασιλεία. The ευς suffix is often used to describe the person related to the thing described by the noun (e.g., ἁλιεύς, "fisherman"; γραμματεύς, "scribe"; ἱερεύς, "priest"). On *F* see p. 134n1 and *MBG*, §27.

4 *Gen* is a combining form meaning, "something produced." Hydro*gen* produces water (ὕδωρ) as the result of burning.

5 *Zoology* is the study of life. Klein argues that this is from the modern Greek ζῳολογία, which in turn is based on ζῷον + λογία.

6 Although this word occurs less than fifty times, we felt you should learn it since it is so similar to its cognate adjective Ἰουδαῖος.

7 Ἰουδαῖος occurs nine times as an adjective, 186 times as a noun; see *EDNT*.

8 No genitive form is given because Ἰσραήλ is indeclinable.

9 *Carpology* is the study of fruit.

10 μείζων occurs only 48 times in the New Testament. We have included it here because it is the comparative form of the adjective μέγας that occurs more frequently. The neuter accusative singular (μεῖζον) can be used adverbially. Be sure to see its full paradigm in the Appendix (a-4b[1]).

It is often followed by a word in the genitive, just like πλείων. You can use the key word "than."

11 *Holistic* education treats the student as a whole person, not just an academic shell. This word often occurs in the predicate position when it is functioning adjectivally.

12 προσκυνέω takes a direct object in either the dative or accusative.

Total word count in the New Testament: 138,162
Number of words learned to date: 210
Number of word occurrences in this chapter: 941
Number of word occurrences to date: 99,207
Percent of total word count in the New Testament: 71.8%

Previous Words

As we meet new tenses, we will list the new tense stems for words you already know in the "Previous words" section. Be sure to update your vocabulary cards.

present	*future*
ἀκούω	ἀκούσω
ἀποκρίνομαι	_ [13]
δύναμαι	δυνήσομαι[14]
λύω	λύσω
πιστεύω	πιστεύσω
πορεύομαι	πορεύσομαι

Stems ending in a stop

βλέπω	βλέψω
ἔχω	ἕξω[15]
συνάγω	συνάξω

Contract stems

ἀγαπάω	ἀγαπήσω
ζητέω	ζητήσω
καλέω	καλέσω[16]
λαλέω	λαλήσω
πληρόω	πληρώσω
ποιέω	ποιήσω
τηρέω	τηρήσω

---

[13] There is no future active or middle form of this word in the New Testament. When this is the case we put a dash in place of a future form.

[14] The alpha has lengthened to an eta just like a contract verb.

[15] Notice that the future has a rough breathing. See *MBG* for an explanation.

[16] καλέω is one of the few contracts that does not lengthen its contract vowel. If you really want to know why, there used to be another letter after the epsilon, a digamma, which has long since dropped off (καλεϝ; see p. 134n1). But because it was there, the verb does not lengthen the epsilon.

Chapter 20

Verbal Roots,
and Other Forms of the Future

Exegetical Insight

One of Jesus' purposes in the Upper Room was to dispel the worries of his followers. They had walked together in Palestine for years and now through death Jesus would depart back to the Father. Were they being abandoned? Left alone without any hope? Were they–are we–alone in this world, particularly when times seem dangerous and the darkness impenetrable?

John's record of Jesus' farewell (John 13:31-17:26) gives us the Lord's answer. The Holy Spirit would not be an ambiguous force or an unnamed power from God. Jesus promises that the Spirit would continue his intimate presence among his followers. In John 14:17 Jesus tells his disciples that they will recognize this Spirit: "you know him for he dwells with you (ὅτι παρ᾽ ὑμῖν μένει) and will be in you (καὶ ἐν ὑμῖν ἔσται).

This verse hides a challenging set of Greek variant readings that interpreters have tried to sort out. Here are our choices.

Option 1:	μένει	ἔσται	The Spirit *dwells* with you and *will be* in you.
Option 2:	μενεῖ	ἔσται	The Spirit *will dwell* with you and *will be* in you.
Option 3:	μένει	ἔστιν	The Spirit *dwells* with you and *is* in you.

The best Greek manuscripts support the first reading (μένει, ἔσται), making the second verb only future. Why is this so important? *Why is this essential?* Jesus is saying that Christ's presence *now with them* will soon be *in them*. Not just any spirit, but Christ's Spirit! Not an ambiguous comfort, but Jesus himself in an utterly new form (compare John 14:23; 20:22; 1 John 4:13). Jesus' promise to return to his flock is addressed therefore on the day of Pentecost. The Holy Spirit is Jesus' personal gift of himself to us!

So we are not alone. He who was with the apostles now can be in us. Like a good shepherd (John 10) Jesus never abandons his sheep, no matter what the danger or the darkness.

Gary M. Burge

Overview

In this chapter you will learn:

- the difference between the verbal "root" of a verb, which is its most basic form, and the "stem" of the verb as it appears in a certain tense;
- that sometimes the verbal root is the same as the present tense stem, and other times it is modified in the formation of the present tense;
- that tense stems are not formed from the present tense stem but from the root;
- liquid futures.

Verbal Roots and Tense Stems

20.1   Before we start discussing the other ways Greek forms its futures, it is important to pause and discuss the difference between a verbal *stem* and its *root*. This may appear to be somewhat technical, but if you can grasp the concept now it will make a tremendous amount of difference later on. And this applies not only to the future tense but to all the other tenses as well.

20.2   *The "root" of a verb is its most basic form.* For example, the root of ἀγαπάω is *ἀγαπα. We always preface the verbal root with an asterisk. This root shows itself in the verb ἀγαπάω as well as the noun ἀγάπη and the adjective ἀγαπητός.

20.3   *The "stem" of a verb is the basic form of that verb in a particular tense.* The verbal root *λυ forms its present tense as λύω and its future as λύσω. In the case of this verb, the same stem (λυ) is used in both tenses.

20.4   *The present tense stem and the verbal root of some verbs are the same.* For example, the root *ἀγαπα is the same as the present tense stem ἀγαπα and forms its present as ἀγαπάω.

In verbs where this is the case, the root is normally used without modification in all the tenses and is therefore quite recognizable. Most call these the "regular" verbs.

ἀγαπάω	present
ἀγαπήσω	future active
ἠγάπησα	aorist active
ἠγάπηκα	perfect active
ἠγάπημαι	perfect middle/passive
ἠγαπήθην	aorist passive

In all these tense forms you can see the same verbal root *ἀγαπα.[1]

20.5 *Some verbs modify their verbal root when forming their different tense stems.* This is especially true in the formation of the present tense. *The present tense is by far the most "irregular" of all the tenses.* If you assume that the present tense stem is the base form of the verb and all other tenses are derived from it, you will become very confused and potentially discouraged since this approach forces you to memorize hundreds of "irregular" forms. However, if you will learn that the *different tense stems are formed from the verbal root and not the present tense stem,* memorization and frustration can be kept to a minimum.

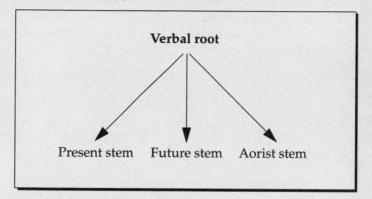

For example, the verbal root *βαλ is modified to form its present tense stem by doubling the lambda: βάλλω ("I throw"). However, when you arrive at the future, you will see that there is only one lambda: βαλῶ. (This is a special future that does not use the sigma as a tense formative, but more about that later.) When you learn the aorist tense (chapter 22), you will see that it as well has only one lambda: ἔβαλον. The point of the illustration is that if you learn the present tense as the base form, both these forms will appear irregular. But if you learn the root as *βαλ, these two forms are perfectly regular. It is the present tense stem that is irregular.

Most grammars describe these changes by saying that the future and aorist tense stems have lost a lambda. Although this may be easier at first, it builds a significant error into your way of thinking and will come back to haunt you. *The present tense stem is never altered to form another tense stem!* The present tense stem is usually a modified form of the verbal root.

This may not sound very significant right now, but it is. You must realize that the present tense stem is the most "irregular" tense stem of all. The verbal root is altered to form the present tense stem more than in all the other tenses put together. You must get away from thinking that the future tense stem is an altered form of the present tense stem. It is not.

---

[1] The change of the initial and final alpha to eta is part of the formation of the tenses and is perfectly regular.

*The present tense stem is built on the verbal root, which sometimes is modified
and sometimes is not modified when forming the present tense stem.*

20.6   **Patterns.** As we see more verbs, patterns will develop as to how the ver-
        bal root has been modified to form the different present tense stems.
        With this correct way of thinking, and with a recognition of these pat-
        terns, you will discover that Greek verbs are not that difficult to learn.
        These patterns are discussed at §20.24.

        All verbs are listed in the vocabulary section with their verbal root. If the
        root is different from the present tense stem, be sure to memorize the
        pattern along with the lexical form, and be sure to mark your vocabulary
        cards accordingly.

        βάλλω   I throw (122; *βαλ)
        βαλῶ

20.7   **Tense stems.** If you look up a verb in the lexicon in this grammar, you
        will see something like the following. This format is standard in all
        Greek texts.[2]

        λύω, λύσω, ἔλυσα, λέλυκα, λέλυμαι, ἐλύθην

        You have learned the first two forms so far, the present and the future
        tenses.

        If a verb is deponent in a tense, that tense stem is listed in its middle or
        passive form. For example, γινώσκω is deponent in the future middle.

        γινώσκω, γνώσομαι, ἔγνων, ἔγνωκα, ἔγνωσμαι, ἐγνώσθην

        If there is a dash instead of a tense stem, it means that tense stem does
        not occur in the New Testament.

        δοκέω, δόξω, ἔδοξα, -, -, -

        So, if you ever want to know what the future of any verb is, you can look
        the word up and check the second form listed. Because the future pas-
        sive is formed from the aorist passive stem, we will discuss it in chapter
        24.

20.8   **Memorization of tense stems.** Whereas most grammars require you to
        memorize all the tenses of the verbs, we restrict this memorization to a
        minimum. When verbs form their tenses very regularly, it is unneces-
        sary to memorize them; they can always be figured out.

---

[2]   These six different forms are almost universally called the "principal parts." We have
      not found this terminology helpful. Some English grammarians use the term "princi-
      pal parts" to describe what others call "parts of speech": nouns, adjectives, verbs, etc.
      Others speak of the three principal parts of the verb: present ("eat"), past ("ate"), past
      perfect ("have eaten"). We call the six different forms of the verbs, "tense forms."

There are also many verbs whose tenses seem a bit irregular but actually follow some secondary rule. Memorization is not required in these cases either, because we will be learning those rules (much like we learned the rules for nouns).

But there are a few verbs whose formation of the different tense stems appears to be so irregular that memorization is the easiest answer. Luckily there are not many verbs that fall into this category, but those that do tend to be common in the New Testament.

In the Appendix there is a list of all verbs occurring fifty times or more in the New Testament with their different tense forms. The forms that you need to memorize are underlined. As you work through the following chapters, keep referring to this chart on a regular basis.

20.9 **"Irregular" tense forms**. We hesitate to use the word "irregular" at all when discussing the formation of tenses. Part of the beauty of the Greek language is that it is so regular, *if you know the rules*. Even the verbs that appear to be extremely irregular are actually quite regular. If you want to see all the rules, check *MBG*. Just look up the verb in the index and go to its proper category.

A danger of discussing "irregular" futures is that you will not learn the regular rules as well as you should. It is easy to let the "irregular" formations govern your thinking, convincing you that futures are difficult to learn and you will simply have to memorize every single form. Resist this temptation. The basic rules govern the vast majority of futures.

20.10 **Consonantal iota.** One of the more important elements in this entire discussion is a letter in the Greek alphabet called the "consonantal iota," usually written in grammars as "ι." It fell out of use many centuries before the time of Koine Greek, but the fact that it used to be present explains the formation of many words.

For example, the second iota in the noun πιστίς actually was a consonantal iota. Sometimes the consonantal iota stayed as an iota as it does here. But notice that in the genitive the form is πίστεως. The consonantal iota shifted to an epsilon.

Another example is the verb βάλλω, "I throw" from the root *βαλ. The future (as we will see) is βαλῶ with the single lambda. Why the change? In the formation of the present tense stem, the consonantal iota was added, and a lambda and consonantal iota form two lambdas: *βαλ + ι › βαλλ › βάλλω.

These illustrations are not important to remember. But do remember that the consonantal iota was a letter in the Greek alphabet, it is no longer present, but its presence is still felt.

ιζω, αζω, *and* ασσω *Verbs*

20.11   **ιζω/αζω verbs**. The present tense stems of verbs that end in ιζω or αζω are generally formed from roots that actually end in a dental.

For example, βαπτίζω ("I baptize") is from the root *βαπτιδ. The final letter of the verbal root was changed to zeta to form the present tense stem (see the Advanced Information section for an explanation). It forms the future as βαπτίσω (*βαπτιδ + σω ‣ βαπτίσω), which is totally regular. Remember, dentals drop out before a sigma.

20.12   **ασσω verbs**. The present tense stem of verbs that end in ασσω are generally formed from roots that actually end in a velar.

For example, ταράσσω ("I trouble") is from the root *ταραχ. The final letter of the verbal root was changed to σσ to form the present tense stem (see Advanced Information). It forms the future regularly as ταράξω (*ταραχ + σω ‣ ταράξω). Remember, velars change to xsi before a sigma.

Variations in the Stem

20.13   When a Greek verb has modified its root to form its present tense stem, the present and future tense stems will usually be different. We do the same thing in English. The past tense of a verb is usually formed by adding "ed" (e.g., "kick" ‣ "kicked"). But we form the past tense of "run" by changing the stem vowel to an "a" ("ran", not "runned"). This is roughly equivalent to what can happen in the Greek future tense.

Usually the variation that occurs is a slight change in the stem of the verb. Often it is a matter of a vowel changing (αἴρω ‣ ἀρῶ), or of a double consonant simplifying (βάλλω ‣ βαλῶ). Observe these patterns. If you can see them, it will greatly help you in the future. At the end of this chapter is a chart of the types of changes you can expect to see.

Exact memorization of verbal roots and present tense stems is essential if you want to use and enjoy the language.

20.14   **Hint**. It is often said that "consonants carry the meaning of a word, not the vowels." If you can think of a verb primarily in terms of its consonants, then the vocalic changes will not be a major problem.

For example, γινώσκω, from the root *γνο,[3] becomes γνώσομαι in the future. If you recognize that the basic consonants carry the word (γν), you can still see them in γνώσομαι.

---

[3]   Advanced trivia: to form the present tense, the initial gamma doubles, separated by an iota, and the second gamma drops off. σκ is then added. *γνω ‣ γιγνω ‣ γινω + σκ + ω ‣ γινώσκω.

Liquid Futures

20.15 The consonants λ, μ, ν, and ρ are called "liquids" because the air flows around the tongue (λ, ρ) or the sound goes through the nose (μ, ν) when pronouncing the letter.[4] If the last letter of the verbal stem is a liquid, that verb is called a "liquid verb." Liquid verbs form their future tense somewhat differently.[5]

20.16 **Chart: Future active indicative**

Future active tense stem + *Tense formative* (εσ) +

Connecting vowel + *Primary active personal endings*

μεν + εσ + ο + μεν ‣ μενοῦμεν

Instead of adding a simple sigma followed by the connecting vowel, a liquid future adds εσ and then the connecting vowel. However, a sigma does not like to stand between two vowels so it drops out, and the epsilon and connecting vowel contract.

μεν + εσ + ο + μεν ‣ μενεομεν ‣ μενοῦμεν

The future of a liquid verb looks just like the present tense epsilon contract verb. This different way of forming the future does not affect the verb's meaning, only its inflection.

20.17 **Future active indicative (liquid)**

The present of ποιέω and μένω are included below for comparison.

---

[4] Technically, only lambda and rho are liquids. Mu and nu are called "nasals." But because they often behave in the same manner, they are usually grouped together under the one heading of "liquid."

[5] Not all verbs whose present tense stem ends in a liquid are classified as a liquid. It depends upon whether or not that liquid consonant is actually part of the stem. (Some verbs add a liquid consonant to the root to form the present. This type of verb cannot have a liquid future since the future stem does not end in a liquid.) The only way really to know whether a verb will take a liquid future is to look it up in the lexicon and memorize it.

	liquid	*definition*	*present contract*	*present liquid*
1 sg	μενῶ	I will remain	ποιῶ	μένω
2 sg	μενεῖς	You will remain	ποιεῖς	μένεις
3 sg	μενεῖ	He/she/it will remain	ποιεῖ	μένει
1 pl	μενοῦμεν	We will remain	ποιοῦμεν	μένομεν
2 pl	μενεῖτε	You will remain	ποιεῖτε	μένετε
3 pl	μενοῦσι(ν)	They will remain	ποιοῦσι(ν)	μένουσι(ν)

20.18   Chart: Future middle indicative (liquid)

> *Future active tense stem + Tense formative (εσ) +*
>
> *Connecting vowel + Primary passive personal endings*
>
> μεν + εσ + ο + μεθα ‣ μενούμεθα

20.19   Future middle indicative (liquid)

	liquid	*definition*	*present contract*	*present liquid*
1 sg	μενοῦμαι	I will remain	ποιοῦμαι	μένομαι
2 sg	μενῇ	You will remain	ποιῇ	μένῃ
3 sg	μενεῖται	He/she/it will remain	ποιεῖται	μένεται
1 pl	μενούμεθα	We will remain	ποιούμεθα	μενόμεθα
2 pl	μενεῖσθε	You will remain	ποιεῖσθε	μένεσθε
3 pl	μενοῦνται	They will remain	ποιοῦνται	μένονται

20.20   Stem changes. Along with the different tense formative, the stems of liquid verbs sometime undergo a change in the present. For example, βαλῶ is the future form of the verbal root *βαλ, which has the present tense form βάλλω. The single lambda of the root has become a double lambda in the present, but stays single in the future.

20.21 **Accents.** The accent can be helpful in identifying a liquid verb. As you can see from the paradigms, a liquid future always has a circumflex over the contracted vowels.[6]

20.22 A **compound verb** is a verb that is made up of two parts, a preposition and a verb. For example, ἐκβάλλω ("I throw out") is a compound of the preposition ἐκ ("out") and the verb βάλλω ("I throw").

Compound verbs form their tense stems the same way as the simple verb. For example, the future of βάλλω is βαλῶ, and the future of ἐκβάλλω is ἐκβαλῶ.

Different Roots Altogether

20.23 Some verbs have totally different forms in the future. For example, the future of ὁράω ("I see," from the root *ορα) is ὄψομαι. ὄψομαι is in fact a regular deponent future. Its root is *οπ.

When the sigma is added, the πσ form a psi according to the regular rules. What happened is that the future of ὁράω ceased being used, as did the present of ὄψομαι. The two forms therefore "got together" and function as if they were the same word.[7] There are only nine verbs in the New Testament that do this (cf. v-8 in *The Morphology of Biblical Greek*). The first three are listed below; six more to go. These must be memorized.

ἔρχομαι	ἐλεύσομαι	"I come," "I will come"	*ερχ; *ἐλευθ
λέγω	ἐρῶ	"I say," "I will say"	*λεγ; *ἐρ
ὁράω	ὄψομαι	"I see," "I will see"	*ορα; *ὀπ

Most of the time when a future tense is deponent and the present is not, or vice versa, the verb uses different roots to form the present and the future, like *ὁρα and *ὀπ.

Patterns

20.24 Some may feel that this section belongs in the *Advanced Information* section. Perhaps it does; but if it can be learned, the benefit in the long run is tremendous.

Here are the types of changes you will see. Remember, the present tense stem does not change to form the other tense stems. The verbal root may

---

[6] Except in the first person plural middle.

[7] This is a rather simplistic definition but sufficient for now.

be modified to form the present tense stem; and usually it appears unmodified, or only slightly modified, in the other tense stems.

Class 1 verbs undergo some changes, but since those changes are regular and easy to identify, be sure to learn them as fully regular. It may be too much to memorize these classifications right now, but at least you can be aware of the types of changes that do occur.

Some verbs could belong to more than one group. ἀποθνῄσκω, the example for class 5, could also belong to class 7 because the root undergoes ablaut.

Some of the examples are taken from vocabulary in this chapter.

1. *Verbal root = present tense stem*

    a. Roots ending in iota or upsilon

        *λυ › λύω › λύσω

    b. Contract verbs

        *ποιε › ποιέω › ποιήσω

    c. Roots ending in a stop

        *συναγ › συνάγω › συνάξω

    d. Liquid verbs

        *μεν › μένω › μενῶ

2. *Verbal root + consonantal iota = present tense stem*[8]

    a. λλ › λ

        *βαλ › βάλλω › βαλῶ

    b. ι

        *ἀρ + ι › ἀρι › αἰρ[9] › αἴρω › ἀρῶ

    c. ιζω

        *σωδ › σῳζω[10] › σώσω

---

[8] When the consonantal iota was added to the stems belonging to each of the groups below, it produced the modification you now see.

λ + ι › λλ

γ + ι › σσ

[9] After the iota was added (which was really the old consonantal iota), the rho and iota changed places ("metathesis", see *MBG*, §17).

[10] The consonantal iota that was added to the delta not only altered the delta to a zeta, but it also forced the insertion of an iota that was subsequently subscripted.

d. σσ

*ταραχ ‣ ταράσσω ‣ ταράξω

3. **Verbal root + nu = present tense stem**

4. **Verbal root + tau = present tense stem**

5. **Verbal root + (ι)σκ = present tense stem**[11]

   *ἀποθαν ‣ ἀποθνήσκω[12] ‣ ἀποθανοῦμαι[13]

   *γνω ‣ γιγνω ‣ γινω[14] + σκω ‣ γινώσκω

6. **μι verbs (chapter 34)**

7. **Verbal root undergoes ablaut to form different tense stems.**

   *ἀποθαν ‣ ἀποθνήσκω ‣ ἀποθανοῦμαι[15]

8. **Verb uses multiple verbal roots to form different tense stems.**

*ἐρχ ‣ ἔρχομαι	I come
*ἐλευθ ‣ ἐλεύσομαι[16]	I will come
*ὁρα ‣ ὁράω	I see
*ὀπ ‣ ὄψομαι	I will see
*λεγ ‣ λέγω	I say
*ἐρ ‣ ἐρῶ	I will say

Summary

1. The "root" of a verb is its most basic form

2. The "stem" of a verb is the basic form of that verb in a particular tense.

3. The present tense stem and the verbal root of some verbs are the same.

4. Some verbs modify their verbal root when forming their different tense stems. This is especially true in the formation of the present tense.

---

[11] διδάσκω does not fit into this category because the final σκ is actually part of the verbal root.

[12] The alpha of the root has dropped out in the present tense stem, and the iota has subscripted.

[13] Liquid future.

[14] See the footnote to §20.14 for an explanation of these changes.

[15] The alpha in the stem drops out in the present but remains in the future.

[16] The theta of the stem has dropped out before the sigma tense formative.

5. Lexicons list verbs with six tense stems (present; future; aorist active; perfect active; perfect passive; aorist passive). So far we have learned the first two tenses.

6. The different future forms are not irregular. They are perfectly regular if you know the rules.

7. Verbs that are deponent in one tense are not necessarily deponent in another.

8. ιζω, αζω, and ασσω verbs have stems which actually end in a dental or velar, respectively.

9. Some verbs alter their roots to produce their different tense stems.

10. Liquid futures add εσ and not just sigma as the tense formative in the future. The sigma drops out and the epsilon contracts with the connecting vowel. They look just like a present tense epsilon contract verb.

11. A compound verb is made up of a preposition and a verb. The compound verb always follows the tense forms of the simple verb.

12. There are eight ways a verbal root is modified to form the present tense stem. Of those eight, we have seen five; we will see examples of #3, #4, and #6 in later chapters.

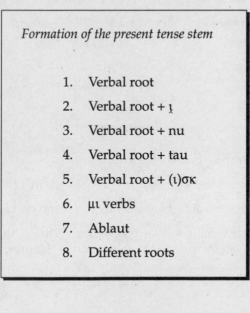

Formation of the present tense stem

1. Verbal root

2. Verbal root + ι

3. Verbal root + nu

4. Verbal root + tau

5. Verbal root + (ι)σκ

6. μι verbs

7. Ablaut

8. Different roots

		Master Verb Chart				
Tense	*Aug/ Redup*	*Tense stem*	*Tense form.*	*Conn. vowel*	*Personal endings*	*1st sing paradigm*
Present act		pres		o/ε	prim act	λύω
Present mid/pas		pres		o/ε	prim mid/pas	λύομαι
Future act		fut act	σ	o/ε	prim act	λύσω
Liquid fut act		fut act	εσ	o/ε	prim act	μενῶ
Future mid		fut act	σ	o/ε	prim mid/pas	πορεύσομαι

Vocabulary

Be sure to check the verbal roots to see which verbs have altered the root in the formation of the present tense stem. If the verb uses more than one root, we will show the different roots.

αἴρω
ἀρῶ
: I raise, take up, take away (101; *ἀρ)[17]

ἀποκτείνω
ἀποκτενῶ
: I kill (74; *ἀποκτεν)

ἀποστέλλω
ἀποστελῶ
: I send (away) (132; *ἀποστελ)[18]

βαπτίζω
βαπτίσω
: I baptize, dip, immerse (77; *βαπτιδ)[19]

γινώσκω
γνώσομαι
: I know, come to know, realize, learn (222; *γνο)[20]

---

[17] See the explanation in §20.24 #2b for the changes to the tense stem. αἴρω can take a direct object in the genitive.

[18] The cognate verb of ἀπόστολος.

[19] *Baptism* is from the cognate noun βάπτισμα. The μα suffix is often used in Greek to specify the result of the action described by the root (cf. *Bl-D* §109[2]).

[20] *Gnostics* were those who claimed to possess certain knowledge.

γλῶσσα, -ης, ἡ	tongue, language (50; *γλωσσα)[21]
ἐγείρω	I raise up, wake (144; *ἐγερ) ἐγερῶ
ἐκβάλλω	I cast out, send out (81; ἐκ + *βαλ)[22] ἐκβαλῶ
ἐκεῖ	there, in that place (105)
κρίνω	I judge, decide, prefer (114; *κριν)[23] κρινῶ
λαός, -οῦ, ὁ	people, crowd (142; *λαο)[24]
μένω	I remain, live (118; *μεν) μενῶ
ὁράω	I see, notice, experience (454;*ὁρα; *ὀπ) ὄψομαι[25]
σοφία, -ας, ἡ	wisdom (51; *σοφια)[26]
στόμα, -ατος, τό	mouth (78; *στοματ)[27]
σώζω[28]	I save, deliver, rescue (106; *σωδ)[29] σώσω

Total word count in the New Testament:	138,162
Number of words learned to date:	226
Number of word occurrences in this chapter:	1,849
Number of word occurrences to date:	101,056
Percent of total word count in the New Testament:	73.14%

---

[21] *Glossolalia* is the spiritual gift of speaking in other tongues, or languages. *Glossology* is the science of language.

[22] ἐκβάλλω retains the meaning of its two parts. This cannot always be assumed in a Greek word.

[23] A *critic* (κριτικός) is one who is able to judge.

[24] *Laity* is actually from "lay" and the suffix "ity." "Lay" is from λαϊκός, which has the same meaning as λαός. The laity are a group of people distinct from the clergy, or any group of people separate from those belonging to a specific profession.

[25] ὁράω and ὄψομαι are formed from two different roots. The root of the future tense form is *ὀπ. Most of the other tense forms of ὁράω are formed from *ὀπ.

[26] *Philosophy* is the love of wisdom.

[27] *Stomatology* is the the study of the diseases of the mouth. *Stomach* (στόμαχος) is also derived from στόμα.

[28] The iota subscript shows that this is actually an ιζω verb.

[29] *Soteriology* is the the study of salvation.

Previous Words

ἔρχομαι   ἐλεύσομαι (*ἐρχ; *ἐλευθ; class 8)

λέγω   ἐρῶ (*λεγ; *ἐρ; class 8)

οἶδα   εἰδήσω[30]

Advanced Information

20.25   **ιζω verbs**

You saw how βαπτίζω forms its future as if its stem ended in a dental. The reason for this is that it does end in a dental. The root of βαπτίζω is actually *βαπτιδ. But what happened with this word, and many like it, is that in order to form the present tense stem from this root, a consonantal iota was added. (This is the same letter we saw in πόλις.) A dental plus a consonantal iota form zeta. But since this consonantal iota was added only to form the present tense, it is not a factor in the other tenses and the word behaves regularly, like any other verb whose stem ends in a dental. So, to form the future, you have βαπτιδ + σ + ω ‣ βαπτίσω.

20.26   **ασσω verbs**

The root of an ασσω verb actually ends in a velar, in this case chi. The root of ταράσσω is *ταραχ. (This root can be seen in its noun cognate ταραχή). When the sigma of the future is added to the stem, the velar and sigma form xsi according to the regular rules (ταράξω).

The present tense of this word was formed basically like ιζω verbs. The consonantal iota was added to the root in order to form the present tense stem, and when a velar and consonantal iota combine they form double sigma (*ταραχ + ι ‣ ταράσσω). But since the consonantal iota is only used in the present tense stem, it is not a factor in the other tenses, and the word follows the regular rules for velars.

---

[30] The future active of this verb occurs only once in the New Testament (Heb 8:11). It may not be worth memorizing; ask your teacher.

Chapter 21

Imperfect Indicative

Exegetical Insight

The Greek imperfect tense is both limited and versatile in its usage. It is limited in that it only occurs in the indicative mood, but in that mood it has some interesting nuances of meaning. Basically, the imperfect expresses linear action in past time. That action may be repetitive, prolonged or just beginning. Sometimes, however, the imperfect expresses repeated *attempts*.

This is true in Galatians 1:13 where Paul says, "For you have heard of my previous way of life in Judaism, how I violently persecuted the church of God and tried to destroy it." Both verbs in the second clause of this verse are imperfects. The first one (ἐδίωκον) simply expresses repeated action in the past. Paul is saying that he often persecuted the church. The second one (ἐπόρθουν) is "tendential," i.e., it expresses attempted action. (This is why the *NIV* adds the word "tried," which does not occur in the Greek.) Paul repeatedly persecuted the church, but his violent acts did not, indeed could not, destroy it. His actions were only attempts, and feeble ones at that. Jesus' promise about his church was true then, as it is now: "The gates of Hades will not overcome it."

Walter W. Wessel

Overview

In this chapter we will learn:

- that the imperfect indicates a continuous action normally occurring in the past;

- that the imperfect is formed with an augment, the present tense stem, a connecting vowel, and secondary personal endings;

- that an augment is a prefix indicating past time. If the verb begins with a consonant, the augment is an epsilon (λύω › ἔλυον); if the verb begins with a vowel, the augment is the lengthened vowel (ἀγαπάω › ἠγάπων);

- secondary active and passive endings, the final two sets of personal endings.

English

21.1   In English there is only one past tense. However, its aspect can be either punctiliar or continuous. For example, "Bob *studied* (punctiliar) last night, but I *was studying* (continuous) until the early hours of the morning."

The past continuous active is formed by using the past tense of the helping verb "was" (for the singular) or "were" (for the plural) and the participial form of the verb (i.e., the "ing" form of the verb). "I *study*." "I *was studying*."

The passive uses the same helping verb but adds the participle "being." "I *was being studied*."

Greek

21.2   **Two past tenses**. Greek also can describe an action occurring in the past, but the difference is that it uses different tenses for different aspects. The **imperfect** tense describes a continuous action normally occurring in the past, while the **aorist** (chapter 22) describes an undefined action normally occurring in the past. ἠγάπων is imperfect (continuous), meaning "I was loving." ἠγάπησα is aorist (undefined), meaning "I loved."[1]

21.3   **Augment**. Greek indicates that a verb is in the past time by adding a prefix. It is called an "augment." We will discuss this in more detail later, but the epsilon added to the beginning of λύω in the paradigm in §21.6 is the augment. It is roughly equivalent to "-ed" in English: "kick"‣ "kicked."

21.4   **Primary and secondary endings**. As we saw in chapter 16, there are two sets of paradigms you need to learn. *The **primary** tenses are defined as those that do not use the augment, and the **secondary** tenses are those that do use the augment.*

Four Sets of Personal Endings

Primary active	Secondary active
Primary passive	Secondary passive

Primary tenses use primary personal endings, and secondary tenses use

---

[1]   The name "imperfect" comes from its basic significance. Because it describes a past continuous action, it does not tell us whether that action was ever completed or not. So it is imperfect, i.e., not completed, not perfected.

secondary personal endings. We have learned the primary in association with the present tense, and we will learn the secondary using the imperfect.

Present active	Imperfect active
Present passive	Imperfect passive

These four sets of endings are all you need to know for the Greek verb. All other paradigms will be slight variations of these four. You already know two of the four. Once you have learned the following two paradigms, you will know all the basic personal endings for verbs. Congratulations.

21.5   One advantage of learning about primary and secondary endings is that when you see a secondary ending you can assume the verb is augmented. This is an extremely significant aid in parsing and should become a regular part of your parsing arsenal. Whenever you see a secondary ending, confirm that the verb has been augmented.

Imperfect Active

21.6   **Chart**. The imperfect active indicative is formed from four parts.

> *Augment + Present active tense stem +*
>
> *Connecting vowel + Secondary active personal endings*
>
> ἐ + λυ + ο + μεν ‣ ἐλύομεν

21.7   **Paradigm: Imperfect active**

The different parts of the verb are separated for convenience, the true connecting vowels and personal endings are listed with explanation, and the present tense form has been included for comparison. Try to list all the similarities you see between the primary and secondary endings. Concentrate on those similarities.

	form	translation	conn. vow.	ending	present
1 sg	ἔ λυ ο ν	I was loosing	ο	ν	λύω
2 sg	ἔ λυ ε ς	You were loosing	ε	ς	λύεις
3 sg	ἔ λυ ε (ν)	He/she/it was loosing	ε	- (ν)²	λύει
1 pl	ἐ λύ ο μεν	We were loosing	ο	μεν	λύομεν
2 pl	ἐ λύ ε τε	You were loosing	ε	τε	λύετε
3 pl	ἔ λυ ο ν	They were loosing	ο	ν³	λύουσι(ν)

Notice that nu is the personal ending for both the first person singular and the third person plural active. The context will help you decide whether a particular form is first singular or third plural.

Imperfect Middle/Passive

21.8   **Chart**. The imperfect middle/passive indicative is formed from four parts.

> *Augment + Present passive tense stem +*
>
> *Connecting vowel + Secondary passive personal endings*
>
> ἐ + λυ + ο + μην ‣ ἐλυόμην

21.9   **Paradigm: Imperfect middle/passive**

The translation is passive.

---

[2]   No personal ending is used, so the connecting vowel stands alone, with the movable nu. This is somewhat the same as we saw in the first person singular active of the primary endings (see §16.10).

[3]   The imperfect active uses the same endings for the first person singular and the third person plural. The context will tell you which is which.

	form	*translation*	*conn. vow.*	*ending*	*pres. pas.*
1 sg	ἐ λυ ό μην	I was being loosed	ο	μην	λύομαι
2 sg	ἐ λύ ο υ	You were being loosed	ε	σο[4]	λύῃ
3 sg	ἐ λύ ε το	He/she/it was being loosed	ε	το	λύεται
1 pl	ἐ λυ ό μεθα	We were being loosed	ο	μεθα	λυόμεθα
2 pl	ἐ λύ ε σθε	You were being loosed	ε	σθε	λύεσθε
3 pl	ἐ λύ ο ντο	They were being loosed	ο	ντο	λύονται

These secondary endings are not that different from the primary endings. This is why we asked you to learn what is really happening in the Greek verb. Otherwise you would not see the similarities as clearly. The connecting vowel is visible in almost every form.

Characteristics of Imperfect Verbs

21.10   **Augment.** The augment indicates past time. There are two different ways a word will augment, depending upon whether the stem of the verb begins with a consonant or a vowel.

a.   If the verb *begins with a consonant*, the augment is an epsilon, always with smooth breathing.[5] For example, λύω is augmented as ἔλυον, because the first letter of the stem is a consonant.

b.   If a word *begins with a vowel*, the augment is formed by lengthening that vowel.[6] For example, ἀγαπάω is augmented as ἠγάπων because the first letter of the stem is a vowel. The lengthening follows the standard pattern discussed in the chapter on contractions, except that an initial alpha lengthens to an eta and not an alpha.

augment		*original*	*augment*		*original*
η	‹	α	ῃ	‹	αι
η	‹	ε	ῃ	‹	ει

---

[4]   This is the only secondary personal ending that has changed significantly. The ending is actually σο. Because a sigma cannot stand between two vowels, it drops out and the connecting vowel and omicron contract to ου.

[5]   This is called a "syllabic" augment since the augment adds another syllable to the word.

[6]   This is called a "temporal" augment because it takes longer to say the word with the vowel being long. Of course, "long" is a relative term; the time difference between saying an omega and an omicron is not that noticeable, but it is present.

augment		original	augment		original
ω	‹	ο	ῳ	‹	οι
η	‹	η	ηυ	‹	αυ
ι	‹	ι	ηυ	‹	ευ[7]
υ	‹	υ			
ω	‹	ω			

c. If a verb *begins with a diphthong*, either the first letter of the diphthong lengthens (εὐχαριστέω › ηὐχαριστουν), or the diphthong is not changed at all (εὑρίσκω › εὕρισκον). Verbs beginning with ευ often do not augment.

21.11 **Present tense stem.** The present tense stem is used to form the imperfect tense. To find the present tense stem, drop the connecting vowel and personal ending from the lexical form. Then, to form the imperfect, add the augment, connecting vowel, and secondary personal endings.

The imperfect form is not usually listed with the other verb tenses in lexicons because it is built on the present tense stem. However, if a verb occurs in the imperfect in the New Testament, we have included the imperfect in our listings, but have put it in parentheses. This way you will always know what the augmented form looks like.

ἔρχομαι, (ἠρχόμην), ἐλεύσομαι, ἦλθον or ἦλθα, ἐλήλυθα, -, -

21.12 **Connecting vowels and secondary personal endings.** The imperfect is formed with the same connecting vowels as the present, but with secondary endings.

21.13 **Recognition.** Even though the personal endings for the imperfect are somewhat different from the present and future tenses, there are still many similarities.

Active

λύεις	ἔλυες	*Second person singular.* Both end in a sigma. This is the only personal ending to do so. Therefore, whenever you see a verb whose personal ending ends in sigma, you know what it is, automatically.
λύομεν	ἐλύομεν	*First person plural.* Identical.
λύετε	ἐλύετε	*Second person plural.* Identical.
λύουσι	ἔλυον	*Third person plural.* The primary ending actually is νσι while the secondary is simply ν.

---

[7] Sometimes the diphthong ευ is not augmented.

Passive

λύομαι   ἐλυόμην   *First person singular*. Both are three letters long beginning with mu.

λύῃ   ἐλύου   *Second person singular*. Both have a sigma that drops out and results in significantly different contractions. This ending is always the most troublesome.

λύεται   ἐλύετο   *Third person singular*. ται in the primary and το in the secondary.

λυόμεθα ἐλυόμεθα *First person plural*. Endings are identical, just like the active.

λύεσθε   ἐλύεσθε   *Second person plural*. Endings are identical, just like the active. While the tau is associated with the active (τε), the theta is characteristic of the passive (σθε); compare also the theta in the first person plural (μεθα).

λύονται ἐλύοντο   *Third person plural*. νται for the primary and ντο for the secondary.

21.14   **Four main paradigms**. You now know the four primary paradigms. All other paradigms are variations of these.

	primary tenses		*secondary tenses*	
active voice	λύω	(-)	ἔλυον	(ν)
	λύεις	(ς)	ἔλυες	(ς)
	λύει	(ι)	ἔλυε(ν)	(-)
	λύομεν	(μεν)	ἐλύομεν	(μεν)
	λύετε	(τε)	ἐλύετε	(τε)
	λύουσι(ν)	(νσι)	ἔλυον	(ν)
middle/passive voice	λύομαι	(μαι)	ἐλυόμην	(μην)
	λύῃ	(σαι)	ἐλύου	(σο)
	λύεται	(ται)	ἐλύετο	(το)
	λυόμεθα	(μεθα)	ἐλυόμεθα	(μεθα)
	λύεσθε	(σθε)	ἐλύεσθε	(σθε)
	λύονται	(νται)	ἐλύοντο	(ντο)

21.15 **Translating an imperfect**. Almost everything in the imperfect tense (person, number, voice, mood) behaves the same as it does in the present tense. The only difference is the aspect and usually the time. In general, the imperfect tense is translated as a past continuous.

21.16 **Deponent verbs.** If a verb is deponent in the present it will always be deponent in the imperfect since both are using the same stem.

21.17 **Compound verbs**. In a compound verb, the augment comes after the preposition and before the stem of the verb. In other words, you augment the verbal part and not the preposition. The imperfect of καταβαίνω is κατεβαίνον.

It makes sense to augment the verbal part of the compound. The augment indicates past time, and a preposition cannot indicate time; so the verbal part of the compound verb must receive the augment.

You will notice that the final alpha from καταβαίνω did not contract with the augment, otherwise it would be κατάβαινον (αε ‣ α). Whenever the preposition ends in a vowel, that final vowel will either drop out before the augment (which is the most common) or in a few cases (such as compounds with περί) it stays but will not contract (e.g., περιπατέω ‣ περιεπάτουν.

When you augment a compound verb beginning with ἐκ, the kappa changes to a xsi (ἐκβάλλω ‣ ἐξέβαλλον).[8]

Contract Verbs

21.18 You should be able to look at the following contracted forms and discover for yourself what vowels were involved in the contractions and why they contracted as they did. If you cannot, go back to chapter 17 and review the rules.

Just as in the present tense, contract verbs contract not with the real connecting vowel/personal ending combination, but with the form seen in the present active and passive.

---

[8] If you really want to know why, the true form of the preposition is ἐξ. The sigma that is part of the xsi is lost when the next letter is a consonant ("interconsonantal sigma"). When the augment is inserted, the sigma is no longer interconsonantal so it does not go away.

	ἀγαπάω	ποιέω	πληρόω
		active	
1 sg	ἠγάπων	ἐποίουν	ἐπλήρουν
2 sg	ἠγάπας	ἐποίεις	ἐπλήρους
3 sg	ἠγάπα	ἐποίει⁹	ἐπλήρου¹⁰
1 pl	ἠγαπῶμεν	ἐποιοῦμεν	ἐπληροῦμεν
2 pl	ἠγαπᾶτε	ἐποιεῖτε	ἐπληροῦτε
3 pl	ἠγάπων	ἐποίουν	ἐπλήρουν
		middle/passive	
1 sg	ἠγαπώμην	ἐποιούμην	ἐπληρούμην
2 sg	ἠγαπῶ	ἐποιοῦ	ἐπληροῦ
3 sg	ἠγαπᾶτο	ἐποιεῖτο	ἐπληροῦτο
1 pl	ἠγαπώμεθα	ἐποιούμεθα	ἐπληρούμεθα
2 pl	ἠγαπᾶσθε	ἐποιεῖσθε	ἐπληροῦσθε
3 pl	ἠγαπῶντο	ἐποιοῦντο	ἐπληροῦντο

21.19   The imperfect of **εἰμί** is as follows. Memorize the paradigm. You now know all the forms of εἰμί in the indicative mood.

1 sg	ἤμην	I was
2 sg	ἦς¹¹	You were
3 sg	ἦν	He/she/it was
1 pl	ἦμεν¹²	We were
2 pl	ἦτε	You were
3 pl	ἦσαν	They were

21.20   **Translation hint**. When you see a verbal form, we recommend that the first question you ask is, "Is this a present tense verb or something else?" (Ignore any augment at this point.) By doing this, you are really asking,

---

⁹   Although there is no personal ending, the stem vowel (ε) is still contracting with the connecting vowel (ε).

¹⁰   Although there is no personal ending, the stem vowel (o) is still contracting with the connecting vowel (ε).

¹¹   There is an alternate form ἦσθα that occurs only twice (Matt 26:69; Mark 14:67).

¹²   This form occurs eight times in the New Testament. The alternate ἤμεθα occurs five times.

"What is the verbal stem?" "Is it the same as the present tense stem or not?"

If the answer is "Yes," then the verb is a present or an imperfect (since the imperfect is built from the present tense stem). If the answer is "No," then it is another tense that may have altered the root. You may want to develop some other method, but the idea is to teach yourself that the verbal root, and whether it has been modified or not, is a tremendously important clue in the identification of verbal forms.

Summary

1. The imperfect indicates a continuous action normally in the past.

2. The imperfect is formed with an augment + present tense stem + connecting vowel + secondary endings. The imperfect is a secondary tense because it employs an augment.

3. The augment is a prefix to the verb indicating past time.

   - If the stem begins with a consonant, the augment is an epsilon.

   - If the stem begins with a vowel, the vowel lengthens.

   - If the stem begins with a diphthong, either the first vowel of the diphthong lengthens or the diphthong is not changed at all.

   - If it is a compound verb, the augment is placed before the verbal part of the compound. If the preposition ends in a vowel it will usually drop off and not contract with the augment.

4. The secondary tense personal endings are much like the primary.

   - Active: ν, ς, -, μεν, τε, ν.

   - Passive: μην, σο, το, μεθα, σθε, ντο.

5. A verb that is deponent in the present will also be deponent in the imperfect, and vice versa.

6. Contract verbs follow the regular rules.

Master Verb Chart

Tense	Aug/ Redup	Tense stem	Tense form.	Conn. vowel	Personal endings	1st sing paradigm
Present act		pres		o/ε	prim act	λύω
Present mid/pas		pres		o/ε	prim mid/pas	λύομαι
Imperfect act	ε	pres		o/ε	sec act	ἔλυον
Imperfect mid/pas	ε	pres		o/ε	sec mid/pas	ἐλυόμην
Future act		fut act	σ	o/ε	prim act	λύσω
Liquid fut act		fut act	εσ	o/ε	prim act	μενῶ
Future mid		fut act	σ	o/ε	prim mid/pas	πορεύσομαι

Vocabulary

Unlike other grammars, we list the imperfect form of verbs if they occur in the New Testament. They are in parentheses before the future tense form.

ἀκολουθέω
I follow, accompany (90; *ἀκολουθε)[13]
(ἠκολούθουν), ἀκολουθήσω

διδάσκω
I teach (97; *δακ)[14]
(ἐδίδασκον), διδάξω[15]

ἐπερωτάω
I ask (for), question, demand of (56; *ἐπερωτα)
(ἐπηρώτων), ἐπερωτήσω

ἐρωτάω
I ask, request, entreat (63; *ἐρωτα)
(ἠρώτων), ἐρωτήσω

θέλω
I will, wish, desire, enjoy (208; *θελ)[16]
(ἤθελον),[17] θελήσω[18]

---

13 Normally takes a direct object in the dative. *Anacoluthon* is a construction in which the grammar does not follow, i.e., it is not correct. An *acolyte* (ἀκόλουθος) is an attendant or a follower, especially an altar attendant.

14 The cognate verb of the noun διδάσκαλος. On the root see *MBG*, v-5a, p. 312.

15 Notice that the sigma of the stem is also absorbed by the xsi.

16 Metzger (*Lexical Aids*) reminds us of the *monothelite* heresy that said Christ had only one will, the divine.

περιπατέω	I walk (around), live (95; *περιπατε)[19] (περιεπάτουν), περιπατήσω
συναγωγή, -ῆς, ἡ	synagogue, meeting (56; *συναγωγη)[20]
Φαρισαῖος, -ου, ὁ	Pharisee (98; *Φαρισαιο)[21]
χρόνος, -ου, ὁ	time (54; *χρονο)[22]

Previous Words[23]

| δύναμαι | (ἐδυνάμην),[24] δυνήσομαι |
| ἔχω | (εἶχον), ἕξω |

Total word count in the New Testament:	138,162
Number of words learned to date:	235
Number of word occurrences in this chapter:	817
Number of word occurrences to date:	101,873
Percent of total word count in the New Testament:	73.73%

Advanced Information

21.21 **Irregular augments.** Some verbs appear to have irregular augments. Actually, they are not irregular, but it is one of those things where the rules governing the augment can become quite complicated. We will explain most apparent "irregularities" in the footnotes, but in some cases it might be simpler for you just to memorize them. Of course, if you can remember the rules, that is much better because the rules that are affecting any one particular augment are probably affecting other verbs as well.

---

[17] θέλω forms its augment as if it were ἐθέλω because its imperfect form is ἤθελον. Actually, its stem used to begin with epsilon, but the epsilon dropped out although the augment remembers that it was there.

[18] Inserts an eta before the tense formative. This is not that unusual.

[19] A *peripatetic* (περιπατητικός) philosopher walked around from place to place, teaching his followers as he traveled.

[20] The *synagogue* is where people gathered together for a meeting.

[21] *Pharisee.*

[22] A *chronograph* measures time. *Chronology* is the science of measuring time.

[23] We have included only those words that form their augment unexpectedly.

[24] δύναμαι also augments as ἠδυνάμην.

For example, lets look at ἔχω. The imperfect of ἔχω is εἶχον. The verbal root is *σεχ. In the present the sigma is replaced by the rough breathing. But because the Greeks did not like the two "aspirate" sounds of the rough breathing and the chi in a row, the rough breathing "deaspirates" to a smooth breathing (*σεχ ‣ ἑχ ‣ ἐχ ‣ ἔχω).

In forming the imperfect, because the verbal root actually begins with a consonant, the augment is the epsilon. But then because the sigma is between two vowels it drops out, and the two epsilons contract to ει (ε + σεχ ‣ εεχ ‣ εἶχον).

The future has a rough breathing (ἕξω). The tense formative sigma joins with the chi to form xsi, but since there are not two aspirates in a row the rough breathing can remain (*σεχ + σ + ω ‣ ἑχσω ‣ ἕξω).

Now, all this may sound complicated and unnecessary, and maybe at this point it is. But it is important you realize that Greek verbs are formed with rhyme and reason, that they do follow specific rules, and that eventually knowing these rules reduces the amount of memorization. As a result, a continuing use of Greek becomes a much greater possibility. And that is, after all, why we are learning this great language: to use it for the rest of our lives to understand and proclaim God's revelation as effectively as possible.

21.22   **Preparatory use of "there."** So far, the only unusual aspect of εἰμί is that it takes a predicate nominative rather than a direct object. There is one other important aspect to the verb. It is permissible to add "There" before εἰμί to make a sensible English translation. Context will show you whether this is necessary or not. For example, ἐστὶν οἶκος παρὰ τὴν θάλασσαν can mean, "There is a house by the sea." But it can also be, "A house is by the sea."

Chapter 22

Second Aorist Active/Middle Indicative

Exegetical Insight

The aorist (ἀόριστος) is the indefinite tense that states only the fact of the action without specifying its duration. When the aorist describes an action as a unit event it may accentuate one of three possibilities, as, imagine, a ball that has been thrown: 1) *let fly* (inceptive or ingressive); 2) *flew* (constative or durative); 3) *hit* (culminative or telic).

These aspects of the indefinite aorist may shed some light on a perplexing saying of Jesus in his Olivet discourse (Mark 13:30 and parallels). "I tell you the truth, this generation will certainly not pass away until all these things γένηται." The difficulty lies in the fact that Jesus has already described the end of the world in vv. 24f. in vivid terms of the sun and moon not giving their light, the stars falling from the sky, and the heavenly bodies being shaken. Unless the expression "this generation" (ἡ γενεὰ αὕτη) is stretched to include the entire age from Jesus' first to his second coming (a less likely option), the aorist γένηται must provide the clue. If we view the verb as an ingressive aorist and translate it from the perspective of initiated action, the saying may be rendered, "I tell you the truth, this generation will certainly not pass away until all these things *begin* to come to pass."

This nuance of the same aorist form may also be seen in the angel Gabriel's words to Zechariah (Luke 1:20): "And now you will be silent and not able to speak until the day γένηται ταῦτα." Not only the birth but the adult ministry of John the Baptist is prophesied by Gabriel in vv. 13-17, yet Zechariah recovers his speech as soon as he writes the name of his infant son John on a tablet (vv. 62-64). Accordingly, v. 20 should be translated, "And now you will be silent and not able to speak until the day these things *begin* to happen."

The student is well advised, then, to pay careful attention to the contextual meaning of the larger sense unit and interpret the aorist as the pericope or paragraph would suggest.

Royce Gordon Gruenler

Overview

In this chapter we will learn that:

- the aorist indicates an undefined action normally occurring in the past. For now, it should be translated with the simple past tense in English ("I *ate*," not

"I *was eating*");

- Greek has two ways to form the aorist. The second aorist uses the unmodified verbal root for its aorist tense stem, which will always be different from the present tense stem;

- the second aorist is formed by using an augment, second aorist tense stem, connecting vowel, and secondary endings.

English

22.1   The past tense of an English verb is formed one of two ways. A **regular**[1] verb forms its past tense by adding "-ed." "I *study* all the time." "I *studied* all last night." An **irregular**[2] verb forms its past tense by altering its actual stem. Usually the vowel is changed. "I *eat* breakfast every morning." "I *ate* last night as well." As far as the meaning of the verb is concerned, it makes no difference which pattern is followed. "Swimmed" and "swam" would have the same meaning, if the former were a real word.

Greek

22.2   In the last chapter, we studied one of the past tenses in Greek. The imperfect describes a continuous action that normally occurs in the past. The second past tense in Greek is the **aorist**. The aorist tense describes an **undefined** action that normally occurs in the past.

As the imperfect is always continuous, the aorist is always undefined. It tells you that the action happened, but nothing more about the aspect of the action (cf. §15.6-7, especially the discussion of the difference between "undefined" and "punctiliar"). This means that in translation you will normally use the simple form of the English past tense: "I studied"; not, "I was studying." As we saw in chapter 15, the English punctiliar is not the same as the Greek undefined, so be careful.

The word "aorist" means "undefined," "indefinite."

22.3   The Greek has two different ways of forming the aorist tense, somewhat as English has two ways of forming the past tense. The Greek tense parallel to the English "regular" formation is called the **first aorist** while the "irregular" is called the **second aorist**. Most Greek grammars begin with the first aorist, but we believe it is easier to begin with the second because it is almost identical to the imperfect.

---

[1]   Also called a "weak" verb.

[2]   Also called a "strong" verb.

A Greek verb will be either first or second aorist, not both. For example, in Greek, "swim" would become "swam" or "swimmed" but never both.[3]

Second Aorist Active

22.4   **Chart.** There are four parts to the second aorist active.

> *Augment + Aorist active tense stem +*
>
> *Connecting vowel +*
>
> *Secondary active personal endings*
>
> ἐ + λαβ + ο + μεν · ἐλάβομεν

λύω has a first aorist active form (chapter 23), so the paradigm uses the second aorist of the verb λαμβάνω (*λαβ), which means "I take." Notice that the endings are identical to those used in the imperfect. The aorist active stem is listed as the third form of the verb in the lexicon (e.g., ἔλαβον).

λαμβάνω, (ἐλάμβανον), λήμψομαι, ἔλαβον, εἴληφα, εἴλημμαι, ἐλήμφθην

	form	translation	conn. vow.	ending	imperfect
1 sg	ἔ λαβ ο ν	I took	ο	ν	ἔλυον
2 sg	ἔ λαβ ε ς	You took	ε	ς	ἔλυες
3 sg	ἔ λαβ ε (ν)	He/she/it took	ε	- (ν)	ἔλυε(ν)
1 pl	ἐ λάβ ο μεν	We took	ο	μεν	ἐλύομεν
2 pl	ἐ λάβ ε τε	You took	ε	τε	ἐλύετε
3 pl	ἔ λαβ ο ν	They took	ο	ν	ἔλυον

22.5   **Augment**. Augmentation for the aorist follows the same rules as it did for the imperfect.

22.6   **Stem**. In the active voice, *a second aorist will always have a different stem from the present because the root will always have been modified to form the*

---
[3]   There are a few exceptions to this rule, but only a few.

present tense stem. Otherwise you could never distinguish an imperfect from a second aorist. This sometimes involves a drastic change, such as when the verb uses different roots to form its tense stems (e.g., λέγω [*λεγ] becomes εἶπον [ϝιπ][4] in the aorist). But most of the time the stem change is minor, and involves either the simplification of a double consonant (e.g., *βαλ ‣ βάλλω ‣ ἔβαλον) or a vowel changing (e.g., *λειπ ‣ λείπω ‣ ἔλιπον).

If you observe the types of changes in vowels that occur between the present and second aorist, it will help you master the second aorist. Once again, this should be a reminder to memorize your lexical forms of verbs very carefully, especially the verbal roots. One letter can make all the difference. Usually, the verbal root has not been modified in the formation of the second aorist tense stem, so if you have been learning your verbal roots the second aorist should be easy.

22.7   **Tense formative**. The second aorist active has no tense formative.

22.8   **Connecting vowels**. The second aorist active uses the same connecting vowels as the present. *If the personal ending begins with mu or nu, the connecting vowel is omicron; the connecting vowel in every other case is epsilon. If no personal ending is used, the connecting vowel can be either omicron or epsilon.*

22.9   **Personal endings**. Because the second aorist is an augmented tense, it uses secondary personal endings. In the active, the endings are identical to the imperfect active endings that you have already learned. It will be easy to confuse these two tenses. The only difference between the imperfect and second aorist active is the tense stem (e.g., ἔβαλλον vs ἔβαλον).

Although the first person singular and the third person plural are identical in form (ἔβαλον), context usually clarifies which one is intended.

22.10   **Translation.** The aorist active describes an undefined action that normally occurs in the past. Use the simple past (e.g., "I *ate*") and not the continuous ("I *was eating*").

22.11   **Vocabulary listing.** If a verb has a second aorist, we will always list it in the vocabulary section. In the Appendix, we have provided a list of all verbs occurring fifty times or more that have second aorists. It may be helpful to make a separate vocabulary card for each second aorist.

---

[4]   ϝ, the digamma, is another letter that, like the consonantal iota, dropped out of the Greek alphabet long before Koine Greek. That it was once present still affects the forms of words. In this case, because the root of εἶπον is *ϝιπ, the iota did not lengthen but rather an epsilon was added as its augment and the digamma dropped out (ε + ϝιπ ‣ εἶπον).

22.12 **"Irregular" second aorists.** What we said about "irregular" future forms applies to the aorist as well. Some aorist forms may appear to be irregular but actually they are not.

Sometimes the shift will be obvious because many verbs follow the same patterns. At other times, however, the variation will be significant. For example, λέγω has the aorist εἶπον that is built on a totally different root. In these cases, it is easier simply to memorize the two stems.

Second Aorist Middle

22.13 **Chart.** There are four parts to the second aorist middle.

> *Augment + Aorist active tense stem +*
>
> *Connecting vowel +*
>
> *Secondary passive personal endings*
>
> ἐ + γεν + ο + μην ‣ ἐγενόμην

	form	translation	conn. vow.	ending	imperfect
1 sg	ἐ γεν ό μην	I became	ο	μην	ἐλυόμην
2 sg	ἐ γέν ο υ	You became	ε	σο[5]	ἐλύου
3 sg	ἐ γέν ε το	He/she/it became	ε	το	ἐλύετο
1 pl	ἐ γεν ό μεθα	We became	ο	μεθα	ἐλυόμεθα
2 pl	ἐ γέν ε σθε	You became	ε	σθε	ἐλύεσθε
3 pl	ἐ γέν ο ντο	They became	ο	ντο	ἐλύοντο

22.14 In the aorist, as in the future, the middle and passive are distinctly different forms. In the paradigm above, the definitions are active because the only aorist middle forms we will see in this chapter are deponent.

---

[5] The sigma drops out because it is intervocalic (i.e., between two vowels), and the vowels contract to ου.

Summary

1. The aorist indicates an undefined action normally occurring in the past. For now it should be translated with the simple past tense in English.

2. Greek has two ways to form the aorist. There is no difference in meaning between the two, only in the form.

3. The second aorist tense stem will usually have a vowel change to differentiate it from the present, although sometimes it will be a consonantal change. It is usually the unmodified form of the verbal root.

4. The second aorist active is formed by using an augment, second aorist tense stem, connecting vowel, and secondary active endings.

5. The second aorist middle is formed by using an augment, second aorist tense stem, connecting vowel, and secondary passive endings.

6. Sometimes the changes in stems are minor. Other times there will be a significant difference because the present and aorist stems are actually from two different roots.

Master Verb Chart						
Tense	Aug/ Redup	Tense stem	Tense form.	Conn. vowel	Personal endings	1st sing paradigm
Present act		pres		o/ε	prim act	λύω
Present mid/pas		pres		o/ε	prim mid/pas	λύομαι
Imperfect act	ε	pres		o/ε	sec act	ἔλυον
Imperfect mid/pas	ε	pres		o/ε	sec mid/pas	ἐλυόμην
Future act		fut act	σ	o/ε	prim act	λύσω
Liquid fut act		fut act	εσ	o/ε	prim act	μενῶ
Future mid		fut act	σ	o/ε	prim mid/pas	πορεύσομαι
2nd aorist act	ε	aor act		o/ε	sec act	ἔλαβον
2nd aorist mid	ε	aor act		o/ε	sec mid/pas	ἐγενόμην

Vocabulary

Be sure to learn these second aorists well; they are common. We will learn the aorist form of προσεύχομαι and a few other verbs we know in the next chapter.

ἀποθνῄσκω	I die, am about to die, am freed from (111; *ἀποθαν) (ἀπέθνῃσκον), ἀποθανοῦμαι, ἀπέθανον
ἄρτος, -ου, ὁ	bread, loaf, food (97; *ἀρτο)
βάλλω	I throw (122; *βαλ) (ἔβαλλον), βαλῶ, ἔβαλον
γῆ, γῆς, ἡ	earth, land, region, humanity (250; *γη)[6]
γίνομαι	I become, am, exist, am born, am created (669; *γεν)[7] (ἐγινόμην), γενήσομαι, ἐγενόμην[8]
εἰσέρχομαι	I come in(to), go in(to), enter (194; εἰσ + *ερχ; εἰσ + *ελευθ) εἰσελεύσομαι, εἰσῆλθον[9]
ἐξέρχομαι	I go out (218; *ἐξ + ερχ; *ἐξ + ελευθ) (ἐξηρχόμην), ἐξελεύσομαι, ἐξῆλθον[10]
ἔτι	still, yet, even (93)
εὑρίσκω	I find (176; *εὑρ)[11] (εὕρισκον or ηὕρισκον), εὑρήσω,[12] εὗρον
λαμβάνω	I take, receive (258; *λαβ) (ἐλάμβανον), λήμψομαι,[13] ἔλαβον
οὔτε	and not, neither, nor (87, adverb)
προσέρχομαι	I come/go to (86; πρός + *ἐρχ) (προσηρχόμην), προσελεύσομαι, προσῆλθον[14]

---

[6] *Geo* is used as a combining form meaning "earth": *geocentric, geology, geodesy.*

[7] Takes a predicate nominative, like εἰμί. γίνομαι has a wide range of meaning. We have found it helpful to think in two categories, "to be," or "to come into being." Most uses fall into one of these two groups.

The root is clearly visible outside of the present tense stem

[8] Aorist middle deponent.

[9] The root undergoes ablaut, dropping out ευ.

[10] The root undergoes ablaut, dropping out ευ.

[11] *Heuristic* is an adjective that describes a person who learns by discovery. *Eureka*, meaning "I found it," is an interjection used by Archimedes when he discovered how to measure the purity of the king's gold crown.

[12] An eta is inserted after the tense stem, just as in γίνομαι.

[13] The future middle deponent is not that irregular. The alpha lengthens to eta (ablaut), the mu is inserted before the beta as it is in the present, and the beta turns to a psi because of the sigma in the tense formative. *λαβ ‣ ληβ ‣ λημβ + σομαι ‣ λήμψομαι.

[14] The root undergoes ablaut, dropping out ευ.

προσεύχομαι   I pray (85; *προσευχ)
                              (προσηυχόμην), προσεύξομαι

πῦρ, πυρός, τό   fire (71; *πυρ)[15]

Total word count in the New Testament:	138,162
Number of words learned to date:	249
Number of word occurrences in this chapter:	2,517
Number of word occurrences to date:	104,390
Percent of total word count in the New Testament:	75.56%

Congratulations! You now know three out of every four word occurrences in the New Testament.

Previous Words

γινώσκω	ἔγνων
ἐκβάλλω	ἐξέβαλον
ἔχω	ἔσχον
ἔρχομαι	ἦλθον
λέγω	εἶπον
ὁράω	εἶδον[16]
συνάγω	συνήγαγον

Advanced Information

22.15   **Translation of the aorist.** So far we have restricted translation of the aorist to the simple past in English. Some grammars also allow for the use of "have." "I have studied all night." This is certainly a valid translation of the aorist; all it must do is indicate past undefined action. However, the last tense we will learn is the perfect, and for didactic reasons it seems better to reserve the use of "have" for the perfect. Once you become used to the verbal system you can be allowed the luxury of using "have" for the aorist as well. However, your teacher may prefer a different didactic method. Be sure to ask.

---

[15] A *pyromaniac* is a person who has a compulsive desire to start destructive fires.

[16] εἶδον is a second aorist without a present tense form. All the other words meaning "see" have their own aorist stems, and yet most grammars associate the word with ὁράω. ὁράω does have its own first aorist middle deponent form, ὠψάμην, but it is quite rare, occurring in the New Testament only in Luke 13:28. We will list εἶδον as the aorist of ὁράω as do most grammars.

Chapter 23

First Aorist Active/Middle Indicative

Exegetical Insight

The aorist tense has often been mishandled by both scholars and preachers. Aorist verbs too frequently are said to denote once-for-all action when the text has no such intention. Bill Mounce makes this abundantly clear in his lucid discussion below. Having been warned of this error, we should not go to the other extreme and fail to see that in some contexts the aorist does denote once-for-all action, not merely because the verb is an aorist but because of the context. Rom 6:10 says of Jesus, ὃ γὰρ ἀπέθανεν, τῇ ἁμαρτίᾳ ἀπέθανεν ἐφάπαξ ("for the death that he died, he died to sin once for all"). The aorist ἀπέθανεν ("he died") clearly refers to the once-for-all death of Jesus, for the verb is modified by the adverb ἐφάπαξ ("once for all"). Paul's purpose is to teach that by virtue of his death Jesus has conquered the power of sin and death once-for-all.

Jesus' victory over sin and death is not of mere historical interest, for Romans 6 teaches that those who belong to Jesus share his victory over sin. Verse 2 says, οἵτινες ἀπεθάνομεν τῇ ἁμαρτίᾳ, πῶς ἔτι ζήσομεν ἐν αὐτῇ ("we who have died to sin, how shall we still live in it?"). The subsequent verses (vv. 3-6) clarify that we died to sin by being baptized into Christ, for when we were baptized into him we were crucified together with Christ. The aorist ἀπεθάνομεν ("we died") in verse 2, therefore, denotes our once-for-all death to sin at our conversion. When we died with Christ the power of sin was broken decisively for us. This does not mean that we cannot sin any longer. Otherwise, the exhortation not to let sin reign in our lives would be superfluous (vv. 12-14). It does mean that the mastery, dominion, and lordship of sin has been broken in a decisive way for believers. Since Christ conquered sin at his death, and since we died with Christ, we now share in his victory over sin. "Therefore do not let sin reign in your mortal body, so that you obey its desires" (v. 12).

Thomas R. Schreiner

Overview

In this chapter we will learn that:

- first aorists are formed "regularly" by adding an augment, tense formative (σα), and secondary endings to the aorist tense stem (e.g., ἔλυσα);
- most first aorist tense stems are identical to their present tense stems;

- when the sigma of the tense formative is added to a stem ending in a stop, the same changes we saw in the future also occur in the first aorist (e.g., βλέπω ‣ ἔβλεψα);

- contract verbs lengthen their final stem vowel before the tense formative, just as they do in the future (e.g., γεννάω ‣ ἐγέννησα).

English

23.1   As we discussed in the previous chapter, English forms its past tense in two different ways. An "irregular" verb alters its stem. "*I am eating* my lunch now." "*I ate* my dinner last night." A "regular" verb adds "-ed" to the stem. "*I clean* my desk every day." "*I cleaned* mine last year."

Greek

23.2   As we also discussed in the previous chapter, Greek has two ways of forming the aorist tense. The second aorist is the Greek equivalent of the English "irregular" formulation; the verb stem is altered to form the different tenses.

The first aorist is the Greek equivalent of the English "regular" formulation. In the first aorist, instead of altering the stem of the verb to form the aorist stem, the tense uses a tense formative (σα). The majority of verbs in Greek follow this pattern.

Characteristics of the First Aorist Active

23.3   **Chart**. There are four parts to the formation of the first aorist active.

> *Augment + Aorist active tense stem +*
>
> *Tense formative (σα) + Secondary active personal endings*
>
> ἐ + λυ + σα + μεν ‣ ἐλύσαμεν

Notice that there are no connecting vowels. The tense formative is σα and therefore a connecting vowel is unnecessary. The imperfect and second aorist have been included for comparison in the following paradigm.

	first aorist	translation	ending	imperfect	second aorist
1 sg	ἔ λυ σα[1]	I loosed	–	ἔλυον	ἔλαβον
2 sg	ἔ λυ σα ς	You loosed	ς	ἔλυες	ἔλαβες
3 sg	ἔ λυ σε (ν)[2]	He/she/it loosed	– (ν)	ἔλυε(ν)	ἔλαβε(ν)
1 pl	ἐ λύ σα μεν	We loosed	μεν	ἐλύομεν	ἐλάβομεν
2 pl	ἐ λύ σα τε	You loosed	τε	ἐλύετε	ἐλάβετε
3 pl	ἔ λυ σα ν	They loosed	ν	ἔλυον	ἔλαβον

23.4 **Augment**. The first aorist is augmented just as the second aorist and imperfect.

23.5 **Stem**. The aorist active is formed from the first aorist tense stem, which is generally the same form as the present tense stem. If the aorist stem of a verb is different from the present, the verb will usually have a second aorist.

23.6 **Tense formative**. Greek adds a tense formative between the stem and the personal endings to form the first aorist in the same way that it adds sigma to form the future. The first aorist active tense formative is σα.[3]

Because the tense formative ends with a vowel there is no need for a connecting vowel, and so the personal endings are added directly to the tense formative.

The tense formative for the active is easy to spot. The only time it alters its form is the third person singular, where instead of the σα it is σε.

23.7 **Personal endings**. The first aorist active uses secondary personal endings because the aorist tense is augmented. This means it has the same personal endings as the imperfect and second aorist.

If you have been memorizing the personal endings as a combination of connecting vowel and personal ending (e.g., ομεν), then you may not see the similarity between the endings in the first aorist and in the imperfect as clearly. But if you have been keeping the connecting vowel and personal ending distinct (e.g., ο + μεν), then you already know the endings used in the first aorist.

---

[1] No ending is used, so the tense formative stands by itself.

[2] No ending is used, but in this case (as opposed to the first person singular) the alpha of the tense formative is changed to an epsilon.

[3] Some argue that the tense formative is sigma, and the alpha is a connecting vowel. But see Smyth, §455-456.

23.8   **Contract verbs**. As was the case in the future, contract verbs lengthen
their contract vowel before the tense formative. ἀγαπάω becomes
ἠγάπησα.

23.9   **Translation**. The aorist active is translated with the simple English past
indicating undefined action. "I studied." Remember that aspect is primary, and all the aorist tells you is that an event occurred; it tells you
nothing more about the aspect of the event. And the aorist is not necessarily punctiliar; it is "undefined."

23.10   **Stems ending in a stop**. We have already seen how the stops change
when followed by a sigma, both in third declension nouns as well as in
verbs in the future. What was true in the future is also true in the first
aorist active. First aorist stems ending in a labial form a psi when joined
to the tense formative. Stems ending in a velar (including ασσω verbs)
form a xsi. Stems ending in a dental (including ιζω and αζω verbs) lose
the dental.

πσ ▸ ψ	βλέπ +	σα ▸	ἔβλεψα
βσ ▸ ψ	τρίβ +	σα ▸	ἔτριψα
φσ ▸ ψ	γράφ +	σα ▸	ἔγραψα
κσ ▸ ξ	πλέκ +	σα ▸	ἔπλεξα
γσ ▸ ξ	πνίγ +	σα ▸	ἔπνιξα
χσ ▸ ξ	βρέχ +	σα ▸	ἔβρεξα
τσ[4] ▸ σ			
δσ ▸ σ	σπεύδ +	σα ▸	ἔσπευσα
θσ ▸ σ	πείθ +	σα ▸	ἔπεισα

23.11   **Second aorist stems with first aorist endings**. Occasionally you will
find certain second aorist forms with an alpha instead of an omicron as
the connecting vowel. Instead of εἶπον you will find εἶπαν, and instead
of ἦλθον you will find ἦλθαν. There is no difference in meaning, just in
form.[5]

---

[4]   There is no example of this combination in aorist verbs in the New Testament.

[5]   Here is the reason if you want to know. Greek, like any language, was always in a state
of change. One type of formation overrides another, things are added, things are
removed. One evidence of this state of flux can be seen in certain second aorist forms.
Koine Greek was in the process of phasing out its second aorist endings while retain-
ing the second aorist stems. As a result, we occasionally run across second aorist stems
with first aorist endings, such as εἶπαν and ἦλθαν.

Liquid Aorists

23.12 **Liquid aorists**. Instead of adding σα as the tense formative, liquid verbs add only alpha and then sometimes modify the tense stem. The paradigmatic verb used below is μένω.

The phenomena of the liquids affect only the future and aorist tenses. They will not come into consideration in any of the remaining chapters.

> *Augment + Aorist active tense stem +*
>
> *Tense formative (α) + Secondary active personal endings*
>
> ἐ + μειν + α + μεν ‣ ἐμείναμεν

23.13 **Forms**. The keys to recognizing a liquid aorist are two:

- the final stem consonant is a liquid;
- the alpha tense formative, not σα.

	aorist liquid	*translation*	*first aorist*
1 sg	ἔμεινα	I remained	ἔλυσα
2 sg	ἔμεινας	You remained	ἔλυσας
3 sg	ἔμεινε(ν)	He/she/it remained	ἔλυσε(ν)
1 pl	ἐμείναμεν	We remained	ἐλύσαμεν
2 pl	ἐμείνατε	You remained	ἐλύσατε
3 pl	ἔμειναν	They remained	ἔλυσαν

As you can see, μένω has altered its stem in the aorist tense: the epsilon has changed to ει. All verbs that occur fifty times or more and have a liquid aorist are listed in the Appendix.

Aorist Middle Indicative

23.14 Like the future, the aorist uses distinct forms for the middle and the passive. (We will learn passives in the next chapter.) Like the future middle, the aorist middle is identical to the aorist active except that it uses passive personal endings.

23.15   **Chart**

> *Augment + Aorist active tense stem +*
>
> *Tense formative (σα) + Secondary passive personal endings*
>
> ἐ + λυ + σα + μην ‣ ἐλυσάμην

23.16   **Paradigm**. The translations are still in the active because all the middles you will see in this chapter are active in meaning.

	first aorist	*translation*	*ending*	*second aorist*
1 sg	ἐ λυ σά μην	I loosed	μην	ἐγενόμην
2 sg	ἐ λύ σ ω⁶	You loosed	σο	ἐγένου
3 sg	ἐ λύ σα το	He/she/it loosed	το	ἐγένετο
1 pl	ἐ λυ σά μεθα	We loosed	μεθα	ἐγενόμεθα
2 pl	ἐ λύ σα σθε	You loosed	σθε	ἐγένεσθε
3 pl	ἐ λύ σα ντο	They loosed	ντο	ἐγένοντο

23.17   You know that a verb is a middle deponent in the aorist if the third tense form of the verb listed in the lexicon ends in "μην."

> ἀρνέομαι   I deny (33, v-1d[2a])
> (ἠρνούμην), ἀρνήσομαι, ἠρνησάμην, -, ἤρνημαι, -

Middle Voice

23.18   Up to this point every middle we have seen is deponent and therefore has an active meaning. There is another situation we need to look at. A few verbs have one meaning in the active and another in the middle. The most common example of this is ἄρχω, which in the active means "I rule" but in the middle (ἄρχομαι) means "I begin."

> ἄρχω   *act:*   I rule
> ἄρχομαι   *mid:*   I begin

---

6   Remember that the actual personal ending is σο. When combined with the tense formative, the second sigma drops out because it is intervocalic (i.e., "between vowels") and the vowels contract to omega (*σα + σο ‣ σαο ‣ σω).

ἅπτω   *act:*   I light (a fire)
ἅπτομαι   *mid:*   I touch

Summary

1. A verb that has a first aorist stem forms its aorist active by adding an augment, tense formative (σα), and secondary personal endings to the aorist tense stem. The aorist middle is a distinct form from the passive, and is formed in the same way as is the active except that it uses passive personal endings.

2. Like the second aorist, the first aorist describes an undefined action, normally occurring in past time.

3. Verbs with stems ending in a stop behave in the aorist as they do in the future in reference to the sigma of the tense formative.

4. Contract verbs lengthen their final stem vowel before the tense formative.

5. Liquid aorists use α and not σα as their tense formative, and sometimes modify their tense stem.

Master Verb Chart						
Tense	*Aug/ Redup*	*Tense stem*	*Tense form.*	*Conn. vowel*	*Personal endings*	*1st sing paradigm*
Present act		pres		o/ε	prim act	λύω
Present mid/pas		pres		o/ε	prim mid/pas	λύομαι
Imperfect act	ε	pres		o/ε	sec act	ἔλυον
Imperfect mid/pas	ε	pres		o/ε	sec mid/pas	ἐλυόμην
Future act		fut act	σ	o/ε	prim act	λύσω
Liquid fut act		fut act	εσ	o/ε	prim act	μενῶ
Future mid		fut act	σ	o/ε	prim mid/pas	πορεύσομαι
1st aorist act	ε	aor act	σα		sec act	ἔλυσα
Liquid aorist act	ε	aor act	α		sec act	ἔμεινα
2nd aorist act	ε	aor act		o/ε	sec act	ἔλαβον
1st aorist mid	ε	aor act	σα		sec mid/pas	ἐλυσάμην
2nd aorist mid	ε	aor act		o/ε	sec mid/pas	ἐγενόμην

Vocabulary

ἀπέρχομαι   I depart (117; ἀπ + *ἐρχ; ἀπ + *ἐλευθ)
                                   ἀπελεύσομαι, ἀπῆλθον

ἄρχω   active: I rule (86; *ἀρχ)
                                   middle: I begin[7]
                                   ἄρξομαι, ἠρξάμην

γράφω   I write (191; *γραφ)[8]
                                   (ἔγραφον), γράψω, ἔγραψα

διό   therefore, for this reason (53)

δοξάζω   I praise, honor, glorify (61; *δοξαδ)[9]
                                   (ἐδόξαζον), δοξάσω, ἐδόξασα

δύναμις, -εως, ἡ   power, miracle (119; *δυναμι)[10]

κηρύσσω   I proclaim, preach (61; *κηρυγ)[11]
                                   (ἐκήρυσσον), κηρύξω, ἐκήρυξα

πίνω   I drink (73; *πι)[12]
                                   (ἔπινον), πίομαι, ἔπιον

Total word count in the New Testament:	138,162
Number of words learned to date:	257
Number of word occurrences in this chapter:	761
Number of word occurrences to date:	105,151
Percent of total word count in the New Testament:	76.11%

---

[7] ἄρχω occurs primarily in the middle in the New Testament. As a prefix it means "chief" (e.g., archbishop, archangel).

[8] Graphic (γραφικός) means, "pertaining to writing."

[9] Verbal cognate of δόξα.

[10] This is the cognate noun of the verb δύναμαι. Dynamite comes from δύναμις, but you cannot define the latter by the former because English was not a language until hundreds of years later. See D.A. Carson, Exegetical Fallacies, pp. 32-33.

[11] The kerygma is a term used by C.H. Dodd to describe the essential nature of the gospel message in the early church. See R.H. Mounce, The Essential Nature of New Testament Preaching (Eerdmans). Kerygma is from the cognate noun κήρυγμα.

[12] πίνω is from the root *πι to which was added a nu in the formation of the present tense stem (class v-3; see §20.24). The future and aorist tense stems are therefore perfectly regular in their formation, the nu belonging only to the present tense stem.

A potion is something you drink (from *πι through the French, potion).

Previous Words

Present	Aorist
ἀκούω	ἤκουσα
δύναμαι	-
θέλω	ἠθέλησα[13]
λύω	ἔλυσα
πιστεύω	ἐπίστευσα
πορεύομαι	-

Stems ending in a stop

βαπτίζω	ἐβάπτισα
βλέπω	ἔβλεψα
διδάσκω	ἐδίδαξα
προσεύχομαι	προσηυξάμην
σῴζω	ἔσωσα

Contract stems

ἀγαπάω	ἠγάπησα
ἀκολουθέω	ἠκολούθησα
γεννάω	ἐγέννησα
ζάω	ἔζησα
ζητέω	ἐζήτησα
καλέω	ἐκάλεσα[14]
λαλέω	ἐλάλησα
πληρόω	ἐπλήρωσα
ποιέω	ἐποίησα
προσκυνέω	προσεκύνησα[15]
τηρέω	ἐτήρησα

---

[13] θέλω augments in the aorist as it does in the imperfect (cf. chapter 21). It also inserts an eta before the tense formative.

[14] As in the future, καλέω does not lengthen its final stem vowel before the tense formative.

[15] Notice that προσκυνέω augments as if it were a compound verb.

Liquid stems

αἴρω	ἦρα
ἀποκτείνω	ἀπέκτεινα
ἀποστέλλω	ἀπέστειλα
ἐγείρω	ἤγειρα
θέλω	ἠθέλησα[16]
κρίνω	ἔκρινα
μένω	ἔμεινα[17]

---

[16] The root of θέλω is *εθελ. It lost the initial epsilon in the present, but its influence can still be seen in the augment.

[17] ε changes to ει (ablaut).

Chapter 24

Aorist and Future Passive Indicative

Exegetical Insight

The biblical writers are so open and direct in speaking of God's actions for us and for our salvation, that it may come as a surprise to students of New Testament Greek that sometimes God's sovereign grace is hidden in grammatical expressions that do not contain the name of God at all. This is the case with the construction Max Zerwick has called the "theological passive." Jewish reticence about speaking of God directly shows up quite often in Jesus' use of the future passive indicative–perhaps as a kind of understatement for rhetorical effect.

There are four classic examples in the Beatitudes, where Jesus says of those he pronounces "Blessed" that "they will be comforted" (Matt 5:4), "they will be filled" (5:6), "they will be shown mercy" (5:7), and "they will be called children of God" (5:9). The meaning is that *God* will comfort them, fill them, show them mercy, and call them his children. In a promise of answered prayer, Jesus says, "Ask and it will be given you ... knock and it will be opened" (Luke 11:9). Clearly, *God* is the One who gives and who opens the door.

The aorist passive is used less often in this way, yet Peter speaks of the prophets to whom "it was revealed" (that is, to whom *God* revealed) that their prophecies were for us (1 Peter 1:12). God's sovereignty embraces even the terrible judgments in Revelation, where four horsemen were "given" (ἐδόθη) power to kill by sword, famine, and disease (Rev 6:8), and John himself was "given" (ἐδόθη) a reed to measure the temple court for judgment (11:1). Here too God is the unexpressed Giver.

In English the passive voice is often considered a sign of weak style, but in Greek it can be a clear signal that God is at work.

J. Ramsey Michaels

Overview

In this chapter we will learn that:

- the aorist and future passives are formed from the same tense stem. It is listed sixth and last in the lexicon;

- the aorist passive is formed with an augment, aorist passive tense stem, tense formative (θη or η), and secondary active endings.

207

- the future passive is formed with the unaugmented aorist passive tense stem, tense formative (θησ or ησ), connecting vowel, and primary passive endings.

English

24.1   In English, the **past passive** is formed by using the helping verb "was"/ "were" and the past participle form of the verb. "*I was flunked* by the Hebrew teacher."

The **future passive** is formed by using the helping verb "will," the helping verb "be," and the past participle form of the English verb. "*I will be flunked* if I do not study."

The **future continuous passive** is formed in the same way except that "being" is inserted. "I will be being flunked," which obviously is not a common tense in English.

Greek

24.2   We have already learned the aorist and future active and middle. In this chapter we will look at the aorist and future passive. Both these tenses are formed from the same tense stem, so it is natural to discuss them at the same time. The aorist passive form is listed sixth and last in the lexicon: ἠγαπήθην. The future passive is not listed as a separate form.

> ἀγαπάω   I love (143; *ἀγαπα)
> ἀγαπήσω, ἠγάπησα, ἠγάπηκα, ἠγάπημαι, ἠγαπήθην

As is true of ἀγαπάω, if the word occurs in the New Testament in the future passive, we list the future passive in the footnote: ἀγαπηθήσομαι.

There are only four or five points to be learned in this chapter. The grammar is very easy.

First Aorist Passive

24.3   **Form**. There are four parts to the formation of the first aorist passive.

> *Augment + Aorist passive stem + Tense formative (θη) +*
> *Secondary active personal endings*
>
> ἐ + λυ + θη + ν ⬧ ἐλύθην

Notice that there are no connecting vowels. The tense formative is **θη**[1] and therefore the connecting vowels are unnecessary. Notice also that the passive uses *active* endings. The imperfect active has been included for comparison.

	first aorist pas.	translation	ending	imperfect act.
1 sg	ἐ λύ θη ν	I was loosed	ν	ἔλυον
2 sg	ἐ λύ θη ς	You were loosed	ς	ἔλυες
3 sg	ἐ λύ θη	He/she/it was loosed	-	ἔλυε
1 pl	ἐ λύ θη μεν	We were loosed	μεν	ἐλύομεν
2 pl	ἐ λύ θη τε	You were loosed	τε	ἐλύετε
3 pl	ἐ λύ θη σαν[2]	They were loosed	σαν	ἔλυον

24.4 **Augment**. The aorist passive stem uses the augment, which normally indicates past time.

24.5 **Tense stem**. The first aorist passive tense stem is generally the same as the present tense stem. If it is different, the verb will usually have a second aorist passive.

The aorist passive tense form of the verb is listed as the sixth form in the lexicon: ἤχθην.

> ἄγω   I lead (67; *ἀγ)
> (ἠγόμην), ἄξω, ἤγαγον, -, -, ἤχθην

24.6 **Tense formative**. The tense formative is θη and easy to spot because it never varies. Almost every time you see the θη you can assume the verb is an aorist passive.[3]

24.7 **Secondary active endings**. The aorist passive uses active endings.

---

[1] Advanced information for the curious: the tense formative actually is θε, which in this form has lengthened to θη. We will see the shortened form in other situations later.

[2] This form uses the alternative ending σαν instead of the nu used in the imperfect and second aorist. We have already seen this ending on the aorist active, third person plural of γινώσκω: ἔγνωσαν.

[3] The only exception to this is an epsilon contract verb like ἀκολουθέω which, when used with a tense formative, has the θη combination because of the lengthened contract vowel (e.g., ἠκολούθησα, which is aorist active, or ἀκολουθήσω, which is future active).

24.8   **Translation**. The aorist passive is translated with the helping verb "was"/"were" and designates an event of undefined aspect, normally in past time. "I was tested." "They were flunked."

24.9   **Stems ending in a stop**. Stops change when immediately followed by a theta, according to the following pattern.[4]

πθ	▸	φθ		*βλεπ + θη	▸	ἐβλέφθην
βθ	▸	φθ		*ἐλημβ + θην	▸	ἐλήμφθην
κθ	▸	χθ		*διωκ + θη	▸	ἐδιώχθην
γθ	▸	χθ		*αγ + θη	▸	ἤχθην
τθ	▸	σθ[5]				
δθ	▸	σθ		*βαπτιδ+ θη	▸	ἐβαπτίσθην
θθ	▸	σθ		*πειθ + θη	▸	ἐπείσθην

Second Aorist Passive

24.10   **Second Aorist Passive Indicative**

> *Augment + Aorist passive tense stem +*
>
> *Tense formative* (η) +
>
> *Secondary active personal endings*
>
> ἐ + γραφ + η + μεν ▸ ἐγράφημεν

---

[4]   For you grammarian experts, this is called "aspiration." In one sense, in English it is what turns "t" to "th," or "p" to "ph," or "c" to "ch." It is like adding the "h" sound (which is an "aspirate"). The same holds true for Greek. Theta is like an aspirated tau.

To put it another way, if you look at the Square of Stops, you can see the pattern.

π	β	φ	▸	φ
κ	γ	χ	▸	χ
τ	δ	θ	▸	σ

If the stop occurs in the left or middle column, the stop shifts to the corresponding stop in the right column.

[5]   There is no example of this combination in aorist verbs in the New Testament.

The paradigm for the second aorist passive uses γράφω. In the case of this particular verb, the second aorist stem has not changed from the present (γράφω ‣ ἐγράφην). This serves to emphasize how important it is to know your personal endings exactly, otherwise you might mistakenly think that one of these forms is a present or imperfect. The New Testament has only 32 words that occur in the second aorist passive (see *MBG*).

The tense formative is eta, there is no connecting vowel, and it uses secondary active personal endings. The first aorist passive is listed for comparison.

	second aorist passive	translation	endings	first aorist passive
1 sg	ἐ γράφ η ν	I was written	ν	ἐλύθην
2 sg	ἐ γράφ η ς	You were written	ς	ἐλύθης
3 sg	ἐ γράφ η	He/she/it was written	-	ἐλύθη
1 pl	ἐ γράφ η μεν	We were written	μεν	ἐλύθημεν
2 pl	ἐ γράφ η τε	You were written	τε	ἐλύθητε
3 pl	ἐ γράφ η σαν	They were written	σαν[6]	ἐλύθησαν

In the passive, sometimes the stem will be the same as in the present, sometimes the same as in the aorist active, and sometimes it will be different from both. It is therefore important to recognize the tense formative and personal endings used in the aorist passive.

24.11 All that we said above regarding the significance and translation of the aorist active applies to the passive as well. In the passive, English uses the past form of "I am" and the past perfect participle form of the verb ("I was asked," "They were asked.")

First Future Passive

24.12 **Form**. The future middle is built on the future active tense stem. The examples we have learned thus far have all been deponent, and have used the primary passive endings: γενήσομαι, γενήσῃ, γενήσεται, γενησόμεθα, γενήσεσθε, γενήσονται.

However, a future passive is formed from the aorist passive tense stem. Note that whereas the aorist passive uses active endings, the future pas-

---

6   Same alternate ending as in the first aorist.

sive uses passive endings.

> *Aorist passive tense stem (without augment)* +
>
> *Tense formative* (θησ) + *Connecting vowel* +
>
> *Primary passive personal endings*
>
> λυ + θησ + ο + μαι ‣ λυθήσομαι

	first fut. pass.	*translation*	*conn. vowel*	*ending*
1 sg	λυ θήσ ομαι	I will be loosed	ο	μαι
2 sg	λυ θήσ ῃ	You will be loosed	ε	σαι[7]
3 sg	λυ θήσ εται	He/she/it will be loosed	ε	ται
1 pl	λυ θησ όμεθα	We will be loosed	ο	μεθα
2 pl	λυ θήσ εσθε	You will be loosed	ε	σθε
3 pl	λυ θήσ ονται	They will be loosed	ο	νται

24.13 **Differences between the future and aorist passive**

- In the future passive there is no augment. It should be obvious why.[8]

- The tense formative is θησ, not θη. If it helps, you could think of the θη as part of the aorist passive stem and the sigma making the necessary alterations to form the future passive (like the sigma in the future active and middle).

- The third person plural passive form -θησαν is aorist and not future. This is the only time in the first aorist passive that you have a sigma after the theta. All other times θησ indicates the future passive.

24.14 **Deponent futures.** The only way to form a future passive is to use the aorist passive tense stem. However, there are two kinds of future deponents: middle deponents built on the future active tense stem (e.g., γενήσομαι); and passive deponents built on the aorist passive tense stem (e.g., φοβηθήσεται).

---

[7] The sigma in the personal ending drops out because it is between two vowels, and the vowels contract normally.

[8] The augment indicates past time, and this is the future.

Second Future Passive

24.15 **Form.** The second future passive is formed just like the first future passive except that the tense formative is ησ.

> *Aorist passive tense stem (without augment) +*
>
> *Tense formative (ησ) + Connecting vowel +*
>
> *Primary passive personal endings*
>
> ἀποσταλ + ησ + ο + μαι ⸰ ἀποσταλήσομαι

	second fut. pas.	translation	conn. vowel	endings
1 sg	ἀπόσταλ ήσ ομαι	I will be sent	ο	μαι
2 sg	ἀπόσταλ ήσ ῃ	You will be sent	ε	σαι[9]
3 sg	ἀπόσταλ ήσ εται	He/she/it will be sent	ε	ται
1 pl	ἀπόσταλ ησ όμεθα	We will be sent	ο	μεθα
2 pl	ἀπόσταλ ήσ εσθε	You will be sent	ε	σθε
3 pl	ἀπόσταλ ήσ ονται	They will be sent	ο	νται

24.16 **Translation.** The future passive is translated with the simple English ("undefined"), almost always referring to a future event: "I will be passed."

Summary

1. The aorist and future passives are formed from the same tense stem. It is listed sixth and last in the lexicon.

2. The aorist passive is formed with an augment, aorist passive tense stem, tense formative (θη or η), and secondary active endings.

---

[9] The sigma in the personal ending drops out because it is between two vowels, and the vowels contract normally.

3. The future passive is formed with the unaugmented aorist passive tense
    stem, tense formative (θησ or ησ), connecting vowel, and primary passive
    endings.

Master Verb Chart

Tense	Aug/ Redup	Tense stem	Tense form.	Conn. vowel	Personal endings	1st sing paradigm
Present act		pres		ο/ε	prim act	λύω
Present mid/pas		pres		ο/ε	prim mid/pas	λύομαι
Imperfect act	ε	pres		ο/ε	sec act	ἔλυον
Imperfect mid/pas	ε	pres		ο/ε	sec mid/pas	ἐλυόμην
Future act		fut act	σ	ο/ε	prim act	λύσω
Liquid fut act		fut act	εσ	ο/ε	prim act	μενῶ
Future mid		fut act	σ	ο/ε	prim mid/pas	πορεύσομαι
1st future pas		aor pas	θησ	ο/ε	prim mid/pas	λυθήσομαι
2nd future pas		aor pas	ησ	ο/ε	prim mid/pas	ἀποσταλήσομαι
1st aorist act	ε	aor act	σα		sec act	ἔλυσα
Liquid aorist act	ε	aor act	α		sec act	ἔμεινα
2nd aorist act	ε	aor act		ο/ε	sec act	ἔλαβον
1st aorist mid	ε	aor act	σα		sec mid/pas	ἐλυσάμην
2nd aorist mid	ε	aor act		ο/ε	sec mid/pas	ἐγενόμην
1st aorist pas	ε	aor pas	θη		sec act	ἐλύθην
2nd aorist pas	ε	aor pas	η		sec act	ἐγράφην

There is only one more tense to learn!

Vocabulary

In chapter 25 we will learn the last tense, the perfect. When grammars list a
verb's tense forms, they place the perfect active and perfect passive between the
aorist active and aorist passive. Since you do not yet know the perfect tense, we
have used dashes in the following listing for the perfect forms.

ἄγω   I lead, bring, arrest (67; *αγ)[10]
                                  (ἦγον), ἄξω, ἤγαγον,[11] -, -, ἤχθην[12]

αἷμα, -ατος, τό   blood (97, *αἱματ)[13]

---

[10] This is the verbal part of the compound συνάγω.

ἕκαστος, -η, -ον
each, every (82; *ἑκαστο/η)

ἱμάτιον, -ου, τό
garment, cloak (60; *ἱματιο)[14]

ὄρος, ὄρους, τό
mountain, hill (63; *ὀρο)[15]

ὑπάγω
I depart (79; ὑπ + *αγ)
(ὑπῆγον), -, -, -, -, -

φοβέομαι[16]
I fear (95; *φοβε)[17]
(ἐφοβούμην), -, -, -, -, ἐφοβήθην

χαίρω
I rejoice (74; *χαρ)[18]
(ἔχαιρον), χαρήσομαι,[19] -, -, -, ἐχάρην[20]

Total word count in the New Testament: 138,162
Number of words learned to date: 265
Number of word occurrences in this chapter: 617
Number of word occurrences to date: 105,768
Percent of total word count in the New Testament: 76.55%

In the following chart, we list the aorist and future passive if they occur in the New Testament.[21]

Previous Words

present active	aorist passive	future passive
ἀκούω	ἠκούσθην[22]	ἀκουσθήσομαι

---

[11] ἄγω undergoes what is called "Attic reduplication." This means that the word both reduplicates and then augments the reduplicated alpha (αγ ‣ αγαγ ‣ ἤγαγον). This is a second aorist.

[12] The gamma has changed to a chi because of the following theta, in compliance with the rules (§24.9).

[13] *Hematology* is the study of blood.

[14] The *himation* is a Greek garment worn over the tunic.

[15] *Orology* and *orography* both mean the study of mountains.

[16] Some do not list φοβέομαι as a deponent, and yet the meaning is always active. In the passive it can mean "I am seized with fear," "I am caused to be fearful."

[17] The English *phobia* derives from this root and is commonly used as a combining form.

[18] χαίρειν (an infinitive, chapter 32) was the common greeting in Koine Greek (cf. Acts 15:23; James 1:1).

[19] The future middle deponent is quite regular. The stem diphthong αι has shifted to alpha (ablaut, as in the aorist passive), and the eta is inserted after the stem. *χαιρ ‣ χαρ ‣ χαρήσομαι.

[20] Second aorist passive.

[21] If neither an aorist or future passive form occurs in the New Testament, there is a dash.

present active	aorist passive	future passive
ἄρχω	-	-
δύναμαι	ἠδυνήθην	-
διδάσκω	ἐδιδάχθην[23]	-
ἔχω	-	-
λύω	ἐλύθην	λυθήσομαι
πιστεύω	ἐπιστεύθην	-
πορεύομαι	ἐπορεύθην	-

Ablaut and stem change

ἀπέρχομαι	-	-
ἀποθνῄσκω	-	-
βάλλω	ἐβλήθην	βληθήσομαι
γίνομαι	ἐγενήθην	-
γινώσκω	ἐγνώσθην	γνωσθήσομαι
ἔρχομαι	-	-
εὑρίσκω	εὑρέθην	εὑρεθήσομαι
λέγω	ἐρρέθην[24]	-
πίνω	ἐπόθην	-
προσέρχομαι	-	-

Stems ending in a stop

βαπτίζω	ἐβαπτίσθην	βαπτισθήσομαι
βλέπω	-	-
γράφω	ἐγράφην	-
δοξάζω	ἐδοξάσθην	-
κηρύσσω	ἐκηρύχθην	κηρυχθήσομαι
λαμβάνω	ἐλήμφθην[25]	-

---

[22] Several verbs insert a sigma after the tense stem and before the tense formative.

[23] The sigma has dropped out, and the kappa has changed to chi in accordance with the rules (§24.9).

[24] The aorist passive of λέγω is formed from a different root: *ερ. The same root is used in the formation of the future active form: ἐρῶ.

[25] The same changes that occur in the future middle deponent occur in the aorist passive as well, along with the change of the final beta to a phi, in accordance with the rules (§24.9).

present active	aorist passive	future passive
προσέρχομαι	-	-
προσεύχομαι	-	-
συνάγω	συνήχθην	συναχθήσομαι
σῴζω	ἐσώθην	σωθήσομαι

Contract stems

ἀγαπάω	-	ἀγαπηθήσομαι
ἀκολουθέω	-	-
γεννάω	ἐγεννήθην	-
ἐρωτάω	-	-
ζάω	-	-
ζητέω	-	ζητηθήσομαι
καλέω	ἐκλήθην	κληθήσομαι
λαλέω	ἐλαλήθην	λαληθήσομαι
ὁράω	ὤφθην[26]	ὀφθήσομαι
πληρόω	ἐπληρώθην	πληρωθήσομαι
ποιέω	-	-
προσκυνέω	-	-
τηρέω	ἐτηρήθην	-

Liquid stems

αἴρω	ἤρθην	ἀρθήσομαι
ἀποκρίνομαι	ἀπεκρίθην	ἀποκριθήσομαι
ἀποκτείνω	ἀπεκτάνθην	-
ἀποστέλλω	ἀπεστάλην	-
βάλλω	ἐβλήθην	βληθήσομαι
ἐγείρω	ἠγέρθην	ἐγερθήσομαι
ἐκβάλλω	ἐξεβλήθην	ἐκβληθήσομαι
θέλω	ἠθελήθην[27]	-
κρίνω	ἐκρίθην	κριθήσομαι
μένω	-	-
χαίρω	ἐχάρην	χαρήσομαι

---

[26] The aorist passive of ὁράω is formed from a different root: *ὀπ. The omicron is augmented, and the pi is altered (i.e., "aspirated") to a phi because of the following theta (cf. §24.9). The same root is used in the formation of the future middle deponent form: ὄψομαι.

[27] Note that it augments here as it does in the imperfect, since the stem originally began with an epsilon.

Chapter 25

Perfect Indicative

Exegetical Insight

It is often the very first and the very last thing we say that is the most important, or the statement that is the most memorable. First impressions and last impressions are the lasting impressions. The same is true for Jesus. The first statement we hear him say is that he should be in his Father's house (Luke 2:49). Even at the age of twelve, he was aware of his divine lineage.

And as he hung on the cross, having lived a sinless life, having paid the penalty for your sins and mine, Jesus uttered his last words before dying. Τετέλεσται. "It is finished" (John 19:30). This one word summary of Jesus' life and death is perhaps the single most important statement in all of Scripture. The word means "to complete," "to bring to perfection." Jesus had fully done the work God the Father sent him to do. Paul spends Romans 5 discussing this very fact, that our salvation is sure because Christ's death totally defeated the effects of Adam's sin, completely.

But the tense of the verb, the "perfect" tense, brings out even more of what Jesus was saying. The perfect describes an action that was fully completed and has present-day consequences. Jesus could have used the aorist, ἐτέλησεν, and simply said, "The work is done." But there is more, there is hope for you and for me. Because Jesus fully completed his task, the ongoing effects are that you and I are offered the free gift of salvation so that we can be with him forever. Praise the Lord. Τετέλεσται.

William D. Mounce

Overview

In this chapter we will learn that:

* the perfect indicates a completed action whose effects are felt in the present. The action normally occurred in the past;
* if a verb begins with a consonant, it receives a consonantal reduplication to form the perfect (λύω ‣ λέλυκα);
* if a verb begins with a vowel, it receives a vocalic reduplication to form the perfect (ἀγαπάω ‣ ἠγάπηκα);
* the perfect uses the tense formative κα and primary personal endings;

- the classical rule of the middle voice is that the subject does the action of the verb in some way that affects itself.

English

25.1 English has no exact counterpart to the Greek perfect tense.

- The English past tense indicates that something happened in the past, whether it was continuous or punctiliar. "I studied" means I did something previously, but it does not say whether I completed my studies.

- When you use the helping verbs "have" or "has," the action described was done in the (recent) past and the statement is accurate up to now.

- The English present can describe an action with current consequences ("It is written"). This is close to the Greek perfect.

Greek

25.2 The Greek perfect is one of the more interesting tenses and is often used to express great theological truths. The Greek perfect *describes an action that was brought to completion and whose effects are felt in the present.*[1] Because it describes a completed action, by implication the action described by the perfect verb normally occurred in the past.

For example, "Jesus died" is a simple statement of an event that happened in the past. In Greek this would be in the aorist. But if we used the Greek perfect to say, "Jesus has died," then we would expect the verse to continue by spelling out the present significance of that past action. "Jesus has died for my sins."

Another example is the verb "to write." When the Bible says, "It is written," this is usually in the perfect tense. Scripture was written in the past but is applicable in the present. That is why some translations choose the present "It is written," instead of "It has been written." This emphasizes its abiding significance.

25.3 It can become somewhat complicated to translate the perfect tense because of the absence of any English parallel. Choose between the two possibilities below, depending upon the needs of the context.

- Use the helping verbs "have/has" and the past participle form of the verb (e.g., "has eaten"). Be sure to remember the true signifi-

---

[1] Present in the time frame of the speaker, not the reader.

cance of the Greek perfect. This will help you differentiate between the aorist ("I ate") and the perfect ("I have eaten").

- Use the English present tense when the current implications of the action of the verb are emphasized by the context ("It is written.")

This is the last tense that you will learn (but see *Advanced Information* for the pluperfect). There are a few more variations, but this is the last actual tense. Once again, congratulations!

Perfect

25.4   Perfect active indicative

The perfect active is formed with four parts. It is a primary tense and uses primary endings. However, because of the alpha in the tense formative there is an apparent similarity to the first aorist.

> *Reduplication + Perfect active tense stem +*
>
> *Tense formative* (κα) + *Primary active personal endings*
>
> λ + ε + λυ + κα + μεν › λελύκαμεν

	perfect active	translation	ending	aorist active
1 sg	λέλυκα	I have loosed	-	ἔλυσα
2 sg	λέλυκας	You have loosed	ς	ἔλυσας
3 sg	λέλυκε(ν)[2]	He/she/it has loosed	- (ν)	ἔλυσε(ν)
1 pl	λελύκαμεν	We have loosed	μεν	ἐλύσαμεν
2 pl	λελύκατε	You have loosed	τε	ἐλύσατε
3 pl	λελύκασι(ν)[3]	They have loosed	σι (ν)	ἔλυσαν

---

[2] The tense formative changes from κα to κε, much like the change in the first aorist from σα to σε.

[3] This is the usual personal ending νσι(ν), but the nu has dropped out because of the sigma.

The third plural can also be λέλυκαν, which resembles the first aorist. There are thirty-one perfect active, third person plural, forms in the New Testament; this "alternate" form occurs nine times.

25.5   Perfect middle/passive indicative

The perfect middle/passive is formed with three parts. There is no tense formative and no connecting vowel. The middle and passive are identical in the perfect, as they are in the present. The paradigm gives the translation of the passive.

> *Reduplication +*
>
> *Perfect middle/passive tense stem +*
>
> *Primary passive personal endings*
>
> λ + ε + λυ + μαι ‣ λέλυμαι

	perfect mid./pas.	translation	ending	present mid./pas.
1 sg	λέλυμαι	I have been loosed	μαι	λύομαι
2 sg	λέλυσαι	You have been loosed	σαι[4]	λύῃ
3 sg	λέλυται	He/she/it has been loosed	ται	λύεται
1 pl	λελύμεθα	We have been loosed	μεθα	λυόμεθα
2 pl	λέλυσθε	You have been loosed	σθε	λύεσθε
3 pl	λέλυνται[5]	They have been loosed	νται	λύονται

25.6   Reduplication. The most notable difference in form between the perfect and other tenses is the reduplication of the initial letter. The fact that it is so obvious makes the identification of the perfect relatively easy. There are several variations to the rules governing reduplication, but here are the basic guidelines.

---

[4]   This is the only place where the true second person singular, primary passive ending appears without contraction obscuring its form. Elsewhere it is preceded by a vowel, the sigma drops out, and the vowels contract.

[5]   The third person plural perfect passive occurs only nine times in the New Testament, six of those being the form ἀφέωνται (from ἀφίημι). See *Advanced Information*.

1. **Consonantal reduplication**. *If a verb begins with a single consonant,*[6] *that consonant is reduplicated and the two consonants are separated by an epsilon.*

   λυ ‣ λελυ ‣ λέλυκα

   • If the consonant that was reduplicated is φ, χ, or θ, the reduplicated consonant will change to π, κ, or τ, respectively.

φανερόω	‣	φεφανερο	‣	πεφανέρωκα
χαρίζομαι	‣	χεχαριζ	‣	κεχάρισμαι
θεραπεύω	‣	θεθεραπευ	‣	τεθεράπευμαι

   As you can see from looking at the Square of Stops, the stop in the right column ("aspirated" stops) is shifting to its corresponding stop in the left column ("voiceless" stops).

voiceless	voiced	aspirates
π	β	φ
κ	γ	χ
τ	δ	θ

2. **Vocalic reduplication**. *If a verb begins with a vowel or diphthong, the vowel is lengthened.*[7] The vocalic reduplication is identical in form to the augment in the imperfect and aorist.

   ἀγαπάω ‣ ἠγάπηκα

   αἰτέω ‣ ᾔτηκα

   However, the functions of the vocalic reduplication and the augment are significantly different. Reduplication indicates the completion of an action. The augment indicates past time.

   Now, when you see an initial augment/vocalic reduplication, the verb can be one of three tenses: imperfect; aorist; perfect. The majority of verbs begin with a consonant, so vocalic reduplication does not occur that frequently.

   ---

   [6] "Single consonant" means that there is not another consonant immediately after it.

   [7] It is common for a diphthong not to reduplicate. For example, the perfect form of εὑρίσκω is εὕρηκα.

- If the verb begins with two consonants,[8] the verb will usually undergo vocalic reduplication and not consonantal reduplication.[9]

    *γνο (γινώσκω) ‣ ἔγνωκα

3. A compound verb reduplicates the verbal part of a compound verb, just like the imperfect and aorist augment the verbal part of a compound.

    ἐκβάλλω ‣ ἐκβέβληκα[10]

25.7 **Stem**. The perfect active tense stem is the fourth verbal form listed in the lexicon, while the perfect passive is the fifth.

ἀγαπάω, ἀγαπήσω, ἠγάπησα, ἠγάπηκα, ἠγάπημαι, ἠγαπήθην

Sometimes the stems are identical to the present tense stem, while at other times they have undergone a change (such as a change in the stem vowel).

25.8 **Tense formative**. The tense formative for the active is κα. The perfect passive has no tense formative.

25.9 **Connecting vowel**. The perfect does not use a connecting vowel. In the active, the tense formative ends in a vowel so no connecting vowel is required. In the passive the endings are attached directly to the stem.

A good clue for recognizing the perfect passive is the absence of both a tense formative and connecting vowels. This situation occurs only in the perfect passive.

25.10 **Personal endings**. Because the perfect is not an augmented tense, it uses the primary personal endings. However, because of the alpha in the tense formative, the perfect active looks similar to the first aorist, which is a secondary tense.

In the passive there is no connecting vowel. The final consonant of the stem and the initial consonant of the personal ending come into direct contact, and as a result the final stem consonant is often changed. In the *Advanced Information* section of this chapter we have spelled out those changes. If this is too confusing, simply remember that in the perfect passive, the consonant immediately preceding the personal ending may have been altered.

---

[8] This is called a "consonant cluster."

[9] If the second consonant is a lambda or rho, then the verb will usually reduplicate (γράφω ‣ γέγραφα).

[10] βέβληκα is the perfect active of βάλλω.

25.11 **Contract verbs**. Contract verbs lengthen their contract vowel in both the active and passive, even though there is no tense formative in the passive.

ἀγαπάω ▸ ἠγάπηκα
ἀγαπάω ▸ ἠγάπημαι

25.12 **Second perfects**. There are only a few second perfects in the New Testament, so they do not warrant a major discussion here. They are identical to the first perfect except that they use the tense formative α and not κα in the active. You know five verbs that have second perfect forms.[11]

ἀκούω ▸ ἀκήκοα   γράφω ▸ γέγραφα
γίνομαι ▸ γέγονα   ἔρχομαι ▸ ἐλήλυθα
λαμβάνω ▸ εἴληθα

Classical Meaning of the Middle

25.13 It is now time to learn the rest of the grammar pertaining to the middle voice.

If a verb is in the active, then the subject does the action of the verb. If the verb is in the passive, then the subject receives the action of the verb. The classical definition of the middle voice is that *the action of a verb in the middle voice in some way affects the subject*. We will call this the "self-interest" nuance of the middle.

This is not the reflexive idea. If the subject of the verb performs an action to itself, Greek requires the reflexive pronoun (ἑαυτοῦ).[12] Rather, in the middle the subject does the action of the verb to the direct object, and yet the action of the verb in some way affects the subject.

Most middle paradigms translate the middle as "I loose *for myself*," "They loose *for themselves*." The problem with learning the middle this way is that the actual force of the middle does not normally connote "self-interest," or else the force of the middle is so subtle that it is scarcely discernible.

25.14 *In the majority of cases, the middle has the same meaning as the active*. Either they are deponents, or their middle meaning is active to the English mind.

---

[11] οἶδα actually is a second perfect.

[12] Many grammars say the middle is "reflexive," but we are uncomfortable with the term. The "direct reflexive" was common in Classical Greek but not in Koine. The only one in the New Testament is at Matt 27:5, but Moule (*Idiom Book*, 24) disputes even this one. See Wallace for discussion. There are a few verbs that are reflexive in the middle, but that has more to do with the meaning of the verb than the function of the middle voice.

25.15   Despite classical usage, the "self-interest" idea is one of the less likely options for the translation of the middle.[13] Context will show whether the "self-interest" nuance is present.

αἰτέω[14]	*active:*	I ask
	middle:	I ask (for myself)
βαπτίζω	*active:*	I baptize
	middle:	I dip myself
εὑρίσκω	*active:*	I find
	middle:	I obtain (for myself)

It is possible that other verbs will have the "self-interest" nuance in specific contexts. As always, context must be the ultimate decider, but *just because a verb is in the middle does not mean the "self-interest" nuance is present.*[15]

25.16   Only a few verbs have both a middle deponent and a passive deponent form. For example, in the aorist γίνομαι has both a middle deponent (ἐγενόμην) and a passive deponent (ἐγενήθην) aorist form.

25.17   **Parsing**. How we parse a middle form is a bit arbitrary; but we need to be consistent, so here are our suggested guidelines. Your teacher may prefer another system.

   •   If you can clearly tell it is a middle (future; aorist), then say it is a middle.

       However, if the middle is deponent, you should say "deponent" and not "middle." The only way to know if a verb is deponent in the middle is to memorize it. In the Appendix, there is a list of all middle

---

13   Cf. Moule, *Idiom Book*, 24.

14   *BAGD* does not say that αἰτέω has the self-interest sense in the New Testament, but see the exercises.

15   A good example of the problems caused by assuming that the classical use of the middle is always present is found in 1 Corinthians 13:8, where Paul says that the gifts of tongues "will cease" (παύσονται). It is argued by some that because παύσονται is middle, Paul is saying the gift of tongues will cease in and of itself.

   Regardless of one's views on the topic of spiritual gifts, we feel this is an incorrect use of the middle. It assumes that the middle here has the classical usage, even though *BAGD* lists no self-interest meaning for the middle of παύω. And when one looks at the other eight occurrences of the verb, it is seen that the verb is a middle deponent and not reflexive. The best example is in Luke 8:24, where Jesus calms the sea. "Jesus rebuked the wind and calmed the water, and *they ceased* and became calm" (ὁ δὲ διεγερθεὶς ἐπετίμησεν τῷ ἀνέμῳ καὶ τῷ κλύδωνι τοῦ ὕδατος· καὶ ἐπαύσαντο καὶ ἐγένετο γαλήνη). The wind and water certainly did not "cease" in and of themselves. The middle of this verb does not designate "self-interest"; it is deponent.

deponent forms of verbs occurring fifty times or more in the New Testament.

- If you cannot tell it is middle (present; imperfect; perfect), always assume it is passive or deponent.

Congratulations

25.18 You now know all the tenses in the indicative. It is important that you spend some time going through the chart entitled *Tense Stems of Verbs Occurring Fifty Times or More in the New Testament* in the Appendix. You need to see which tense stems you know and which ones you need to work on. If you can master this chart, verbs will be much easier for you.

In the Appendix there is a chart of λύω in all the tenses and voices. This would be a good time to review it, making sure you can recognize every different form.

There is a class of verbs you will not meet until chapter 34 whose lexical forms end in μι and not ω. Ignore these words until then.

25.19 **Master Verb Chart**. The *Master Verb Chart* is now complete for the indicative. To indicate reduplication we have simply entered λε as if we were reduplicating λύω. But remember that the perfect can also undergo vocalic reduplication to form the perfect.

Master Verb Chart

Tense	Aug/ Redup	Tense stem	Tense form.	Conn. vowel	Personal endings	1st sing paradigm
Present act		pres		o/ε	prim act	λύω
Present mid/pas		pres		o/ε	prim mid/pas	λύομαι
Imperfect act	ε	pres		o/ε	sec act	ἔλυον
Imperfect mid/pas	ε	pres		o/ε	sec mid/pas	ἐλυόμην
Future act		fut act	σ	o/ε	prim act	λύσω
Liquid fut act		fut act	εσ	o/ε	prim act	μενῶ
Future mid		fut act	σ	o/ε	prim mid/pas	πορεύσομαι
1st future pas		aor pas	θησ	o/ε	prim mid/pas	λυθήσομαι
2nd future pas		aor pas	ησ	o/ε	prim mid/pas	ἀποσταλήσομαι
1st aorist act	ε	aor act	σα		sec act	ἔλυσα
Liquid aorist act	ε	aor act	α		sec act	ἔμεινα
2nd aorist act	ε	aor act		o/ε	sec act	ἔλαβον
1st aorist mid	ε	aor act	σα		sec mid/pas	ἐλυσάμην
2nd aorist mid	ε	aor act		o/ε	sec mid/pas	ἐγενόμην
1st aorist pas	ε	aor pas	θη		sec act	ἐλύθην
2nd aorist pas	ε	aor pas	η		sec act	ἐγράφην
1st perfect act	λε	perf act	κα		prim act	λέλυκα
2nd perfect act	λε	perf act	α		prim act	γέγονα
Perfect mid/pas	λε	perf pas			prim mid/pas	λέλυμαι

Summary

1. The perfect indicates a completed action whose effects are felt in the present. The action normally occurred in the past.

2. Verbs that begin with a single consonant reduplicate to form the perfect. If the initial consonant was φ, χ, or θ, the reduplicated consonant will be π, κ, or τ, respectively.

3. Verbs beginning with a consonant cluster or a vowel usually undergo a vocalic reduplication (lengthening). Although this looks like an augment, it is essentially different in function. Diphthongs usually do not reduplicate.

4. The perfect active uses κα for its tense formative and primary active endings. The perfect middle/passive has neither tense formative nor connecting vowels. The middle and passive forms are identical.

5. Contract verbs lengthen their contract vowel in both active and passive.

6. The classical rule of the middle voice is that the subject does the action of the verb in some way that affects itself. Only context and the use of the word elsewhere can determine if this nuance is present in a specific verse. It cannot be automatically assumed.

    In most cases, a middle has the same meaning as the active. Either the middle is a true middle with an active meaning, or it is a deponent.

7. When parsing middles, if you can clearly tell that it is a middle, say so. If it is a middle deponent, say so. If you cannot tell whether a form is middle or passive, assume it is passive.

Vocabulary

αἰτέω	I ask, demand (70; *αιτε) (ἤτουν), αἰτήσω, ᾔτησα, ᾔτηκα, -, -
μᾶλλον	more, rather (81)[16]
μαρτυρέω	I bear witness, testify (76; *μαρτυρε)[17] (ἐμαρτύρουν), μαρτυρήσω, ἐμαρτύρησα, μεμαρτύρηκα, μεμαρτύρημαι, ἐμαρτυρήθην

Total word count in the New Testament:	138,162
Number of words learned to date:	268
Number of word occurrences in this chapter:	281
Number of word occurrences to date:	105,995
Percent of total word count in the New Testament:	76.72%

Previous Words

present	perfect active	perfect middle/passive
ἀκούω	ἀκήκοα	-
ἄρχω	-	-
δύναμαι	-	-
διδάσκω	-	-
ἔχω	ἔσχηκα	-
θέλω	-	-

---

[16] When used with ἤ, ἤ is usually translated "than," not "or."

[17] The cognate noun μάρτυς means *witness*. A *martyr* is one who witnesses to the faith by dying.

present	perfect active	perfect middle/passive
λύω	-	λέλυμαι
πιστεύω	πεπίστευκα	πεπίστευμαι
πορεύομαι	-	πεπόρευμαι

Ablaut and stem change

ἀπέρχομαι	ἀπελήλυθα	-
ἀποθνῄσκω	-	-
βάλλω[18]	βέβληκα	βέβλημαι
γίνομαι	γέγονα	γεγένημαι
γινώσκω	ἔγνωκα	ἔγνωσμαι
ἔρχομαι	ἐλήλυθα	-
εὑρίσκω	εὕρηκα	-
λέγω	εἴρηκα	εἴρημαι[19]
πίνω	πέπωκα	-

Stems ending in a stop

ἄγω	-	-
βαπτίζω	-	βεβάπτισμαι
βλέπω	-	-
γράφω	γέγραφα	γέγραμμαι
δοξάζω	-	δεδόξασμαι
κηρύσσω	-	-
λαμβάνω	εἴληφα	-
προσέρχομαι	προσελήλυθα	-
προσεύχομαι	-	-
συνάγω	-	συνήγμαι,
σῴζω	σέσωκα	σέσωσμαι
ὑπάγω	-	-

---

[18] The same basic change has occurred to both perfect forms (see καλέω below). The root of βάλλω is *βαλ. The stem vowel has dropped out (ablaut), and the eta has been inserted after the stem.

[19] The perfect tense stem is built from the root *ερ, as is the aorist passive.

present	perfect active	perfect middle/passive
Contract stems		
ἀγαπάω	ἠγάπηκα	ἠγάπημαι
ἀκολουθέω	ἠκολούθηκα	-
γεννάω	γεγέννηκα	γεγέννημαι
ζάω	-	-
ζητέω	-	-
καλέω[20]	κέκληκα	κέκλημαι
λαλέω	λελάληκα	λελάλημαι
ὁράω	ἑώρακα	-
πληρόω	πεπλήρωκα	πεπλήρωμαι
ποιέω	πεποίηκα	πεποίημαι
προσκυνέω	-	-
τηρέω	τετήρηκα	τετήρημαι
Liquid stems		
αἴρω	ἦρκα	ἦρμαι
ἀποκτείνω	-	-
ἀποστέλλω	ἀπέσταλκα	ἀπέσταλμαι
βάλλω	βέβληκα	βέβλημαι
ἐγείρω	-	ἐγήγερμαι
ἐκβάλλω	-	-
κρίνω	κέκρικα	κέκριμαι
μένω	μεμένηκα[21]	-
χαίρω	-	-

Advanced Information

25.20 Third person plural, perfect middle/passive. The third person plural perfect passive occurs only nine times in the New Testament, six of those

---

[20] The same basic change has occurred to both perfect forms (see βάλλω above). The root of καλέω is *καλεϝ. The stem vowel (ablaut) and digamma have dropped out, and the final epsilon has lengthened to eta.

[21] The perfect of μένω does not occur in the New Testament, but the pluperfect does once, and the pluperfect is formed from the perfect tense stem.

being the form ἀφέωνται (from ἀφίημι). The third person plural middle never occurs in the New Testament.

Part of this absence is explained by what is called a *periphrastic construction*. This construction uses the third person plural present form of εἰμί and the perfect participle of the verb (see chapter 30) as a "round about" way of stating the third person plural. Here is the rule that governs whether a verb will form its third person plural, perfect middle/passive, periphrastically or not.[22]

Verbs formed periphrastically:

- stems ending in a consonant (except nu; for stems in stops, see below);

- stems adding a sigma to form the perfect passive tense stem.

Verbs not formed periphrastically:

- stems ending in nu drop the nu and are formed regularly;

- contract stems lengthen their final stem vowel.

25.21 **Stems ending in a stop**. Verbal roots that end in a stop undergo significant change in the perfect passive because they are placed immediately next to the consonant of the personal ending. Here is the full paradigm of changes (cf. Smyth, §409).

	labial (π β φ)	*velar* (κ γ χ)	*dental* (τ δ θ)
	γράφω	διώκω	πείθω
μαι	γέγραμμαι	δεδίωγμαι	πέπεισμαι
σαι	γέγραψαι	δεδίωξαι	πέπεισαι
ται	γέγραπται	δεδίωκται	πέπεισται
μεθα	γεγράμμεθα	δεδιώγμεθα	πεπείσμεθα
σθε	γέγραφθε	δεδίωχθε	πέπεισθε
νται	εἰσὶ γεγραμμένοι	εἰσὶ δεδιωγμένοι	εἰσὶ πεπεισμένοι

In the second personal plural, in the labials the expected psi has become a phi (γεγραφσθε ‣ γεγραψθε ‣ γέγραφθε), and in the velars the expected xsi has become a chi (δεδιωκσθε ‣ δεδιωξθε ‣ δεδίωχθε), contrary to the normal rules.

---

[22] Cf. cf. Smyth, §408. Periphrasitic (περί + φράσις) constructions occur in other situations as well.

25.22   **Pluperfect**. There is one more tense that we should mention. It does not occur very frequently, so some teachers may prefer not to discuss it now. There are 22 verbs in the New Testament that appear as a pluperfect.

The pluperfect is used to describe an action that was completed and whose effects are felt at a time after the completion but before the time of the speaker. (The effects of the an action described by the perfect is felt at the time of the speaker.)

The pluperfect is formed from the perfect tense stem. Preceding the reduplication can be an augment, although this is not necessary, so we have placed the augment in parentheses. The first pluperfect is formed with the tense formative (κ) but the second pluperfect has none. Following the tense formative are the connecting vowels ει and secondary endings.

	1 pluperfect	*2 pluperfect*
	active	
1 sg	(ἐ)λελύκειν	(ἐ)γεγράφειν
2 sg	(ἐ)λελύκεις	(ἐ)γεγράφεις
3 sg	(ἐ)λελύκει(ν)	(ἐ)γεγράφει(ν)
1 pl	(ἐ)λελύκειμεν	(ἐ)γεγράφειμεν
2 pl	(ἐ)λελύκειτε	(ἐ)γεγράφειτε
3 pl	(ἐ)λελύκεισαν	(ἐ)γεγράφεισαν

middle/passive

The middle/passive of the pluperfect follows the same pattern as the active except that it is formed from the perfect middle/passive tense form, and does not use a tense formative or connecting vowel.

1 sg	(ἐ)λελύμην	*1 pl*	(ἐ)λελύμεθα
2 sg	(ἐ)λέλυσο	*2 pl*	(ἐ)λέλυσθε
3 sg	(ἐ)λέλυτο	*3 pl*	(ἐ)λέλυντο

25.23   **Future perfect**. The future perfect appears six times in the New Testament, every time in a periphrastic construction (Matt 16:19; 18:18; John 20:23). There is a question as to their precise meaning; see the survey by D.A. Carson[23] and the *Exegetical Insight* for chapter 15.

---

[23]   "Matthew," *The Expositor's Bible Commentary*, 8:370-72.

Chapter 26

Introduction to Participles

Overview

In this chapter we will learn that:

* a participle is an "-ing" word like "eating," sleeping," "procrastinating";
* a participle is a verbal adjective, sharing characteristics of both a verb and an adjective;
* as a verb, a participle has tense (present, aorist, perfect) and voice (active, middle, passive);
* as an adjective, a participle agrees with the noun it modifies in case, number, and gender.

English

26.1   Participles are formed by adding "-ing" to a verb.[1] "The man, *eating* by the window, is my Greek teacher." "After *eating*, I will go to bed."[2]

26.2   *Participles are verbal adjectives.*

A participle has verbal characteristics. "*After eating*, my Greek teacher gave us the final." In this example, *eating* is a participle that tells us something about the verb *gave*. The teacher gave us the final after he was done eating. (*After* is an adverb that emphasizes when the action of the participle occurred.)

A participle also has adjectival aspects. "The woman, *sitting by the window*, is my Greek teacher." In this example, *sitting* is a participle telling us something about the noun "woman."

---

[1] More correctly stated, "-ing" is added to form the active participle. "-ed" is added to form the passive participle. "Moved by the sermon, they all began to cry."

[2] English has both *participles* and *gerunds*. When the -ing form is functioning adjectivally or adverbially, it is considered a participle. If it is functioning as a noun it is considered a gerund. The two are identical in form.

Greek has no gerund, so we will use the term *participle* to describe what in English are gerunds and participles. (Actually, Greek uses an infinitive (chapter 32) when English uses a gerund. For example, the sentence "Seeing is believing" in Greek would be "To see is to believe.")

26.3   When a participle has modifiers such as a direct object or an adverb, the participle and modifiers form a **participial phrase**. In translation it is important to identify the beginning and the end of the participial phrase, much like you do with a relative clause.

26.4   In a sentence like, "While *eating*, he saw her." English requires that "he" is the one who is eating, not "her," since "he" is closer in word order to the participle.

Greek

26.5   Almost everything said above about the English participle applies to the Greek as well. It is important to realize this. The Greek participle can be somewhat frustrating to learn if you do not see its many similarities with English.

Also realize that it is essential to learn the Greek participle if you are to translate the New Testament with any proficiency. Participles are common and very important.

Chapters 26 through 30 all deal with the participle. Although the chapters may seem lengthy, there is not that much new to learn. Most of the grammar of participles is in this chapter, and the majority of the other four chapters deals with the form of the participle. And participles follow the normal first, second, and third declension inflection patterns, so there are no new case endings to learn.

Do not try to memorize the Greek forms you see in this chapter. They are just illustrations. Concentrate on learning the grammar.

26.6   Because a participle is a verbal adjective, it shares the characteristics of both verbs and adjectives. As a *verb* participles have tense (present, aorist, perfect) and voice (active, middle, passive). As an *adjective* they agree with the word they are modifying in case, number, and gender. It may sound strange at first to think that a word can have both tense and case, but the Greek participle does. We will start our discussion by looking at the verbal characteristics of the participle, and then its adjectival characteristics.

26.7   A participle can be built on any verb.

The participle λύων is built on λύω.

The participle πιστεύων is built on πιστεύω.

The participle morpheme is ων. A "morpheme" is the smallest unit of meaning in the formation of a word.

26.8 **Aspect**. The key to understanding participles is to recognize that their significance is primarily one of aspect, i.e., type of action. This is the genius, the essence, of participles. They do not necessarily indicate when an action occurs ("time": past, present). Because there are three aspects, there are three participles.

The *present* participle describes a *continuous* action and is formed from the present stem of a verb.

The *aorist* participle describes an action without commenting on the nature of the action (*undefined*) and is formed from the aorist stem of a verb.

The *perfect* participle describes a *completed action with present effects*, and is formed from the perfect stem of a verb.

26.9 **Two basic uses of the participle**. Because a participle is a verbal adjective, it performs two basic functions depending on whether its verbal or its adjectival aspect is emphasized.

If it is an **adverbial participle**, the action described by the participle is directed toward the verb. This kind of participle is usually translated with an adverbial phrase. "While *studying* for his Greek final, Ian fell asleep."

If it is an **adjectival participle**, the action described by the participle modifies a noun or pronoun. This kind of participle is usually translated as an adjectival phrase. "Ian saw Kathy *sitting* by the window." (If you inserted "while" before "sitting," it would be adverbial.)

Context determines whether a participle is adverbial or adjectival. Its form does not vary.

Adverbial Side of the Participle

26.10 **Tense**. Participles can be built on the present, aorist, or perfect tense stems.[3] The participle morphemes are in bold type. Memorize the morphemes.[4]

The **present** participle λύοντος is built on the present tense stem of λύω (λυ + ο + **ντ** + ος).

The **aorist** participle λύσαντος is built on the aorist tense stem of λύω (λυ + σα + **ντ** + ος). Notice that there is no augment.

---

[3] There also is a participle which is built on the future tense stem, but it occurs only twelve times in the New Testament. See *Advanced Information* in chapter 28.

[4] We use the genitive singular forms below since they show the unmodified participle morpheme.

The **perfect** participle λελυκότος is built on the perfect tense stem of λύω (λε + λυ + κ + **οτ** + ος).

26.11   **Voice**. A participle can also be active, middle, passive, or deponent. If the verb is deponent, its corresponding participle will be deponent. Greek uses different participles for the different voices.

ἀκούοντος is active, which means the word it is modifying is doing the action of the participle.

ἀκουομένου is passive, which means the word it is modifying is receiving the action of the participle.

ἐρχομένου is deponent, because ἔρχομαι, the verb on which it is built, is deponent.

26.12   **Modifiers, etc.** A participle has other characteristics which it shares with verbs.

It can have a direct object in the accusative. "After studying *her Greek*, the student thought she had died and gone to heaven." "Greek" is the direct object of the participle "studying."

A participle can also have modifiers such as prepositional phrases, adjectives, etc. "After studying *quietly for a long time*, I finally understood the paradigm." "Quietly" is an adverb, and "for a long time" is a prepositional phrase, both modifying the participle "studying."

26.13   **Negation**. The negation οὐ is only used in the indicative. Since the participle is not an indicative form, participles are negated by μή. It has the same meaning as οὐ.

26.14   You will notice that the participle does not use personal verb endings. It is not a finite verbal form and therefore is not limited by a subject.

Adjectival Side of the Participle

26.15   As an adjective, the participle must agree with the noun it modifies in case, number, and gender.

"The man, *eating* the chocolate, is my brother."

If this were in Greek, *eating* would be nominative singular masculine because *eating* is modifying "man" (ἄνθρωπος), which is nominative singular masculine.

ἔβλεψε τὸν ἄνθρωπον τὸν διδάσκοντα τὴν κοινήν.
He saw the man who was teaching the Koine.

Because the participle is modifying ἄνθρωπον, and because ἄνθρωπον is accusative singular masculine, the participle διδάσκοντα must also be accusative singular masculine. This is how an adjective behaves, so the grammar is not new.

26.16 **Subject**. A participle technically does not have a subject. However, because a participle must agree in case, number, and gender with the word it is modifying, it is a relatively easy task to discover who is doing the action of the participle. For example, if you were to say in Greek, "He saw her, while studying," the participle *studying* would be either nominative masculine (if he was studying) or accusative feminine (if she was studying). Greek does not use word order as does English in this situation.

In the example ἔβλεψε τὸν ἄνθρωπον διδάσκοντα τὴν κοινήν, you can tell that it was not the "He" (ἔβλεψε) who was teaching but the "man" (ἄνθρωπον), since the participle (διδάσκοντα) is accusative. If "He" were teaching, the participle would be διδάσκων (nominative).

26.17 **Parsing**. Because the participle is a verbal adjective, there are eight things to remember. Start with its verbal characteristics and then move on to its adjectival. (As before, this is only a suggestion, and teachers will differ on their preferences.)

Tense; voice; "participle";[5] case; number; gender; lexical form; meaning of inflected form.

ἀκούοντος: present active participle, genitive singular masculine, from ἀκούω, meaning "hearing."

The Following Chapters

26.18 To make the participle easier to learn, we have separated its basic uses into different chapters.

- Chapter 27 deals with present adverbial participles.

- Chapter 28 discusses aorist adverbial participles.

- Chapter 29 covers the adjectival use of participles.

- Chapter 30 introduces the perfect participle.

You have now learned the majority of the grammar of participles. It remains only to learn their forms, and you already know all their case endings from your study of adjectives.

---

5   A participle is not technically a "mood" like the indicative, but for simplicity's sake say it is a participle where you normally place the mood.

Summary

1. A participle is a verbal adjective, sharing characteristics of both a verb and an adjective.

2. As a verb, it has tense (present, aorist, perfect) and voice (active, middle, passive). If the verb is deponent, its corresponding participle will be deponent.

3. As an adjective, it agrees with the noun it modifies in case, number, and gender.

Chapter 27

Present (continuous) Adverbial Participles

Exegetical Insight

At the heart of the Christian experience is a radical transformation from what we were by nature into what God intends us to become by grace. Nowhere is that transformation stated with greater clarity than in 2 Corinthians 3:18. And at the heart of this verse is a present middle participle that reveals the secret of Christian growth and maturity.

What this verse tells us is that a wonderful change is taking place in the life of the believer. Although a veil remains over the mind of the unbeliever (v. 15), that veil is lifted for those who are in Christ (vv. 14, 16). They are being changed into the image of Christ from one degree of glory to the next.

The secret of divine transformation lies in the participle κατοπτριζόμενοι. It comes from a verb which, in the middle, originally meant "to look into a mirror." Then it came to mean "to gaze upon" or "to contemplate." Taking the participle in the instrumental sense we read, "We all are being changed into the image of Christ *by beholding* the glory of the Lord."

Transformation into the likeness of Christ is the inevitable result of gazing upon his glory. We become like that which dominates our thoughts and affections. Like Nathaniel Hawthorne's "great stone face," which shaped the life of the one who spent his days looking at that craggy representation of all that was held to be good and pure, so also does the believer gradually take on a family resemblance to his Lord as he spends his time contemplating the glory of God.

Note that the participle is present tense. It is a continual contemplation that effects the transformation. As the participle is present tense, so also is the finite verb "are being changed" (μεταμορφούμεθα). The transformation keeps pace with the contemplation. They are inextricably bound together. By continuing to behold the glory of the Lord we are continually being transformed into his image.

Robert H. Mounce

Overview

In this chapter you will learn that:

- there is no time significance to a participle;

- the present participle is built on the present tense stem of the verb and indicates a continuous action;

- the present participle is formed with the present tense stem + connecting vowel + participle morpheme + case ending;

- to translate you must first discover the participle's aspect, voice, and meaning. You can usually translate it with the "-ing" form of the verb, sometimes with the key word "while."

Greek

27.1   In this chapter we will learn the present adverbial participle. Here are the guidelines.

a.   The present participle is built on the present tense stem of the verb.

b.   It describes a continuous action.

It will often be difficult to carry this "on-going" nuance into your translation, but this must be the foremost consideration in your mind. Everything else pales in light of the aspect of the participle.

c.   In this chapter we are learning the adverbial participle, which means that *the action described by the participle is related to the verb*.

The adverbial participle is usually translated as a type of adverbial clause. In this chapter we will use a temporal phrase to translate the participle. Use the -ing form of the participle in translation and, if possible, preface the translation of the participle with the adverb *while*.[1]

ὁ ἄνθρωπος ἀπέθανε *διδάσκων* τὴν κοινήν.
"The man died *while teaching* koine." He was currently teaching the language when he died. He died very happily!

d.   Even though the participle is adverbial, it still must agree with a noun or pronoun. If the participle is active, the word it modifies does the action of the participle,[2] and the participle agrees with it in case, number, and gender.

For example, if the noun is ἄνθρωπος, the participle would be διδάσκων (nominative singular masculine).

e.   The adverbial participle is always anarthrous (i.e., not preceded by the article). See the example in §27.1c. above.

---

[1]   As you advance in your understanding of the language, you will find that there are other ways to translate this participle, but at your present stage this practice is highly recommended.

[2]   If the participle is passive, then the word receiving the action of the participle controls the form of the participle.

27.2 Most grammars use the term "present" participle because this participle is built on the present tense stem of the verb. This nomenclature is helpful in learning the form of the participle. However, it tends to do a serious disservice because the student may infer that the present participle describes an action occurring in the present time, which it may not. It describes a continuous action. Because the participle is not in the indicative, there is no time significance to the participle.[3] We suggest adopting the terminology "continuous participle" because it rightly emphasizes the true significance of the participle that is built on the present tense stem: its aspect.

27.3 **Summary of form**. The present (continuous) participle is formed with four parts.

> *Present tense stem + Connecting vowel +*
>
> *Participle morpheme + Case endings*
>
>
> πιστευ + ο + ντ + ες

To form a participle you add the participle morpheme to the end of the verb (with connecting vowel), and add the case ending to the participle morpheme.

Participles are formed from only four morphemes (which undergo some slight variations in the different tenses and genders).

- ντ is the usual active morpheme. It appears as ντ in the masculine and neuter, and is third declension.

- ουσα is the active morpheme in the present feminine.[4] In most of the participles, the feminine form is somewhat different from the masculine and neuter. It also differs substantially in the three tenses. The feminine participle is always first declension.

---

[3] There is an implied time relationship between the time of the participle and the time of the main verb, but it is secondary to the true significance of the participle. See *Advanced Information*.

[4] ουσα and ντ actually are the same participle. If you want to learn why the changes are so drastic, see *MBG*, §91.

- μενο/η is the middle/passive morpheme.[5]

	masc	fem	neut
act	ντ	ουσα	ντ
mid/pas	μενο	μενη	μενο

- οτ is the active morpheme used with the perfect. We will meet this form in chapter 30.

Learn to view the participle morpheme as an important indicator, much like the tense formatives. When you see a "οντ + case ending," you can be quite sure the word is an active participle. When you see a "vowel + μεν + case ending," it is probably a middle/passive participle.

Paradigm of the Present (Continuous) Participle

27.4   The **active** participle morpheme in the masculine and neuter is ντ, which, when joined with the connecting vowel, looks like οντ. The masculine and neuter follow the third declension (λύοντες).

The feminine active participle morpheme is ουσα and follows the first declension (λύουσαι).

27.5   **Active chart and paradigm**

> *Present tense stem + Connecting vowel +*
> *Active participle morpheme + Case endings*
>
> πιστευ + ο + ντ + ες

The participle paradigms list the genders left to right (masculine, feminine, neuter). The singular is given first (in normal case order) and below it the plural.

---

5   The slash means it sometimes is μενο (masculine and neuter) and other times μενη (feminine).

Advanced information: the actual morpheme is μεν; but in order to function as a first and second declension form it had to end with a vowel, so the usual declension vowels were added. Treat the vowel as part of the morpheme.

	3 masc	1 fem	3 neut
nom sg	λύων[6]	λύουσα	λῦον[7]
gen sg	λύοντος	λυούσης[8]	λύοντος
dat sg	λύοντι	λυούσῃ	λύοντι
acc sg	λύοντα	λύουσαν	λῦον
nom pl	λύοντες	λύουσαι	λύοντα
gen pl	λυόντων	λυουσῶν	λυόντων
dat pl	λύουσι(ν)[9]	λυούσαις	λύουσι(ν)[10]
acc pl	λύοντας	λυούσας	λύοντα

One of the keys to learning the participle is to memorize the main six forms of each participle listed below (nominative and genitive singular, all three genders, with the connecting vowel and case endings). Once you see the changes between nominative and genitive forms, it is easy to recognize the other forms. You may want to list the dative plural under the genitive singular forms as well, especially for third declension forms.

	masc	fem	neut
nom sg	ων	ουσα	ον
gen sg	οντος	ουσης	οντος

---

[6] No case ending is used, the tau drops off because it cannot stand at the end of a word (rule 8), and the omicron lengthens to omega to compensate for the loss (*λυ + οντ + - ‣ λυον ‣ λύων).

[7] As with the nominative singular masculine, no case ending is used, the tau drops out (rule 8), but in the neuter the connecting vowel does not lengthen.

[8] As you will remember, if the letter before the final stem vowel is epsilon, iota, or rho, then the genitive stays ας. Otherwise, it shifts to ης (cf. chapter 8, footnote to the vocabulary word θάλασσα).

[9] The ντ drops out because of the sigma, and the omicron lengthens to ου in order to compensate for the loss (οντσι ‣ οσι ‣ ουσι). Be sure not to confuse this form with the third person plural indicative (λύουσι, "they loose").

[10] See the footnote to the masculine plural form.

27.6   The **middle/passive** participle morpheme is **μενο/η**. The masculine and
neuter are second declension (μενο) while the feminine is first (μενη).
This participle is completely regular.

27.7   **Middle/passive chart and paradigm**

> *Present tense stem + Connecting vowel +*
>
> *Middle/passive participle morpheme + Case endings*
>
> λυ + ο + μενο + ς

	2 *masc*	1 *fem*	2 *neut*
nom sg	λυόμενος	λυομένη	λυόμενον
gen sg	λυομένου	λυομένης	λυομένου
dat sg	λυομένῳ	λυομένῃ	λυομένῳ
acc sg	λυόμενον	λυομένην	λυόμενον
nom pl	λυόμενοι	λυόμεναι	λυόμενα
gen pl	λυομένων	λυομένων	λυομένων
dat pl	λυομένοις	λυομέναις	λυομένοις
acc pl	λυομένους	λυομένας	λυόμενα

	masc	*fem*	*neut*
nom sg	ομενος	ομενη	ομενον
gen sg	ομενου	ομενης	ομενου

27.8   **Contract verbs**. Contract verbs are totally regular in their participial
forms. The contract vowel contracts with the connecting vowel, as it
does in the indicative.

ἀγαπα + οντος ‣ ἀγάπωντος

27.9 **εἰμί.** Obviously there can be no passive form of εἰμί. Here are the active forms. Notice that they look like the participle morpheme with case endings. They always have a smooth breathing. Translate them with the English participle "being."

	3	1	3
	masc	*fem*	*neut*
nom sg	ὤν	οὖσα	ὄν
gen sg	ὄντος	οὔσης	ὄντος
dat sg	ὄντι	οὔσῃ	ὄντι
acc sg	ὄντα	οὖσαν	ὄν
nom pl	ὄντες	οὖσαι	ὄντα
gen pl	ὄντων	οὐσῶν	ὄντων
dat pl	οὖσι(ν)	οὔσαις	οὖσι(ν)
acc pl	ὄντας	οὔσας	ὄντα

Translation Procedure

27.10 **Initial questions.** You must ask the following three questions of any participle before you can attempt a translation.

1. **Aspect?** If the participle is formed on the present tense stem, then it is a present participle. This means that your translation must be continuous if possible.

2. **Voice?** The voice of a participle will be either active, middle, or passive, depending on the verb's stem and participle morpheme. (Do not forget about deponent verbs.)

3. **Meaning?** What does the lexical form of the verb actually mean? This includes finding the participle's case, number, and gender so you can see which word it is modifying.

27.11 **Translation.** Once you have the answers to all three questions, you can understand what the participle is saying. There are many different ways to translate an adverbial participle, but the following three are quite common. Context will show you which one to use.

- If possible, translate with the simple -ing form of the English verb.

    ἀπεκρίθη λέγων ...
    "He answered saying ...."

- Some participles require using the key word "while" before the -ing form. This is called the "temporal" use of the participle.

    λέγων ἐγὼ ἔρχομαι ...
    "While speaking I come ...."

- If the participle is passive, use "being" and a form of the participle that is not the -ing form.

    δοξαζόμενος, ὁ θεός ...
    "While being glorified, God ...."

As we will see later, there are many other uses of the participle and other ways to translate it, but these three are sufficient for the time being.

It will often be impossible to convey the full force of the participle's aspect in your English translation, but you can in your preaching, teaching, and studying.

Summary

1. The present participle is built on the present tense stem of the verb and indicates a continuous action. There is no time significance to a participle. We encourage students to adopt the terminology "continuous" participle.

2. An adverbial participle describes an action that is related to the verb. Its form is determined by the word it modifies.

3. The adverbial participle is anarthrous.

4. The present participle is formed with the present tense stem, connecting vowel, participle morpheme, and case ending.

5. In the active, ντ (third declension) is the morpheme for the masculine and neuter, and ουσα (first declension) is the morpheme for the feminine.

    Present active (continuous): οντ, ουσα

ων	ουσα	ον
οντος	ουσης	οντος

6. In the middle/passive, μενο/η is the morpheme for all three genders. The masculine and neuter follow the second declension and the feminine follows the first.

    Present middle/passive (continuous): μενο/η

ομενος	ομενη	ομενον
ομενου	ομενης	ομενου

7. Always memorize the nominative and genitive singular forms of the participle (listed above). Remember that in third declension forms, the type of morphological change that occurs in the nominative because of the initial sigma will also occur in the dative plural.

8. The participle of εἰμί looks like the participle morpheme with a case ending, always with smooth breathing.

9. To translate you must first discover the participle's aspect, voice, and meaning. You can usually translate it with the "-ing" form of the verb, sometimes with the key word "while."

Vocabulary

ἀναβαίνω	I go up, come up (82; ἀνά + *βα) (ἀνέβαινον), ἀναβήσομαι, ἀνέβην, ἀναβέβηκα, -, -
ἀρχιερεύς, -έως, ὁ	chief priest, high priest (122; *ἀρχιερεϜ)[11]
δεξιός, -ιά, -ιόν	right (54; *δεξιο/α)[12]
δύο[13]	two (135)[14]
ἕτερος, -α, -ον	other, another, different (99; *ἑτερο/α)[15]
εὐαγγελίζω	I bring good news, preach (54; *εὐαγγελιδ)[16] (εὐηγγέλιζον), -, εὐηγγέλισα, -, εὐηγγέλισμαι, εὐηγγελίσθην
θεωρέω	I look at, behold (58; *θεωρε) -, ἐθεώρησα, -, -, -

---

[11] The two parts to this compound noun were switched in the word ἱεράρχης meaning "hierarch" (*sacred* [ἱερός] + *ruler* [ἀρχός]).

[12] You will usually have to add a word to your translation of this word. Context will tell you what it should be. Normally it will be "hand" or "side." It is related to the Latin word "dextra" that gave rise to the English adjective "dextral," which means "right-handed."

[13] δύο is declined as follows.

nom pl	δύο
gen pl	δύο
dat pl	δυσί(ν)
acc pl	δύο

[14] A *dyarchy* (also *diarchy*) is a dual government system. A *dyad* (δυάς) is two units viewed as one.

[15] *Heterdoxy* (ἑτερόδοξος) is unorthodoxy, holding a position different from the right one.

[16] The preacher *evangelizes* the audience with the good news of the gospel.

Ἰεροσόλυμα, τά or ἡ[17]	Jerusalem (62; *Ἰεροσόλυμα). Indeclinable.
κάθημαι	I sit (down), live (91; *καθη)[18] (ἐκαθήμην), καθήσομαι, -, -, -, -
καταβαίνω	I go down, come down (81; κατά + *βα) (κατέβαινον), καταβήσομαι, κατέβην, καταβέβηκα, -, -
οὗ[19]	where (54; adverb)
παρακαλέω	I call, urge, exhort, comfort (109; παρά + *καλεϝ)[20] (παρεκάλουν), -, παρεκάλεσα, -, παρακέκλημαι, παρεκλήθην
πείθω	I persuade (52; *πειθ) (ἔπειθον), πείσω, ἔπεισα, πέποιθα, πέπεισμαι, ἐπείσθην
τρεῖς, τρία	three (68; *τρες)[21]

Total word count in the New Testament:	138,162
Number of words learned to date:	282
Number of word occurrences in this chapter:	1,121
Number of word occurrences to date:	107,116
Percent of total word count in the New Testament:	77.53%

Advanced Information

27.12   If you want to use this advanced information in translating the exercises, do your exercises first before reading this section. Then come back, read this discussion, and redo your exercises.

27.13   Most grammars view the following material as an essential part of the participle, and certainly in the long run it is important. But because there is already so much to learn about the participle, we thought it best to include the discussion of a participle's relative time in this *Advanced* section. If you can learn it as well as everything else in this chapter, then by

---

[17]   Ἰεροσόλυμα can be either neuter plural or feminine singular.

[18]   When the pope speaks "ex cathedra" (which is actually from the Latin but with obvious links to the Greek), he is speaking with the full authority of the pope, as one who is sitting on the seat of authority.

[19]   Do not confuse this word with the negation (οὐ) or relative pronoun (οὗ).

[20]   Jesus used the cognate noun παράκλητος, "Paraclete," for the Holy Spirit, one who is called (κλητός) alongside (παρά) to encourage and help Christians (John 14:26).

[21]   A *triad* (τριάς) is a group of three things. A *tricycle* has three wheels.

all means do so. If you are struggling, ignore it for the time being. But, eventually you should come back and learn it.

27.14 **Relative Time.** There is an important distinction between absolute and relative time. An indicative verb indicates **absolute** time. For example, if an indicative verb is present tense, then it usually indicates an action occurring in the present. If the Greek participle indicated absolute time, then the present participle would indicate an action occurring in the present.

However, the Greek participle does not indicate absolute time. It indicates **relative** time. This means that the time of the participle is relative to the time of the main verb. *The present participle describes an action occurring at the same time as the main verb.*[22]

27.15 In order to indicate relative time, you must change the way you translate the participle by using a helping verb ("studying" becomes "was studying.") You may want to add the appropriate pronoun (e.g., "he was studying").

- If the main verb is aorist, then the present participle will be translated as the past continuous (e.g., "was praying').

  ἦλθε προσευχόμενος.
  He went *while he was praying*.

- If the main verb is a present, then the present participle is translated as the present continuous (e.g., "is praying").

  ἔρχεται προσευχόμενος.
  He goes *while he is praying*.

Which pronoun you use is determined by the word the participle is modifying. Which helping verb you use is determined by the time of the main verb.

This is what is meant by "relative time." The time of the participle is relative to the time of the main verb.

27.16 When this distinction of relative time is taken into consideration in the translation of the participle, it must never overrule the significance of the aspect in your translation. *Aspect is always primary to time. When English allows your translation to indicate clearly only aspect or time, you must always choose aspect.*

27.17 **"Subject" of the participle.** Technically speaking, the participle does not have a subject. However, because the participle must agree with the

---

[22] The aorist participle, which is formed from the aorist tense stem, often indicates an action occurring *before* the time of the main verb. This will be discussed in chapter 29.

noun it is modifying, you can almost always identify who or what is doing the action of the participle. Indicating the "subject" of the participle will help greatly in exegesis. (This "subject" is the pronoun we suggested adding in §27.15.)

A way to indicate both the aspect and the "subject" is to include the appropriate pronoun and verb form. "*While he was studying*, the teacher (διδάσκαλος) told the students (μαθητάς) about the exam." "*While they were studying*, the teacher (διδάσκαλος) told the students (μαθητάς) about the exam."

Choose the pronoun that makes the identification most clear as to who or what is doing the participle. Be sure to use the continuous form of the finite verb as well. What you will discover is that it is often difficult, if not impossible, to translate this way word for word. You must ask yourself, "Now that I know what all the parts mean in Greek, how can I say exactly the same thing in English?" Allow yourself a little freedom in your translation.

27.18   If you are struggling with the translation of the participle, then pay no attention right now to this *Advanced* discussion. Work with the basics of the participle until you are very comfortable with them, and then start adding the pronoun and relative time. If you can use the pronoun now, then do so.

Chapter 28

Aorist (undefined) Adverbial Participles

Exegetical Insight

When the aorist participle is used adverbially it is one of the flexible syntactical constructions in Koine Greek. It can be used to indicate almost any type of adverbial clause and is therefore one of the most common grammatical constructions in the New Testament. But its flexibility also creates some real problems for translators and biblical exegetes (as well as beginning students of Koine Greek). Since the meaning of the aorist adverbial participle is always determined by its relationship to the main verb in context, some of the most heated arguments in the interpretation of the New Testament center around the meaning of an aorist participle.

There is probably no better example of such an argument than the ongoing debate about the correct understanding of the aorist participle πιστεύσαντες in Acts 19:2. The meaning of this participle determines the meaning of Paul's question: Εἰ πνεῦμα ἅγιον ἐλάβετε πιστεύσαντες; The King James Version translated this question: "Have ye received the Holy Ghost since ye believed?" One of the common uses of the aorist participle is to indicate an action that occurs before the action of the main verb. The King James translation understands the aorist participle in this way and indicates that the believing would have occurred before the receiving of the Holy Spirit. Pentecostals have used this translation to support their claim that receiving the Holy Spirit is an event distinct from and subsequent to believing in Christ. But traditional Protestant exegetes have argued that this interpretation is based on a misunderstanding of the use of the aorist participle. Koine Greek frequently uses the aorist participle to express action that is part of the action of an aorist finite verb and this is clearly the case in Paul's question. Believing and receiving the Holy Spirit are both part of one experience. Most recent translations agree with this understanding of πιστεύσαντες and follow the Revised Standard Version's translation: "Did you receive the Holy Spirit when you believed?"

So which interpretation is right? It is essential to recognize that both are based on legitimate understandings of the use of the aorist adverbial participle in Koine Greek. Even in context, it is virtually impossible to prefer one over the other and theological concerns usually determine which interpretation is chosen. So both interpretations can be considered correct understandings of Paul's question in Acts 19:2. The moral of this little exegetical note is that when dealing with the aorist adverbial participle, flexibility and a willingness to consider the valid-ity of interpretations that differ from one's own are just as important as a knowledge of the complexities of Greek grammar.

J. M. Everts

Overview

In this chapter we will learn:

*   that the aorist participle is formed from the unaugmented aorist tense stem;
*   that the aorist participle indicates an undefined action;
*   that the aorist participle uses the participle morpheme ντ in the active and passive, and μεν in the middle;
*   to use "after" in your translation for the time being.

Introduction

28.1   In this chapter we will look at the aorist adverbial participle. The basic grammar of the aorist participle is the same as the present adverbial; the only two differences are the participle's form and aspect. This chapter may look long, but there is not that much new information to learn. It is mostly paradigms, and you already know most of the forms.

Aorist (Undefined) Adverbial Participle

28.2   **Summary**. The aorist participle is formed on the aorist stem and indicates an undefined action.

Most grammars use the term "aorist" participle because this participle is built on the aorist tense stem of the verb. This nomenclature is helpful in learning the form of the participle. However, it tends to do a serious disservice because the student may infer that the aorist participle describes an action occurring in the past, which it does not. It describes an undefined action. Because the participle is not in the indicative, there is no time significance to the participle.[1] We suggest adopting the terminology "undefined participle" because it rightly emphasizes the true significance of the participle that is built on the aorist tense stem, its aspect.

28.3   **Translation**. The most important thing to remember about the aorist participle is its aspect. It indicates an undefined action. It tells you nothing about the aspect of the action other than it occurred.

---

[1]   There is an implied time relationship between the time of the participle and the time of the main verb, but it is secondary to the true significance of the participle. This relative time significance is covered in the *Advanced Information* section.

Just as you use "while" in translating the present participle, use "after" with the aorist participle. We will discuss this in more detail below.

φάγοντες, ἦλθον ....
After eating, they went ....

It is very difficult if not impossible to carry the aspect of the aorist participle over into English using the -ing form of the verb. In the *Advanced Information* section we will discuss a few alternative methods for translation. But even if you are unable to indicate the true aspect of the aorist participle in your translation, you can always explain it in your teaching and preaching. In other words, it is your responsibility always to remember the true significance of the aorist participle, and if an accurate translation is not possible without butchering the English language, you must at least explain the concept in words your audience can understand.

Never forget: the participle formed on the aorist tense stem indicates an undefined action.

Formation of the Aorist (undefined) Participle

28.4   **Form**. The aorist participle is formed with the

- unaugmented aorist tense stem,

- tense formative (if the verb is a first aorist),

- the participle morpheme (which varies depending whether the verb has a first or second aorist),

- and the appropriate case endings (which follow the normal first, second, and third declension endings).

28.5   **Augment**. An augment is used in the indicative mood to indicate past time. To be more specific, it indicates absolute past time. However, since the participle does not indicate absolute time, the aorist participle cannot have an augment. Therefore, the aorist participle is formed from the unaugmented aorist tense stem.

This process of unaugmenting is easy to spot if the augment is a simple epsilon. ἔλαβον unaugments to *λαβ. However, if the augment is a lengthened initial vowel it can be a bit confusing. For example, ἐλθών looks like a present active participle, but actually it is from ἔρχομαι which has the second aorist ἦλθον. The initial eta is a lengthened epsilon which, in the formation of the aorist participle, goes back to the original epsilon (*ἐλθ ▸ ἠλθ ▸ ἦλθον ▸ ἐλθων).

This whole process can get especially tricky in a compound verb like ἐξελθών. You can spend a long time thumbing through a lexicon looking for some form like ξελθόω, perhaps assuming this form is an imperfect contract verb. The moral of the story? Know your vocabulary! Know your verbal roots!

28.6   Tense formative. Although the augment is dropped, you will still see the familiar σα or θη tense formatives if the verb has a first aorist.

First Aorist

28.7   If a verb has a first aorist indicative, it will use that first aorist stem in the formation of the aorist participle.

> *Unaugmented first aorist stem + Tense formative*
>
> *Participle morpheme + Case endings*
>
> λυ + σα + ντ + ος

28.8   First aorist active participle

	masc	*fem*	*neuter*
nom sg	λύσας[2]	λύσασα[3]	λῦσαν[4]
gen sg	λύσαντος	λυσάσης	λύσαντος
dat sg	λύσαντι	λυσάσῃ	λύσαντι
acc sg	λύσαντα	λύσασαν	λῦσαν
nom pl	λύσαντες	λύσασαι	λύσαντα
gen pl	λυσάντων	λυσασῶν	λυσάντων
dat pl	λύσασι(ν)	λυσάσαις	λύσασι(ν)
acc pl	λύσαντας	λυσάσας	λύσαντα

---

[2]   As is usual in the masculine third declension, the sigma case ending causes the preceding ντ to drop off.

[3]   ια was added to ντ, which then changed to σα, not to be confused with the tense formative. ια is involved in the formation of all the feminine participles, and is responsible for their significant difference from the masculine and neuter (cf. *MBG*, §91).

[4]   As is usual in the neuter third declension, no case ending is used in the nominative/accusative, and therefore the final tau must drop off.

The **active** participle morpheme is **ντ**, which looks like **σαντ** with the tense formative. In the feminine the ντ has been replaced by σα.

	masc	*fem*	*neut*
nom sg	σας	σασα	σαν
gen sg	σαντος	σασης	σαντος

28.9   First aorist middle participle

	masc	*fem*	*neuter*
nom sg	λυσάμενος	λυσαμένη	λυσάμενον
gen sg	λυσαμένου	λυσαμένης	λυσαμένου
dat sg	λυσαμένῳ	λυσαμένη	λυσαμένῳ
acc sg	λυσάμενον	λυσαμένην	λυσάμενον
nom pl	λυσάμενοι	λυσάμεναι	λυσάμενα
gen pl	λυσαμένων	λυσαμένων	λυσαμένων
dat pl	λυσαμένοις	λυσαμέναις	λυσαμένοις
acc pl	λυσαμένους	λυσαμένας	λυσάμενα

The **middle** participle morpheme is **μενο/η**, which looks like **σαμενο/η** with the tense formative.

	masc	*fem*	*neut*
nom sg	σαμενος	σαμενη	σαμενον
gen sg	σαμενου	σαμενης	σαμενου

28.10   First aorist passive participle

	masc	*fem*	*neuter*
nom sg	λυθείς[5]	λυθεῖσα[6]	λυθέν[7]
gen sg	λυθέντος	λυθείσης	λυθέντος
dat sg	λυθέντι	λυθείσῃ	λυθέντι
acc sg	λυθέντα	λυθεῖσαν	λυθέν
nom pl	λυθέντες	λυθεῖσαι	λυθέντα
gen pl	λυθέντων	λυθεισῶν	λυθέντων
dat pl	λυθεῖσι(ν)[8]	λυθείσαις	λυθεῖσι(ν)[9]
acc pl	λυθέντας	λυθείσας	λυθέντα

The **passive** participle morpheme is **ντ**. The eta in the tense formative (θη) shortens to epsilon (θε), and the participle then looks like **θεντ**. In the feminine the ντ has been replaced by ισα.

	masc	*fem*	*neut*
nom sg	θεις	θεισα	θεν
gen sg	θεντος	θεισης	θεντος

---

[5]   The case ending is sigma, the ντ drops out because of the sigma, and the epsilon lengthens to compensate for the loss (*θε + ντ + ς › θες › θεις).

[6]   As in the active, consonantal iota was added to ντ which then changed to ισα.

[7]   No case ending is used, and the tau drops off because it cannot end a word (rule 8).

[8]   The ντ drops out because of the sigma, and the epsilon lengthens to ει in order to compensate for the loss.

[9]   The ντ drops out because of the sigma, and the epsilon lengthens to ει in order to compensate for the loss.

Second Aorist

28.11 If a verb has a second aorist form in the indicative, the aorist participle of that verb will use the second aorist stem.

> *Unaugmented second aorist stem +*
>
> *Connecting vowel +*
>
> *Participle morpheme + Case endings*
>
> βαλ + ο + ντ + ος

There is one point that bears emphasis. The active and middle aorist participle formed from the second aorist stem will look just like the present participle except for the verbal stem.

	present participle	*second aorist participle*
active	βάλλων	βαλών
middle/passive	βαλλόμενος	βαλόμενος

This similarity is heightened by the fact that the stem of the aorist participle is unaugmented. For example, if you see the form βαλών you could easily assume that it is a present participle from the verb βάλω. However, there is no such verb. βαλών is rather the aorist participle from βάλλω, which has a second aorist ἔβαλον. The only indication of which is which, short of looking it up in a lexicon, is a good knowledge of Greek vocabulary and verbal roots.

28.12 Second aorist active participle

	masc	*fem*	*neuter*
nom sg[10]	βαλών	βαλοῦσα	βαλόν
gen sg	βαλόντος	βαλούσης	βαλόντος
dat sg	βαλόντι	βαλούσῃ	βαλόντι
acc sg	βαλόντα	βαλοῦσαν	βαλόν

---

[10] The changes to the participle morpheme in the nominative singular are the same as in the present active participle. See there for an explanation.

nom pl	βάλοντες	βάλουσαι	βάλοντα
gen pl	βαλόντων	βαλουσῶν	βαλόντων
dat pl	βάλουσι(ν)	βαλούσαις	βάλουσι(ν)
acc pl	βάλοντας	βαλούσας	βάλοντα

The **active** participle morpheme is **ντ**, which looks like **οντ** with the connecting vowel. In the feminine the ντ has been replaced by ουσα.

	masc	*fem*	*neut*
nom sg	ων	ουσα	ον
gen sg	οντος	ουσης	οντος

28.13   Second aorist middle participle

	masc	*fem*	*neuter*
nom sg	γενόμενος	γενομένη	γενόμενον
gen sg	γενομένου	γενομένης	γενομένου
dat sg	γενομένῳ	γενομένη	γενομένῳ
acc sg	γενόμενον	γενομένην	γενόμενον
nom pl	γενόμενοι	γενόμεναι	γενόμενα
gen pl	γενομένων	γενομένων	γενομένων
dat pl	γενομένοις	γενομέναις	γενομένοις
acc pl	γενομένους	γενομένας	γενόμενα

The **middle** participle morpheme is **μενο/η** which looks like **ομενο/η** with the connecting vowel.

	masc	*fem*	*neut*
nom sg	ομενος	ομενη	ομενον
gen sg	ομενου	ομενης	ομενου

28.14   Second aorist passive participle

	masc	*fem*	*neuter*
nom sg	γραφείς[11]	γραφεῖσα[12]	γραφέν[13]
gen sg	γραφέντος	γραφείσης	γραφέντος
dat sg	γραφέντι	γραφείσῃ	γραφέντι
acc sg	γραφέντα	γραφεῖσαν	γραφέν
nom pl	γραφέντες	γραφεῖσαι	γραφέντα
gen pl	γραφέντων	γραφεισῶν	γραφέντων
dat pl	γραφεῖσι(ν)	γραφείσαις	γραφεῖσι(ν)
acc pl	γραφέντας	γραφείσας	γραφέντα

The **passive** participle morpheme is **ντ**. The tense formative (η) shortens to epsilon (ε), and the participle then looks like **εντ**. In the feminine the ντ has been replaced by ισα.

	masc	*fem*	*neut*
nom sg	εις	εισα	εν
gen sg	εντος	εισης	εντος

Because in the aorist the middle and passive are distinct forms, there should be no confusion between present and second aorist passive participles.

28.15   Case endings. The following rules hold true whether the participle is present or aorist.

- The feminine participle always uses first declension endings (λύουσα, λυσαμένη).

---

[11] The case ending is sigma, the ντ drops out because of the sigma (rule #7), and the epsilon lengthens to compensate for the loss (rule #8; *ε + ντ + ς ▸ ες ▸ εις).

[12] As in the active, ι̥α was added to ντ, which then changed to ισα.

[13] No case ending is used, and the tau drops off because it cannot end a word (rule #8).

- The feminine participle always uses first declension endings (λύουσα, λυσαμένη).

- When the masculine and neuter participles are active, they are third declension (λύων, λύον).

- When the masculine and neuter participles are present middle or passive, or aorist middle, they are second declension (λυόμενος, λυό-μενον; λυσάμενος, λυσάμενον), and when they are aorist passive they use third declension (λυθείς, λυθέν).

28.16   Here is a list of the verbs that could give you some trouble. They all occur more than fifty times in the New Testament. Be sure to note the differences between γίνομαι (*γεν) and γινωσκω (*γνο).

present		*aorist*	
ἄγω	▸ ἄγων	ἤγαγον	▸ ἀγαγών
αἴρω	▸ αἴρων	ἦρα	▸ ἄρας
ὁράω	–	εἶδον	▸ ἰδών
ἔρχομαι	▸ ἐρχόμενος	ἦλθον	▸ ἐλθών
εὑρίσκω	▸ εὑρίσκων	εὗρον	▸ εὑρών
ἔχω	▸ ἔχων	ἔσχον	▸ σχών
θέλω	▸ θέλων	ἠθέλησα	–
λέγω	▸ λέγων	εἶπον	▸ εἰπών

Summary

1. The aorist participle is formed from the unaugmented aorist tense stem and indicates an undefined action. For the time being, use "after" in your translation.

2. The forms you should learn are as follows.

First aorist active: σαντ, σασα

σας	σασα	σαν
σαντος	σασης	σαντος

First aorist middle: σαμενο/η

σαμενος	σαμενη	σαμενον
σαμενου	σαμενης	σαμενου

First aorist passive: θεντ, θεισα

θεις	θεισα	θεν
θεντος	θεισης	θεντος

Second aorist active: οντ, ουσα

ων	ουσα	ον
οντος	ουσης	οντος

Second aorist middle: ομενο/η

ομενος	ομενη	ομενον
ομενου	ομενης	ομενου

Second aorist passive: εντ, εισα

εις	εισα	εν
εντος	εισης	εντος

Vocabulary

ἀσπάζομαι	I greet, salute (59; *ἀσπαδ) (ἠσπαζόμην), -, ἠσπασάμην, -, -, -
γραμματεύς, -έως, ὁ	scribe (63; *γραμματεϝ)[14]
ἐφή[15]	He/she/it was saying; he/she/it said
ἱερόν, -οῦ, τό	temple (71; * ἱερο)[16]
κράζω	I cry out, call out (56; *κραγ)[17] (ἔκραζον), κράξω, ἔκραξα, κέκραγα, -, -
οὐχί	not (54, adverb)
παιδίον, -ου, τό	child, infant (52; *παιδιο)[18]

---

[14] *Grammar* is from the Greek γραμματική, meaning the skill (τέχνη) of writing (γράμμα).

[15] Third person singular of φημί; it can be either imperfect active or second aorist active. This one form occurs forty-three times in the New Testament. We have included it as a vocabulary word because it is very difficult for a first year student to recognize.

[16] *Hieroglyphics* is Egyptian writing, from the cognate ἱερός ("sacred," "holy") and γλύφω ("to carve, note down [on tablets]").

[17] This is one of the very few αζω verbs whose stem does not actually end in a dental; cf. v-2a(2) in *MBG*.

[18] A child is one who learns, who needs to be taught. *Paideutics* (παιδευτικός) and *pedagogy* are the art of teaching. The combining form *pedo* is also common, as in *pedobaptism*.

σπείρω   I sow (52, *σπερ)
                                    -, ἔσπειρα, -, ἔσπαρμαι, -

Total word count in the New Testament:	138,162
Number of words learned to date:	289
Number of word occurrences in this chapter:	407
Number of word occurrences to date:	107,523
Percent of total word count in the New Testament:	77.82%

Advanced Information

28.17 **Relative time**. Whereas the present participle indicates an action occurring at the same time as the main verb, the aorist participle generally indicates an action occurring *before* the time of the main verb. There are, however, many exceptions to this general rule. (That is why it is only a *general* rule.) For example, many aorist participles indicate an action occurring at the same time as the main verb.

It is especially difficult to indicate relative time for the aorist participle using the -ing form of the verb. Using "after" instead of "while" when appropriate does help. It will also help to follow the advice in the *Advanced Information* section in the previous chapter.

28.18 The following chart shows the relationship among main verbs, present participles, and aorist participles. If you are confused with the names of the English tenses, the appropriate helping verbs are listed below their names. See the Appendix for a further discussion of English tenses.

main verb	*present participle*	*aorist participle*
Future	"While" + future continuous *will be eating*	"After" + present *eating*
Present	"While" + present continuous *is eating*	"After" + simple past *eating*
Imperfect	"While" + past continuous *was eating*	"After" + past perfect *had eaten*
Aorist	"While" + past continuous *was eating*	"After" + past perfect *had eaten*
Perfect	"While" + perfect continuous *have been eating*	"After" + past perfect *had eaten*

28.19 **Future participle**. The future participle is used to describe what is "purposed, intended, or expected" in the future (Smyth, §2044). The future participle occurs twelve times in the New Testament. The forms are quite obvious, and we felt they did not require specific comment. Here they are.

Matt. 27:49   οἱ δὲ λοιποὶ ἔλεγον, Ἄφες ἴδωμεν εἰ ἔρχεται Ἡλίας **σώσων** αὐτόν.

Luke 22:49   ἰδόντες δὲ οἱ περὶ αὐτὸν τὸ **ἐσόμενον** εἶπαν, Κύριε, εἰ πατάξομεν ἐν μαχαίρῃ;

John 6:64   ἀλλ᾽ εἰσὶν ἐξ ὑμῶν τινες οἳ οὐ πιστεύουσιν. ᾔδει γὰρ ἐξ ἀρχῆς ὁ Ἰησοῦς τίνες εἰσὶν οἱ μὴ πιστεύοντες καὶ τίς ἐστιν ὁ **παραδώσων** αὐτόν.

Acts 8:27   καὶ ἀναστὰς ἐπορεύθη· καὶ ἰδοὺ ἀνὴρ Αἰθίοψ εὐνοῦχος δυνάστης Κανδάκης βασιλίσσης Αἰθιόπων, ὃς ἦν ἐπὶ πάσης τῆς γάζης αὐτῆς, ὃς ἐληλύθει **προσκυνήσων** εἰς Ἰερουσαλήμ,

Acts 20:22   καὶ νῦν ἰδοὺ δεδεμένος ἐγὼ τῷ πνεύματι πορεύομαι εἰς Ἰερουσαλήμ, τὰ ἐν αὐτῇ **συναντήσοντά** μοι μὴ εἰδώς,

Acts 22:5   ὡς καὶ ὁ ἀρχιερεὺς μαρτυρεῖ μοι καὶ πᾶν τὸ πρεσβυτέριον· παρ᾽ ὧν καὶ ἐπιστολὰς δεξάμενος πρὸς τοὺς ἀδελφοὺς εἰς Δαμασκὸν ἐπορευόμην **ἄξων** καὶ τοὺς ἐκεῖσε ὄντας δεδεμένους εἰς Ἰερουσαλὴμ ἵνα τιμωρηθῶσιν.

Acts 24:11   δυναμένου σου ἐπιγνῶναι ὅτι οὐ πλείους εἰσίν μοι ἡμέραι δώδεκα ἀφ᾽ ἧς ἀνέβην **προσκυνήσων** εἰς Ἰερουσαλήμ,

Acts 24:17   δι᾽ ἐτῶν δὲ πλειόνων ἐλεημοσύνας **ποιήσων** εἰς τὸ ἔθνος μου παρεγενόμην καὶ προσφοράς,

1 Cor 15:37   καὶ ὃ σπείρεις, οὐ τὸ σῶμα τὸ **γενησόμενον** σπείρεις ἀλλὰ γυμνὸν κόκκον εἰ τύχοι σίτου ἤ τινος τῶν λοιπῶν·

Heb 3:5   καὶ Μωϋσῆς μὲν πιστὸς ἐν ὅλῳ τῷ οἴκῳ αὐτοῦ ὡς θεράπων εἰς μαρτύριον τῶν **λαληθησομένων**,

Heb 13:17   Πείθεσθε τοῖς ἡγουμένοις ὑμῶν καὶ ὑπείκετε, αὐτοὶ γὰρ ἀγρυπνοῦσιν ὑπὲρ τῶν ψυχῶν ὑμῶν ὡς λόγον **ἀποδώσοντες**, ἵνα μετὰ χαρᾶς τοῦτο ποιῶσιν καὶ μὴ στενάζοντες, ἀλυσιτελὲς γὰρ ὑμῖν τοῦτο.

1 Pet 3:13   Καὶ τίς ὁ **κακώσων** ὑμᾶς ἐὰν τοῦ ἀγαθοῦ ζηλωταὶ γένησθε;

Chapter 29

Adjectival Participles

Exegetical Insight

In Romans 1:3-4 it is imperative to see that the two attributive participles (τοῦ γενομένου, "who was," and τοῦ ὁρισθέντος, "who was appointed") modify the word "son" (υἱοῦ) that appears at the beginning of verse 3. The two participial phrases communicate two complementary truths about the Son. First, "he was of the seed of David according to the flesh" (τοῦ γενομένου ἐκ σπέρματος Δαυὶδ κατὰ σάρκα). Since Jesus was a descendant of David, he fulfilled the Old Testament prophecies that a ruler would come from David's line (2 Sam 7:12-16; Isa 11:1-5, 10; Jer 23:5-6; 33:14-17; Ezek 34:23-24).

In saying that Jesus was David's descendant "according to the flesh," no criticism of his Davidic origin is implied. Nonetheless, the second attributive participle introduces something greater than being the fleshly descendant of David. The Son "was appointed to be the Son of God in power according to the Spirit of holiness by the resurrection of the dead" (τοῦ ὁρισθέντος υἱοῦ θεοῦ ἐν δυνάμει κατὰ πνεῦμα ἁγιωσύνης ἐξ ἀναστάσεως νεκρῶν).

The two stages of salvation history are present here. During his earthly life Jesus was the Messiah and the Son of David, but upon his resurrection he was appointed as the ruling and reigning Messiah. The title "Son of God" in verse 4, then, refers to the messianic kingship of Jesus, not his deity. Paul is not suggesting that Jesus was adopted as God's Son upon his resurrection. Remember that the phrase introduced with the attributive participle τοῦ ὁρισθέντος in verse 4 modifies the word "Son" (υἱοῦ) in verse 3. The "Son" was appointed by God to be "the Son of God." In other words, Jesus was already the Son before he was appointed to be the Son of God! The first usage (v. 3) of the word "Son," then, refers to Jesus' pre-existent divinity that he shared with the Father from all eternity. Jesus' appointment as "the Son of God" (v. 4) refers to his installment as the messianic King at his resurrection.

How great Jesus Christ is! He is the eternal Son of God who reigns with the Father from all eternity. But he also deserves our worship as the messianic King, the God-Man who was appointed as the Son of God in power when he was raised from the dead.

Thomas R. Schreiner

Overview

In this chapter we will learn that:

- an *adjectival* participle modifies a noun or pronoun, or it performs a function like a noun;

- if an adjectival participle is functioning as an adjective, it is called an *attributive* participle and behaves like an adjective;

- if an adjectival participle is functioning as a noun, it is called a *substantival* participle and behaves like a noun.

English

29.1 A participle is a verbal adjective. As such, it not only has verbal but also adjectival characteristics. In other words, a participle can do whatever an adjective can do. For example, it can modify a noun. "The man eating by the window is my Greek teacher." In this example, the participle *eating* tells us something about the *man*.

29.2 But a participle can do more than simply modify a noun. One of its most obvious other talents is to act like a noun. In other words, a participle can be used substantivally. "The living have hope." In this example, the participle *living* is serving as a noun, specifically as the subject of the sentence.[1]

Greek

29.3 Almost everything we have learned about participles so far applies here as well. The formation of the participle, its aspect, agreement with the word it modifies–all these apply to all participles. However, the specific participle we have been studying is the adverbial participle, and it is now time to learn the other type, the adjectival.

29.4 **Adjectival**. Because a participle is a verbal adjective, it can behave not only as an adverb (which has been the case so far) but also as an adjective. This is called the "adjectival" participle. The participle will modify some other noun or pronoun in the sentence, and will agree with that word in case, number, and gender, just like an adjective. For the time being, it can be translated simply with the "ing" form.

> ὁ ἄνθρωπος ὁ λέγων τῷ ὀχλῷ ἐστιν ὁ διδάσκαλός μου.
> The man *speaking* to the crowd is my teacher.

---

[1] As we said before, when an -ing word is used in English as a noun, it is technically called a "gerund" and not a participle. In Greek there are no gerunds, but the participle in Greek can function as a noun.

29.5 **Substantival**. Since an adjective can also function as a noun, so also can a participle. Remember: a participle is a *verbal adjective*, and anything an adjective can do a participle can do, usually better.

> ὁ τῷ ὀχλῷ λέγων ἐστὶν ὁ διδάσκαλός μου.
> The *one who is speaking* to the crowd is my teacher.

You will also notice that there is no difference in form between the adverbial and adjectival participle. There are no new forms to learn here. Context will show whether a participle is adverbial or adjectival.

The key words "while" and "after" apply only to adverbial participles. They are not used with adjectival participles.

29.6 **Adverbial or adjectival?** It now becomes important to decide whether a participle is being used adverbially or adjectivally. There are two clues to the answer to this question.

- The first is whether or not the participle is preceded by the **article**. As a general rule,[2] *the adverbial participle is anarthrous while the adjectival participle is articular.*[3] ("Anarthrous" means it is not preceded by the article, and "articular" means it is preceded by the article.) The article will always agree with the participle in case, number, and gender.[4]

  > ὁ ἄνθρωπος λέγων τῷ ὀχλῷ ἐστιν ὁ διδάσκαλός μου.

  According to this general guideline, this example would be translated, "The man, while speaking to the crowd, is my teacher." This of course makes no sense, which leads us to the second clue.

- **Context**. Often, the only clue available to us is the context of the verse. Which makes more sense? Adverbial or adjectival? Trying to translate the participle one way, and then the other, will be the only clue. In the example ὁ ἄνθρωπος λέγων τῷ ὀχλῷ ἐστιν ὁ διδάσκαλός μου, the only possible translation of λέγων is as an adjectival participle, even though there is no definite article before λέγων. "The man who is speaking to the crowd is my teacher."

29.7 **Substantival**. The key to this next point is to remember that a participle is a verbal adjective, and anything an adjective can do a participle can also do. One of the functions of an adjective is to act like a noun, i.e., substantivally. The same is true of participles. In other words, the

---

2 Which does allow for some exceptions.

3 An adverbial participle must be anarthrous. The adjectival participle can be either articular or anarthrous. See Wallace on participles for a further discussion.

4 You should expect this, since this is also true of an adjective. Sometimes a word or phrase will be inserted between the article and participle, as is the case with adjectives (e.g., ὁ τῷ ὀχλῷ λέγων).

adjectival participle has two functions, *attributive* (if it functions as an adjective) and *substantival* (if it functions as a noun).

What will determine the case, number, and gender of a participle used substantivally?

> ὁ λέγων τῷ ὄχλῳ ἐστιν ὁ διδάσκαλός μου.
> *The one who is speaking*[5] to the crowd is my teacher.

Correct! The case is determined by the function of the participle in the sentence (just like it does with a substantival adjective). In the example above, it is nominative because the participle is the subject of the sentence.

Its number and gender are determined by what or who it is representing. In this case, there is only one teacher (i.e., singular) and he is a man (i.e., masculine).

Since a participle can function either as an adjective or as a noun, how can you tell which is which? Again the answer is *context*. Take the example, ὁ λέγων τῷ ὄχλῳ ἐστιν ὁ διδάσκαλός μου. How can you tell whether ὁ λέγων is adjectival or substantival? Simple. Try translating it as adjectival. You cannot. Therefore it must be substantival.

29.8   **Translation of the substantival use**. You will also notice a slight difference in the translation of the substantival participle. We had to use "one who is" in the translation. Try translating without these words.

> ὁ λέγων τῷ ὄχλῳ ἐστιν ὁ διδάσκαλός μου.
> The *speaking* to the crowd is my teacher.

Does not make much sense does it? This gets back to a point we made several chapters back. The translation of the Greek participle is often quite idiomatic. You must look at what the Greek means, and then figure out how to say the same thing in English. Going word for word will usually not work.

Use common sense in the words you add (like "one who is"). If the participle is singular you could use "one," "he," "she," or perhaps "that" if it is neuter. If it is plural you could use "they" or perhaps "those." Instead of "who" you might use "which," especially if the concept described by the participle is neuter. There is quite a bit of flexibility possible here, and the best way to figure out what you want to use is to figure it out first in Greek and then switch to English. Additional rules would just confuse you now.

What case, number, and gender would a participle be if the translation is as follows?

---

[5]   We will discuss why we added "one who is" in §29.8.

	case	number	gender

"The ones who"

"That which"

"To those who"

"Of that which"

Summary

Four different terms are important to know.

1. **Adverbial**. An adverbial participle agrees with a noun or pronoun in the sentence, but the action described by the participle is directed toward the verb. It uses the key words *while* or *after*, depending upon whether it is present or aorist.

2. **Adjectival**. An adjectival participle modifies a noun or pronoun, or functions like a noun.

    a. **Attributive**. If an adjectival participle is functioning as an adjective, i.e., if it is attributing something to a noun or pronoun, it is called an attributive participle. For the time being, the simple "ing" form of the English verb is sufficient for translation. It will agree in case, number, and gender with the word it is modifying.

    b. **Substantival**. If an adjectival participle is functioning as a noun, then it is called a substantival participle. You must insert some extra words into your translation to make sense of this construction. Use those words that enable you to repeat in English the true significance of the participle in Greek. Its case is determined by its function, its gender and number by the word it is replacing.

3. The following chart illustrates the process of translating participles.

The Seven Questions to Ask of any Participle You Meet

1. What is the case, number, and gender of the participle, and why (i.e., what word is it modifying)?

2. Is the action (or state of being) in the participle directed toward a verb (adverbial) or a noun (adjectival)?

3. If it is adverbial, do you use "while" or "after"?

4. If it is adjectival, is it attributive or substantival?

5. What is the aspect of the participle? Continuous (present) or undefined (aorist)?

6. What is the voice of the participle?

7. What does the verb mean?

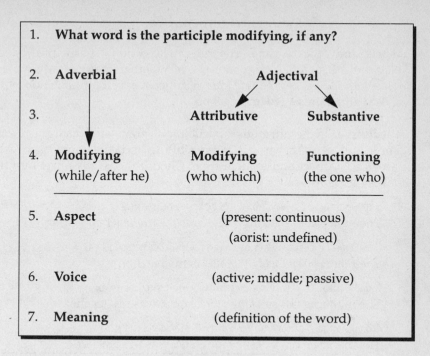

1. **What word is the participle modifying, if any?**

2. **Adverbial**   **Adjectival**

3.   **Attributive**   **Substantive**

4. **Modifying**   **Modifying**   **Functioning**
   (while/after he)   (who which)   (the one who)

   ---

5. **Aspect**   (present: continuous)
                               (aorist: undefined)

6. **Voice**   (active; middle; passive)

7. **Meaning**   (definition of the word)

Vocabulary

δέχομαι — I take, receive (56; *δεχ)
δέξομαι, ἐδεξάμην, -, δέδεγμαι, ἐδέχθην

δοκέω — I think, seem (62; *δοκ)[6]
(ἐδόκουν), δόξω, ἔδοξα, -, -, -

ἐσθίω — I eat (158; *ἐσθι; *φαγ)[7]
(ἤσθιον), φάγομαι, ἔφαγον, -, -, -

πέμπω — I send (79, *πεμπ)
πέμψω, ἔπεμψα, -, -, ἐπέμφθην

φέρω — I carry, bear, produce (66; *φερ; *οι; *ενεχ)[8]
(ἔφερον), οἴσω, ἤνεγκα, ἐνήνοχα, ἐνήνεγμαι,
ἠνέχθην

Total word count in the New Testament:	138,162
Number of words learned to date:	294
Number of word occurrences in this chapter:	421
Number of word occurrences to date:	107,944
Percent of total word count in the New Testament:	78.13%

---

[6] *Docetism* was an early Christian heresy that taught Jesus only appeared to be human. Epsilon is added to form the present tense stem.

[7] *Esophagus* is formed from the second root, *φαγ.

[8] *Christopher* (Χρίστοφερ) means *bearing Christ*. See *MBG* for explanation of tense stems.

Advanced Information

29.9   **Aspect and relative time**. The present and aorist participles have a relative time significance regardless of whether they are adverbial or adjectival. However, keeping this significance in the translation of the adjectival requires a few more steps.

29.10   **Attributive**. If the attributive participle is translated using a relative clause and a finite verb, it is possible to indicate more clearly the participle's aspect and relative time. Choose the relative pronoun that makes the correct sense.

ὁ ἄνθρωπος ὁ λέγων τῷ ὀχλῷ ἐστιν ὁ διδάσκαλός μου.
The man *who is speaking to the crowd* is my teacher.

ὁ ἄνθρωπος ὁ εἰπὼν τῷ ὀχλῷ ἐστιν ὁ διδάσκαλός μου
The man *who spoke to the crowd* is my teacher.

ὁ ἄνθρωπος ὁ λέγων τῷ ὀχλῷ ἦν ὁ διδάσκαλός μου.
The man *who was speaking to the crowd* was my teacher.

ὁ ἄνθρωπος ὁ εἰπὼν τῷ ὀχλῷ ἦν ὁ διδάσκαλός μου.
The man *who had spoken to the crowd* was my teacher.

29.11   **Substantival**. Because you already know how to use personal and relative pronouns in the translation of the substantival participles, there is really nothing else to learn here, except that you should concentrate on using a verbal form that shows the proper aspect and the correct relative time significance.

29.12   **Alternate translations for participles**. So far we have learned only one way to translate adverbial participles: present with "while"; aorist with "after." This is an excellent way to start, but there are participles that cannot be translated very well this way. As you become more familiar with participles, and as you become grounded in the basics of the participle (i.e., the significance of aspect), other ways of translating the participle will become possible. Following are two of those possibilities:

- **Causal participle**. Some adverbial participles indicate the reason for an action. You can use the key word "because" with the participle.

- **Instrumental participle**. Adverbial participles can indicate the means by which an action occurred. You may use the key word "by." πιστεύων can mean, "by believing."

- **Telic participle**. Adverbial participles can also give the goal or purpose for something, and the key phrase "in order to" may be used. (πειράζω means "I tempt.")

  τὸ πνεῦμα αὐτὸν ἐκβάλλει εἰς τὴν ἔρημον πειραζόμενον.
  The Spirit led him out into the desert *in order to be tempted.*

Chapter 30

Perfect Participles and Genitive Absolutes

Exegetical Insight

Ἰδοὺ δέδωκα ἐνώπιόν σου θύραν ἠνεῳγμένην (Rev 3:8). "Behold, I have set before thee an open door" (*KJV*); "See, I have placed before you an open door" (*NIV*); "Behold, I have put before you an open door" (*NASB*).

Here is a classic example of the weakness or inadequacy of translations. In the first place each of these versions obscures the basic meaning of the verb, δέδωκα, telling the reader that it means "I have set," or "I have placed," or "I have put," when it really means, "I have given." The resurrected, exalted Christ personally addresses the hearer of this word (note the σου ["you"], second person singular) and says, "Look, I have given *you* something special right before your eyes–it is my permanent (the force of the perfect tense, δέδωκα) gift to you!"

And in the second place they all translate the words stating what this gift is, θύραν ἠνεῳγμένην, as "an open door." In doing so they fail to communicate to the reader that it is not just "an open door," as if by chance it happened to be "open." It is in fact "an *opened* door," since the adjective modifying door, ἠνεῳγμένην, is a participle in the passive voice, a "divine passive," implying that the door is not simply open, but that it is a divinely opened door–a door opened by God.

And further, something that is especially important for this lesson, none of these translations takes note of the fact that this passive participle is also in the perfect tense, *the* tense that stresses the idea that not only *did* God open the door, but having done so *it stands presently and permanently open*. Is it any wonder, then, that the speaker from heaven here goes on to say, "Hence, no one is able to shut it."

Thus, reading this text in Greek and not in translation causes me to sit up and take notice. For I see the door as one permanently opened for me by God and graciously given right into my hands as an irrevocable gift by the risen Christ. I see it as a metaphor of life with its God-given, boundless, inexhaustible range of immediate opportunities–opportunities to do something worthwhile in life limited only by my failure to see them and take advantage of them. "Look," says our Lord, "I have given you a God-opened door." Hence, I have stopped hoping for Friday, for the end of term, for graduation, for a job. Instead I say to myself, "Look, today opens before me with every imaginable God-given opportunity– from studying Greek to speaking a word in kindness.

Gerald F. Hawthorne

Overview

In this chapter we will learn that:

- the perfect participle is formed from the perfect active tense stem (including reduplication) and indicates a completed action with results continuing into the present.

- a genitive absolute is a participial construction in which the participle in the genitive is not connected to the rest of the sentence;

- a periphrastic construction consists of a participle and a form of εἰμί and is used in place of a finite verbal form.

Perfect Participle

30.1   This is the last participle you will learn. The perfect participle is formed on the perfect tense stem and carries the same significance that the perfect does in the indicative. It indicates a completed action which has consequences in the present.[1]

30.2   **Reduplication**. The perfect participle is built on the perfect tense stem. The vocalic reduplication is retained, since it is not the same thing as the augment indicating past time.

30.3   **Paradigm of the first perfect active participle**[2]

If a verb has a first perfect indicative, it will use that first perfect stem in the formation of the perfect participle.

> *Reduplication + Perfect tense stem +*
>
> *Tense formative* (κ) +
>
> *Participle morpheme + Case endings*
>
>
> λε + λυ + κ + οτ + ες ⸱ λελυκότες

---

[1] As was true in the indicative, the time is present from the point of view of the speaker, not necessarily the reader.

[2] The second perfect participle is quite rare. It is discussed in *Advanced Information*, §30.12.

	masc	*fem*	*neut*
nom sg	λελυκώς³	λελυκυῖα⁴	λελυκός⁵
gen sg	λελυκότος	λελυκυίας	λελυκότος
dat sg	λελυκότι	λελυκυίᾳ	λελυκότι
acc sg	λελυκότα	λελυκυῖαν	λελυκός
nom pl	λελυκότες	λελυκυῖαι	λελυκότα
gen pl	λελυκότων	λελυκυιῶν	λελυκότων
dat pl	λελυκόσι(ν)	λελυκυίαις	λελυκόσι(ν)
acc pl	λελυκότας	λελυκυίας	λελυκότα

The **active** participle morpheme is **οτ** that looks like **κοτ** with the tense formative.

	masc	*fem*	*neut*
nom sg	κως	κυια	κος
gen sg	κοτος	κυιας	κοτος

30.4 Paradigm of the first perfect middle/passive participle

Reduplication + Perfect tense stem +
Participle morpheme + Case endings

λε + λυ + μενο + ς › λελυμένος

---

³ The case ending is a sigma. The tau drops out (rule #7) and the omicron lengthens to omega in order to compensate for the loss (rule #5). κοτς › κος › κως.

⁴ As is the case in the other participles, the feminine participle is quite different from the masculine and neuter. See *MBG*, §91.5.

⁵ The case ending is a sigma. The tau drops out (rule #7) but the omicron does not lengthen. κοτς › κος.

	masc	*fem*	*neut*
nom sg	λελυμένος	λελυμένη	λελυμένον
gen sg	λελυμένου	λελυμένης	λελυμένου
dat sg	λελυμένῳ	λελυμένῃ	λελυμένῳ
acc sg	λελυμένον	λελυμένην	λελυμένον
nom pl	λελυμένοι	λελυμέναι	λελυμένα
gen pl	λελυμένων	λελυμένων	λελυμένων
dat pl	λελυμένοις	λελυμέναις	λελυμένοις
acc pl	λελυμένους	λελυμένας	λελυμένα

The **middle/passive** morpheme is **μενο/η**. There is no tense formative and no connecting vowel. This is a very important indicator of the perfect middle/passive.[6]

	masc	*fem*	*neut*
nom sg	μενος	μενη	μενον
gen sg	μενου	μενης	μενου

30.5 **Translation**. As has been the case previously, the most important part in the translation of the participle is its aspect. The perfect participle indicates a completed action that has continuing results.

A general suggestion is to use "(After) having ..." and the past perfect form of the verb (e.g., "after having eaten"). The use of "after" is optional depending upon context.

Genitive Absolute

30.6 The grammatical definition of an "absolute" construction is a construction that has no grammatical relationship to the rest of the sen-

---

[6] The accent will always be on the next to the last syllable, the "penult" (μέν).

tence.[7] The primary example of an absolute construction in Greek is the genitive absolute.

A genitive absolute is *a noun or pronoun and a participle in the genitive that are not grammatically connected to the rest of the sentence.*[8] In other words, there will be no word in the sentence that the noun, pronoun, or participle modifies.

> Καὶ εὐθὺς ἔτι αὐτοῦ λαλοῦντος παραγίνεται Ἰούδας (Mark 14:43)
> And immediately, *while he is still speaking*, Judas comes.

Notice how αὐτοῦ functions as the "subject" of the participle. The genitive absolute is often used when the noun or pronoun doing the action of the participle is different from the subject of the sentence. It is also possible for the participle to have modifiers such as a direct object.

The genitive absolute tends to occur at the beginning of a sentence.

In English we have a similar construction called the "nominative absolute." It is a noun or pronoun with a participle that is not grammatically linked to the sentence. "*Weather permitting*, we will eat soon."

30.7   **Translation**. Most genitive absolutes in the New Testament are temporal. Using "while" or "after" will normally make proper sense. In our example above, ἔτι is already there.[9]

The translation of the genitive absolute is highly idiomatic. You cannot translate word for word. See what it says in Greek, and then say the same basic thing in English, trying to emphasize the aspect of the participle. If you use an absolute construction in your translation, your English will actually be poor English, but for the time being this is okay.

30.8   These guidelines provide a starting point for translation.

1. Translate the genitive absolute as a temporal clause, using "while" if the participle is present and "after" if the participle is aorist. If there is a word in the genitive, use the appropriate pronoun and the finite form of the verb.

---

7 "Absolute" means "separated." It comes from the Latin "absolutus," which means "loosed."

8 It is possible not to have the noun or pronoun, but this is unusual (see *Bl-D* §423.6). If one is not present, you may assume it in your translation.

9 If you are translating with relative time as discussed in the *Advanced Information* sections in previous chapters, maintain the notion of relative time in connection with the main verb.

ἀκούοντος αὐτοῦ ....
While he heard ....

ἀκούσαντος αὐτοῦ ....
After he heard ....

2.   If there is no noun or pronoun in the genitive, translate with the -ing form of the verb

ἀκούοντος ....
While hearing ....

ἀκούσαντος ....
After hearing ....

30.9   In the following examples, differentiate among the regular participles and the genitive absolutes. Parse each participle.

εἰπόντες ταῦτα οἱ μαθηταὶ ἀπῆλθον ....
εἰπόντων προφήτων ταῦτα οἱ μαθηταὶ ἀπῆλθον ....
εἰπόντων προφήτων ταῦτα τῶν ἀποστόλων οἱ μαθηταὶ ἀπῆλθον ....

λεγόντες ταῦτα οἱ μαθηταὶ ἀπῆλθον ....
λεγοντῶν προφήτων ταῦτα οἱ μαθηταὶ ἀπῆλθον ....
λεγόντος αὐτοῦ ταῦτα οἱ μαθηταὶ ἀπῆλθον ....

διδαχθέντες ὑπὸ τοῦ κυρίου ἐξῆλθον εἰς τὴν ἔρημον οἱ δοῦλοι.
διδαχθέντων προφήτων ὑπὸ τοῦ κυρίου ἐξῆλθον εἰς τὴν ἔρημον οἱ δοῦλοι.
τῶν μαθητῶν διδαχθέντων ὑπὸ τοῦ κυρίου ἐξῆλθον εἰς τὴν ἔρημον οἱ δοῦλοι.

Periphrastic Constructions

30.10   One of the basic differences we have seen between English and Greek is that the different Greek tenses do not use helping verbs. English uses "will" to make a verb future and "be" to make it passive. Greek just uses different tense formatives, etc.

There is one situation, however, when Greek uses εἰμί and a participle together to state a single idea, and this is called a periphrastic construction.[10] Originally a periphrastic construction was used to emphasize the continuous force of the participle (which is why the aorist participle never occurs in this construction). However, by the time of Koine Greek, this emphasis is often totally lost. In fact, Koine Greek normally uses a periphrastic construction for the third person plural, perfect middle/passive.

---

[10] "Periphrastic" means a "round about" way of saying something, from περί and φράσις.

Translate the periphrastic construction just as you would the regular formation of the tense; perhaps the continuous idea will be emphasized, but that is up to the context and not the verbal form.

Following are all the different forms a periphrastic construction can take. The form of εἰμί and the participle can be separated by several words.

periphrastic tense	*construction*		
Present	present of εἰμί	+	present participle
Imperfect	imperfect of εἰμί	+	present participle
Future	future of εἰμί	+	present participle
Perfect	present of εἰμί	+	perfect participle
Pluperfect	imperfect of εἰμί	+	perfect participle
Future perfect	future of εἰμί	+	perfect participle

For a discussion of the pluperfect, see *Advanced Information* in chapter 25.

Summary

1. The perfect participle indicates a completed action with results continuing into the present.

2. The perfect active participle is formed from the perfect active tense stem (including vocalic reduplication). The participle morphemes and case endings are κως, κυια, and κος.

3. The perfect middle/passive participle is formed from the perfect middle/passive tense stem (including vocalic reduplication). The participle morphemes and case endings are μενος, μενη, and μενον.

4. A genitive absolute is a participial construction in which the participle in the genitive is unconnected to the rest of the sentence. It usually includes a noun or pronoun in the genitive that acts as the "subject" of the participle, and it can have modifiers. Translate the genitive absolute as a temporal clause using "while" and "after" unless the context does not allow it.

5. A periphrastic construction consists of a participle and a form of εἰμί that are used instead of a finite verbal form. It was originally designed to emphasize the continuous aspect of an action, but this cannot be assumed in Koine Greek. It is normally used in place of a third person plural perfect middle/passive.

A Summary of the Forms of the Greek Participle

1. What is nice about the inflection of Greek participles is that you already know all the different forms. There are no new endings to learn. All you really need to know are the actual participles and a little grammar.

2. If the participle is used as an adverb, its form must still agree with the noun or pronoun that is doing the action of the participle. In other words, if the person/thing doing the action of the participle is the subject of the verb, then the participle must be in the nominative. If the person/thing doing the action of the participle is the indirect object of the verb, then the participle must be in the dative. The same applies to number.

3. If the participle is used as an adjective, then it must agree with the word it is modifying in case, number, and gender, just like any other adjective. (Remember, the participle is a verbal adjective.)

4. If the participle is used as a noun, then like any noun its case is determined by its function in the sentence. Its number and gender will be determined by the number and gender of the word to which it is referring (like a substantival adjective).

5. Because the participle does not indicate absolute time, the aorist participle cannot have an augment. Therefore, the aorist participle will unaugment. The perfect participle does not lose its vocalic reduplication.

6. There are only a few participles. The following charts list the tense formatives, connecting vowels, and participle morphemes. The nominative forms are in parentheses.

Present active and second aorist active

*   The masculine and neuter active is οντ (ων, ον).

*   The feminine active is ουσα.

First aorist active

*   The masculine and neuter active is σαντ (σας, σαν).

*   The feminine active is σασα.

Aorist passive

*   The masculine and neuter passive is θεντ (θεις, θεν).

*   The feminine passive is θεισα.

Perfect active

*   The masculine and neuter perfect active is κοτ (κως, κος).

*   The feminine perfect active is κυια.

μενο/η is used in the following participles;

- Present middle/passive, second aorist middle: ομενο/η.

- First aorist middle: σαμενο/η.

- Perfect middle/passive: μενο/η.

The aorist participles formed on second aorist stems use the same participle morphemes and case endings as the present participle. Only the stem is different.

7. The participle uses first, second, and third declension endings.

- All feminine participles use first declension endings.

- When the masculine and neuter participle is formed with μεν, both genders use second declension case endings.

- When the masculine and neuter participle is formed with ντ or οτ, both genders use third declension case endings (οντ, σαντ, κοτ).

8. In the Appendix there is a summary chart of all the participle forms you should know. Check it out.

Vocabulary

μηδέ   but not, nor, not even (56)

πρεσβύτερος, α, ον   elder (66; *πρεσβυτερο/α)[11]

Total word count in the New Testament:	138,162
Number of words learned to date:	296
Number of word occurrences in this chapter:	122
Number of word occurrences to date:	108,066
Percent of total word count in the New Testament:	78.22%

Advanced Information

30.11   Following are two more ways to translate a participle.

- As a **regular verb**. In certain constructions where a participle accompanies a verb, the participle is best translated as a finite verb.

---

[11] The word can be used adjectivally to describe an older person, or as a noun to describe an official in the church.

ὁ δὲ Ἰησοῦς ἀποκριθεὶς εἶπεν ....
But Jesus *answered* (and) said ....

- **"Though."** Some participles state a concessive idea and the key phrase is "though." (ἁμαρτάνω means "I sin.")

  ἁμαρτάνοντα γὰρ ὁ θεὸς ἀγαπᾷ με.
  "For *though (I am) a sinner*, God loves me."

30.12   Second perfect participles

There are six verbs (excluding compound forms) that have second perfects. Instead of memorizing paradigms, it is easier to see the forms and know them well enough to recognize them. They are all quite regular.

Their forms are identical to the first perfect except that the tense formative is α and not κα. Since the middle/passive does not use a tense formative, second perfects can only be found in the active.

If the form occurs only once, we will list the inflected form and reference. If a form occurs more than once, we will list the nominative and genitive singular masculine forms, and the number of times all related forms occur.

lexical form	*participle*	*reference or number of occurrences*
ἀκούω	ἀκηκοότας	John 18:21
ἀνοίγω	ἀνεῳγότα	John 1:51
γίνομαι	γεγονώς, ότος	14
ἔρχομαι	ἐληλυθώς, ότος	4
λαμβάνω	εἰληφώς	Matt 25:24
πείθω	πεποιθώς, ότος	9

Chapter 31

Subjunctive Mood

Exegetical Insight

When we listen to someone we care about and respect deeply, we listen for more than the surface meaning. The content is important, but we are keen to catch also the attitude of the speaker, what his words imply about our relationship with him, what is most significant to him, what he emphasizes as he speaks, and so forth. When we study the New Testament we can look for such elements of meaning as well.

This chapter describes a fascinating combination used by the Greek language to show emphasis: it is the use of the two negatives οὐ μή with a subjunctive verb to indicate a strong negation about the future. The speaker uses the subjunctive verb to suggest a future possibility, but in the same phrase he emphatically denies (by means of the double negative) that such could ever happen. This linguistic combination occurs about eighty-five times in the New Testament, often in significant promises or reassurances about the future.

In Jesus' description of himself as the Good Shepherd in John 10, he gives one of the most treasured of these promises: "My sheep listen to my voice; I know them, and they follow me. I give them eternal life, and they shall never perish [οὐ μή ἀπόλωνται]" (10:27-28a *NIV*). It would have been enough to have οὐ with a future indicative verb here, but Jesus is more emphatic. The subjunctive combination strongly denies even the possibility that any of Jesus' sheep would perish: "they will certainly not perish," "they will by no means perish," is the sense of Jesus' assertion. This is reinforced by the addition of the phrase εἰς τὸν αἰῶνα, "forever." Jesus' emphatic promise is the bedrock of assurance and godly motivation for every one of his sheep!

Buist M. Fanning

Overview

In this chapter we will learn that:

- the subjunctive mood is used when a verb expresses a possibility, probability, exhortation, or axiomatic concept;
- a verb in the subjunctive has no time significance; its only significance is one of aspect;

- the present subjunctive is built on the present tense stem and indicates a continuous action;

- the aorist subjunctive is built on the unaugmented aorist tense stem and indicates an undefined action;

- the sign of the subjunctive is the lengthened connecting vowel (e.g., λύωμεν). The endings are exactly the same in the aorist as in the present.

English

31.1   So far we have studied only the indicative mood. If a verb is making a statement or asking a factual question, the verb is in the indicative. As it is normally stated, the indicative is the mood of reality. It states what is.

> The book is red.
>
> Greek is fun.
>
> Hebrew is too hard.
>
> Why am I procrastinating?

31.2   The subjunctive does not describe what is, but what may (or might) be. In other words, it is the mood not of reality but of possibility (or probability). There may be a subtle distinction between "may" and "might," but for our purposes they can be viewed as identical.[1]

> I might learn Hebrew.
>
> If we were wealthy, we would buy more Greek Bibles.

31.3   A quite common use of the subjunctive in English is in an "if" clause. "If I were a rich man, I would hire a Greek tutor." If in fact the speaker were rich, he would not have used the subjunctive "were" but the indicative form: "I *am* rich and therefore I will hire a tutor." This would be a statement of fact, the mood being one of reality. However, if he were not rich, the speaker would use the subjunctive form "were": "If I were rich ...."[2]

31.4   Because the action described by a verb in the subjunctive is unfulfilled, it often refers to a future event.

---

[1]   The technical distinction is that if the main verb is a present or future tense, you use "may;" if the main verb is a past tense, you use "might."

[2]   "Were" is perhaps not the best example since it can be used both as an indicative and as a subjunctive, but it is the most common subjunctive. "If I were rich" is correct English grammar, regardless of current usage.

Greek

31.5 The basic definition of the subjunctive and indicative moods in Greek is the same as in English. There are, however, several significant differences.

31.6 **Aspect**. A Greek verb has time significance only in the indicative. The only significance that a verb in the subjunctive has is one of aspect. This is the same as with the participle.

A verb in the present subjunctive indicates a continuous action; a verb in the aorist subjunctive indicates an undefined action. There is no concept of absolute past or present time in the subjunctive. Most grammars call the subjunctive formed from the present tense stem the "present subjunctive," and the subjunctive formed from the aorist tense stem the "aorist subjunctive." As is the case with participles, we urge you to adopt the terminology "continuous subjunctive" and "undefined subjunctive," because their true significance is aspect and not time.

It will be difficult to bring out the aspect in translation. One way is to use the key word "continue" with the present subjunctive. If you cannot translate this way, be sure to emphasize the aspect in your teaching or preaching.

There are only two tenses that form the subjunctive, present and aorist.[3] There is no future subjunctive. Because the aorist subjunctive is built on the unaugmented aorist tense stem, a first aorist subjunctive may look like a future (e.g., ἀγαπήσω). But remember, there is no future subjunctive.

31.7 **Form**. The good news is that the subjunctive uses the same endings as the indicative. All forms of the subjunctive use primary endings. The subjunctive merely lengthens the connecting vowel to indicate that the verb is in the subjunctive. Omicron lengthens to omega (e.g., λύωμεν) and epsilon lengthens to eta (e.g., λύητε).[4]

31.8 **Present (continuous) subjunctive**. The present subjunctive uses the present tense stem of the verb but lengthens the connecting vowel. λύομεν in the indicative becomes λύωμεν in the subjunctive.

---

[3] There actually are a few examples of the perfect subjunctive; see *Advanced Information*.

[4] ουσι(ν) goes to ωσι(ν) and η stays as η.

> Present tense stem + Lengthened connecting vowel (ω/η) +
>
> Primary personal endings
>
> λυ + ω + μεν › λύωμεν

We have included the active subjunctive of εἰμί. It has no passive. For the forms of contract verbs in the subjunctive, see the Appendix.

	subjunctive	(εἰμί)	indicative
		active	
1 sg	λύω	ὦ	λύω
2 sg	λύῃς	ᾖς	λύεις
3 sg	λύῃ	ᾖ[5]	λύει
1 pl	λύωμεν	ὦμεν	λύομεν
2 pl	λύητε	ἦτε	λύετε
3 pl	λύωσι(ν)	ὦσι(ν)	λύουσι(ν)
		middle/passive	
1 sg	λύωμαι		λύομαι
2 sg	λύῃ		λύῃ
3 sg	λύηται		λύεται
1 pl	λυώμεθα		λυόμεθα
2 pl	λύησθε		λύεσθε
3 pl	λύωνται		λύονται

Notice that the endings are all regular. You do not have to memorize any new endings; just one rule. Notice also that the ending η occurs in third singular active and second singular middle/passive.

31.9   Aorist (undefined) subjunctive. The aorist subjunctive uses the aorist tense stem of the verb. Because the subjunctive does not indicate abso-

---

[5]   Do not confuse this form with similar words; see the Appendix.

lute past time, the augment must be removed, just as in the aorist participle. The aorist subjunctive uses exactly the same personal endings as the present subjunctive. Just as the aorist passive indicative uses active endings, so also the aorist passive subjunctive uses active endings. The main clue showing the difference between tenses is that the aorist subjunctive is formed from the aorist tense stem (and tense formative, if there is one) of the verb.

Unaugmented aorist tense stem + (Tense formative +)

Lengthened connecting vowel + Primary personal endings

λυ + σ + ω + μεν ‣ λύσωμεν

If it is a first aorist, you will see the tense formative. If it is a second aorist, it will have the altered stem.

	subjunctive		*indicative*	
	1st aorist	*2nd aorist*	*1st aorist*	*2nd aorist*

active

	1st aorist	*2nd aorist*	*1st aorist*	*2nd aorist*
1 sg	λύσω	λάβω	ἔλυσα	ἔλαβον
2 sg	λύσῃς	λάβῃς	ἔλυσας	ἔλαβες
3 sg	λύσῃ	λάβῃ	ἔλυσε(ν)	ἔλαβε(ν)
1 pl	λύσωμεν	λάβωμεν	ἐλύσαμεν	ἐλάβομεν
2 pl	λύσητε	λάβητε	ἐλύσατε	ἐλάβετε
3 pl	λύσωσι(ν)	λάβωσι(ν)	ἔλυσαν	ἔλαβον

middle

	1st aorist	*2nd aorist*	*1st aorist*	*2nd aorist*
1 sg	λύσωμαι	γένωμαι	ἐλυσάμην	ἐγενόμην
2 sg	λύσῃ	γένῃ	ἐλύσω	ἐγένου
3 sg	λύσηται	γένηται	ἐλύσατο	ἐγένετο

1 pl	λυσώμεθα	γενώμεθα	ἐλυσάμεθα	ἐγενόμεθα
2 pl	λύσησθε	γένησθε	ἐλύσασθε	ἐγένεσθε
3 pl	λύσωνται	γένωνται	ἐλύσαντο	ἐγένοντο

passive

1 sg	λυθῶ	γραφῶ	ἐλύθην	ἐγράφην
2 sg	λυθῇς	γραφῇς	ἐλύθης	εγράφης
3 sg	λυθῇ	γραφῇ	ἐλύθη	ἐγράφη
1 pl	λυθῶμεν	γραφῶμεν	ἐλύθημεν	ἐγράφημεν
2 pl	λυθῆτε	γραφῆτε	ἐλύθητε	ἐγράφητε
3 pl	λυθῶσι(ν)	γραφῶσι(ν)	ἐλύθησαν	ἐγράφησαν

Remember: there is no future subjunctive. It is easy to see an aorist subjunctive and think it is a future indicative or subjunctive. Also, do not confuse the lengthened connecting vowel of the subjunctive with the lengthened contract vowel in the indicative.

31.10   **Clues**. There are other clues indicating that a verb is in the subjunctive, and these are important to note. For example, the verb in a ἵνα clause is almost always in the subjunctive.

> ὁ κύριος ἦλθεν ἵνα σωθῶμεν.
> The Lord came in order that *we might be saved*.

When you see the ἵνα, start looking for a subjunctive. Here are some other words that are generally (but not always) followed by the subjunctive.

* ὅταν (ὅτε + ἄν)   whenever
* ἐάν (εἰ + ἄν)   if
* ὃς ἄν   whoever
* ὅπου ἄν   wherever
* ἕως   until
* ἕως ἄν   until

You will notice how many times ἄν is involved in requiring the subjunctive. All in all, the subjunctive is easy to learn and to recognize.

Uses of the Subjunctive

31.11 **Different uses**. The subjunctive has a wider variety of uses in Greek than in English. The idea of "probability" is only one. The first two occur in independent clauses, the second two in dependent clauses.

31.12 **1. Hortatory subjunctive**. The first person subjunctive, either singular or plural, can be used as an exhortation. It will usually be plural and occur at the beginning of the sentence. Use "Let us" in your translation.

> προσευχώμεθα.
> Let us pray.

Just because a verb is first person subjunctive does not mean it is necessarily hortatory. Context will decide.[6]

31.13 **2. Deliberative subjunctive.** When a person asks a question and expects the audience to think about the answer, the verb in the question is put in the subjunctive.

> μὴ οὖν μεριμνήσητε λέγοντες, τί φάγωμεν; ἤ· τί πίωμεν; ἤ· τί περι-βαλώμεθα; (Matt 6:31)[7]
>
> Therefore do not worry saying, "What *should we eat?*", "What *should we drink?*", or, "What *should we wear?*'"

31.14 **3. ἵνα and the subjunctive**. ἵνα is almost always followed by the subjunctive and can indicate purpose.

The phrases ἵνα μή and ὅπως μή can be translated "lest" or some equivalent. They are idiomatic phrases.

> ἔρχομαι πρὸς τὸν οἶκον ἵνα προσεύχωμαι.
> I am going to the house in order that *I may pray*.
>
> ἐρχόμεθα πρὸς τὸν οἶκον ἵνα μὴ ἁμαρτάνωμεν.
> We are going to the house lest *we sin*.

31.15 **4. Conditional statement**. A conditional statement is an "If ... then ...." sentence. "If I were smart, I would have taken Hebrew." The "if" clause is called the "protasis" and the "then" clause is called the "apodosis."

The issue of how to categorize and translate conditional sentences is debated. At this early time in your training we cannot go into the debate in detail. In the exercises there are two types of conditional sentences and we will discuss those here. In the *Appendix* there is a summary of

---

[6] Rom 5:1 can read either ἔχωμεν or ἔχομεν. What is the difference in meaning, especially as you look at the overall argument of Romans?

[7] You may have noticed that μὴ μεριμνήσητε states a prohibition. This is another use of the subjunctive and will be discussed in §33.15.

conditional sentences. For a detailed discussion see Wallace, *GGBB*. We will use his terminology and definitions.

Conditional sentences are classified by their form and are given the titles "first class," "second class," "third class," and "fourth class." Third class conditional sentences always have a protasis introduced by ἐάν and a verb in the subjunctive. The verb in the apodosis can be any tense or mood. There are two subdivisions of third class conditions.

1. **Future more probable**. A future condition says that if something might happen, then something else will definitely happen.

    ἐὰν ἁμαρτάνω, ἔτι θεὸς ἀγαπήσει με.
    If I might sin, God will still love me.

    Exegesis raises the important question here as to whether the protasis can be assumed to be true or not. The Bible has examples of future more probable conditions in which the protasis is likely to be true and others in which the protasis is hypothetical. As always, context is the key.

2. **Present general**. A general condition is identical in form to the future more probable condition except that the verb in the apodosis must be in the present tense.

    Its meaning is slightly different from the future more probable. Instead of saying something about a specific event, about something that might happen, it is stating a general truth, an axiomatic truth. The subjunctive is appropriate because the truth of the statement is timeless.

    ἐὰν ἁμαρτάνω, ἔτι θεὸς ἀγαπᾷ με.
    If I sin, God still loves me.

You will notice that this example is the same as the one above, except that "might" was not used in the translation of the protasis and "loves" is present tense. This illustrates a problem in conditional sentences. Apart from the tense of the verb in the apodosis, only context can tell you if the speaker is making a specific statement or stating a general truth. If you feel that this sentence is making a general statement, then "may" or "might" would be inappropriate because the truth of the "if" clause is not in question.

Odds and Ends

31.16   **Negation**. The basic rule is that οὐ is used to negate a verb in the indicative while μή is used to negate everything else, including the subjunctive.

There is one specific construction using the subjunctive that needs to be stressed. The construction οὐ μή followed by the aorist subjunctive is a strong negation of a future situation, stronger than simply saying οὐ.[8] The two negatives do not negate each other; they strengthen the construction to say "No!" more emphatically. See the *Exegetical Insight* for an example.

31.17   Questions. There are three ways to ask a question.

- No indication is given as to the answer expected by the speaker.

- If the question begins with οὐ, the speaker expects an affirmative answer.[9]

    Διδάσκαλε, οὐ μέλει σοι ὅτι ἀπολλύμεθα; (Mark 4:38)
    Teacher, it is a concern to you that we are perishing, isn't it?

    The disciples were expecting Jesus to answer, "Yes, it is a concern."

- If the question begins with μή the speaker expects a negative answer.

    μὴ πάντες ἀπόστολοι; (1 Cor 12:29)
    All are not apostles, are they?

Contrary to the practice of many translations, if the Greek indicates the answer, so should your translation. Most translations translate the above as, "Are all apostles?" We have this same idiom in English, so our translation should also indicate the expected answer.

Summary

1. The subjunctive mood is used when a verb expresses a possibility, probability, exhortation, or axiomatic concept.

2. A verb in the subjunctive has no time significance. Its only significance is one of aspect. The present subjunctive is built on the present tense stem and indi-

---

8   To emphasize to his disciples that they would see the truth of his definition of discipleship in the Kingdom of God, Jesus says: Ἀμὴν λέγω ὑμῖν ὅτι εἰσίν τινες ὧδε τῶν ἑστηκότων οἵτινες οὐ μὴ γεύσωνται θανάτου ἕως ἂν ἴδωσιν τὴν βασιλείαν τοῦ θεοῦ ἐληλυθυῖαν ἐν δυνάμει. "Truly I say to you that there are some standing here who *will most assuredly not taste death* (οὐ μὴ γεύσωνται) until they see that the kingdom of God has come in power" (Mark 9:1).

9   Just because a question has an οὐ does not mean it expects an affirmative answer. καὶ ἔρχονται καὶ λέγουσιν αὐτῷ, Διὰ τί οἱ μαθηταὶ Ἰωάννου καὶ οἱ μαθηταὶ τῶν Φαρισαίων νηστεύουσιν, οἱ δὲ σοὶ μαθηταὶ οὐ νηστεύουσιν; (Mark 2:18). "And they come and say to him, 'Why do the disciples of John and the disciples of the Pharisees fast, but your disciples do not fast?'" Here the οὐ immediately precedes the verb and negates it. But when οὐ is indicating the expected answer, that answer is "Yes."

cates a continuous action. The aorist subjunctive is built on the unaugmented aorist tense stem and indicates an undefined action.

3.   The sign of the subjunctive is the lengthened connecting vowel. The endings are exactly the same in the aorist as in the present.

4.   Among many uses, the subjunctive is used in a hortatory comment (to which we add the helping phrase "Let us"), in clauses that begin with specific words like ἵνα indicating, among other things, purpose, and in conditional statements.

Signs of the Subjunctive

1.   Lengthened connecting vowel (ω/η).
2.   No augment in the aorist.
3.   ἵνα or ἄν clause

Vocabulary

λίθος, -ου, ὁ   stone (59; *λιθο)[10]

τοιοῦτος, -αύτη, -οῦτον   such, of such a kind (57; *τοιουτο; *τοιαυτη)

Total word count in the New Testament: 138,162

Number of words learned to date: 298

Number of word occurrences in this chapter: 116

Number of word occurrences to date: 108,182

Percent of total word count in the New Testament: 78.3%

Advanced Information

31.18   **Perfect subjunctive**. The perfect subjunctive occurs only ten times in the New Testament. All ten are forms of οἶδα. There are other examples of the perfect subjunctive but they are all periphrastic.[11] It denotes an action as completed with permanent results.

---

[10]   *Lithography* is a printing method that originally used a flat stone but now uses metal. *Lithomancy* is divination using stone.

[11]   Cf. Fanning, 396-7.

1 sg	εἰδῶ	1 Cor 13:2; 14:11
2 sg	εἰδῇς	1 Tim 3:15
3 sg	-	
1 pl	εἰδῶμεν	1 Cor 2:12
2 pl	εἰδῆτε	Mt 9:6; Mk 2:10; Lk 5:24; Eph 6:21; 1 Jn 2:29; 5:13
3 pl	-	

Chapter 32

Infinitive

Exegetical Insight

Infinitives often complete important ideas. No more important idea exists than the one Paul makes in 1 Corinthians 15:25. Here he says, "For it is necessary that he (Jesus) be reigning (βασιλεύειν) until he (God) has put all things in subjection under his (Jesus') feet." Now a Greek infinitive contains tense, something that is not clear in English infinitives. The tense in the case of this verse is a present tense, which describes a continuous action. So this present infinitive explains what is necessary about what God is in the process of doing through Jesus. (Remember that tense highlights type of action.) So Paul stresses that Jesus is in the process of ruling until the job of subjecting everything under his feet is complete. The remark about subjection is an allusion to Psalm 110:1, one of the New Testament's favorite Old Testament passages.

This idea is important because some think only of Jesus' rule as one anticipated in the future. There will be a total manifestation of that authority one day as the rest of 1 Corinthians 15 makes clear, but the process has already started in the second Adam, the one who reverses the presence of sin in the world and does so in each one of us daily as an expression of his authority to redeem us from the curse of sin. May his rule be manifest in us!

Darrell L. Bock

Overview

In this chapter we will learn that:

- the Greek infinitive is a verbal noun. It is not declined;
- it does not have a subject, but there will often be a word in the accusative functioning as if it were the subject;
- all infinitive morphemes, except for the present and second aorist active, end in αι;
- the infinitive has no time significance, only aspect: continuous; undefined; perfected;
- there are five main ways in which an infinitive is used.

English

32.1 An infinitive is a verbal noun, much like the participle is a verbal adjective. It is most easily recognized as a verb preceded by the word "to." "*To study* is my highest aspiration." In this case, the infinitive *to study* is the subject of the sentence. "I began *to sweat* when I realized finals were three weeks away." In this sentence, the infinitive *to sweat* is completing the action of the verb *began*.

Greek

32.2 The same is true of the infinitive in Greek, although here it is capable of somewhat wider use. The infinitive is a verbal noun. It is always indeclinable (which means it has no case), but is viewed as singular neuter. When it is preceded by a definite article, the article is always neuter singular and is declined according to the function of the infinitive. For example, if the infinitive is the subject, the article will be in the nominative.

An infinitive can have a direct object and adverbial modifiers. "To study *for a long time* brings one into a state of ecstasy." In this case, the prepositional phrase *for a long time* modifies the infinitive *to study*. An infinitive also has tense and voice, but this will be discussed below.

The infinitive has no person and no number!

32.3 **Subject**. Because an infinitive is not a finite[1] verbal form, it technically cannot have a subject. However, there is often a noun *in the accusative* that acts as if it were the subject of the infinitive. A parallel to this is the genitive absolute, where the noun or pronoun in the genitive acts as if it were the subject of the participle.[2]

If the infinitive has a direct object, it can sometimes become interesting to determine which word in the accusative is the "subject" and which is the direct object. Usually context will make it clear. As a general rule, the first accusative will be the "subject" and the second the direct object. βλέπειν αὐτὸν αὐτήν would usually mean, "he (αὐτόν) to see her (αὐτήν)." (βλέπειν is an infinitive.)

---

[1] A "finite" verbal form is one that is limited, specifically by a subject. In the sentence "Tom reads books," the verb *reads* is finite, limited. It does not apply to everyone, just the subject *Tom*.

Similarly, an "infinitive" (the "in-" negates the following word) is not limited by a subject; it is infinite, an infinitive.

[2] Technically, this accusative is called an "accusative of reference." If you were to read βλέπειν αὐτόν, this would be translated "to see with reference to him." αὐτόν behaves as if it were the subject of the infinitive.

Two exceptions to this are the verbs ἔξεστιν ("it is lawful") and παραγγέλλω ("I command") that take a "subject" in the dative. Verbs that take their direct object in the dative will take the "subject" of their infinitive in the dative as well.

32.4   **Form**. There are primarily five forms of the infinitive, built on stems from three tenses.

- The *present* infinitive is built on the present tense stem.

- The *aorist active/middle* infinitive is built on the aorist active tense stem (without the augment).

  The *aorist passive* infinitive is built on the aorist passive tense stem (without the augment).

- The *perfect active* infinitive is formed on the perfect active tense stem.

  The *perfect middle/passive* infinitive is formed on the perfect middle/passive tense stem.

Once again we would urge adoption of the terminology *continuous* infinitive, *undefined* infinitive, and *completed* infinitive.

	present	*1st aorist*	*2nd aorist*	*perfect*
active	ειν	σαι	ειν	ναι
middle	εσθαι	σασθαι	εσθαι	σθαι
passive	εσθαι	θηναι	ηναι	σθαι

In the paradigm below, the meanings are given for the aorist. If you wish to differentiate between the present and aorist, add "continue to" to your translation.

present active	λύειν	to loose
present middle	λύεσθαι	to loose for oneself
present passive	λύεσθαι	to be loosed
first aorist active	λῦσαι	to loose
first aorist middle	λύσασθαι	to loose, to loose for oneself
first aorist passive	λυθῆναι	to be loosed
second aorist active	λαβεῖν	to throw
second aorist middle	λαβέσθαι	to throw for oneself
second aorist passive	γραφῆναι	to be written

perfect active	λελυκέναι	to have loosed
perfect middle	λελύσθαι	to have loosed for oneself
perfect passive	λελύσθαι	to have been loosed

The aorist infinitive that is built on the second aorist stem looks just like the present except for the stem change (and the accent). Note that all the infinitives, except the present and second aorist active, end in αι.

Do not forget about the irregular contractions that occur with contract verbs in the present active infinitive. Alpha contracts form -ᾶν instead of the expected -αν, while omicron contract verbs form οῦν instead of οῖν.[3]

νικαειν ▸ νικαιν ▸ νικᾶν

πληροειν ▸ πληρουν ▸ πληροῦν

The present infinitive of εἰμί is εἶναι, "to be." It has no aorist form.

32.5   **Aspect.** As is the case in the participle and subjunctive, the infinitive has no time significance whatsoever. The only difference between the infinitive built on the present stem and that built on the aorist stem is one of aspect. The infinitive built on the present stem indicates a continuous action; the infinitive built on the aorist stem indicates an undefined action; the infinitive built on the perfect stem indicates a completed action with ongoing implications.

Due to the limitations of English, it is usually impossible to carry this significance across into English. You will probably use the present punctiliar form of the verb in your translation of all infinitives (e.g., "to see," "to eat").

To help enforce the significance of the aspect in your mind, you may at first want to use "continue" in your translation of the present infinitive. βλέπειν means "to continue to see," while βλέψαι means "to see." You certainly would not want to use this technique when producing a finished translation, but for now it is a good idea. But most importantly, in your studies and teaching you can always bring out the true significance of aspect.

32.6   **Negation.** Because the infinitive is not the indicative mood, it is negated by μή and not οὐ.

32.7   **Parsing.** The necessary elements for parsing the infinitive are tense, voice, "infinitive," lexical form, and inflected meaning.

βλέψαι. Aorist active infinitive, from βλέπω, meaning "to see."

---

3   This is because ειν is actually a contraction of εεν. When you contract αεεν and οεεν, you end with αν and ουν according to the usual rules.

32.8   **Deponent**. If a verb is deponent in a tense, its infinitive will be deponent in the same tense. The present deponent infinitive of ἔρχομαι is ἔρχεσθαι, meaning "to come."

Translation

32.9   **1. Substantive**. Because the infinitive is a verbal noun, it can perform any function that a substantive can. When used as a substantive, it will usually, but not always, be preceded by the definite article. Translate this construction using "to" and the verb. This is a common construction, and yet its translation can be quite idiomatic, so feel free not to go "word-for-word."

> τὸ ἐσθίειν ἐστὶν ἀγαθόν.
> *To eat* is good.

32.10   **2. Complementary infinitive**. A finite verb's meaning may be incomplete apart from some additional information. An infinitive is often used to complete that meaning.

For example, δεῖ ("it is necessary") requires an infinitive to complete its meaning: δεῖ ἐσθίειν ("It is necessary to eat."). When an infinitive is used this way it is called a "complementary infinitive," because the meaning of the infinitive complements the meaning of the verb.

The following five verbs will always be followed by a complementary infinitive. Translate the infinitive using "to" and the verb.

> δεῖ αὐτὴν ἐσθίειν.
> It is necessary for her *to eat*.
>
> ἔξεστιν ἐσθίειν αὐτῷ.
> It is lawful for him *to eat*.
>
> μέλλω ἐσθίειν.
> I am about *to eat*.
>
> δύναμαι ἐσθίειν.
> I am able *to eat*.
>
> ἄρχομαι ἐσθίειν.
> I am beginning *to eat*.

The complementary infinitive can be used with other verbs but less frequently (e.g., θέλω, "I wish"; κελεύω, "I command"; ὀφείλω, "I ought").

32.11   **3. Articular infinitive and preposition**. When the infinitive is preceded by the article, it is called an "articular infinitive." We have already seen how this infinitive can be used as a substantive. But when the articular infinitive is preceded by a preposition, there are specific rules of translation. These should be learned well because the construction is common.

The preposition will always precede the infinitive, never follow. The case of the definite article is determined by the preposition.

This is perhaps the most difficult use of the infinitive; it certainly is the most idiomatic. Any attempt to translate word for word must be abandoned because we have no construction like it in English. You must look at the phrase in Greek, see what it means in Greek, and then say the same thing in English. You should make a separate vocabulary card for each of the following possibilities.

Below are listed six common constructions, the two most common being εἰς and μετά. We have listed the preposition, the case of the article, and the key word/phrase that you should associate with that preposition.

1. διά (accusative) meaning *because* (indicating reason)

    διὰ τὸ βλέπειν αὐτόν.
    Because he sees.

    ὁ ᾿Ιησοῦς χαρήσεται διὰ τὸ βλέπειν αὐτὸν ὅτι ἡμεῖς ἀγαπῶμεν αὐτόν.
    Jesus will rejoice because he sees that we love him.

2. εἰς (accusative) meaning *in order that* (indicating purpose)

    εἰς τὸ βλέπειν αὐτόν.
    In order that he sees.

    καθίζω ἐν ἐκκλησίᾳ εἰς τὸ ἀκούειν με τὸν λόγον τοῦ θεοῦ.
    I sit in church in order that I might hear the word of God.

3. ἐν (dative) meaning *when/while* (indicating time)

    ἐν τῷ βλέπειν αὐτόν.
    When he sees.

    ὁ κύριος κρινεῖ ἡμᾶς ἐν τῷ ἔρχεσθαι αὐτὸν πάλιν.
    The Lord will judge us when he comes again.

4. μετά (accusative) meaning *after* (indicating time)

    μετὰ τὸ βλέπειν αὐτόν.
    After he sees.

    μετὰ τὸ βλέψαι τὸν ᾿Ιησοῦν τοὺς ἁμαρτωλούς, ἔκλαυσε.
    After Jesus saw the sinners, he wept.

5. πρό (genitive) meaning *before* (indicating time)

    πρὸ τοῦ βλέπειν αὐτόν.
    Before he sees.

    ὁ ᾿Ιησοῦς ἠγάπησεν ἡμᾶς πρὸ τοῦ γνῶναι ἡμᾶς αὐτόν.
    Jesus loved us before we knew him.

6.   πρός (accusative) meaning *in order that* (indicating purpose)

πρὸς τὸ βλέπειν αὐτόν.
In order that he sees.

κηρύσσομεν τὸν εὐαγγέλιον πρὸς τὸ βλέψαι ὑμᾶς τὴν ἀλήθειαν.
We proclaim the gospel so that you may see the truth.

There are two tricks that will help you translate the articular infinitive. The first is to remember the key words (listed above) associated with each preposition when used with an articular infinitive. The second is to use the phrase "the act of." For example, the key word associated with διά is *because*. What does διὰ τὸ βλέπειν αὐτόν mean? "Because of the act of seeing with reference to him." Sometimes it is necessary to translate in this stilted manner, to see what it means; then put it into proper English: "Because he sees."

32.12   **4. Purpose**. Another function of the infinitive is to express purpose, "in order that."

1.   Purpose can be expressed using the articular infinitive preceded by εἰς or πρός (discussed above).

2.   The articular infinitive with the article in the genitive (no preposition) can also express purpose.

ὁ Ἰησοῦς ἀπέθανον τοῦ εἶναι ἡμᾶς σὺν αὐτῷ εἰς τὸν αἰώνιον.
Jesus died *in order that we (may) be* with him forever.

3.   The infinitive all by itself (without a preposition or the article) can express purpose.

πορεύομαι νικᾶν.
I come *in order to conquer.*

32.13   **5. Result**. A common way of indicating the result of some action is to use a clause introduced by ὥστε. In this case ὥστε will not be followed by a finite verb as one might expect but by an infinitive. Because we have no similar use of the infinitive in English, we must translate this infinite with a finite verb.

ὁ Ἰησοῦς ἀγαπᾷ με ὥστε με ἀγαπᾶν αὐτόν.
Jesus loves me *which results in the fact that I love* him.

It is often extremely difficult to differentiate between "purpose" and "result."

Summary

1.   The Greek infinitive is a verbal noun. It is not declined, although it is considered singular neuter and any accompanying article will be declined.

2. Technically it does not have a subject, but there will often be a word in the accusative functioning as if it were the subject.

3. The basic forms are λύειν, λύεσθαι, λῦσαι, λύσασθαι, λυθῆναι, λελυκέναι, and λελῦσθαι. Note that all forms except the present active and second aorist active end in αι.

4. The infinitive has no time significance, only aspect. The present infinitive is built on the present tense stem and indicates a continuous action. The aorist infinitive is built on the unaugmented aorist tense stem and indicates an undefined action. The perfect infinitive is built on the perfect tense stem and indicates a perfected action.

5. There are five main ways in which an infinitive is used.

    a. Substantive.

    b. Complementary infinitive.

    c. Articular infinitive preceded by a preposition.
       - διά   because
       - εἰς   in order that
       - ἐν   when, while
       - μετά   after
       - πρό   before
       - πρός   in order that

    d. Purpose.
       - εἰς/πρός with an infinitive
       - Articular infinitive with the definite article in the genitive
       - Infinitive by itself

    e. Result, expressed by ὥστε with the infinitive. Translate the infinitive as a finite verb.

Vocabulary

δίκαιος, -αία, -αιον   right, just, righteous (79, *δικαιο/α)

μέλλω   I am about to (109, *μελλε)[4]
          (ἔμελλον or ἤμελλον), μελλήσω, -, -, -, -

Total word count in the New Testament:	138,162
Number of words learned to date:	300
Number of word occurrences in this chapter:	188
Number of word occurrences to date:	108,370
Percent of total word count in the New Testament:	78.44%

---

[4]   The second epsilon is lost in the present and imperfect tenses but remains in the future.

Advanced Information

32.14   **Indirect discourse**. *Direct discourse* is reporting what someone else said. Since it is your intention to report exactly what the other person said, you use quotation marks. *The teacher said, "Hand in the tests!"*

If you intend to repeat the basic idea of what someone else said, while not claiming to use exactly the same words, you use *indirect discourse* (also called *indirect speech*). Instead of quotation marks, you use the connecting word *that. He said that he wanted to study some more.*

In Greek, indirect discourse is usually expressed with ὅτι followed by a verb in the indicative. However, indirect discourse can also be expressed with an infinitive.

32.15   A rather peculiar thing happens to the tense of the English verb in indirect discourse, and most of us are probably not aware of it. All of the following, except for the last paragraph, pertains to English grammar. When we are done with the English grammar, we will then see that Greek behaves differently.

John says, "I *want* to eat." When you tell someone else what John said with indirect discourse, if the main verb of the sentence is present ("says"), then the verb in the indirect discourse retains the same tense as the original saying. "John says that he *wants* to eat." If John originally said, "I *wanted* to eat," we would say, "John says that he *wanted* to eat."

However, when the main verb of the sentence is a past tense (e.g., "said"), then we shift the tense of the verb in the indirect discourse back one step in time.

For example, if the tense of the original saying is present, in indirect speech it will be in the past.

    Original (present):   "I *want* to eat."
    Indirect speech: John said that he *wanted* to eat.

If it originally were past, then in indirect speech it will be past perfect.

    Original (past):   "I *wanted* to eat."
    Indirect speech: John said that he *had wanted* to eat.

If it originally were future, then we use the subjunctive mood ("would").

    Original (future):   "I *will want* to eat."
    Indirect speech: John said that he *would want* to eat.

If the original were past perfect, then in indirect discourse it would remain the same since English has no tense "farther back" in time.

    Original (past perfect):   "I *had wanted* to eat."
    Indirect speech: John said that he *had wanted* to eat.

The point of all this is that *whereas English switches the tense and sometimes the mood of the verb in indirect speech, Greek does not.* The tense and mood of the verb in Greek indirect discourse will always be the same tense and mood as the verb in the original statement. Of course, to make a good translation you must switch the tense and mood of your English translation.

Chapter 33

Imperative

Exegetical Insight

There is no more forceful way in the Greek language to tell someone to do something than a simple imperative–particularly the second person imperative. Especially when such a command is given regarding a specific situation, the one giving that command sees himself as an authority figure. He expects those addressed to do exactly as he has ordered.

On his third missionary journey, the apostle Paul expended much energy in attempting to get the churches he had organized to participate in the collection "for the poor among the saints in Jerusalem" (Rom 15:26). When he addressed this issue in 1 Corinthians 16:1-4, he simply told the Corinthians to get busy regularly collecting money for this cause, using the second person imperative ποιήσατε (v. 1), followed by a third person imperative τιθέτω (v. 2). He gives no other reason than this is what he had also "told" (διέταξα) the churches in Galatia to do.

Paul returns to the same issue in 2 Corinthians 8 and 9. But there one is struck by the numerous ways he uses in order to try to motivate the Corinthians to participate in the collection. Most surprising is the fact that in these thirty-nine verses, there is only *one* imperative (ἐπιτελέσατε, 2 Cor 8:11). The other places where the *NIV* inserts an imperative (8:7,24; 9:7) are substantially weaker forms of expressing an imperatival idea. Such a radical shift in Paul's approach strongly suggests that he had lost much of his authority in Corinth, mostly because of the influence of his opponents. Other elements in this letter bear out this same factor.

Undoubtedly one main reason why Paul was losing his influence in Corinth was because he was trying to run the church from a distance (i.e., from Ephesus). That simply cannot be done. Unless pastors consistently take the necessary time to nurture good, wholesome relationships with their parishioners, they risk losing their ability to motivate the church to pay attention to their preaching of God's Word and to live the Christian life.

Verlyn Verbrugge

Overview

In this chapter we will learn that:

- the imperative mood is used when making a command (e.g., "Eat!");

302

- the imperative occurs in the present and aorist tenses, and its only significance is its aspect;

- there are five different types of prohibitions using the indicative, imperative, and subjunctive.

English

33.1 The verb is in the imperative mood when it is making a command. In English, it is the second person form of the indicative, usually with an exclamation mark as the sentence's punctuation. "Study!" The understood subject of this sentence is "You."

The English imperative is usually not inflected. There are other words that we can add to the sentence to strengthen or further define the intent of the imperative. "Go quickly!"

Greek

33.2 The imperative is basically the same in Greek as it is in English. It is the mood of command. However, as is the case with participles and infinitives, the imperative has a greater range of meaning in Greek. It has second and third person, and the aspect is significant. However, it does not indicate time and there is no first person.

33.3 **Person**. In English all imperatives are second person; in Greek there are second and third person imperatives. Because there is no English equivalent to a third person imperative, your translation must be a little idiomatic. βλέπε (second person singular) means "(You) look!" βλεπέτω (third person singular) means "Let him look!" or "He must look!" The key words "let" or "must," and a pronoun supplied from the person of the verb ("him"), can be added to make sense of the construction.

33.4 **Aspect**. The imperative built on the present tense stem is called the *present* imperative and indicates a continuous action. The imperative built on the aorist tense stem (without augment) is called the *aorist* imperative and indicates an undefined action. There is no time significance with the imperative. Once again we urge the adoption of the terminology "continuous imperative" and "undefined imperative."

Sometimes, to get the significance of the aspect into English, you must use the key word "continually" in your translation of the present imperative, although this is somewhat stilted English: "continually eat."

Form

33.5   There are primarily two imperatives in Greek, present and aorist.[1] The imperative morphemes in the present active and aorist active are identical, as they are in the present middle and aorist middle. The morphemes in the aorist passive are identical to the aorist active.

The second singular forms must be memorized; the remaining are regular. The translation is the same for both imperatives.[2]

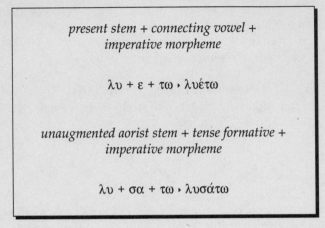

present stem + connecting vowel +
imperative morpheme

λυ + ε + τω ‣ λυέτω

unaugmented aorist stem + tense formative +
imperative morpheme

λυ + σα + τω ‣ λυσάτω

33.6   The second person singular imperatives seem to be irregular.[3] They should just be memorized. The other forms are delightfully regular.

	active and aorist passive	mid/pas
2 sg	-	-
3 sg	τω	σθω
2 pl	τε	σθε
3 pl	τωσαν	σθωσαν

Think of the σθ in the middle/passive (e.g., σθε) as replacing the tau in the active (τε).

---

1   There are four perfect imperatives in the New Testament; cf. §33.17.

2   If you want to differentiate between the present and the aorist, use "go on" or "continue" for the present. We list the translation of the aorist in the paradigm.

3   Of course, they are not; cf. *MBG*, §70.

	present	first aorist	translation

active

| 2 sg | λῦε | λῦσον | (You) Loose! |
| 3 sg | λυέτω | λυσάτω | Let him loose! |

| 2 pl | λύετε | λύσατε | (You) loose! |
| 3 pl | λυέτωσαν | λυσάτωσαν | Let them loose! |

middle

| 2 sg | λύου | λῦσαι | (You) loose for yourself! |
| 3 sg | λυέσθω | λυσάσθω | Let him loose for himself! |

| 2 pl | λύεσθε | λύσασθε | (You) loose! |
| 3 pl | λυέσθωσαν | λυσάσθωσαν | Let them loose! |

passive

| 2 sg | λύου | λύθητι | (You) be loosed! |
| 3 sg | λυέσθω | λυθήτω | Let him be loosed! |

| 2 pl | λύεσθε | λύθητε | (You) be loosed! |
| 3 pl | λυέσθωσαν | λυθήτωσαν | Let them be loosed! |

If you can remember these forms, the imperative will be simple. In the present be sure to add the connecting vowel epsilon, and in the aorist drop the augment but keep the tense formative σα.

33.7 Confusing forms

- Do not be fooled by the imperative second person plural (active and middle) endings (ετε, εσθε; σατε, σασθε). They are the same as the indicative. In the present, context will usually decide whether a particular form is a statement or a command. In the aorist, there will be no augment.

  For example, Jesus says to his disciples, "ἔχετε πίστιν θεοῦ (Mark 11:22)." Is ἔχετε an indicative in which case Jesus is making a statement, or is it an imperative in which case Jesus is telling them to have faith? Interestingly there is a textual variant here: some manuscripts add εἰ before ἔχετε πίστιν θεοῦ, "If you have faith in God...", making ἔχετε an indicative.[4]

- The ending of λύου (second singular passive) looks just like the second person singular middle ending of the imperfect indicative (without the augment, ἐλύου).

- The ending of λῦσαι makes it look like it is the aorist active infinitive.

33.8   **Second aorist**. The aorist imperative that is built on a second aorist stem uses the same endings as the present imperative. The only difference is the tense stem. The second aorist passive imperative looks just like the first aorist passive except for the absence of the theta.

	active	*middle*	*passive*
2 sg	λάβε	γενοῦ	γράφητι
3 sg	λαβέτω	γενέσθω	γραφήτω
2 pl	λάβετε	γένεσθε	γράφητε
3 pl	λαβέτωσαν	γενέσθωσαν	γραφήτωσαν

33.9   **Contract verbs**. The contractions with the imperative are all regular. Of course, there will be contractions only in the present. The present active is as follows. See the Appendix for the full paradigms.

	α contract	*ε contract*	*o contract*
2 sg	ἀγάπα	ποίει	πλήρου
3 sg	ἀγαπάτω	ποιείτω	πληρούτω
2 pl	ἀγαπᾶτε	ποιεῖτε	πληροῦτε
3 pl	ἀγαπάτωσαν	ποιείτωσαν	πληρούτωσαν

33.10   **εἰμί**. To form the imperative of εἰμί, normal endings are added to the root *εσ. εἰμί has no aorist form.

2 sg	ἴσθι
3 sg	ἔστω
2 pl	ἔστε
3 pl	ἔστωσαν

---

[4]   See the difficult translation of John 14:1-2.

33.11 **Deponent**. If a verb is deponent, so also will be its imperative. The present imperative of ἔρχομαι is ἔρχου, meaning "Come!"

33.12 **Parsing**. When parsing an imperative, we suggest you list the tense, voice, "imperative," person, number, lexical form, definition of inflected meaning.

ποιείτω. Third person singular, present active imperative, from ποιέω, meaning "Let him do!"

Meaning

33.13 **Aspect**. As has been the case in all non-indicative moods, the only significance of the imperative is its aspect. It has no time significance. Because of the differences between Greek and English, it will often be impossible to carry this over into English. At first you may want to use "continue" or "keep on" in your translation of the present imperative. For example, βλέπε (present) means "Keep on looking!" while βλέψον (aorist) means "Look!"

33.14 **Command**. The imperative mood is used when a verb expresses a command. It is also used to encourage or ask someone to do something.[5]

Prohibition and Other Types of Negation

33.15 In Greek there are several different ways to say, "No!" The beauty of the constructions is that each one has its own slightly different nuance, information available to those who understand Greek. Unfortunately these nuances are seldom carried over into the translations. In the *Advanced Information* we fine tune our understanding of the significance of the present and aorist imperatives used in prohibitions.

1. *οὐ with the indicative*, or μή with a non-indicative form (except those below). This is the simple negation. Included here is the use of οὐ with the future indicative. "Thou shalt not covet."

2. *μή plus the present imperative*. Because it is a present imperative, you know that the action being prohibited is a continuous action.

3. *μή plus the aorist imperative*. Because it is an aorist imperative, you know that the action being prohibited is an undefined action.

---

[5] This is called the "Imperative of Entreaty." You do not "command" God to do something; you "entreat" him, both in English and in Greek, e.g., "Give us this day our daily bread." ("Give" is an imperative.)

4. *μή plus the aorist subjunctive.* This construction says "No!" more strongly than #1 above.[6]

5. *οὐ μή plus the aorist subjunctive.* When Greek uses a double negative, one does not negate the other as in English. The οὐ and μή combine in a very firm, "This will certainly not occur!" This is stronger than #4 above and refers to a future situation.[7]

Summary

1. The imperative is the form of the verb used for commands.

2. It occurs in the second person (like English) and the third (in which case you use the key word "Let" and supply a pronoun).

3. The imperative built on the present tense stem is called the present imperative and indicates a continuous action. The imperative built on the aorist tense stem (without augment) is called the aorist imperative and indicates a simple action. There is no time significance with the imperative.

4. You must memorize the second person singular. The remaining forms are quite regular: τω, τε, τωσαν; σθω, σθε, σθωσαν.

5. The difference between aspect is difficult to carry over into English. You can use "continue" in the translation of the present.

6. There are five different kinds of prohibitions using the indicative, imperative, and subjunctive.

   • οὐ with indicative verbs, and μή with non-indicative (excluding those below).

   • μή plus the present imperative. Prohibits a continuous action.

   • μή plus the aorist imperative. Prohibits an undefined action.

   • μή plus the aorist subjunctive. "No!"

   • οὐ μή plus the aorist subjunctive. "This will certainly not occur!"

---

6   Some grammarians argue that #1 and #4 have the same force.

7   There is one other way to express a prohibition (which actually is a negative wish). It uses the optative mood. Fifteen times in the New Testament Paul uses the expression μὴ γένοιτο, which is often translated "God forbid!" For example, Paul asks the rhetorical question, "Should we continue in sin in order that grace might abound? God forbid!" (Rom 6:1-2). On the optative mood see *Advanced Information* in chapter 35.

Vocabulary

ἀπόλλυμι[8]

active: I destroy, kill (90; ἀπ᾽ + *ὀλ)[9]
middle: I perish, die
(ἀπώλλυον), ἀπολέσω, ἀπώλεσα, ἀπόλωλα, -, -

ἀπολύω

I release (66; ἀπό + *λυ)
(ἀπέλυον), ἀπολύσω, ἀπέλυσα, -, ἀπολέλυμαι,
ἀπελύθην

εἴτε

if, whether (65; particle)

Total word count in the New Testament:	138,162
Number of words learned to date:	303
Number of word occurrences in this chapter:	221
Number of word occurrences to date:	108,591
Percent of total word count in the New Testament:	78.6%

Advanced Information

33.16 **Recent research on prohibitions**. For many years it has been argued
that the force of the present imperative has the basic meaning, "Stop
doing what you are presently doing!" while the force of the aorist imperative is "Don't start!" Moulton[10] recounts a discussion with Davidson
who was learning modern Greek and thought he had discovered the difference between the continuous and the undefined imperative in a prohibition. His friend spoke modern Greek, and one day he was yelling at
a dog to stop barking. He used the continuous imperative. "Stop barking!" Davidson went to Plato's *Apology* and reasoned that what is true in
modern Greek was also true in Classial Greek. The present tense prohibition is used to prohibit an action already in process. This has been carried over into Koine Greek.

---

[8] The stem of this verb is *ὀλ. It belongs to a class of verbs that add νυ to the root to form
the present tense stem, but the nu assimilates to a lambda (cf. *MBG*, §13). *ὀλ + νυ ›
ολλυ › ὄλλυμι. This is why there is a single lambda in the other tenses.

Because ἀπόλλυμι is a compound verb the alpha does not augment, but the omicron
does.

In the present tense this verb follows the athematic conjugation (chapter 34). In the
other tenses it follows the thematic conjugation we have been learning so far.

[9] *Apollyon*, from Ἀπολλύων, is the destroying angel in Rev 9:11. On the stem see *MBG*,
309.

[10] *A Grammar of New Testament Greek* (T & T Clark, 1985) 3rd edition, 1:122.

However, it is currently being questioned whether this is accurate.[11] Our position is that a prohibition with the present tense is prohibiting a continuous action while a prohibition with the aorist in prohibiting an undefined action. The neighbor was telling the dog to stop its continual barking.

Following Fanning, we also hold that the present tense prohibition tends to be used for "attitudes and conduct" ("general precept") while the aorist tends to be used for "specific cases" ("specific command").[12]

This has tremendously important ramifications for exegesis. For example, Paul tells Timothy to have nothing to do with silly myths, using a present imperative (παραιτοῦ; 1 Tim 4:7). If the present imperative commands cessation from an action currently under way, this means Timothy was participating in the myths. This creates a picture of Timothy that is irreconcilable with his mission at Ephesus and what we know of him elsewhere. But if a present imperative does not carry this meaning, then Paul is stating a command regarding a "general precept" that is continuous in nature–continually stay away from the myths–and is saying nothing about Timothy's current involvement, or non-involvement, in the Ephesian myths.

33.17   **Perfect imperative.** There are four perfect imperatives in the New Testament.

πεφίμωσο	φιμόω	Mark 4:39
ἔρρωσθε	ῥώννυμι	Acts 15:29
ἴστε	οἶδα	Eph 5:5; James 1:19

---

[11]   See the discussion in Fanning (325-388) and Wallace.

[12]   327; citing *Bl-D*, §335. Fanning adds, "The present pictures an occurrence from an internal perspective, focusing on the course or internal details of the occurrence but with no focus on the end-points, while the aorist views it from an external perspective, seeing the occurrence as a whole from beginning to end without focus on the internal details which may be involved" (p. 388).

Chapter 34

μι Verbs

Active Indicative of δίδωμι

Exegetical Insight

The imperfect (chapter 21) form of the verb is usually described as having reference to continued action in past time (*I was loosing*) in contrast to the aorist form that denotes simple past (*I loosed*). But the Greek imperfect may have other shades of meaning that are not always easy to establish and that may depend largely upon context.

One of these variations is known as the *inceptive imperfect*, which is found frequently in the New Testament. In Mark 1:21, for example, the *RSV* reads, "Jesus went into the synagogue and *began* to teach." This seems to be a natural reading of the text.

In other places this is not immediately evident but might perhaps be intended. Luke's "Emmaus Road" resurrection narrative is a case in point. The two disciples of Jesus who were returning to Emmaus after their Passover visit to Jerusalem were joined by an apparent stranger. In the ensuing conversation they communicated the deep hopes they once had concerning Jesus and his significant role in their religious tradition.

The usual translation of Luke 24:21 is, "We had hoped (ἠλπίζομεν) that he was the one who was going to redeem Israel"(*RSV*). This suggests to the reader that these disciples once held such an opinion but that the recent events that led to Jesus' death now ruled out such a possibility. However, if in fact what we have here is the inceptive imperfect then the text could be translated, "We were beginning to hope that he was the one who was going to redeem Israel."

We often represent the contemporaries of Jesus as people who had a clear understanding of his message and mission. Here there is pause for thought. Even with such close contact the entire story is not self evident. The disciples had a glimmer of insight–but more was needed to bring that to a firm faith.

E. Margaret Howe

Overview

In this chapter we will learn:

- a different category of verbs that, especially in the present, are formed differently;
- the five rules that govern their formation.

English

34.1   There is nothing remotely like μι verbs in English.

Greek

34.2   So far, the endings used by verbs have all been basically the same. Due to contractions and consonantal changes, these endings have sometimes looked a little different, but for the most part they have been the same. The first person singular active ends in omega, and most of the tenses use connecting vowels. All the forms we know are said to belong to the *thematic conjugation* because of the use of the thematic vowel, or what we have called the "connecting vowel."

The only two variations we have seen were slight. In the third person plural, perfect active indicative we saw that some verbs have κασι(ν) while others have καν. And, of course, the verb εἰμί seems to follow its own rules.

34.3   Actually there is another conjugation that goes by several names. It is sometimes called the *athematic*[1] *conjugation* because it does not use a thematic vowel. At other times it is called the *μι conjugation*, or *μι verbs*, because the lexical form ends not in omega (λύω) but in μι (δίδωμι, "I give").

There is good news and bad news about these verbs. The bad news is that their forms change so drastically that they can become almost unrecognizable. The good news is that there are only very few of them. The bad news is that these few μι verbs are common. The good news is that most of the changes occur only in the present tense.

Like declensions, the differences do not affect the meaning of the words, only their form. It does not matter whether δίδωμι was formed as a μι

---

[1]   The English word "athematic" is a compound of the Greek alpha privative (much like the prefixes "un-" ["unlikely"] or "ir-" ["irregular"] in English) with the noun "thematic," which refers to the use of a thematic vowel. Hence, "athematic" means "without a thematic vowel."

verb or as a thematic verb (δίδω, which is not a real word). It would still mean, "I give."

Actually, εἰμί is a μι verb, but it is so different from the regular μι verbs that the comparison is not helpful.

34.4   There are two ways to learn the forms of μι verbs. The first is to memorize all of them, but this is nearly impossible because the forms are so varied and unusual. The second is a much better approach. If you memorize the five basic rules below, you can figure out what the different inflected forms mean when you see them. This is easier and in the long run better since memorizing another 330 forms is difficult.

The only disadvantage of learning μι verbs this way is that you will not have the security of knowing the full paradigm. But even those people who use Greek regularly have trouble in reproducing the μι verb paradigms from rote memory. It simply is not necessary. It is much better to learn five rules and concentrate on recognition.

There is something else that helps us learn μι verbs. While μι verbs are common, they do not occur in many forms. If you memorized the complete paradigm, you would be learning hundreds of forms that never occur in the New Testament. So why learn them?

34.5   **Four classes**. μι verbs are classified by their stem vowel. δίδωμι has an o-class vowel for its stem vowel (*δο), and all other μι verbs with an o-class vowel follow the same pattern as δίδωμι. This is like contract verbs in which all alpha contracts inflect the same way. In this chapter we will learn the pattern of δίδωμι. The other vowel classes are taught in the next chapter.

The other three classes are the alpha (*στα ‣ ἵστημι), epsilon (*θε ‣ τίθημι), and upsilon (*δεικνυ ‣ δείκνυμι). These three classes are discussed in the next chapter. What is nice about μι verbs is that if you know one pattern you know them all. In other words, whatever δίδωμι does in the future, τίθημι will also do in the future, although the stem vowel will be an eta instead of omega.

The Rules

34.6   **Rule One:** *μι verbs reduplicate their initial stem letter to form the present, and separate the reduplicated consonant with an iota.*

The root of δίδωμι is *δο. To form the present tense stem the initial delta is reduplicated, separated with an iota, and the personal ending μι is added (see rule three below). In the present singular the omicron lengthens to omega (rule 4).

δο ‣ διδο ‣ διδω ‣ δίδωμι

It is therefore essential that you always memorize the root of a μι verb along with its lexical form. As always, they are listed in the vocabulary section. The only time you will see the reduplication with the iota is in the present and imperfect. As we have already learned, the different tenses are not formed from the present tense stem but from the verbal root.

For example, parse δώσω. If you are working from the present tense form you will not be able to. But if you recognize that the actual verb is *δο, then this is clearly the first person singular future and is regular (with a lengthened stem vowel; rule 4).

δω + σ + ω ‣ δώσω

If you reduplicate the verbal root to form the present tense stem, how can you tell the difference between the present and the perfect? Think about it. Right. The perfect will also have reduplication, but there the vowel separating the reduplicated consonant is an epsilon, just like in the thematic conjugation. *δο ‣ δεδο ‣ δέδωκα.

	present	aorist	perfect
1 sg	δίδωμι	ἔδωκα	δέδωκα
2 sg	δίδως	ἔδωκας	δέδωκας
3 sg	δίδωσι(ν)	ἔδωκε(ν)	δέδωκε(ν)
1 pl	δίδομεν	ἐδώκαμεν	δεδώκαμεν
2 pl	δίδοτε	ἐδώκατε	δεδώκατε
3 pl	διδόασι(ν)	ἔδωκαν	δέδωκαν

34.7   **Rule Two:** *μι verbs do not ordinarily use a connecting (i.e., "thematic") vowel in the indicative.* The personal ending is added directly to the stem.

δι + δο + μεν ‣ δίδομεν.

A connecting vowel is used in the imperfect singular and future. (See the chart at §34.11.)

34.8   **Rule Three:** *μι verbs employ three different personal endings in the present active.* Compare the following chart of the present active indicative.

	μι verbs		thematic conjugation	
1 sg	δίδωμι	μι	λύω	-
2 sg	δίδως	ς	λύεις	ς
3 sg	δίδωσι(ν)	σι	λύει	ι
1 pl	δίδομεν	μεν	λύομεν	μεν
2 pl	δίδοτε	τε	λύετε	τε
3 pl	διδόασι(ν)	ασι	λύουσι(ν)	νσι

As you can see, μι verbs use the same endings as the thematic conjugation in three places, δίδως, δίδομεν, and δίδοτε. But in the other three places the endings are different: δίδωμι; δίδωσι(ν); διδόασι(ν). These must simply be memorized.

However, the present active is the only place that μι verbs use different endings. In all other tenses, they use the same endings as the thematic conjugation. This does not mean they will look absolutely identical (although in most places they do); it means that if you have been learning the true personal endings, there is nothing more to learn. For example, in the present middle/passive the paradigm is as follows.

	μι verbs		thematic conjugation	
1 sg	δίδομαι	μαι	λύομαι	μαι
2 sg	δίδοσαι	σαι	λύῃ	σαι
3 sg	δίδοται	ται	λύεται	ται
1 pl	διδόμεθα	μεθα	λυόμεθα	μεθα
2 pl	δίδοσθε	σθε	λύεσθε	σθε
3 pl	δίδονται	νται	λύονται	νται

Even though the second person singular looks a little unusual, as we learned with the perfect, this is the real form of the personal ending; it has undergone contractions in most of the thematic forms because the sigma drops out.[2]

---

[2]   It does not drop out in the athematic conjugation because it is not preceded by a connecting vowel and is therefore not intervocalic.

34.9   **Rule Four:** *the stem vowel of μι verbs can lengthen, shorten, or drop out (ablaut).* Although there are rules governing when the stem vowel is long or short, or has dropped out, all that we are concerned with is recognition; therefore these rules are just burdensome. You do not have to know when they shorten; you just have to recognize that they do.

For example, in the present active paradigm the vowel is long in the singular (δίδωμι) but short in the plural (δίδομεν). In the middle/passive it is always short. Take the form δώσω. It does not really matter whether you see the form δώσω or δόσω. Once you recognize that the verbal root is *δο, δώσω could only be one form: future.

See the paradigm in §34.11 if you are curious about the length of the stem vowel.

34.10   **Rule Five:** *Most of the μι verbs use κα as their tense formative in the aorist.* These are called "kappa aorists." Compare the paradigm for the aorist active.

	μι verbs	*thematic conjugation*
1 sg	ἔδωκα	ἔλυσα
2 sg	ἔδωκας	ἔλυσας
3 sg	ἔδωκε(ν)	ἔλυσε(ν)
1 pl	ἐδώκαμεν	ἐλύσαμεν
2 pl	ἐδώκατε	ἐλύσατε
3 pl	ἔδωκαν	ἔλυσαν

Everything is identical except for the tense formative. But how can you tell the difference between the aorist of a μι verb and the perfect of a verb in the thematic conjugation that also uses κα as its tense formative? Right. The perfect has reduplication (with an epsilon separating the reduplicated consonants). ἔδωκα vs. λέλυκα.

34.11   **δίδωμι in the indicative (active).** Concentrate on recognition.

	present	*imperfect*	*future*	*aorist*	*perfect*
1 sg	δίδωμι	ἐδίδουν	δώσω	ἔδωκα	δέδωκα
2 sg	δίδως	ἐδίδους	δώσεις	ἔδωκας	δέδωκας
3 sg	δίδωσι(ν)	ἐδίδου	δώσει	ἔδωκε(ν)	δέδωκε(ν)

1 pl	δίδομεν	ἐδίδομεν	δώσομεν	ἐδώκαμεν	δεδώκαμεν
2 pl	δίδοτε	ἐδίδοτε	δώσετε	ἐδώκατε	δεδώκατε
3 pl	διδόασι(ν)	ἐδίδοσαν	δώσουσι(ν)	ἔδωκαν	δέδωκαν

In the imperfect singular, the endings are formed with a connecting vowel. In the future they are identical to the forms in the thematic conjugation.

To see the indicative middle and passive as well as non-indicative forms, check the Appendix.

Summary

1. μι verbs reduplicate their initial stem letter to form the present and separate the reduplicated consonant with an iota. It is therefore essential that you always memorize the root of a μι verb along with its lexical form.

2. μι verbs do not ordinarily use a connecting vowel in the indicative ("athematic").

3. μι verbs employ three different personal endings in the present active indicative: δίδωμι; δίδωσι(ν); διδόασι(ν).

4. The stem vowel of μι verbs can lengthen, shorten, or drop out. It is not so important to know when this will happen, but merely to recognize that it does.

5. Most of the μι verbs use κα for the tense formative in the aorist.

Let's Practice

Let's look at several inflected forms and see how easy it is to apply the rules.[3]

δώσετε   We have the bare verbal root (*δο) without augment, reduplication, or κα. It can only be a future: second person plural.

ἐδίδους   The reduplication with an iota shows it is the present tense stem; the augment confirms that this is an imperfect. Second person singular.

ἔδωκα   The simple verbal root plus augment and tense formative κα means this must be aorist. First person singular.

δίδωσιν   The reduplicated stem with an iota and without an augment confirms this is a present. Third person singular.[4]

---

3   A colleague once suggested the following mnemonic to help remember the different tense stems. It requires an understanding of "perfection" in which the "end goal" of life is death. "Do (δω) is past, did (διδ) is present, dead (δεδ) is perfect."

4   It could also be subjunctive, but that is discussed in the next chapter.

δέδωκε   The reduplication may suggest present, but notice that the interven-
           ing vowel is an epsilon. This must therefore be a perfect, third per-
           son singular.

Vocabulary

δίδωμι   I give (out), entrust, give back, put   (415; *δο)[5]
                                (ἐδίδουν) δώσω, ἔδωκα, δέδωκα, δέδομαι, ἐδόθην

ἔθνος, -ους, τό   nation (162, *ἔθνες)[6]
                                the Gentiles (plural)

λοιπός, -ή, -όν   adjective: remaining (55; *λοιπο/η)
                                noun: (the) rest
                                adverb: for the rest, henceforth

Μωϋσῆς, -έως, ὁ   Moses (80)[7]

παραδίδωμι   I entrust, hand over, betray (119; παρά + *δο)
                                (παρεδίδουν), παραδώσω, παρέδωκα,
                                παραδέδωκα, παραδέδομαι, παρεδόθην

πίπτω   I fall (90; *πετ)[8]
                                (ἔπιπτον), πεσοῦμαι, ἔπεσον or ἔπεσα,[9] πέπτωκα,
                                -, -

ὑπάρχω   I am, exist (60; *ὑπ’ + *ἀρχ)
                                (ὑπῆρχον), -, -, -, -, -
                                τά ὑπάρχοντα: one’s belongings

Total word count in the New Testament: 138,162
Number of words learned to date: 310
Number of word occurrences in this chapter: 981
Number of word occurrences to date: 109,572
Percent of total word count in the New Testament: 79.31%

---

5   An *antidote* (ἀντί + δοτος) is something given to work against something else, such as
    poison.

6   *Ethnic.*

7   Μωϋσῆς has an irregular declension pattern: Μωϋσῆς, Μωϋσέως, Μωϋσεῖ, Μωϋσῆν.

8   The verbal root loses its stem vowel epsilon in the present and the stem is reduplicat-
    ed, even though it is not a μι verb (*πετ › πτ › πιπτ + ω › πίπτω). The tau drops out before
    the sigma in the future and aorist but remains in the perfect active.

9   Has both a second and a first aorist.

Chapter 35

Additional μι Verbs, and Non-Indicative Forms

(ἵστημι, τίθημι, δείκνυμι)

Exegetical Insight

In the doxology at the end of Romans 11 (v. 36), Paul spells out three distinct theological concepts as he discusses the relationship between God and all things. His use of three different Greek prepositions (chapter 8) shows his structure distinctly, and he is relying on the specific differences in meaning among the three prepositions to convey his message. This kind of precision and exactness can be lost in English translations.

> ἐξ αὐτοῦ καὶ δι' αὐτοῦ καὶ εἰς αὐτὸν τὰ πάντα·
> αὐτῷ ἡ δόξα εἰς τοὺς αἰῶνας· ἀμήν.

1. All things come *out of* (ἐξ) him in that he is the *source* or *origin* of all things.
2. All things come *through* (δι') him in that he is the *agent* or *guide* of all things.
3. All things come *unto* or *to* (εἰς) him in that he is the ultimate *goal* of all things.

Glory be to God, our Creator, Sustainer, and Exalted Lord, the One who is the source, guide, and goal of all things!

Deborah Gill

Overview

In this chapter we will learn that:

- what was true of δίδωμι is also true of the other μι verbs;
- the secret is to watch what happens to the verbal root of δίδωμι, and see that the same types of changes occur to the roots of the other μι verbs.

Greek

35.1   In the previous chapter we learned the essentials of μι verbs and how the rules apply to μι verbs with a stem vowel of omicron (δίδωμι) in the

319

indicative. All that remains is to see that what is true of δίδωμι is also true of the other μι verbs whose stem vowel is alpha (ἵστημι), epsilon (τίθημι), or upsilon (δείκνυμι). We will also look at some of the non-indicative forms of δίδωμι.

35.2   In the following chart of the present active indicative you can see the similarity among the different μι verbs. They use the same endings. They reduplicate to form the present tense stem (although that reduplication is hidden in ἵστημι and absent in δείκνυμι). And what happens to the stem vowel in δίδωμι also happens to the other stem vowels even though they are different vowels (except for δείκνυμι, which stays the same).

	*στα	*θε	*δο	*δεικνυ
1 sg	ἵστημι	τίθημι	δίδωμι	δείκνυμι
2 sg	ἵστης	τίθης	δίδως	δεικνύεις
3 sg	ἵστησι(ν)	τίθησι(ν)	δίδωσι(ν)	δείκνυσι (ν)
1 pl	ἵσταμεν	τίθεμεν	δίδομεν	δείκνυμεν
2 pl	ἵστατε	τίθετε	δίδοτε	δείκνυτε
3 pl	ἱστᾶσι(ν)	τιθέασι(ν)	διδόασι(ν)	δεικνύασι(ν)

The stem of ἵστημι is *στα. When it reduplicates, the reduplicated sigma drops out and is replaced by a rough breathing.

> στα ▸ σιστα ▸ ἵστημι

Except for its personal endings, δείκνυμι behaves more like a thematic verb.

35.3   The most effective thing to do at this point is to look through the μι verb paradigms in the Appendix. You can see all the forms of δίδωμι and the other μι verbs. Look at the patterns. See how the rules are put into effect. Concentrate on recognition. You do not need to know if the stem vowel is long or short; you just need to recognize that it varies and that it is not significant for parsing.

35.4   In Koine Greek, μι verbs were slowly being replaced by the thematic conjugation. As a result, μι verbs sometimes occur in the athematic and at other times as a "regular" thematic form with no difference in meaning. For example, both ἵστημι and ἱστάνω occur.[1]

Non-Indicative Forms of δίδωμι

35.5 **Subjunctive.** The non-indicative forms of μι verbs are even easier to identify than the indicative forms. In the subjunctive the reduplicated stem is the only difference between the present and the aorist. Here are the active forms.[2]

	present	*second aorist*
1 sg	διδῶ	δῶ
2 sg	διδῷς	δῷς
3 sg	διδῷ	δῷ[3]
1 pl	διδῶμεν	δῶμεν
2 pl	διδῶτε	δῶτε
3 pl	διδῶσι(ν)	δῶσι(ν)

35.6 **Imperative.** The imperatives are also easy to recognize. Remember that μι verbs do not use a thematic vowel, so the imperative morpheme is added directly to the verbal root. Here are the active forms.

	present	*second aorist*
2 sg	δίδου	δός
3 sg	διδότω	δότω
2 pl	δίδοτε	δότε
3 pl	διδότωσαν	δότωσαν

35.7 **Infinitive**

	present	*second aorist*
active	διδόναι	δοῦναι
middle	δίδοσθαι	δόσθαι
passive	δίδοσθαι	δοθῆναι

---

[1] Nu was added to the verbal root in order to form the present tense stem; class 3 verbs. Cf. §20.24.

[2] δίδωμι has first aorist forms in the indicative and second aorist forms elsewhere.

[3] In Mark 8:37 it is written as δοῖ.

35.8   Participle

	present	*aorist*
active	διδούς, διδοῦσα, διδόν	δούς, δοῦσα, δόν
	διδόντος, διδούσης, διδόντος	δόντος, δούσης, δόντος
middle	διδόμενος, η, ον	δόμενος, η, ον
	διδομένου, ης, ου	δομένου, ης, ου
passive	διδόμενος, η, ον	δοθείς, δοθεῖσα, δοθέν
	διδομένου, ης, ου	δοθέντος, δοθείσης, δοθέντος

Take some time now and browse through all the charts on δίδωμι in the Appendix, since we have not included all of its forms above. Concentrate on recognition and applying the five μι rules. See how the other μι verbs follow the same pattern set by δίδωμι.

Summary

1. μι verbs with stem vowels in alpha (ἵστημι) and epsilon (τίθημι) behave just like μι verbs with stem vowels in omicron (δίδωμι). δείκνυμι, however, is somewhat different and in many ways much more like the thematic conjugation.

2. The athematic conjugation was in the process of being lost in Koine Greek, and subsequently some μι verbs have thematic forms.

3. Be sure to spend some time browsing through the μι verb charts in the Appendix. Concentrate on recognition.

Vocabulary

In chapter 33 you learned ἀπόλλυμι, and in 34 you learned δίδωμι and παραδίδωμι, three of the nine μι verbs that occur fifty times or more in the New Testament. The other six such μι verbs are listed in this vocabulary. These six are not all used in the exercises for this chapter, but you should learn them.

ἀνίστημι   intransitive: I rise, get up (108; ἀνά + *στα)
                                          transitive: I raise
                                          ἀναστήσω, ἀνέστησα, -, -, -

ἀνοίγω[4]	I open (77; ἀν + *Ϝοιγ) ἀνοίξω, ἠνέῳξα or ἀνέῳξα, ἀνέῳγα, ἀνέῳγμαι or ἠνέῳγμαι, ἠνεῴχθην or ἠνοίχθην
ἀφίημι[5]	I let go, leave, permit (143; ἀφ + *σε)[6] (ἤφιον), ἀφήσω, ἀφῆκα, -, ἀφέωμαι, ἀφέθην
δείκνυμι	I show, explain (33; *δεικνυ)[7] δείξω, ἔδειξα, δέδειχα, -, ἐδείχθην
ἴδιος, -α, -ον	one's own (114; * ἰδιο/α)[8]
ἵστημι	intransitive:[9] I stand (154; *στα) transitive:[10] I cause to stand (ἵστην), στήσω, ἔστησα,[11] ἕστηκα,[12] ἕσταμαι, ἐστάθην
μέσος, -η, -ον	middle, in the midst (58; *μεσο/η)[13]

---

[4] This verb was originally a compound verb, and at times it is augmented as if it still were compound, and at other times as if it were a simple verb. You also can see two augments in places.

[5] The root of this verb is *σε. Like ἵστημι, the reduplicated sigma dropped off and was replaced with a rough breathing. The initial sigma was also dropped because it was intervocalic. σε ‣ σισε ‣ ἱσε ‣ ἵημι.

It is a compound with ἀπό and the pi has aspirated to a phi because of the rough breathing that actually is there, although unseen. ἵημι occurs in the New Testament only as a compound.

[6] *Aphesis* is the gradual loss of an initial unaccented vowel, such as in the English*esquire* to *squire* (cf. *MBG*, §7.10).

[7] Even though this word occurs less than fifty times, it has been included so the paradigms can be complete. Outside of the present and imperfect tenses, it forms its tense stems from the root *δεικ and is not a μι verb.

In grammar, a *deictic* word is one that is demonstrative, one that points out, such as the demonstrative pronoun.

[8] Can be used in the sense of one's own "people" or "land." It can also be used adverbially to mean "individually." *Idiosyncrasy* (συνκρᾶσις, "a mixing together") is a temperament or behavior peculiar to one person or group.

[9] ἵστημι is intransitive in the second aorist (ἔστην) and perfect. "Intransitive" means it does not take a direct object.

[10] ἵστημι is transitive in the present, future, and first aorist. "Transitive" means it takes a direct object.

[11] This is the one μι verb that does not use a kappa aorist. It has a second aorist, ἔστην.

[12] Notice the shift to the rough breathing.

[13] *Meso* is a combining form that when added to another word carries the meaning of "middle," such as "mesomorphic" (the state between liquid and crystalline), "mesoplast" (the nucleus of a cell), and "Mesozoic" (the age between the Paleozoic and Cenozoic ages).

τίθημι   I put, place (100; *θε)[14]
                                          (ἐτίθουν), θήσω, ἔθηκα, τέθεικα, τέθειμαι, ἐτέθην

φημί   I say, affirm (66; *φε)
                                          (ἔφη), -, ἔφη[15], -, -, -, -

Total word count in the New Testament:	138,162
Number of words learned to date:	319
Number of word occurrences in this chapter:	853
Number of word occurrences to date:	110,425
Percent of total word count in the New Testament:	79.92%

Contratulations! You know all 319 words that occur most frequently in the New Testament, and almost four out of five word occurrences in the New Testament.

Where Do We Go From Here?

Congratulations. You have finished learning the building blocks of biblical Greek; now the real fun begins. But what should you do next?

1. There is no substitute at this point for reading the biblical text, reading as much as you can. You need to be exposed to large sections of the New Testament to have fun (if for no other reason).

2. For this reason we wrote a third volume in this series, *A Graded Reader of Biblical Greek*. It starts with easy passages and slowly works into more difficult Greek. We start with Mark and John because you are so familiar with them; most of our exercises came from the early chapters of Mark. Pay close attention to the footnotes in this text. They will help carry you into the next stage by exposing you to intermediate Greek grammar inductively.

3. The *Graded Reader* is tied into Daniel B. Wallace's *Greek Grammar Beyond the Basics: An Exegetical Syntax of the New Testament* (volume four in this series). Read the sections of this grammar as it is cross-indexed in the *Graded Reader*. It is essential at some time that you sit down and read through a complete grammar. However, the further you are into the *Graded Reader*, the easier it will be to remember grammatical constructions.

4. *The Morphology of Biblical Greek* (volume five in this series) is designed to show you what is really happening to the forms of the Greek words you meet. Read the introductory discussion so you can see how to use the text; and as you come across forms that you do not understand, look up the word in the index and from there go to its relevant discussion. But do not become

---

14 The cognate θέσις is a "placing," a "proposition." In logic a "thesis" is an unprovable statement, a proposition, assumed to be true.

15 ἔφη can be either imperfect or aorist, and is third singular. We learned this as a vocabulary word earlier.

bogged down in this process right away. It is much better to have some fun and read lots of Greek.

5.   *The Analytical Lexicon to the Greek New Testament* by William D. Mounce can help you with those difficult parsings. Be sure to read the introductory discussion "How to Use the Analytical" for warnings about the misuse of the book. The lexicon contained in the *Anaytical* is especially well-suited for the second year Greek student.

6.   Do not forget to review. This is essential. You will lose all pleasure in the language if you have to look up every other verb in order to parse it, or every other word in the lexicon to discover its meaning. Purchase Warren Trenchard's *The Student's Complete Vocabulary Guide to the Greek New Testament* or Bruce Metzger's *Lexical Aids for Students of New Testament Greek*. They will help you review your vocabulary, fill out the definitions, and make it easy to memorize more vocabulary if you wish.

You already know all of the words that occur fifty times or more. As we said in the introduction, there are only 313 words occurring fifty times or more in the New Testament and they account for almost 80 percent of the total word count in the text. Beyond fifty occurrences it is debatable how significant vocabulary acquisition becomes.

7.   But most importantly, do not forget why you have learned the language of God's Word. It is a tool for ministry, helping you to get closer to what God has said through his writers. It is a tool that allows you to use other tools such as good commentaries.

I once heard a story, perhaps apocryphal, about a sailor who was in love with a woman from another country. He wanted to be married and so he tried to familiarize himself with her native country. He studied its customs, history, etc. But finally he realized that if he really wanted to understand her, he would have to learn her native language. I believe that learning Greek is nothing more than a natural extension of our loving relationship with Jesus Christ. Although many translations are good, they are one step further removed from what Jesus said. Ultimately, we want to know him and his message as well as possible. A knowledge of the Greek language is essential to achieve this goal.

May your days be filled with blessing and your ministry fruitful as you seek to share your love and knowledge of Jesus Christ with those around you.

William D. Mounce

Advanced Information

35.9   **Optative**. There is one more mood in Koine Greek, the optative. Whereas the subjunctive is the mood of probability or possibility, the optative is the mood of "wish." Whereas the subjunctive is one step removed from reality, the optative is two.

There are sixty-eight examples of the optative in the New Testament. It is found only in the present (continuous aspect; twenty-three times) and aorist (undefined aspect; forty-five times). It occurs twenty-eight times in Luke -Acts and thirty-one times in Paul. εἴη occurs twelve times and γένοιτο seventeen times, fifteen of which are the Pauline phrase μὴ γένοιτο, "God forbid!"

* Because the optative can have no real time significance, it can have no augment.

* The connecting vowel is omicron.

* The tense formative for the aorist active/middle is σα, which contracts with the mood formative so that all forms have σαι.

  The tense formative for the aorist passive in θε, and the mood formative in ιη, which result in θειη in all forms.

* Its mood formative in the thematic conjugation is ι (except in the aorist passive where it is ιη), and in the athematic conjugation it is ιη. All forms of the present optative will have this οι.

* The optative uses secondary personal endings except in the first person singular active where it uses μι.

To see fuller paradigms, see *MBG* or *Analytical*.

	present	*future*	*first aorist*	*second aorist*
		active		
1 sg	λύοιμι	λύσοιμι	λύσαιμι	βάλοιμι
2 sg	λύοις	λύσοις	λύσαις	βάλοις
3 sg	λύοι	λύσοι	λύσαι	βάλοι
1 pl	λύοιμεν	λύσοιμεν	λύσαιμεν	βάλοιμεν
2 pl	λύοιτε	λύσοιτε	λύσαιτε	βάλοιτε
3 pl	λύοιεν	λύσοιεν	λύσαιεν	βάλοιεν
		middle		*passive*
1 sg	λυοίμην	λυσοίμην	λυσαίμην	λυθείην
2 sg	λύοιο	λύσοιο	λύσαιο	λυθείης
3 sg	λύοιτο	λύσοιτο	λύσαιτο	λυθείη
1 pl	λυοίμεθα	λυσοίμεθα	λυσαίμεθα	λυθείημεν
2 pl	λύοισθε	λύσοισθε	λύσαισθε	λυθείητε
3 pl	λύοιντο	λύσοιντο	λύσαιντο	λυθείησαν

Appendix

In this section we have collected all the charts you need to read Greek. The listing is not exhaustive; if you want to see every chart, see *MBG*.

Remember, the charts are not for you to memorize. You should memorize the eight rules on case endings, the definite article, and the ten verbal rules. Use the rest of the charts to test yourself, to see if you really know the rules.

Crasis in the New Testament

καὶ ἐγώ   ▸   κἀγώ

καὶ ἐμοί   ▸   κἀμοί

καὶ ἐκεῖ   ▸   κἀκεῖ

καὶ ἐκεῖθεν   ▸   κἀκεῖθεν

καὶ ἐκεῖνος   ▸   κἀκεῖνος

καὶ ἐάν or ἄν   ▸   κἄν

When Accents and Breathings Are Especially Important

1. τις, τίς
2. ἡ, ἤ, ἥ, ᾗ, ῇ
3. οἱ, αἱ; οἵ, αἵ
4. ὁ, ὅ; ὄν, ὅν
5. ὤν, ὦν
6. ἧς, ἧς; ἥν, ἤν

7. αὐτή, αὕτη
8. αὐταί, αὗται
9. οὐ, οὗ
10. ἔξω, ἔξω
11. ἐν, ἕν
12. ὦ, ὧ, ᾧ

13. ἀλλά, ἄλλα
14. εἰ, εἶ
15. εἰς, εἷς
16. ποτέ, πότε
17. ἄρα, ἆρα
18. Liquid futures

Square of Stops

		orders			
		voiceless	*voiced*	*aspirate*	
	labial	π	β	φ	
classes	*velar*	κ	γ	χ	cognate
	dental	τ	δ	θ	
		coordinate			

Spatial Representation of Prepositions

General guidelines for the cases

Genitive: Indicates motion away from ("separation"; ἀπό)

Dative: Indicates rest (ἐν)

Accusative: Indicates motion (εἰς)

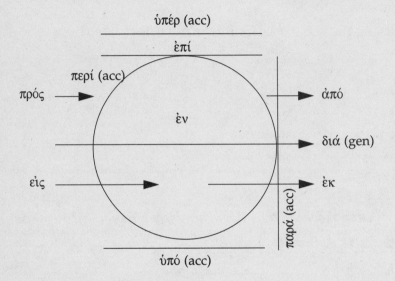

Other prepositions that are not spatially diagrammed

ἀντί	gen:	instead of, for
διά	acc:	on account of
ἐπί	gen:	on, over, when
	dat:	on the basis of, at
κατά	gen:	against
	acc:	according to
μετά	gen:	with
	acc:	after
παρά	gen:	from
	dat:	beside, in the presence of
περί	gen:	concerning, about
ὑπέρ	gen:	in behalf of
ὑπό	gen:	by

Contractions of Single Vowels

Following is a chart of all possible contractions of single vowels. The four most common (and troublesome) are bolded and enlarged.

	α	ε	η	ι	υ	ο	ω
α	α	α	α	αι	αυ	ω	ω
ε	η	**ει**	η	ει	ευ	**ου**	ω
η	η	η	η	ῃ	ηυ	ω	ω
ο	ω	**ου**	ω	οι	ου	**ου**	ω
ω	ω	ω	ω	ῳ	ωυ	ω	ω

Contraction of vowels and diphthongs

	α/αι	ει [1]	ει [2]	η	οι	ου [3]	ῳ
α	ᾳ	ᾳ	α	ᾳ	ῳ	ω	ῳ
ε	η	ει	ει	η	οι	ου	ῳ
η	η	ῃ	η	η	ῳ		ῳ
ο	ῳ	οι	ου	οι	οι	ου	ῳ

---

[1] "Genuine" diphthong (not formed by a contraction)
[2] "Spurious" diphthong (formed by a contraction)
[3] Spurious

Conditional Sentences

This is a brief overview of conditional sentences. Be sure to study the relevant sections in Wallace, *GGBB*.

1.   The "if" clause is the *protasis*; the "then" clause is the *apodosis*.

2.   Conditional sentences are most easily classified by their structure, specifically, the word that introduces the protasis, the tense and mood of the verb in the apodosis, and sometimes the tense of the verb in the apodosis.

class	protasis	apodosis
First class	εἰ + indicative any tense; negated by οὐ	any mood; any tense
Second class	εἰ + indicative past tense; negated by μή	ἄν + indicative same tense as in the protasis
Third class	ἐάν + subjunctive negated by μή	any mood; any tense
Fourth class	εἰ + optative	ἄν + optative

3.   Only the protasis is conditional. If the protasis is true, then the apodosis must be true (if the statement is in fact a factually correct statement).

4.   Language is only a portrayal of reality. Whether the protasis is actually true or not, regardless of what the author says (see second class conditions), is decided by context and the reader.

5.   Conditional sentences can overlap; see Wallace, *GGBB*.

First class   Also called "conditions of fact." These sentences are saying that if something is true, and let's assume for the sake of the argument that it is true, then such and such will occur.

Sometimes the apodosis is clearly true, and you can translate "Since such and such, then such and such." At other times the protasis is not so obvious and you cannot use "since."

Second class   Also called "contrary to fact." These sentences are saying that if something is true, even though it is not, then such and such would occur. The falseness of the protasis is assumed in the argument.

Third class   Presents a condition that might be true in the future, or is generally true at all times. It does not necessarily suggest that it is likely to occur; sometimes the protasis is hypothetical (see §31.15).

Fourth class   No complete illustration in the New Testament.

Greek Cases

This is a summary of all the cases. The "Question" is what you can ask of a word to help determine its case. The "Key word" is what you should use in your translation of words in that case.

English cases	Greek cases and uses	Question	Key word
1. Subjective (he)	1. *NOMINATIVE*	Who? What?	
	a. Subject of the verb		
	b. Predicate of "is"		
	VOCATIVE (direct address)		"O"
2. Possessive (his)	2. *GENITIVE*	Whose?	
	a. Possessive		"of"
	b. Object of Preposition		
	c. Direct object		
	d. Ablative (separation)		"from"
3. Objective (him)	3. *DATIVE*		
	a. Indirect object	to whom? to what?	"to" /"for"
	b. Object of Preposition		
	c. Direct object		
	d. Instrumental (means)	by what?	"by"/"with"
	e. Locative (place)	where?	"in"
4. Objective (him)	4. *ACCUSATIVE*		
	a. Direct object of the verb	whom? what?	
	b. Object of preposition		

The word has the ____ case ending, so I know that it functions as the _____ in the sentence; therefore I translate it with the key word _____ .

Always precede a word in a certain case with a "key word" for that case, if there is one.

Master Case Ending Chart

A dash means that no case ending is used. An underline means that the final stem vowel changes to the one listed in the chart (rule 5). The case endings for the masc/fem in the declension are repeated for the sake of clarity, even though in several cases they are the same as in the first and second declensions.

	first/second declension			third declension	
	masc	fem	neut	masc/fem	neut
nom sg	ς	-	ν	ς -	-^{1}
gen sg	υ^2	ς	υ	ος	ος
dat sg	ι^3	ι	ι	ι^4	ι
acc sg	ν	ν	ν	α/ν^5	-
nom pl	ι	ι	α	ες	α^6
gen pl	ων	ων	ων	ων	ων
dat pl	ις	ις	ις	σι(ν)^7	σι(ν)
acc pl	υς^8	ς	α	ας^9	α

1   Be prepared for the final stem letter to undergo changes (rule 8).

2   The ending is actually omicron, which contracts with the final stem vowel and forms ου (rule 5).

3   The vowel lengthens (rule 5) and the iota subscripts (rule 4).

4   Because third declension stems end in a consonant, the iota cannot subscript as it does in the first and second declensions; so it remains on the line ("iota adscript").

5   The case ending alternates between alpha and nu.

6   As opposed to the first and second declensions, this alpha is an actual case ending and not a changed stem vowel. This is also true of the accusative plural.

7   The nu is a movable nu. Notice that the ending σι is a flipped version of ις found in the first and second declensions.

8   The actual case ending for the first and second declension is νς, but the nu drops out because of the following sigma. In the first declension the alpha simply joins with the sigma (ωρα + νς ‣ ὥρας), but in the second declension the final stem omicron lengthens to ου (rule 5; λογονς ‣ λογος ‣ λόγους).

9   As opposed to the first declension (e.g. ὥρα), the alpha here is part of the case ending.

The Basic Rules Governing Case Endings

1. *Stems ending in alpha or eta are in the first declension, stems in omicron are in the second, and consonantal stems are in the third.*

2. *Every neuter word has the same form in the nominative and accusative.*

3. *Almost all neuter words end in alpha in the nominative and accusative plural.*

   - In the second declension the alpha is the changed stem vowel; in the third it is the case ending.

4. *In the dative singular, the iota subscripts if possible.*

   - Because an iota can subscript only under a vowel (in which case the vowel lengthens), it subscripts only in the first and second declensions.

5. *Vowels often change their length ("ablaut").*

   - "Contraction" occurs when two vowels meet and form a different vowel or diphthong.

     λογο + ι ‣ λόγῳ   (dative singular)

     λογο + ο ‣ λόγου   (genitive singular)

     γραφη + ων ‣ γραφῶν   (genitive plural)[1]

   - "Compensatory lengthening" occurs when a vowel is lengthened to compensate for the loss of another letter.

     λογο + νς ‣ λόγος ‣ λογους   (accusative plural)

6. *In the genitive and dative, the masculine and neuter will always be identical.*

7. *The Square of Stops*

Labials	π	β	φ
Velars	κ	γ	χ
Dentals	τ	δ	θ

   - Labials + sigma form psi; velars plus sigma form xsi; dentals plus sigma form sigma.

   - The ντ combination drops out when followed by sigma (παντ + ς ‣ πᾶς).

   - Whatever happens in the nominative singular third declension also happens in the dative plural. σαρκ + σ ‣ σαρξ. σαρκ + σι ‣ σάρξι.

8. *A tau cannot stand at the end of a word and will drop off.*

   - When no case ending is used in stems ending in -ματ, the tau drops out.

     ὀνοματ + - ‣ ὀνοματ ‣ ὄνομα.

---

[1] The omega of the genitive plural will absorb any preceding vowel.

Noun System

The paradigms in the following pages illustrate the forms of the more common noun and verb patterns. They cover the words you need to learn in this grammar. For a full set of paradigms see *MBG* or *Analytical*.

The nomenclature for the following noun and adjective charts is discussed in full in the introduction to the Lexicon (below). We have included the paradigms for all classes of words occurring in the exercises.

The Article

	masc	*fem*	*neut*		*masc*	*fem*	*neut*
nom sg	ὁ	ἡ	τό	nom pl	οἱ	αἱ	τά
gen sg	τοῦ	τῆς	τοῦ	gen pl	τῶν	τῶν	τῶν
dat sg	τῷ	τῇ	τῷ	dat pl	τοῖς	ταῖς	τοῖς
acc sg	τόν	τήν	τό	acc pl	τούς	τάς	τά

First Declension Nouns

	n-1a	*n-1b*	*n-1c*	*n-1d*
nom sg	ὥρα	γραφή	δόξα	νεανίας
gen sg	ὥρας	γραφῆς	δόξης	νεανίου
dat sg	ὥρᾳ	γραφῇ	δόξῃ	νεανίᾳ
acc sg	ὥραν	γραφήν	δόξαν	νεανίαν
voc sg	ὥρα	γραφή	δόξα	νεανία
n/v pl	ὧραι	γραφαί	δόξαι	νεανίαι
gen pl	ὡρῶν	γραφῶν	δοξῶν	νεανιῶν
dat pl	ὥραις	γραφαῖς	δόξαις	νεανίαις
acc pl	ὥρας	γραφάς	δόξας	νεανίας

First Declension Nouns

	n-1e	n-1f	n-1g	n-1h
nom sg	σατανᾶς	προφήτης	Μανασσῆς	μνᾶ
gen sg	σατανᾶ	προφήτου	Μανασσῆ	μνᾶς
dat sg	σατανᾷ	προφήτῃ	-	μνᾷ
acc sg	σατανᾶν	προφήτην	Μανασσῆ	μνᾶν
voc sg	σατανᾶ	προφῆτα	-	μνᾶ
n/v pl	-	προφῆται	-	μναῖ
gen pl	-	προφητῶν	-	μνῶν
dat pl	-	προφήταις	-	μναῖς
acc pl	-	προφήτας	-	μνᾶς

Second Declension Nouns

	n-2a	n-2b	n-2c	n-2d(1)	n-2d(2)	n-2e
nom sg	λόγος	ὁδός	ἔργον	χειμάρρους	ὀστοῦν	κῶς
gen sg	λόγου	ὁδοῦ	ἔργου	χειμάρρου	ὀστοῦ	κῶ
dat sg	λόγῳ	ὁδῷ	ἔργῳ	χειμάρρῳ	ὀστῷ	κῷ
acc sg	λόγον	ὁδόν	ἔργον	χειμάρρουν	ὀστοῦν	-
voc sg	λόγε	ὁδέ	ἔργον	χειμάρρους	ὀστοῦν	κῶς
n/v pl	λόγοι	ὁδοί	ἔργα	χείμαρροι	ὀστᾶ	-
gen pl	λόγων	ὁδῶν	ἔργων	χειμάρρων	ὀστῶν	-
dat pl	λόγοις	ὁδοῖς	ἔργοις	χειμάρροις	ὀστοῖς	-
acc pl	λόγους	ὁδούς	ἔργα	χειμάρρους	ὀστᾶ	-

Third Declension Nouns

	n-3a(1)	n-3a(2)	n-3b(1)	n-3b(1)	n-3b(2)	n-3b(3)
nom sg	λαῖλαψ	ἄραψ	σάρξ	γυνή	σάλπιγξ	θρίξ[2]
gen sg	λαίλαπος	ἄραβος	σάρκος	γυναικός	σάλπιγγος	τριχός
dat sg	λαίλαπι	ἄραβι	σαρκί	γυναικί	σάλπιγγι	τριχί
acc sg	λαίλαπα	ἄραβα	σαρκά	γυναῖκα	σάλπιγγα	τρίχα
voc sg	λαῖλαψ	ἄραψ	σάρξ	γύναι	σάλπιγξ	θρίξ
n/v pl	-	ἄραβες	σάρκες	γυναῖκες	σάλπιγγες	τρίχες
gen pl	-	ἀράβων	σαρκῶν	γυναικῶν	σαλπίγγων	τριχῶν
dat pl	-	ἄραψι(ν)	σαρξί(ν)	γυναιξί(ν)	σάλπιγξι(ν)	θριξί(ν)
acc pl	-	ἄραβας	σάρκας	γυναῖκας	σάλπιγγας	τρίχας

	n-3c(1)	n-3c(2)	n-3c(3)	n-3c(4)	n-3c(5a)	n-3c(5b)
n/v sg	χάρις	ἐλπίς	ὄρνις	ὄνομα	ὀδούς	ἄρχων
gen sg	χάριτος	ἐλπίδος	ὄρνιθος	ὀνόματος	ὀδόντος	ἄρχοντος
dat sg	χάριτι	ἐλπίδι	ὄρνιθι	ὀνόματι	ὀδόντι	ἄρχοντι
acc sg	χάριν	ἐλπίδα	ὄρνιθα	ὄνομα	ὀδόντα	ἄρχοντα
n/v pl	χάριτες	ἔλπιδες	ὄρνιθες	ὀνόματα	ὀδόντες	ἄρχοντες
gen pl	χαρίτων	ἐλπίδων	ὀρνίθων	ὀνομάτων	ὀδόντων	ἀρχόντων
dat pl	χάρισι(ν)	ἔλπισι(ν)	ὄρνισι(ν)	ὀνόμασι(ν)	ὀδοῦσι	ἄρχουσι(ν)
acc pl	χάριτας	ἔλπιδας	ὄρνιθας	ὀνόματα	ὀδόντας	ἄρχοντας

	n-3c(6a)	n-3c(6b)	n-3c(6c)	n-3c(6d)	n-3d(1)	n-3d(2a)
n/v sg	τέρας	ὕδωρ	φῶς	γόνυ	γήρας	σωσθένης
gen sg	τέρατος	ὕδατος	φωτός	γόνατος	γήρως	σωσθένους
dat sg	τέρατι	ὕδατι	φωτί	-	γήρει	-
acc sg	τέρας	ὕδωρ	φῶς	-	-	σωσθένην

---

[2] With this particular word, the initial letter varies between theta and tau depending upon whether the final consonant is a xsi or a chi in the nominative singular and dative plural. See *MBG* for an explanation.

Third Declension Nouns

	n-3c(6a)	n-3c(6b)	n-3c(6c)	n-3c(6d)	n-3d(1)	n-3d(2a)
n/v pl	τέρατα	ὕδατα	φῶτα	-	-	-
gen p	τεράτων	ὑδάτων	φώτων	-	-	-
dat pl	τέρασι(ν)	ὕδασι(ν)	-	-	-	-
acc pl	τέρατα	ὕδατα	φῶτα	γόνατα	-	-

	n-3d(2b)	n-3d(3)	n-3e(1)	n-3e(2)	n-3e(3)
nom sg	γένος	αἰδώς	ἰχθύς	ναῦς	βασιλεύς
gen sg	γένους	αἰδοῦς	ἰχθύος	νεώς	βασιλέως
dat sg	γένει	-	ἰχθύι	-	βασιλεῖ
acc sg	γένος	-	ἰχθύν	ναῦν	βασιλέα
voc sg	γένος	αἰδώς	ἰχθύ	-	βασιλεῦ
n/v pl	γένη	-	ἰχθύες	-	βασιλεῖς
gen pl	γενῶν	-	ἰχθύων	-	βασιλέων
dat pl	γένεσι(ν)	-	ἰχθύσι(ν)	-	βασιλεῦσι(ν)
acc pl	γένη	-	ἰχθύας	-	βασιλεῖς

	n-3e(4)	n-3e(5a)	n-3e(5b)	n-3e(6)
nom sg	νοῦς	νῆστις	πόλις	πείθω
gen sg	νοός	-	πόλεως	πειθοῦς
dat sg	νοΐ	-	πόλει	πειθοῖ
acc sg	νοῦν	-	πόλιν	-
voc sg	νοῦ	-	πόλι	-
n/v pl	νόες	-	πόλεις	-
gen pl	νοῶν	-	πόλεων	-
dat pl	νουσί(ν)	-	πόλεσι(ν)	-
acc pl	νόας	νήστεις	πόλεις	-

Third Declension Nouns

	n-3f(1a)	n-3f(1b)	n-3f(1c)	n-3f(2a)	n-3f(2b)
nom sg	αἰών	ἡγεμών	κύων	σωτήρ	ῥήτωρ
gen sg	αἰῶνος	ἡγεμόνος	κυνός	σωτῆρος	ῥήτορος
dat sg	αἰῶνι	ἡγεμόνι	-	σωτῆρι	ῥήτορι
acc sg	αἰῶνα	ἡγεμόνα	-	σωτῆρα	ῥήτορα
voc sg	αἰών	ἡγεμών	κύων	-	ῥῆτορ
n/v pl	αἰῶνες	ἡγεμόνες	κύνες	σωτῆρες	ῥήτορες
gen pl	αἰώνων	ἡγεμόνων	-	σωτήρων	ῥητόρων
dat pl	αἰῶσι(ν)	ἡγεμόσι(ν)	κυσίν	σωτῆρσι(ν)	ῥήτορσι(ν)
acc pl	αἰῶνας	ἡγεμόνας	κύνας	σωτῆρας	ῥήτορας

	n-3f(2c)	n-3f(2c)	n-3f(2c)	n-3f(2c)	n-3g(1)
nom sg	ἀνήρ	θυγάτηρ	πατήρ	μήτηρ	Μωϋσῆς
gen sg	ἀνδρός	θυγατρός	πατρός	μητρός	Μωϋσέως
dat sg	ἀνδρί	θυγατρί	πατρί	μητρί	Μωϋσεῖ
acc sg	ἄνδρα	θυγατέρα	πατέρα	μητέρα	Μωϋσῆν
voc sg	ἄνερ	θυγάτερ	πάτερ	μῆτερ	-
n/v pl	ἄνδρες	θυγατέρες	πατέρες	-	-
gen pl	ἀνδρῶν	θυγατέρων	πατέρων	-	-
dat pl	ἀνδράσι(ν)	-	πατράσι(ν)	-	-
acc pl	ἄνδρας	θυγατέρας	πατέρας	μητέρας	-

Adjectives

a-1a (2-1-2)

	masc	fem	neut		masc	fem	neut
nom sg	ἅγιος	ἁγία	ἅγιον	*nom pl*	ἅγιοι	ἅγιαι	ἅγια
gen sg	ἁγίου	ἁγίας	ἁγίου	*gen pl*	ἁγίων	ἁγίων	ἁγίων
dat sg	ἁγίῳ	ἁγίᾳ	ἁγίῳ	*dat pl*	ἁγίοις	ἁγίαις	ἁγίοις
acc sg	ἅγιον	ἁγίαν	ἅγιον	*acc pl*	ἁγίους	ἁγίας	ἅγια
voc sg	ἅγιε	ἁγία	ἅγιον	*voc pl*	ἅγιοι	ἅγιαι	ἅγια

Adjectives

a-1a(2a) (2-1-2)

	masc	fem	neut		masc	fem	neut
nom sg	ἀγαθός	ἀγαθή	ἀγαθόν	nom pl	ἀγαθοί	ἀγαθαί	ἀγαθά
gen sg	ἀγαθοῦ	ἀγαθῆς	ἀγαθοῦ	gen pl	ἀγαθῶν	ἀγαθῶν	ἀγαθῶν
dat sg	ἀγαθῷ	ἀγαθῇ	ἀγαθῷ	dat pl	ἀγαθοῖς	ἀγαθαῖς	ἀγαθοῖς
acc sg	ἀγαθόν	ἀγαθήν	ἀγαθόν	acc pl	ἀγαθούς	ἀγαθάς	ἀγαθά
voc sg	ἀγαθέ	ἀγαθή	ἀγαθόν	voc pl	ἀγαθοί	ἀγαθαί	ἀγαθά

a-1a(2b) (2-1-2)

	masc	fem	neut		masc	fem	neut
nom sg	οὗτος	αὕτη	τοῦτο	nom pl	οὗτοι	αὗται	ταῦτα
gen sg	τούτου	ταύτης	τούτου	gen pl	τούτων	τούτων	τούτων
dat sg	τούτῳ	ταύτῃ	τούτῳ	dat pl	τούτοις	ταύταις	τούτοις
acc sg	τοῦτον	ταύτην	τοῦτο	acc pl	τούτους	ταύτας	ταῦτα

a-1a(2a) (2-1-2)

	masc	fem	neut		masc	fem	neut
nom sg	μέγας	μεγάλη	μέγα	nom pl	μεγάλοι	μεγάλαι	μεγάλα
gen sg	μεγάλου	μεγάλης	μεγάλου	gen pl	μεγάλων	μεγάλων	μεγάλων
dat sg	μεγάλῳ	μεγάλη	μεγάλῳ	dat pl	μεγάλοις	μεγάλαις	μεγάλοις
acc sg	μέγαν	μεγάλην	μέγα	acc pl	μεγάλους	μεγάλας	μεγάλα

a-1a(2a) (2-1-2)

	masc	fem	neut		masc	fem	neut
nom sg	πολύς	πολλή	πολύ	nom pl	πολλοί	πολλαί	πολλά
gen sg	πολλοῦ	πολλῆς	πολλοῦ	gen pl	πολλῶν	πολλῶν	πολλῶν
dat sg	πολλῷ	πολλῇ	πολλῷ	dat pl	πολλοῖς	πολλαῖς	πολλοῖς
acc sg	πολύν	πολλήν	πολύ	acc pl	πολλούς	πολλάς	πολλά

Adjectives

a-1a(2b) (2-1-2)

	masc	fem	neut		masc	fem	neut
nom sg	ὅς	ἥ	ὅ	nom pl	οἵ	αἵ	ἅ
gen sg	οὗ	ἧς	οὗ	gen pl	ὧν	ὧν	ὧν
dat sg	ᾧ	ᾗ	ᾧ	dat pl	οἷς	αἷς	οἷς
acc sg	ὅν	ἥν	ὅ	acc pl	οὕς	ἅς	ἅ

a-1a(2b) (3-3-3)

	masc	fem	neut		masc	fem	neut
nom sg	ὅστις	ἥτις	ὅτι	nom pl	οἵτινες	αἵτινες	ἅτινα
gen sg	οὗτινος	ἧστινος	οὗτινος	gen pl	ὧντινων	ὧντινων	ὧντινων
dat sg	ᾧτινι	ᾗτινι	ᾧτινι	dat pl	οἷστισι(ν)	αἷστισι(ν)	οἷστισι(ν)
acc sg	ὅντινα	ἥντινα	ὅτι	acc pl	οὕστινας	ἅστινας	ἅτινα

a-2a (3-1-3)

	masc	fem	neut		masc	fem	neut
nom sg	πᾶς	πᾶσα	πᾶν	nom pl	πάντες	πᾶσαι	πάντα
gen sg	παντός	πάσης	παντός	gen pl	πάντων	πασῶν	πάντων
dat sg	παντί	πάσῃ	παντί	dat pl	πᾶσι	πάσαις	πᾶσι
acc sg	πάντα	πᾶσαν	πᾶν	acc pl	πάντας	πάσας	πάντα

a-2b (3-1-3)

	masc	fem	neut		masc	fem	neut
nom sg	ταχύς	ταχεῖα	ταχύ	nom pl	ταχεῖς	ταχεῖαι	ταχέα
gen sg	ταχέως	ταχείας	ταχέως	gen pl	ταχέων	ταχειῶν	ταχέων
dat sg	ταχεῖ	ταχείᾳ	ταχεῖ	dat pl	ταχέσι	ταχείαις	ταχέσι
acc sg	ταχύν	ταχεῖαν	ταχύ	acc pl	ταχεῖς	ταχείας	ταχέα

Adjectives

a-3a (2-2)

	masc & fem	neut		masc & fem	neut
nom sg	ἁμαρτωλός	ἁμαρτωλόν	*nom pl*	ἁμαρτωλοί	ἁμαρτωλά
gen sg	ἁμαρτωλοῦ	ἁμαρτωλοῦ	*gen pl*	ἁμαρτωλῶν	ἁμαρτωλῶν
dat sg	ἁμαρτωλῷ	ἁμαρτωλῷ	*dat pl*	ἁμαρτωλοῖς	ἁμαρτωλοῖς
acc sg	ἁμαρτωλόν	ἁμαρτωλόν	*acc pl*	ἁμαρτωλούς	ἁμαρτωλά
voc sg	ἁμαρτωλέ	ἁμαρτωλόν	*voc pl*	ἁμαρτωλοί	ἁμαρτωλά

a-4a (3-3)

	masc & fem	neut		masc & fem	neut
nom sg	ἀληθής	ἀληθές	*nom pl*	ἀληθεῖς	ἀληθῆ
gen sg	ἀληθοῦς	ἀληθοῦς	*gen pl*	ἀληθῶν	ἀληθῶν
dat sg	ἀληθεῖ	ἀληθεῖ	*dat pl*	ἀληθέσι(ν)	ἀληθέσι(ν)
acc sg	ἀληθῆ	ἀληθές	*acc pl*	ἀληθεῖς	ἀληθῆ

a-4b(1) (3-3)

	masc & fem	neut		masc & fem	neut
nom sg	πλείων	πλεῖον	*nom pl*	πλείονες	πλείονα
gen sg	πλείονος	πλείονος	*gen pl*	πλειόνων	πλειόνων
dat sg	πλείονι	πλείονι	*dat pl*	πλείοσι(ν)	πλείοσι(ν)
acc sg	πλείονα	πλεῖον	*acc pl*	πλείονας	πλείονα

a-4b(1) (3-3)

	masc & fem	neut		masc & fem	neut
nom sg	μείζων	μεῖζον	*nom pl*	μείζονες	μείζονα
gen sg	μείζονος	μείζονος	*gen pl*	μειζόνων	μειζόνων
dat sg	μείζονι	μείζονι	*dat pl*	μείζοσι(ν)	μείζοσι(ν)
acc sg	μείζονα	μεῖζον	*acc pl*	μείζονας	μείζονα

Adjectives

a-4b(2) (3-3; interrogative)

	masc & fem	neut		masc & fem	neut
nom sg	τίς	τί	nom pl	τίνες	τίνα
gen sg	τίνος	τίνος	gen pl	τίνων	τίνων
dat sg	τίνι	τίνι	dat pl	τίσι(ν)	τίσι(ν)
acc sg	τίνα	τί	acc pl	τίνας	τίνα

a-4b(2) (3-3; indefinite)

	masc & fem	neut		masc & fem	neut
nom sg	τις	τι	nom pl	τινές	τινά
gen sg	τινός	τινός	gen pl	τινῶν	τινῶν
dat sg	τινί	τινί	dat pl	τισί(ν)	τισί(ν)
acc sg	τινά	τι	acc pl	τινάς	τινά

a-4b(2) (3-1-3)

	masc	fem	neut
nom sg	εἷς	μία	ἕν
gen sg	ἑνός	μιᾶς	ἑνός
dat sg	ἑνί	μιᾷ	ἑνί
acc sg	ἕνα	μιᾶν	ἕν

a-5

	1st person	2nd person		1st person	2nd person
nom sg	ἐγώ	σύ	nom pl	ἡμεῖς	ὑμεῖς
gen sg	ἐμοῦ (μου)	σοῦ (σου)	gen pl	ἡμῶν	ὑμῶν
dat sg	ἐμοί (μοι)	σοί (σοι)	dat pl	ἡμῖν	ὑμῖν
acc sg	ἐμέ (με)	σέ (σε)	acc pl	ἡμᾶς	ὑμᾶς

Verb System

English Verb Tenses

This is the basic verb chart and terminology followed in this grammar. It is possible to be much more complex; but for the basic task of learning a foreign language, this is sufficient. All forms are listed in the active and then in the passive, starting first with a regular verb (e.g., "study") and then an irregular (e.g., "eat").

	Past simple	*Past progressive*	*Past perfect*
reg act	I studied	I was studying	I had studied
irreg act	I ate	I was eating	I had eaten
reg pas	I was studied	I was being studied	I had been studied
irreg pas	I was eaten	I was being eaten	I had been eaten

	Present simple	*Present progressive*	*Present perfect*
reg act	I study	I am studying	I have studied
irreg act	I eat	I am eating	I have eaten
reg pas	I am studied	I am being studied	I have been studied
irreg pas	I am eaten	I am being eaten	I have been eaten

	Future simple	*Future progressive*	*Future perfect*
reg act	I will study	I will be studying	I will have studied
irreg act	I will eat	I will be eating	I will have eaten
reg pas	I will be studied	I will be being studied	I will have been studied
irreg pas	I will be eaten	I will be being eaten	I will have been eaten

Master Verb Chart

Tense	Aug/ Redup	Tense stem	Tense form.	Conn. vowel	Personal endings	1st sing paradigm
Present act		pres		ο/ε	prim act	λύω
Present mid/pas		pres		ο/ε	prim mid/pas	λύομαι
Imperfect act	ε	pres		ο/ε	sec act	ἔλυον
Imperfect mid/pas	ε	pres		ο/ε	sec mid/pas	ἐλυόμην
Future act		fut act	σ	ο/ε	prim act	λύσω
Liquid fut act		fut act	εσ	ο/ε	prim act	μενῶ
Future mid		fut act	σ	ο/ε	prim mid/pas	πορεύσομαι
1st future pas		aor pas	θησ	ο/ε	prim mid/pas	λυθήσομαι
2nd future pas		aor pas	ησ	ο/ε	prim mid/pas	ἀποσταλήσομαι
1st aorist act	ε	aor act	σα		sec act	ἔλυσα
Liquid aorist act	ε	aor act	α		sec act	ἔμεινα
2nd aorist act	ε	aor act		ο/ε	sec act	ἔλαβον
1st aorist mid	ε	aor act	σα		sec mid/pas	ἐλυσάμην
2nd aorist mid	ε	aor act		ο/ε	sec mid/pas	ἐγενόμην
1st aorist pas	ε	aor pas	θη		sec act	ἐλύθην
2nd aorist pas	ε	aor pas	η		sec act	ἐγράφην
1st perfect act	λε	perf act	κα		prim act	λέλυκα
2nd perfect act	λε	perf act	α		prim act	γέγονα
Perfect mid/pas	λε	perf pas			prim mid/pas	λέλυμαι

Verbal Rules

1. Primary and Secondary endings

	primary			secondary		
	regular	*alternate*[1]		*regular*		*alternate*

active

	regular	*alternate*[1]		*regular*		*alternate*
1 sg	λύω	ο -[2]	μι	ἔλυον	ο ν	
2 sg	λύεις	ε ς		ἔλυες	ε ς	
3 sg	λύει	ε ι	σι(ν)	ἔλυε	ε -	
1pl	λύομεν	ο μεν		ἐλύομεν	ο μεν	
2 pl	λύετε	ε τε		ἐλύετε	ε τε	
3 pl	λύουσι(ν)	ο νσι(ν)[3]	ασι(ν)	ἔλυον	ο ν	σαν

middle/passive

	regular	*alternate*[1]		*regular*		*alternate*
1 sg	λύομαι	ο μαι		ἐλυόμην	ο μην	
2 sg	λύῃ	ε σαι[4]		ἐλύου	ε σο[5]	
3 sg	λύεται	ε ται		ἐλύετο	ε το	
1 pl	λυόμεθα	ο μεθα		ἐλυόμεθα	ο μεθα	
2 pl	λύεσθε	ε σθε		ἐλύεσθε	ε σθε	
3 pl	λύονται	ο νται		ἐλύοντο	ο ντο	

---

[1] Alternate endings are used for μι verbs and a few thematic forms.

[2] No ending is used. The omega that stands at the end of the first person singular of verbs in the thematic conjugation is really the lengthened connecting vowel omicron.

[3] In every case the nu will drop out because of the following sigma. What happens to the preceeding vowel varies.

[4] In almost every case (except perfect passive), the sigma drops out and the vowels contract. This is why this ending varies from tense to tense.

[5] In almost every case, the sigma drops out because it is intervocalic and the vowels contract. This is why this ending varies from tense to tense.

Primary Endings are used on the unaugmented tenses. In the indicative these are the present, future, and perfect. In the subjunctive it is all tenses.

Secondary Endings are used on the augmented tenses. In the indicative these are the imperfect, aorist, and pluperfect. In the optative it is all tenses (even though the optative is not augmented).

The thematic conjugation uses the regular endings while the μι conjugation uses the alternate endings.

2. *Augments occur in the imperfect, aorist, and pluperfect.*
   • It is removed in the non-indicative moods.

3. *Reduplication occurs in the perfect and present.*
   • Consonantal reduplication reduplicates the initial consonant; vocalic reduplication lengthens the initial vowel.
   • Reduplication with an epsilon always signals a perfect.
   • Reduplication with an iota signals the present of a μι verb.

4. *Verbal roots*
   • Altered verbal stems show some patterns, but others should be memorized. See *Verbal Stems of Words Occurring More than Fifty Times* below.

5. *Differences among tense stems*
   • Double consonants simplify to single consonants (v-1)
   • Verbs containing an iota lose the iota (v-2)
   • Verbs containing a nu lose the nu (v-3)
   • Verbs containing a tau lose the tau (v-4)
   • Verbs ending in ισκ lose the ισκ (v-5)
   • μι verbs (v-6)
   • Vowels lengthen, shorten, or drop out altogether (v-7)
   • Verbs that use different roots to form their different tense stems (v-8)

6. *Tense Formatives*
   • σ   Future (includes a connecting vowel)
   • σα   First aorist active/middle
                σε in the third singular active
                Middle uses passive endings
   • α   Liquid aorists
                ε in the third singular active

            Second perfects
                ε in the third singular active

- κα   Perfect
           κε in the third singular
           Third plural varies between καν and κασι(ν)
- θη   Aorist passive
           θησαν occurs in the third plural (cf. future passive)
- η   Second aorist passive
- θησ   Future passive
- ησ   Second future passive (or contract verb in future or aorist)

7. *Participles*

   Morphemes

   - ντ   Active participle (present masculine/neuter; third declension)
              Passive participle (aorist)
   - μενο/η Middle passive participle
              Feminine follows first declension, masculine/neuter the second
   - τ   Active participle (perfect)

   Forms to memorize (masc, fem, neut, nominative and genitive singular)

   Present active: οντ, ουσα

ων	ουσα	ον
οντος	ουσης	οντος

   Present middle/passive: ομενο/η

ομενος	ομενη	ομενον
ομενου	ομενης	ομενου

   First aorist active: σαντ, σασα

σας	σασα	σαν
σαντος	σασης	σαντος

   First aorist middle: σαμενο/η

σαμενος	σαμενη	σαμενον
σαμενου	σαμενης	σαμενου

   First aorist passive: θεντ, θεισα

θεις	θεισα	θεν
θεντος	θεισης	θεντος

   Second aorist active: οντ, ουσα

ων	ουσα	ον
οντος	ουσης	οντος

Second aorist middle: ομενο/η

ομενος	ομενη	ομενον
ομενου	ομενης	ομενου

Second aorist passive: εισα, εντ

εις	εισα	εν
εντος	εισης	εντος

First perfect active: κοτ, κυια

κως	κυια	κος
κοτος	κυιας	κοτος

First perfect middle/passive: μενο/η

μενος	μενη	μενον
μενου	μενης	μενου

8. *Vowels*

- Connecting vowels (o/ε) are used in the present, imperfect, future, second aorist, and participles.
- Contract vowels contract in the present and imperfect. Elsewhere they lengthen before the tense formative or personal ending.
- Contractions also occur in liquid futures.

9. *Second singular passive.* The sigma usually drops out.

- σαι
- σο

10. *Miscellaneous*

- ξ/ψ   When these occur at the end of a verbal stem, they are usually the result of a stop plus a sigma.
- φ/χ   When these occur before a theta, they are probably an aspirated labial or velar.
- Stops in the middle/passive

Overview of Indicative

	present	imperfect	future	1st aorist	2nd aorist	perfect
active indicative						
1 sg	λύω	ἔλυον	λύσω	ἔλυσα	ἔλαβον	λέλυκα
2 sg	λύεις	ἔλυες	λύσεις	ἔλυσας	ἔλαβες	λέλυκας
3 sg	λύει	ἔλυε(ν)	λύσει	ἔλυσε(ν)	ἔλαβε(ν)	λέλυκε(ν)
1 pl	λύομεν	ἐλύομεν	λύσομεν	ἐλύσαμεν	ἐλάβομεν	λελύκαμεν
2 pl	λύετε	ἐλύετε	λύσετε	ἐλύσατε	ἐλάβετε	λελύκατε
3 pl	λύουσι(ν)	ἔλυον	λύσουσι(ν)	ἔλυσαν	ἔλαβον	λελύκασι(ν)
middle indicative						
1 sg	λύομαι	ἐλυόμην	λύσομαι	ἐλυσάμην	ἐγενόμην	λέλυμαι
2 sg	λύῃ	ἐλύου	λύσῃ	ἐλύσω	ἐγένου	λέλυσαι
3 sg	λύεται	ἐλύετο	λύσεται	ἐλύσατο	ἐγένετο	λέλυται
1 pl	λυόμεθα	ἐλυόμεθα	λυσόμεθα	ἐλυσάμεθα	ἐγενόμεθα	λελύμεθα
2 pl	λύεσθε	ἐλύεσθε	λύσεσθε	ἐλύσασθε	ἐγένεσθε	λέλυσθε
3 pl	λύονται	ἐλύοντο	λύσονται	ἐλύσαντο	ἐγένοντο	λέλυνται
passive indicative						
1 sg	λύομαι	ἐλυόμην	λυθήσομαι	ἐλύθην	ἐγράφην	λέλυμαι
2 sg	λύῃ	ἐλύου	λυθήσῃ	ἐλύθης	ἐγράφης	λέλυσαι
3 sg	λύεται	ἐλύετο	λυθήσεται	ἐλύθη	ἐγράφη	λέλυται
1 pl	λυόμεθα	ἐλυόμεθα	λυθησόμεθα	ἐλύθημεν	ἐγράφημεν	λελύμεθα
2 pl	λύεσθε	ἐλύεσθε	λυθήσεσθε	ἐλύθητε	ἐγράφητε	λέλυσθε
3 pl	λύονται	ἐλύοντο	λυθήσονται	ἐλύθησαν	ἐγράφησαν	λέλυνται

Overview of Subjunctive

	present	*first aorist*	*second aorist*
active			
1 sg	λύω	λύσω	λάβω
2 sg	λύῃς	λύσῃς	λάβῃς
3 sg	λύῃ	λύσῃ	λάβῃ
1 pl	λύωμεν	λύσωμεν	λάβωμεν
2 pl	λύητε	λύσητε	λάβητε
3 pl	λύωσι (ν)	λύσωσι (ν)	λάβωσι (ν)
middle			
1 sg	λύωμαι	λύσωμαι	γένωμαι
2 sg	λύῃ	λύσῃ	γένῃ
3 sg	λύηται	λύσηται	γένηται
1 pl	λυώμεθα	λυσώμεθα	γενώμεθα
2 pl	λύησθε	λύσησθε	γένησθε
3 pl	λύωνται	λύσωνται	γένωνται
passive			
1 sg	λύωμαι	λυθῶ	γραφῶ
2 sg	λύῃ	λυθῇς	γραφῇς
3 sg	λύηται	λυθῇ	γραφῇ
1 pl	λυώμεθα	λυθῶμεν	γραφῶμεν
2 pl	λύησθε	λυθῆτε	γραφῆτε
3 pl	λύωνται	λυθῶσι (ν)	γραφῶσι (ν)

Overview of Imperative

	present	*first aorist*	*second aorist*
active			
2 sg	λῦε	λῦσον	λάβε
3 sg	λυέτω	λυσάτω	λαβέτω
2 pl	λύετε	λύσατε	λάβετε
3 pl	λυέτωσαν	λυσάτωσαν	λαβέτωσαν
middle			
2 sg	λύου	λῦσαι	γένου
3 sg	λυέσθω	λυσάσθω	γενέσθω
2 pl	λύεσθε	λύσασθε	γένεσθε
3 pl	λυέσθωσαν	λυσάσθωσαν	γενέσθωσαν
passive			
2 sg	λύου	λύθητι	γράφηθι
3 sg	λυέσθω	λυθήτω	γραφήτω
2 pl	λύεσθε	λύθητε	γράφητε
3 pl	λυέσθωσαν	λυθήτωσαν	γραφήτωσαν

Overview of Infinitive

	present	*first aorist*	*second aorist*	*perfect*
active				
	λύειν	λῦσαι	λαβεῖν	λελυκέναι
middle				
	λύεσθαι	λύσασθαι	γένεσθαι	λέλυσθαι
passive				
	λύεσθαι	λυθῆναι	γραφῆναι	λέλυσθαι

εἰμί

	present	*imperfect*	*future*

Indicative

	present	imperfect	future
1 sg	εἰμί	ἤμην	ἔσομαι
2 sg	εἶ	ἦς	ἔσῃ
3 sg	ἐστί(ν)	ἦν	ἔσται
1 pl	ἐσμέν	ἦμεν, ἤμεθα	ἐσόμεθα
2 pl	ἐστέ	ἦτε	ἔσεσθε
3 pl	εἰσί(ν)	ἦσαν	ἔσονται

Non-indicative

	subjunctive	*imperative*	*active infinitive*
1 sg	ὦ		εἶναι
2 sg	ἦς	ἴσθι	
3 sg	ἦ	ἔστω	
1 pl	ὦμεν		
2 pl	ἦτε	ἔστε	
3 pl	ὦσι(ν)	ἔστωσαν	

Participle

	masc	*fem*	*neut*		*masc*	*fem*	*neut*
nom sg	ὤν	οὖσα	ὄν	*nom pl*	ὄντες	οὖσαι	ὄντα
gen sg	ὄντος	οὔσης	ὄντος	*gen pl*	ὄντων	οὐσῶν	ὄντων
dat sg	ὄντι	οὔσῃ	ὄντι	*dat pl*	οὖσι(ν)	οὔσαις	οὖσι(ν)
acc sg	ὄντα	οὖσαν	ὄν	*acc pl*	ὄντας	οὔσας	ὄντα

Verb Paradigms

The section numbers following the centered headings refer to the relevant sections in *MBG*.

Present Indicative (§41)

Thematic: uncontracted present

	active	middle/passive
1 sg	λύω	λύομαι
2 sg	λύεις	λύῃ
3 sg	λύει	λύεται
1 sg	λύομεν	λυόμεθα
2 sg	λύετε	λύεσθε
3 sg	λύουσι(ν)	λύονται

Thematic: contracted present

active

1 sg	γεννῶ	ποιῶ	φανερῶ
2 sg	γεννᾷς	ποιεῖς	φανεροῖς
3 sg	γεννᾷ	ποιεῖ	φανεροῖ
1 pl	γεννῶμεν	ποιοῦμεν	φανεροῦμεν
2 pl	γεννᾶτε	ποιεῖτε	φανεροῦτε
3 pl	γεννῶσι(ν)	ποιοῦσι(ν)	φανεροῦσι(ν)

middle/passive

1 sg	γεννῶμαι	ποιοῦμαι	φανεροῦμαι
2 sg	γεννᾷ	ποιῇ	φανεροῖ
3 sg	γεννᾶται	ποιεῖται	φανεροῦται
1 pl	γεννώμεθα	ποιούμεθα	φανερούμεθα
2 pl	γεννᾶσθε	ποιεῖσθε	φανεροῦσθε
3 pl	γεννῶνται	ποιοῦνται	φανεροῦνται

Athematic present

active

1 sg	ἵστημι (*στα)	τίθημι (*θε)	δίδωμι (*δο)	δείκνυμι (*δεικνυ)
2 sg	ἵστης	τίθης	δίδως	δεικνύεις
3 sg	ἵστησι(ν)	τίθησι(ν)	δίδωσι(ν)	δείκνυσι(ν)
1 pl	ἵσταμεν	τίθεμεν	δίδομεν	δείκνυμεν
2 pl	ἵστατε	τίθετε	δίδοτε	δείκνυτε
3 pl	ἱστᾶσι	τιθέασι(ν)	διδόασι(ν)	δεικνύασι(ν)

middle/passive

1 sg	ἵσταμαι	τίθεμαι	δίδομαι	δείκνυμαι
2 sg	ἵστασαι	τίθεσαι	δίδοσαι	δείκνυσαι
3 sg	ἵσταται	τίθεται	δίδοται	δείκνυται
1 pl	ἱστάμεθα	τιθέμεθα	διδόμεθα	δεικνύμεθα
2 pl	ἵστασθε	τίθεσθε	δίδοσθε	δείκνυσθε
3 pl	ἵστανται	τίθενται	δίδονται	δείκνυνται

Imperfect Indicative (§42)

Thematic: uncontracted imperfect

	active	*middle/passive*
1 sg	ἔλυον	ἐλυόμην
2 sg	ἔλυες	ἐλύου
3 sg	ἔλυε(ν)	ἐλύετο
1 pl	ἐλύομεν	ἐλυόμεθα
2 pl	ἐλύετε	ἐλύεσθε
3 pl	ἔλυον	ἐλύοντο

Thematic: contracted imperfect

active

1 sg	ἐγέννων	ἐποίουν	ἐφανέρουν
2 sg	ἐγέννας	ἐποίεις	ἐφανέρους
3 sg	ἐγέννα	ἐποίει	ἐφανέρου
1 pl	ἐγεννῶμεν	ἐποιοῦμεν	ἐφανεροῦμεν
2 pl	ἐγεννᾶτε	ἐποιεῖτε	ἐφανεροῦτε
3 pl	ἐγέννων	ἐποίουν	ἐφανέρουν

middle/passive

1 sg	ἐγεννώμην	ἐποιούμην	ἐφανερούμην
2 sg	ἐγεννῶ	ἐποιοῦ	ἐφανεροῦ
3 sg	ἐγεννᾶτο	ἐποιεῖτο	ἐφανεροῦτο
1 pl	ἐγεννώμεθα	ἐποιούμεθα	ἐφανερούμεθα
2 pl	ἐγεννᾶσθε	ἐποιεῖσθε	ἐφανεροῦσθε
3 pl	ἐγεννῶντο	ἐποιοῦντο	ἐφανεροῦντο

Athematic imperfect

active

1 sg	ἵστην	ἐτίθην	ἐδίδουν	ἐδείκνυν
2 sg	ἵστης	ἐτίθεις	ἐδίδους	ἐδείκνυς
3 sg	ἵστη	ἐτίθει	ἐδίδου	ἐδείκνυ
1 pl	ἵσταμεν	ἐτίθεμεν	ἐδίδομεν	ἐδείκνυμεν
2 pl	ἵστατε	ἐτίθετε	ἐδίδοτε	ἐδείκνυτε
3 pl	ἵστασαν	ἐτίθεσαν	ἐδίδοσαν	ἐδείκνυσαν

middle/passive

1 sg	ἱστάμην	ἐτιθέμην	ἐδιδόμην	ἐδεικνύμην
2 sg	ἵστασο	ἐτίθεσο	ἐδίδοσο	ἐδείκνυσο
3 sg	ἵστατο	ἐτίθετο	ἐδίδοτο	ἐδείκνυτο
1 pl	ἱστάμεθα	ἐτιθέμεθα	ἐδιδόμεθα	ἐδεικνύμεθα
2 pl	ἵστασθε	ἐτίθεσθε	ἐδίδοσθε	ἐδείκνυσθε
3 pl	ἵσταντο	ἐτίθεντο	ἐδίδοντο	ἐδείκνυντο

Future Indicative (§43)

Thematic: uncontracted future

	active	middle
1 sg	λύσω	πορεύσομαι
2 sg	λύσεις	πορεύσῃ
3 sg	λύσει	πορεύσεται
1 pl	λύσομεν	πορευσόμεθα
2 pl	λύσετε	πορεύσεσθε
3 pl	λύσουσι(ν)	πορεύσονται

Athematic future

	active	middle
1 sg	δώσω	δώσομαι
2 sg	δώσεις	δώσῃ
3 sg	δώσει	δώσεται
1 pl	δώσομεν	δωσόμεθα
2 pl	δώσετε	δώσεσθε
3 pl	δώσουσι(ν)	δώσονται

Liquid future

	present	future active	future middle
1 sg	μένω	μενῶ	μενοῦμαι
2 sg	μένεις	μενεῖς	μενῇ
3 sg	μένει	μενεῖ	μενεῖται
1 pl	μένομεν	μενοῦμεν	μενούμεθα
2 pl	μένετε	μενεῖτε	μενεῖσθε
3 pl	μένουσι(ν)	μενοῦσι(ν)	μενοῦνται

Aorist Active/Middle Indicative (§44)

Thematic: aorist active/middle

first aorist

	active	middle
1 sg	ἔλυσα	ἐλυσάμην
2 sg	ἔλυσας	ἐλύσω
3 sg	ἔλυσε	ἐλύσατο
1 pl	ἐλύσαμεν	ἐλυσάμεθα
2 pl	ἐλύσατε	ἐλύσασθε
3 pl	ἔλυσαν	ἐλύσαντο

liquid aorist

	active	middle
1 sg	ἔμεινα	ἐμεινάμην
2 sg	ἔμεινας	ἐμείνω
3 sg	ἔμεινε	ἐμείνατο
1 pl	ἐμείναμεν	ἐμεινάμεθα
2 pl	ἐμείνατε	ἐμείνασθε
3 pl	ἔμειναν	ἐμείναντο

second aorist

	active	middle
1 sg	ἔβαλον	ἐγενόμην
2 sg	ἔβαλες	ἐγένου
3 sg	ἔβαλε(ν)	ἐγένετο
1 pl	ἐβάλομεν	ἐγενόμεθα
2 pl	ἐβάλετε	ἐγένεσθε
3 pl	ἔβαλον	ἐγένοντο

Athematic: second aorist

	ἵστημι	τίθημι	δίδωμι
active			
1 sg	ἔστην	ἔθην	ἔδων[6]
2 sg	ἔστης	ἔθης	ἔδως
3 sg	ἔστη	ἔθη	ἔδω
1 pl	ἔστημεν	ἔθεμεν	ἔδομεν
2 pl	ἔστητε	ἔθετε	ἔδοτε
3 pl	ἔστησαν	ἔθεασαν	ἔδοσαν
middle			
1 sg	ἐστάμην	ἐθέμην	ἐδόμην[7]
2 sg	ἔστω	ἔθου	ἔδου
3 sg	ἔστατο	ἔθετο	ἔδοτο
1 pl	ἐστάμεθα	ἐθέμεθα	ἐδόμεθα
2 pl	ἔστασθε	ἔθεσθε	ἔδοσθε
3 pl	ἔσταντο	ἔθεντο	ἔδοντο

Perfect Active Indicative (§45)

Thematic: perfect active

first perfect

1 sg	λέλυκα	*1 pl*	λελύκαμεν
2 sg	λέλυκας	*2 pl*	λελύκατε
3 sg	λέλυκε(ν)	*3 pl*	λελύκασι(ν)

second perfect

1 sg	γέγονα	*1 pl*	γεγόναμεν
2 sg	γέγονας	*2 pl*	γεγόνατε
3 sg	γέγονε(ν)	*3 pl*	γεγόνασι(ν)

---

[6]   First aorist, ἔδωκα.

[7]   First aorist, ἐδωκάμην.

Perfect Middle/Passive Indicative (§46)

1 sg	λέλυμαι		1 pl	λελύμεθα
2 sg	λέλυσαι		2 pl	λέλυσθε
3 sg	λέλυται		3 pl	λέλυνται

Aorist/Future Passive (§47)

first aorist

1 sg	ἐλύθην		1 pl	ἐλύθημεν
2 sg	ἐλύθης		2 pl	ἐλύθητε
3 sg	ἐλύθη		3 pl	ἐλύθησαν

second aorist

1 sg	ἐγράφην		1 pl	ἐγράφημεν
2 sg	ἐγράφης		2 pl	ἐγράφητε
3 sg	ἐγράφη		3 pl	ἐγράφησαν

first future

1 sg	λυθήσομαι		1 pl	λυθησόμεθα
2 sg	λυθήσῃ		2 pl	λυθήσεσθε
3 sg	λυθήσεται		3 pl	λυθήσονται

second future

1 sg	γραφήσομαι		1 pl	γραφησόμεθα
2 sg	γραφήσῃ		2 pl	γραφήσεσθε
3 sg	γραφήσεται		3 pl	γραφήσονται

Subjunctive (§50)

Thematic: uncontracted subjunctive

	present	*aorist*	*perfect*
active subjunctive			
1 sg	λύω	λύσω	λελύκω
2 sg	λύῃς	λύσῃς	λελύκῃς
3 sg	λύῃ	λύσῃ	λελύκῃ
1 pl	λύωμεν	λύσωμεν	λελύκωμεν
2 pl	λύητε	λύσητε	λελύκητε
3 pl	λύωσι(ν)	λύσωσι(ν)	λελύκωσι(ν)
middle subjunctive			
1 sg	λύωμαι	λύσωμαι	λελυμένος ὦ
2 sg	λύῃ	λύσῃ	λελυμένος ᾖς
3 sg	λύηται	λύσηται	λελυμένος ᾖ
1 pl	λυώμεθα	λυσώμεθα	λελυμένοι ὦμεν
2 pl	λύησθε	λύσησθε	λελυμένοι ἦτε
3 pl	λύωνται	λύσωνται	λελυμένοι ὦσι
passive subjunctive			
1 sg	λύωμαι	λυθῶ	λελυμένος ὦ
2 sg	λύῃ	λυθῇς	λελυμένος ᾖς
3 sg	λύηται	λυθῇ	λελυμένος ᾖ
1 pl	λυώμεθα	λυθῶμεν	λελυμένοι ὦμεν
2 pl	λύησθε	λυθῆτε	λελυμένοι ἦτε
3 pl	λύωνται	λυθῶσι(ν)	λελυμένοι ὦσι

Thematic: contracted subjunctive

	-άω	-έω	-όω
present active subjunctive			
1 sg	γεννῶ	ποιῶ	φανερῶ
2 sg	γεννᾷς	ποιῇς	φανεροῖς
3 sg	γεννᾷ	ποιῇ	φανεροῖ
1 pl	γεννῶμεν	ποιῶμεν	φανερῶμεν
2 pl	γεννᾶτε	ποιῆτε	φανερῶτε
3 pl	γεννῶσι(ν)	ποιῶσι(ν)	φανερῶσι(ν)
present middle/passive subjunctive			
1 sg	γεννῶμαι	ποιῶμαι	φανερῶμαι
2 sg	γεννᾷ	ποιῇ	φανεροῖ
3 sg	γεννᾶται	ποιῆται	φανερῶται
1 pl	γεννώμεθα	ποιώμεθα	φανερώμεθα
2 pl	γεννᾶσθε	ποιῆσθε	φανερῶσθε
3 pl	γεννῶνται	ποιῶνται	φανερῶνται

Athematic subjunctive

present active subjunctive			
1 sg	ἱστῶ	τιθῶ	διδῶ
2 sg	ἱστῇς	τιθῇς	διδῷς
3 sg	ἱστῇ	τιθῇ	διδῷ
1 pl	ἱστῶμεν	τιθῶμεν	διδῶμεν
2 pl	ἱστῆτε	τιθῆτε	διδῶτε
3 pl	ἱστῶσι(ν)	τιθῶσι(ν)	διδῶσι(ν)

	*στα	*θε	*δο

present middle/passive subjunctive

1 sg	ἱστῶμαι	τιθῶμαι	διδῶμαι
2 sg	ἱστῇ	τιθῇ	διδῷ
3 sg	ἱστῆται	τιθῆται	διδῶται
1 pl	ἱστώμεθα	τιθώμεθα	διδώμεθα
2 pl	ἱστῆσθε	τιθῆσθε	διδῶσθε
3 pl	ἱστῶνται	τιθῶνται	διδῶνται

second aorist active subjunctive

1 sg	στῶ[8]	θῶ	δῶ
2 sg	στῇς	θῇς	δῷς
3 sg	στῇ	θῇ	δῷ
1 pl	στῶμεν	θῶμεν	δῶμεν
2 pl	στῆτε	θῆτε	δῶτε
3 pl	στῶσι(ν)	θῶσι(ν)	δῶσι(ν)

second aorist middle subjunctive

1 sg	στῶμαι[9]	θῶμαι	δῶμαι
2 sg	στῇ	θῇ	δῷ
3 sg	στῆται	θῆται	δῶται
1 pl	στώμεθα	θώμεθα	δώμεθα
2 pl	στῆσθε	θῆσθε	δῶσθε
3 pl	στῶνται	θῶνται	δῶνται

---

[8] First aorist, στήσω.
[9] First aorist, στήσωμαι.

Imperative (§70)

Thematic: uncontracted imperative

	present	*1 aorist*	*2 aorist*	*perfect*
active imperative				
2 sg	λῦε	λῦσον	βάλε	λέλυκε
3 sg	λυέτω	λυσάτω	βαλέτω	λελυκέτω
2 pl	λύετε	λύσατε	βάλετε	λελύκετε
3 pl	λυέτωσαν	λυσάτωσαν	βαλέτωσαν	λελυκέτωσαν

middle/passive imperative   **1st aorist pas.**

2 sg	λύου	λῦσαι	βαλοῦ	λέλυσο	λύθητι
3 sg	λυέσθω	λυσάσθω	βαλέσθω	λελύσθω	λυθήτω
2 pl	λύεσθε	λύσασθε	βάλεσθε	λέλυσθε	λύθητε
3 pl	λυέσθωσαν	λυσάσθωσαν	βαλέσθωσαν	λελύσθωσαν	λυθήτωσαν

Thematic: contracted imperative

present active imperative

2 sg	γέννα	ποίει	φανέρου
3 sg	γεννάτω	ποιείτω	φανερούτω
2 pl	γεννᾶτε	ποιεῖτε	φανεροῦτε
2 pl	γεννάτωσαν	ποιείτωσαν	φανερούτωσαν

present middle/passive imperative

2 sg	γεννῶ	ποιοῦ	φανεροῦ
3 sg	γεννάσθω	ποιείσθω	φανερούσθω
2 pl	γεννᾶσθε	ποιεῖσθε	φανεροῦσθε
3 pl	γεννάσθωσαν	ποιείσθωσαν	φανερούσθωσαν

Athematic imperative

	*στα	*θε	*δο	*δεικνυ

present active imperative

	*στα	*θε	*δο	*δεικνυ
2 sg	ἵστη	τίθει	δίδου	δείκνυθι
3 sg	ἱστάτω	τιθέτω	διδότω	δεικνύτω
2 pl	ἵστατε	τίθετε	δίδοτε	δείκνυτε
3 pl	ἱστάτωσαν	τιθέτωσαν	διδότωσαν	δεικνύτωσαν

present middle/passive imperative

	*στα	*θε	*δο	*δεικνυ
2 sg	ἵστασο	τίθεσο	δίδοσο	δείκνυσο
3 sg	ἱστάσθω	τιθέσθω	διδόσθω	δεικνύσθω
2 pl	ἵστασθε	τίθεσθε	δίδοσθε	δείκνυσθε
3 pl	ἱστάσθωσαν	τιθέσθωσαν	διδόσθωσαν	δεικνύσθωσαν

aorist active imperative

	*στα	*θε	*δο
2 sg	στῆθι	θές	δός
3 sg	στήτω	θέτω	δότω
2 pl	στῆτε	θέτε	δότε
3 pl	στήτωσαν	θέτωσαν	δότωσαν

aorist middle imperative

	*στα	*θε	*δο
2 sg	στῶ	θοῦ	δοῦ
3 sg	στάσθω	θέσθω	δόσθω
2 pl	στάσθε	θέσθε	δόσθε
3 pl	στάσθωσαν	θέσθωσαν	δόσθωσαν

Infinitive (§80)

Active infinitive

present	future	1st aorist	2nd aorist	1st perfect	2nd perfect

thematic

λυείν	λύσειν	λῦσαι	βαλεῖν	λελυκέναι	γεγονέναι

contract

γεννᾶν	γεννήσειν	γεννῆσαι	γεγεννηκέναι
ποιεῖν	ποιήσειν	ποιῆσαι	πεποιηκέναι
φανεροῦν	φανερώσειν	φανερῶσαι	πεφανερωκέναι

μι

ἱστάναι	στήσειν	στῆσαι	στῆναι	ἑστηκέναι
τιθέναι	θήσειν		θεῖναι	τεθεικέναι
διδόναι	δώσειν		δοῦναι	δεδωκέναι
δεικνύναι				
εἶναι				

liquid

μένειν	μενεῖν	μεῖναι

Mid./pas. infinitive   ## Middle infinitive

present	perfect	future	1st aorist	2nd aorist

thematic

λύεσθαι	λελύσθαι	λύσεσθαι	λύσασθαι

contract

γεννᾶσθαι	γεννῆσθαι	γεννήσεσθαι	γεννήσασθαι
ποιεῖσθαι	πεποιῆσθαι	ποιήσεσθαι	ποιήσασθαι
φανεροῦσθαι	πεφανερῶσθαι	φανερώσεσθαι	φανερώσασθαι

Mid./pas. infinitive   ## Middle infinitive

present	*perfect*	*future*	*1st aorist*	*2nd aorist*
μι				
ἵστασθαι	ἑστάναι	στήσεσθαι	στήσασθαι	στάσθαι
τίθεσθαι		θήσεσθαι		θέσθαι
δίδοσθαι		δώσεσθαι		δόσθαι
		δείκνυσθαι		
		ἔσεσθαι		
liquid				
μένεσθαι		μενεῖσθαι	μείνασθαι	

Passive infinitive

	future	*first aorist*	*second aorist*
thematic	λυθήσεσθαι	λυθῆναι	γραφῆναι
contract (a)	γεννηθήσεσθαι	γεννηθῆναι	
contract (e)	ποιηθήσεσθαι	ποιηθῆναι	
contract (o)	φανερωθήσεσθαι	φανερωθῆναι	

Participle (§90)

Thematic (Uncontracted)

present active participle

nom sg	λύων	λύουσα	λῦον
gen sg	λύοντος	λυούσης	λύοντος
dat sg	λύοντι	λυούσῃ	λύοντι
acc sg	λύοντα	λύουσαν	λῦον
nom pl	λύοντες	λύουσαι	λύοντα
gen pl	λυόντων	λυουσῶν	λυόντων
dat pl	λύουσι(ν)	λυούσαις	λύουσι(ν)
acc pl	λύοντας	λυούσας	λύοντα

present middle/passive participle

nom sg	λυόμενος	λυομένη	λυόμενον
gen sg	λυομένου	λυομένης	λυομένου
dat sg	λυομένῳ	λυομένη	λυομένῳ
acc sg	λυόμενον	λυομένην	λυόμενον
nom pl	λυόμενοι	λυόμεναι	λυόμενα
gen pl	λυομένων	λυομένων	λυομένων
dat pl	λυομένοις	λυομέναις	λυομένοις
acc pl	λυομένους	λυομένας	λυόμενα

future participle

active	nom sg	λύσων	λύσουσα	λῦσον
	gen sg	λύσοντος	λυσούσης	λύσοντος
middle	nom sg	λυσόμενος	λυσομένη	λυσόμενον
	gen sg	λυσομένου	λυσομένης	λυσομένου
first passive	nom sg	λυθησόμενος	λυθησομένη	λυθησόμενον
	gen sg	λυθησομένου	λυθησομένης	λυθησομένου
second passive	nom sg	γραψόμενος	γραψομένη	γραψόμενον
	gen sg	γραψομένου	γραψομένης	γραψομένου

first aorist active participle

nom sg	λύσας	λύσασα	λῦσαν
gen sg	λύσαντος	λυσάσης	λύσαντος
dat sg	λύσαντι	λυσάσῃ	λύσαντι
acc sg	λύσαντα	λύσασαν	λῦσαν
nom pl	λύσαντες	λύσασαι	λύσαντα
gen pl	λυσάντων	λυσασῶν	λυσάντων
dat pl	λύσασι(ν)	λυσάσαις	λύσασι(ν)
acc pl	λύσαντας	λυσάσας	λύσαντα

first aorist middle participle

nom sg	λυσάμενος	λυσαμένη	λυσάμενον
gen sg	λυσαμένου	λυσαμένης	λυσαμένου

first aorist passive participle

nom sg	λυθείς	λυθεῖσα	λυθέν
gen sg	λυθέντος	λυθείσης	λυθέντος
dat sg	λυθέντι	λυθείσῃ	λυθέντι
acc sg	λυθέντα	λυθεῖσαν	λυθέν
nom pl	λυθέντες	λυθεῖσαι	λυθέντα
gen pl	λυθέντων	λυθεισῶν	λυθέντων
dat pl	λυθεῖσι(ν)	λυθείσαις	λυθεῖσι(ν)
acc pl	λυθέντας	λυθείσας	λυθέντα

second aorist participle

active	*nom sg*	βαλών	βαλοῦσα	βαλόν
	gen sg	βαλόντος	βαλούσης	βαλόντος
middle	*nom sg*	βαλόμενος	βαλομένη	βαλόμενον
	gen sg	βαλόμενου	βαλομένης	βαλόμενου
passive	*nom sg*	γραφείς	γραφεῖσα	γραφέν
	gen sg	γραφέντος	γραφείσης	γραφέντος

perfect active participle

nom sg	λελυκώς	λελυκυῖα	λελυκός
gen sg	λελυκότος	λελυκυίας	λελυκότος
dat sg	λελυκότι	λελυκυίᾳ	λελυκότι
acc sg	λελυκότα	λελυκυῖαν	λελυκός
nom pl	λελυκότες	λελυκυῖαι	λελυκότα
gen pl	λελυκότων	λελυκυιῶν	λελυκότων
dat pl	λελυκόσι(ν)	λελυκυίαις	λελυκόσι(ν)
acc pl	λελυκότας	λελυκυίας	λελυκότα

perfect middle/passive participle

nom sg	λελυμένος	λελυμένη	λελυμένον
gen sg	λελυμένου	λελυμένης	λελυμένου

Athematic participle

present active participle

nom sg	ἱστάς	ἱστᾶσα	ἱστάν
gen sg	ἱστάντος	ἱστάσης	ἱστάντος
nom sg	τιθείς	τιθεῖσα	τιθέν
gen sg	τιθέντος	τιθείσης	τιθέντος
nom sg	διδούς	διδοῦσα	διδόν
gen sg	διδόντος	διδούσης	διδόντος
nom sg	δεικνύς	δεικνῦσα	δεικνύν
gen sg	δεικνύντος	δεικνύσης	δεικνύντος

present middle/passive participle

nom sg	ἱστάμενος	ἱσταμένη	ἱστάμενον
gen sg	ἱσταμένου	ἱσταμένης	ἱσταμένου
nom sg	τιθέμενος	τιθεμένη	τιθέμενον
gen sg	τιθεμένου	τιθεμένης	τιθεμένου
nom sg	διδόμενος	διδομένη	διδόμενον
gen sg	διδομένου	διδομένης	διδομένου

nom sg	δεικνύμενος	δεικνυμένη	δεικνυμένον
gen sg	δεικνυμένου	δεικνυμένης	δεικνυμένου

future active participle   future middle participle

nom sg	στήσων	στησόμενος
gen sg	στήσοντος	στησομένου

nom sg	θήσων	θησόμενος
gen sg	θήσοντος	θησομένου

nom sg	δώσων	δωσόμενος
gen sg	δώσοντος	δωσομένου

first aorist active participle

nom sg	στήσας	θήκας
gen sg	στήσαντος	θηκάντος

second aorist active participle

nom sg	στάς	στᾶσα	στάν
gen sg	στάντος	στάσης	στάντος

nom sg	θείς	θεῖσα	θέν
gen sg	θέντος	θείσης	θέντος

nom sg	δούς	δοῦσα	δόν
gen sg	δόντος	δούσης	δόντος

first aorist middle participle

nom sg	στησάμενος	θηκάμενος
gen sg	στησαμένου	θηκομένου

second aorist middle participle

nom sg	στάμενος	σταμένη	στάμενον
gen sg	σταμένου	σταμένης	σταμένου

nom sg	θέμενος	θεμένη	θέμενον
gen sg	θεμένου	θεμένης	θεμένου

| nom sg | δόμενος | δομένη | δόμενον |
| gen sg | δομένου | δομένης | δομένου |

first aorist passive participle

| nom sg | σταθείς | σταθεῖσα | σταθέν |
| gen sg | σταθέντος | σταθείσης | σταθέντος |

| nom sg | τεθείς | τεθεῖσα | τεθέν |
| gen sg | τεθέντος | τεθείσης | τεθέντος |

perfect active participle

| nom sg | ἑστηκώς | τεθεικώς | δεδωκώς |
| gen sg | ἑστκότος | τεθεικότος | δεδωκότος |

Tense Stems of Verbs Occurring Fifty Times or More in the New Testament

The chart on the following pages lists the verbs occurring fifty times or more in the New Testament, including their principal parts (the six different basic tense forms).

Three Verb categories

As far as memorization is concerned, there are three different classes of verbs.

- *Regular verbs.* You should not memorize the tense forms of these verbs. There is no reason to.

- *Verbs that undergo regular changes.* As we worked through *The Basics of Biblical Greek*, we saw patterns in the formation of the different tense stems. If you know the rules governing these changes, there is no reason to memorize these verbs either. The rules that you need to know are listed below, and the changes are explained in the footnotes to the tense forms.

- *Verbal forms that you need to memorize.* Some tense forms seem so irregular that it is easiest simply to memorize them. These forms are underlined in the following chart. Resist the temptation to memorize forms that are not so marked. Learn the rules and memorize as few forms as possible.

  If a compound verb has a tense stem that should be memorized, only the simple form of that verb is underlined. For example, the aorist passive of βάλλω (ἐβλήθην) is underlined, but the aorist passive of ἐκβάλλω (ἐξεβλήθην) is not underlined. If you know the first you should know the second.

You should work through the chart and confirm which forms you need to memorize and which ones you will recognize by knowing the lexical form and the rules. If there are forms you will not recognize that are not underlined, be sure to mark them so you will memorize them.

Rules governing the chart

1. Do not memorize the entire chart. If you rely on rote memory, then you probably will not be able to continue using Greek throughout your ministry.

    Forms you probably will want to memorize are underlined. If you feel the need to mark others, do so, but keep them to a minimum.

2. The tense stems follow the usual order: present, future active/middle, aorist active/middle, perfect active, perfect middle/passive, aorist/future passive.

3. If the verb–in simple or compound form–does not occur in a specific tense in the Greek Testament, it is not listed. There is a dash in its place.

4. Changes to a compound verb are explained in the listing of the simple verb. For example, εἰσέρχομαι is explained under ἔρχομαι.

    If the simple verb is not included in this chart, one of the compound verbs has the explanations and the other compounds with the same simple verb reference that compound. For example, the root *βαινω does not occur. We have described the changes of the root *βαινω under ἀναβαίνω, and κατα-βαίνω refers you to ἀναβαίνω.

5. These 90 verbs are the most important to memorize. The basic rule is that the more a word is used, the more "irregular" or modified it becomes. Therefore, as you learn verbs that occur less than fifty times, there is an increased chance that they will be fully regular.

6. "Regular" and "irregular" are unfortunate choices of terms, because Greek verbs are regular. It is just that in some cases the rules governing the changes are so esoteric that it is simplest to memorize the verbal form and not the rules.

7. All explanations of changes assume you know the verbal root(s) of the verb. Roots are listed in the footnote to the present tense stem, preceded by an asterisk (e.g., *ἀγαπα).

8. If something is not explained in the footnotes for a tense, look first to the footnote on the present tense form. If it is not explained there, then one of the basic rules listed below governs the change.

Rules governing the morphological changes in these stems

If you learn the following rules, the only verb tenses that you need to memorize are those that are underlined in the following chart. As we said above, resist the temptation to memorize forms that are not so marked. Learn the rules and keep the memory work to a minimum. This will increase the chances of you being able to use Greek in the years to come.

1. The present tense is by far the most irregular because the verbal root has often undergone some change in the formation of the present tense stem.

   • Single lambda becomes double lambda (*βαλ ‣ βάλλω ‣ ἔβαλον).

   • Iota is added to form the present tense stem (*αρ ‣ αρι ‣ αιρ ‣ αἴρω ‣ ἦρα).

2. Verbs ending in αζω and ιζω have roots ending in a dental. Once you recognize that, the tense stems are usually regular.

   *βαπτιδ, βαπτίζω, βαπτίσω, ἐβάπτισα, -, βεβάπτισμαι, ἐβαπτίσθην.

3. When a verb undergoes ablaut, it is seldom necessary to know what stem vowel will be used in a certain tense.

   It is most important to use this clue to tell you whether a verbal form is in the present or not. If there has been ablaut, then you know it is not in the present tense, and you can find other clues as to its proper parsing (ἀποστέλλω ‣ ἀπέστειλα ‣ ἀπέσταλκα).

   If a verb undergoes ablaut throughout the tenses, it is usually noted in the footnote to the present tense form.

4. Liquids use the tense formative εσ in the future, which means that the sigma drops out when followed by the connecting vowel, and the contraction looks like that of a present tense epsilon contract verb (αἴρω ‣ ἀρω).

   Liquids also use the tense formative α in the aorist active (αἴρω ‣ ἀρα).

5. It is common for a verb to insert an eta (καλέω ‣ ἐκλήθην) or a sigma (ἀκούω ‣ ἠκούσθην) before the tense formative in the aorist passive and sometimes before the ending in the perfect middle/passive (βάλλω ‣ βέβλημαι; δοξάζω ‣ δεδόξασμαι).

   This is especially common in ιζω and αζω type verbs (βαπτίζω ‣ ἐβαπτίσθην).

6. The letter before the tense formative in the perfect middle/passive and aorist passive is often changed, especially if the stem ends in a stop (ἄγω ‣ ἤχθην). It is usually not important to be able to predict what the new consonant will be; just get used to seeing an unusual consonant there and look elsewhere for clues as to the verb's parsing.

7. Square of stops plus sigma.

labials (π β φ)	+ σ ‣ ψ	βλεπ + σω ‣ βλέψω
velars (κ γ χ)	+ σ ‣ ξ	κηρυγ + σω ‣ κηρύξω
dentals (τ δ θ)	+ σ ‣ σ	βαπτιδ + σω ‣ βαπτίσω

present	future	aorist act	perfect act	perfect mid/pas	aorist pas
ἀγαπάω[1]	ἀγαπήσω	ἠγάπησα	ἠγάπηκα	ἠγάπημαι	ἠγαπήθην
ἄγω[2]	ἄξω	ἤγαγον[3]	-	ἦγμαι	ἤχθην[4]
αἴρω[5]	ἀρῶ	ἦρα	ἦρκα	ἦρμαι	ἤρθην
αἰτέω[6]	αἰτήσω	ᾔτησα	ᾔτηκα	ᾔτημαι	-
ἀκολουθέω[7]	ἀκολουθήσω	ἠκολούθησα	ἠκολούθηκα	-	-
ἀκούω[8]	ἀκούσω	ἤκουσα	ἀκήκοα[9]	-	ἠκούσθην[10]
ἀναβαίνω[11]	ἀναβήσομαι[12]	ἀνέβην[13]	ἀναβέβηκα	-	-
ἀνίστημι[14]	ἀναστήσω	ἀνέστησα	ἀνέστηκα	ἀνέστημαι	ἀνεστάθην
ἀνοίγω[15]	-	ἀνέῳξα[16]	-	-	ἀνεῴχθην[17]

---

[1] *αγαπα

[2] *αγ

[3] *αγ. An unusual second aorist. There actually is a reduplication and an augment. The stem reduplicates (*αγ ‣ αγαγ) and then the reduplicated vowel lengthens (αγαγ ‣ ηγαγ ‣ ἤγαγον).

[4] The final gamma of the stem has been changed to a chi because of the theta.

[5] *αρ. The iota is added to the root to form the present tense stem and it consequently does not occur in the other tenses.

αἴρω is a liquid verb and uses εσ and alpha as the tense formatives in the future and aorist active tenses.

[6] *αἰτε

[7] *ακολουθε. It is easy to mistake the θη in the other tense forms as the aorist passive tense formative. This is the only commonly used Greek verb that ends in θε, so this is not a frequent mistake.

[8] *ακου.

[9] An unusual perfect. Because it is a second perfect, the tense formative is alpha, not κα.

[10] Inserts a sigma before the theta of the tense formative.

[11] *αναβα. A compound of ἀνα and *βαίνω. The stem of βαίνω is *βα, to which is added ιν to form the present tense stem; therefore ιν does not occur in the other tenses.

In the other tense stems, the alpha lengthens to an eta.

[12] Deponent future middle.

[13] Second aorist.

[14] *ανιστα. Compound verb formed by ἀνα plus *στα. See ἵστημι.

[15] *ανοιγ. This is a strange word, one of the most troublesome when it comes to augments. It used to be a compound verb (ἀν[α] plus οἴγω), but in Koine it is beginning to "forget" it was a compound, and the augment is sometimes placed at the beginning of the preposition or sometimes at both places.

[16] Shows a double augment with the iota subscripting (ανοιγ + σα ‣ ανεοιξα ‣ ανεωιξα ‣ ἀνέῳξα). Can also be ἠνέῳξα, which adds a third augment by lengthening the first vowel.

present	future	aorist act	perfect act	perfect mid/pas	aorist pas
ἀπέρχομαι[1]	ἀπελεύσομαι	ἀπῆλθον	ἀπελήλυθα	-	-
ἀποθνῄσκω[2]	ἀποθανοῦμαι[3]	ἀπέθανον[4]	-	-	-
ἀποκρίνομαι[5]	-	ἀπεκρινάμην[6]	-	-	ἀπεκρίθην[7]
ἀποκτείνω[8]	ἀποκτενῶ[9]	ἀπέκτεινα[10]	-	-	ἀπεκτάνθην[11]
ἀπόλλυμι[12]	ἀπολέσω	ἀπώλεσα	ἀπόλωλα[13]	-	-
ἀπολύω[14]	ἀπολύσω	ἀπέλυσα	-	ἀπολέλυμαι	ἀπελύθην

---

[17] Shows the same augmentation pattern as in the aorist active. Here the final stem gamma has changed to a chi because of the theta in the tense formative. Can also be ἠνεῴχθην .

[1] *απερχ. A compound verb formed with ἀπό plus *ἐρχ. See ἔρχομαι.

[2] *αποθαν. ἀποθνῄσκω is a compound verb, ἀπό plus *θαν, as you can see by the augment in the aorist active (ἀπέθανον). If you recognize that the root is *ἀποθαν, knowing how it was altered in the present tense is not essential.

But in case you want to know: in the formation of the present tense, the alpha dropped out (ablaut), eta and ισκ were added, and the iota subscripts. αποθαν ‣ αποθν ‣ αποθνη ‣ αποθνηισκ ‣ ἀποθνῄσκω.

[3] Future middle deponent.

[4] Second aorist.

[5] *αποκριν. All forms of this liquid word are deponent.

[6] Liquid aorist (απεκριν + α + μην ‣ ἀπεκρινάμην).

[7] Loses its stem nu before the theta. This is not normal.

[8] *αποκτεν. A liquid verb. Notice the ablaut of the final stem vowel/diphthong.

[9] Liquid future (αποκτεν + εσ + ω ‣ ἀποκτενῶ).

[10] Due to ablaut, the stem vowel has shifted from epsilon to ει. Because it is a liquid aorist, the tense formative is alpha.

[11] Due to ablaut, the stem vowel has changed from ε to α.

[12] *απολ. This is a compound verb, as you can tell from the augment in the aorist active (ἀπώλεσα). We underlined the present tense form because it is difficult to remember how the stem is altered in the formation of the present. On the root see *MBG*, 309.

[13] Second perfect.

[14] *απολυ.

present	future	aorist act	perfect act	perfect mid/pas	aorist pas
ἀποστέλλω[1]	ἀποστελῶ[2]	ἀπέστειλα[3]	ἀπέσταλκα[4]	ἀπέσταλμαι[5]	ἀπεστάλην[6]
ἄρχω[7]	ἄρξομαι[8]	ἠρξάμην[9]	-	-	-
ἀσπάζομαι[10]	-	ἠσπασάμην[11]	-	-	-
ἀφίημι[12]	ἀφήσω	ἀφῆκα[13]	-	ἀφέωμαι[14]	ἀφέθην[15]
βάλλω[16]	βαλῶ[17]	ἔβαλον[18]	βέβληκα[19]	βέβλημαι[20]	ἐβλήθην[21]
βαπτίζω[22]	βαπτίσω	ἐβάπτισα	-	βεβάπτισμαι	ἐβαπτίσθην

1   *ἀποστελ. The lambda was doubled for the present tense stem. There is therefore a single lambda throughout the other tenses.

   It is a liquid verb, so it uses εσ and alpha for its tense formatives in the future and aorist active tenses. Notice also the ablaut in the final stem vowel/diphthong.

   These changes are all normal, so you should not have to memorize the tense forms.

2   Liquid future.

3   Liquid aorist. The stem vowel has changed due to ablaut.

4   The stem vowel has changed due to ablaut.

5   The stem vowel has changed due to ablaut.

6   Second aorist. The stem vowel has changed due to ablaut.

7   *αρχ.

8   Future middle deponent.

9   Aorist middle deponent.

10   *ασπαδ.

11   Middle deponent.

12   Although this is not actually correct, think of the root of this verb as *αφη, which inserts an iota in the present tense stem (ἀφίημι). It is a μι verb and follows the usual rules.

13   κα aorist.

14   Inserts an ω before the personal ending.

15   The stem vowel shortens from η to ε due to ablaut.

16   *βαλ. The lambda doubles in the formation of the present tense stem. It is a liquid verb.

17   Liquid future (*βαλ + εσ + ω ▸ βαλῶ).

18   Usually liquid aorists are first aorist and use the alpha as the tense formative. βάλλω follows the pattern of a normal second aorist.

19   Due to ablaut, the stem vowel has dropped out and an eta has been inserted before the tense formative. This form follows the normal rules, but many students still have trouble with it so you may want to memorize it.

20   See the explanation for the perfect active tense form.

21   See the explanation for the perfect active tense form.

22   *βαπτιδ.

present	future	aorist act	perfect act	perfect mid/pas	aorist pas
βλέπω[1]	βλέψω	ἔβλεψα	-	-	-
γεννάω[2]	γεννήσω	ἐγέννησα	γεγέννηκα	γεγέννημαι	ἐγεννήθην
γίνομαι[3]	γενήσομαι[4]	ἐγενόμην[5]	γέγονα[6]	γεγένημαι[7]	ἐγενήθην[8]
γινώσκω[9]	γνώσομαι[10]	ἔγνων[11]	ἔγνωκα	ἔγνωσμαι[12]	ἐγνώσθην[13]
γράφω[14]	γράψω	ἔγραψα	γέγραφα[15]	γέγραμμαι[16]	ἐγράφην[17]
δεῖ[18]	-	-	-	-	-

---

[1] *βλεπ.

[2] *γεννα.

[3] The root of γίνομαι is *γεν. This is important to note in keeping it separate from γεννάω (*γεννα) and γινώσκω (*γνο). Here are some hints for keeping these three words separate.

- γίνομαι will always have a vowel between the gamma and nu. Usually it will be an epsilon.
- γεννάω always has the double nu and is fully regular.
- γινώσκω, except in the present tense, does not have a vowel between the gamma and nu.

[4] Future middle deponent.

[5] Second aorist middle deponent.

[6] The stem vowel has shifted from epsilon to omicron due to ablaut. It is a second perfect and therefore uses the tense formative alpha.

[7] Inserts the eta before the personal ending.

[8] Inserts the eta before the personal ending.

[9] *γνο. See the discussion of γίνομαι above.

The root is *γνο, to which was added ισκ to form the present tense stem. Actually, the iota in the present tense stem is the result of reduplication, after which the original gamma dropped off and the stem vowel lengthened: γνο ‣ γιγνο ‣ γινο + σκω ‣ γινώσκω. The stem vowel lengthens from o to ω in the other tenses.

[10] Future middle deponent.

[11] Second aorist.

[12] Inserts a sigma before the tense formative.

[13] Inserts a sigma before the tense formative.

[14] *γραφ.

[15] Second perfect.

[16] The φμ combination forms μμ.

[17] Second aorist.

[18] This is an impersonal, third person singular, form that never changes.

present	future	aorist act	perfect act	perfect mid/pas	aorist pas
δέχομαι[1]	δέξομαι[2]	ἐδεξάμην[3]	-	δέδεγμαι[4]	ἐδέχθην
διδάσκω[5]	διδάξω	ἐδίδαξα	-	-	ἐδιδάχθην[6]
δίδωμι[7]	δώσω	ἔδωκα	δέδωκα	δέδομαι	ἐδόθην
δοκέω[8]	δόξω	ἔδοξα	-	-	-
δοξάζω[9]	δοξάσω	ἐδόξασα	-	δεδόξασμαι[10]	ἐδοξάσθην[11]
δύναμαι[12]	δυνήσομαι[13]	-	-	-	ἠδυνήθην[14]
ἐγείρω[15]	ἐγερῶ	ἤγειρα[16]	-	ἐγήγερμαι[17]	ἠγέρθην
εἰμί[18]	ἔσομαι	ἤμην[19]	-	-	-
εἰσέρχομαι[20]	εἰσελεύσομαι	εἰσῆλθον	εἰσελήλυθα	-	-
ἐκβάλλω[21]	ἐκβαλῶ	ἐξέβαλον	ἐκβέβληκα	ἐκβέβλημαι	ἐξεβλήθην
ἐξέρχομαι[22]	ἐξελεύσομαι	ἐξῆλθον	ἐξελήλυθα	-	-

---

[1] *δεχ.

[2] Future middle deponent.

[3] Aorist middle deponent.

[4] The χμ combination forms γμ.

[5] *διδασκ. Unlike words like ἀποθνήσκω where the σκ is added to form the present tense stem, the σκ is part of this root. It also is not a μι verb. The σ is swallowed up in the contractions in the future and aorist active.

[6] The σ is lost altogether when the κθ combination forms χθ.

[7] *δο. δίδωμι is regular if you know the rules for the formation of μι verbs.

[8] *δοκε.

[9] *δοξαδ.

[10] The δμ combination forms σμ.

[11] The δθ combination forms σθ.

[12] *δυν. Uses an alpha as the connecting vowel in the present.

[13] Future middle deponent.

[14] The verb augments in the aorist passive as if the root began with a vowel.

[15] *εγερ. An iota is added in the formation of the present tense stem. It is a liquid verb. Notice the ablaut throughout the different tense stems.

[16] Stem change due to ablaut.

[17] Reduplicates and undergoes vocalic reduplication: εγερ ‣ εγεγερ ‣ εγηγερ ‣ ἐγήγερμαι.

[18] Just memorize this verb.

[19] Actually an imperfect, but we have included it here for clarity's sake.

[20] See ἔρχομαι.

[21] See βάλλω.

[22] See ἔρχομαι.

present	future	aorist act	perfect act	perfect mid/pas	aorist pas
ἐπερωτάω[1]	ἐπερωτήσω	ἐπηρώτησα	-	-	-
ἔρχομαι[2]	ἐλεύσομαι[3]	ἦλθον[4]	ἐλήλυθα[5]	-	-
ἐρωτάω[6]	ἐρωτήσω	ἠρώτησα	-	-	-
ἐσθίω[7]	φάγομαι[8]	ἔφαγον[9]	-	-	-
εὐαγγελίζω[10]	-	εὐηγγέλισα	-	εὐηγγέλισμαι[11]	εὐηγγελίσθην[12]
εὑρίσκω[13]	εὑρήσω[14]	εὗρον[15]	εὕρηκα[16]	-	εὑρέθην[17]

---

[1] *ἐπερωτα. A compound verb.

[2] *ἐρχ. The different tense stems of this verb are actually quite regular. They look so different because they are based on different verbal roots. Most find it easiest to memorize them.

[3] *ελευθ. Future middle deponent.

[4] *ελευθ, just like the future. The ευ has dropped out due to ablaut (*ελευθ ‣ ελθ ‣ ἦλθον). Second aorist.

[5] *ελευθ, just like the future. The form has both reduplicated and then undergone vocalic reduplication, and the ε has dropped out. It is a second perfect. *ελευθ ‣ ελελευθ ‣ εληλυθ ‣ ἐλήλυθα.

[6] *ερωτα.

[7] Formed from two different stems, *εσθι (used in the present) and *φαγ (used in the future and aorist).

[8] *φαγ. Future middle deponent.

[9] *φαγ. Second aorist.

[10] *ευαγγελιδ. A compound verb as seen by the augment.

[11] The δμ combination forms σμ.

[12] The δθ combination forms σθ.

[13] The stem is *εὑρ. ισκ was added to form the present tense stem.

[14] An eta was added before the tense formative.

[15] Second aorist. Does not augment.

[16] An eta was added before the tense formative.

[17] An epsilon was added before the tense formative.

present	future	aorist act	perfect act	perfect mid/pas	aorist pas
ἔχω[1]	ἕξω	ἔσχον	ἔσχηκα	-	-
ζάω[2]	ζήσω[3]	ἔζησα	-	-	-
ζητέω[4]	ζητήσω	ἐζήτησα	-	-	ἐζητήθην
θέλω[5]	θελήσω	ἠθέλησα	-	-	ἠθελήθην
θεωρέω[6]	-	ἐθεώρησα	-	-	-
ἵστημι[7]	στήσω	ἔστησα	ἕστηκα[8]	ἕσταμαι	ἐστάθην
κάθημαι[9]	καθήσομαι	-	-	-	-
καλέω[10]	καλέσω	ἐκάλεσα	κέκληκα	κέκλημαι	ἐκλήθην
καταβαίνω[11]	καταβήσομαι	κατέβην	καταβέβηκα	-	-

---

[1] What happens to ἔχω is quite fascinating, but perhaps at first you might just want to memorize the tense stems. If you are really interested in what is happening, here it is.

The root is *σεχ. In the present tense the sigma is replaced by the rough breathing so you just have ἔχω. But because the Greeks did not like the two "aspirate" sounds of the rough breathing and the chi in a row, the rough breathing "deaspirates" to a smooth breathing (σεχ ‣ ἑχ ‣ ἐχ ‣ ἔχω).

Therefore, in forming the imperfect, because the verbal root actually begins with a consonant, the augment is the epsilon. But then the sigma is between two vowels, so it drops out and εε contract to ει (ε + σεχ ‣ εεχ ‣ εῖχον).

In the future the tense formative sigma joins with the chi to form xsi, but then there are not two aspirates in a row, so the rough breathing can remain.

In the aorist and perfect active, the ε between the sigma and chi drops out. In the perfect, an eta is added before the tense formative.

[2] *ζα.

[3] Some list as a deponent: ζήσομαι.

[4] *ζητε.

[5] The stem of θέλω originally was *εθελ. This explains the eta before the tense formative in the future active, the augment in the aorist active, and the augment and lengthened contract vowel in the aorist passive. An eta is inserted before the tense formative in the aorist active and passive.

[6] *θεωρε.

[7] *στα. When the initial sigma reduplicated in the formation of the present tense stem, the sigma was dropped in accordance with the rules and was replaced with a rough breathing. The same phenomena occurs in the perfect active.

[8] For a discussion of the rough breathing see the footnote to the present tense stem.

[9] κατα + *εμ. Formed from the present tense stem *καθη.

[10] The stem of this word used to have a digamma (an old Greek letter written as Ϝ in the grammars) after the epsilon (καλεϜ), and therefore the epsilon does not always lengthen as you might expect. In the final three tense stems, the alpha drops out (ablaut) and the epsilon lengthens. You might find it easier to memorize these forms.

[11] See ἀναβαίνω.

present	future	aorist act	perfect act	perfect mid/pas	aorist pas
κηρύσσω[1]	κηρύξω	ἐκήρυξα	-	κεκήρυγμαι	ἐκηρύχθην[2]
κράζω[3]	κράξω	ἔκραξα	κέκραγα[4]	-	-
κρατέω[5]	κρατήσω	ἐκράτησα	κεκράτηκα	κεκράτημαι	-
κρίνω[6]	κρινῶ	ἔκρινα	κέκρικα	κέκριμαι	ἐκρίθην
λαλέω[7]	λαλήσω	ἐλάλησα	λελάληκα	λελάλημαι	ἐλαλήθην
λαμβάνω[8]	λήμψομαι[9]	ἔλαβον[10]	εἴληφα[11]	εἴλημμαι[12]	ἐλήμφθην[13]

---

[1] *κηρυγ.

[2] The γθ combination changes to χθ.

[3] *κραγ.

[4] Second perfect.

[5] *κρατε.

[6] *κριν. A liquid verb. The ν is lost in the final three tenses.

[7] *λαλε.

[8] *λαβ. Actually, the same root is used to form all the tense stems. We give explanations for the different tense stems, and they are quite straightforward, but you may want to memorize the different forms

The key to remember with these different tenses is that the root is *λαβ, and these three letters are always present in some form. The alpha undergoes ablaut, and the beta is changed by the letter that follows it, but the three letters are always present. A mu is inserted in the present, future, and aorist passive stems.

[9] *λαβ. The alpha lengthens to eta, a mu is inserted, and the beta joins with the sigma of the tense formative to form psi. It is a future middle deponent. *λαβ › ληβ › λημβ + σομαι › λήμψομαι.

[10] *λαβ. Second aorist.

[11] *λαβ. The vocalic reduplication is ει instead of the usual epsilon (see *MBG* for an explanation), the stem vowel alpha lengthens to eta (ablaut), and the beta is aspirated to a phi. It is a second perfect, so the tense formative is alpha and not κα. *λαβ › ειλαβ › ειληβ › ειληφ › εἴληφα.

[12] The same changes present in the perfect active are present here as well. The beta has changed to mu because of the following mu.

[13] The same changes present in the perfect active are present here as well, except that the augment is the simple epsilon. The beta has changed to phi because of the following theta.

present	future	aorist act	perfect act	perfect mid/pas	aorist pas
λέγω[1]	ἐρῶ[2]	εἶπον[3]	εἴρηκα[4]	εἴρημαι[5]	ἐρρέθην[6]
μαρτυρέω[7]	μαρτυρήσω	ἐμαρτύρησα	μεμαρτύρηκα	μεμαρτύρημαι	ἐμαρτυρήθην
μέλλω[8]	μελλήσω[9]	-	-	-	-
μένω[10]	μενῶ[11]	ἔμεινα[12]	μεμένηκα[13]	-	-
οἶδα[14]	εἰδήσω	ᾔδειν	-	-	-
ὁράω[15]	ὄψομαι[16]	εἶδον[17]	ἑώρακα[18]	-	ὤφθην[19]
ὀφείλω[20]	-	-	-	-	-

---

[1] Three different stems are used to form this verb: *λεγ (present), *ερ (future, perfect, aorist passive), and *ιπ (aorist active). Memorize the forms.

[2] *Ϝερ Liquid future. The digamma (Ϝ) has dropped out.

[3] *Ϝιπ. Second aorist. It receives a syllabic augment, the digamma (Ϝ) drops out because it is between vowels, and they contract. ε + Ϝιπ + ο + ν ‣ εἶπον.

[4] *Ϝερ It received the syllabic augment and the digamma (Ϝ) dropped out. It inserts an eta before the tense formative. ε + Ϝερ + η + κα ‣ εερηκα ‣ εἴρηκα.

[5] Follows the same pattern of change as in the perfect active.

[6] *Ϝερ When the digamma (Ϝ) was lost, evidently the rho doubled. This is common in verbs beginning with rho. An epsilon was inserted before the tense formative, much like an eta can be inserted.

[7] *μαρτυρε.

[8] *μελλ.

[9] There used to be an epsilon in the root after the second lambda (*μελλε). This is visible only in the future.

[10] *μεν. A liquid, and the stem vowels change due to ablaut.

[11] Liquid future.

[12] Liquid aorist, with a stem vowel change (ablaut).

[13] An eta is inserted before the tense formative.

[14] A very strange verb. οἶδα actually is a perfect form functioning as a present, and ᾔδειν is actually a pluperfect functioning as an aorist. Just memorize the forms. If you want an explanation, see *MBG*.

[15] The stem *ορα is used to form the present and perfect active. In the aorist the root is *Ϝιδ. The other tense stems use the stem *οπ, which is altered according to the regular rules.

[16] *οπ. Future middle deponent.

[17] There is the second aorist middle deponent form ὠψάμην that is formed from the same root as the future active and aorist passive: *οπ. It only occurs at Luke 13:28. Most view εἶδον as the aorist of ὁράω.

[18] There is both a lengthening and an augment: ορα ‣ ωρα ‣ εωρα ‣ ἑώρακα.

[19] *οπ. The πθ combination forms φθ.

[20] *οφειλ.

present	future	aorist act	perfect act	perfect mid/pas	aorist pas
παραδίδωμι[1]	παραδώσω	παρέδωκα	παραδέδωκα	παραδέδομαι	παρεδόθην
παρακαλέω[2]	παρακαλέσω	παρεκάλεσα	παρακέκληκα	παρακέκλημαι	παρεκλήθην
πείθω[3]	πείσω	ἔπεισα	πέποιθα[4]	πέπεισμαι[5]	ἐπείσθην[6]
περιπατέω[7]	περιπατήσω	περιεπάτησα	-	-	περιεπατήθην
πίνω[8]	πίομαι[9]	ἔπιον[10]	πέπωκα[11]	-	ἐπόθην[12]
πίπτω[13]	πεσοῦμαι[14]	ἔπεσον[15]	πέπτωκα[16]	-	-
πιστεύω[17]	-	ἐπίστευσα	πεπίστευκα	πεπίστευμαι	ἐπιστεύθην
πληρόω[18]	πληρώσω	ἐπλήρωσα	πεπλήρωκα	πεπλήρωμαι	ἐπληρώθην
ποιέω[19]	ποιήσω	ἐποίησα	πεποίηκα	πεποίημαι	ἐποιήθην
πορεύομαι[20]	πορεύσομαι[21]	-	-	πεπόρευμαι	ἐπορεύθην

[1] παρα + *δο. See δίδωμι.

[2] παρα + *καλεϝ. See καλέω.

[3] *πειθ.

[4] The stem vowels change from ει to οι due to ablaut. Second perfect.

[5] The θμ combination form σμ.

[6] The dental + mu combination usually forms σμ.

[7] *περιπατε. A compound verb, but the simple πατέω does not occur. Notice that contrary to most compound verbs, περί does not lose its iota ("elision") when the augment is added.

[8] *πι. The nu is added to the root to form the present tense stem.

[9] Future middle deponent.

[10] Second aorist.

[11] The stem vowel iota has shifted to omega due to ablaut.

[12] The stem vowel iota has shifted to omicron due to ablaut.

[13] Memorize the different forms. The stem is actually *πετ. The pi reduplicated and the epsilon dropped out in the formation of the present tense: *πετ ‣ πτ ‣ πιπτ ‣ πίπτω.

[14] The tau has dropped out because of the sigma tense formative, and for some reason there is a contraction. *πετ + σ + ο + μαι ‣ πεσομαι ‣ πεσοῦμαι.

[15] Second aorist. The tau has dropped out because of the sigma, which implies that πίπτω would have a first aorist. But actually it is a second aorist.

[16] The epsilon has dropped out and an omega has been inserted before the tense formative.

[17] *πιστευ.

[18] *πληρο.

[19] *ποιε.

[20] *πορευ.

[21] Future middle deponent.

present	future	aorist act	perfect act	perfect mid/pas	aorist pas
προσέρχομαι[1]	προσελεύσομαι	προσῆλθον	προσελήλυθα	-	-
προσεύχομαι[2]	προσεύξομαι[3]	προσηυξάμην[4]	-	-	-
προσκυνέω[5]	προσκυνήσω	προσεκύνησα	-	-	-
σπείρω	-	ἔσπειρα	-	ἔσπαρμαι	-
συνάγω[6]	συνάξω	συνήγαγον	-	συνῆγμαι	συνήχθην
σῴζω[7]	σώσω[8]	ἔσωσα[9]	σέσωκα[10]	σέσωσμαι[11]	ἐσώθην[12]
τηρέω[13]	τηρήσω	ἐτήρησα	τετήρηκα	τετήρημαι	ἐτηρήθην
τίθημι[14]	θήσω	ἔθηκα[15]	τέθεικα[16]	τέθειμαι[17]	ἐτέθην[18]
ὑπάγω[19]	ὑπάξω	ὑπήγαγον	-	ὑπῆγμαι	ὑπήχθην
ὑπάρχω[20]	ὑπάρξομαι[21]	ὑπηρξάμην[22]	-	-	-

---

[1] *προσερχ. See ἔρχομαι.

[2] *προσευχ.

[3] Future middle deponent.

[4] Aorist middle deponent.

[5] *προσκυνε.

[6] *συναγ. See ἄγω.

[7] *σωδ. Lexicons vary as to whether the iota subscript should be included.

[8] Dentals drop out before a sigma.

[9] Dentals drop out before a sigma.

[10] The delta has dropped out.

[11] The δμ combination forms σμ.

[12] The δθ combination usually produces σθ, although here the sigma has dropped out. It is not unusual for the final sigma to drop out of a word in the aorist passive.

[13] *τηρε.

[14] *θε. τίθημι forms its stems as a regular μι verb, except for the ablaut in the perfect and for the transfer of aspiration in the aorist passive (θ ‣ τ).

[15] μι verbs use κα for their tense formative in the aorist active.

[16] The stem vowel has shifted to ει due to ablaut.

[17] The stem vowel has shifted to ει due to ablaut.

[18] Believe it or not, this form is regular. What is a little confusing is that the root *θε has shifted to τε ("transfer of aspiration"). When the θη is added for the aorist passive, there is the θεθ combination. The Greeks tried to avoid two aspirates (theta is an "aspirate") in successive vowels, so they "deaspirated" the first one, i.e., shifted it to a tau. ε + *θε + θη + ν ‣ εθεθην ‣ ἐτέθην.

[19] *υπαγ. See ἄγω.

[20] *ὑπαρχ.

[21] Future middle deponent.

[22] Aorist middle deponent.

present	future	aorist act	perfect act	perfect mid/pas	aorist pas
φέρω[1]	οἴσω	ἤνεγκα	ἐνήνοχα[2]	ἐνήνεκμαι	ἠνέχθην
φημί[3]	-	-	-	-	-
φοβέομαι	-	-	-	-	ἐφοβήθην
χαίρω[4]	χαρήσομαι[5]	-	-	-	ἐχάρην[6]

Liquid Verbs Occurring
Fifty Times and More in the New Testament

αἴρω	I take up, take away ἀρῶ, ἦρα, ἦρκα, ἦρμαι, ἤρθην
ἀποθνήσκω	I die ἀποθανοῦμαι, ἀπέθανον, -, -, -
ἀποκρίνομαι	I answer -, ἀπεκριναμην, -, -, ἀπεκρίθην
ἀποκτείνω	I kill ἀποκτενῶ, ἀπέκτεινα, -, -, ἀπεκτάνθην
ἀποστέλλω	I send ἀποστελῶ, ἀπέστειλα, ἀπέσταλκα, ἀπέσταλμαι, ἀπεστά-λην
βάλλω	I throw, put βαλῶ, ἔβαλον, βέβληκα, βέβλημαι, ἐβλήθην
ἐγείρω	I raise up ἐγερῶ, ἤγειρα, -, ἐγήγερμαι, ἠγέρθην
εἰμί	I am ἔσομαι, ἤμην, -, -, -
ἐκβάλλω	I cast out ἐκβαλῶ, ἐξέβαλον, ἐκβέβληκα, ἐκβέβλημαι, ἐξεβλήθην

---

[1] Just memorize the different forms. There are three different stems present here. See *MBG* for an explanation

[2] Second perfect.

[3] See *MBG* for an explanation. This actually is a compound verb.

[4] *χαρ. The iota was added to form the present tense stem and is therefore not present in the other tense stems.

[5] An eta has been added before the tense formative. It is a future deponent.

[6] Second aorist.

κρίνω   I judge, decide
                        κρινῶ, ἔκρινα, κέκρικα, κέκριμαι, ἐκρίθην

λέγω   I say, speak
                        ἐρῶ, εἶπον, εἴρηκα, εἴρημαι, ἐρρέθην

μέλλω   I am about to
                        μελλήσω, -, -, -, -,

μένω   I remain
                        μενῶ, ἔμεινα, μεμένηκα, -, -,

πίνω   I drink
                        πίομαι, ἔπιον, πέπωκα, -, ἐπόθην

φέρω   I carry
                        οἴσω, ἤνεγκα, ἐνήνοχα, ἐνήνεκμαι, ἠνέχθην

χαίρω   I rejoice
                        χαρήσομαι, -, -, -, ἐχάρην

Second Aorist Actives of Verbs Occurring Fifty Times and More in the New Testament

ἄγω   I lead
                        ἄξω, ἤγαγον, -, ἦγμαι, ἤχθην

ἀναβαίνω   I go up
                        ἀναβήσομαι, ἀνέβην, -, -, -

ἀπέρχομαι   I depart
                        ἀπελεύσομαι, ἀπῆλθον, ἀπελήλυθα, -, -

ἀποθνήσκω   I die
                        ἀποθανοῦμαι, ἀπέθανον, -, -, -

βάλλω   I throw
                        βαλῶ, ἔβαλον, βέβληκα, βέβλημαι, ἐβλήθην

γίνομαι   I become
                        γενήσομαι, ἐγενόμην, γέγονα, γεγένημαι, ἐγενήθην

γινώσκω   I know
                        γνώσομαι, ἔγνων, ἔγνωκα, ἔγνωσμαι, ἐγνώσθην

εἶδον   I saw

εἰσέρχομαι   I go into
                        εἰσελεύσομαι, εἰσῆλθον, εἰσελήλυθα, -, -

ἐκβάλλω   I cast out
                        ἐκβαλῶ, ἐξέβαλον, ἐκβέβληκα, ἐκβέβλημαι, ἐξεβλήθην

ἐξέρχομαι	I go out ἐξελεύσομαι, ἐξῆλθον, ἐξελήλυθα, -, -
ἔρχομαι	I come ἐλεύσομαι, ἦλθον, ἐλήλυθα, -, -
ἐσθίω	I eat φάγομαι, ἔφαγον, -, -, -
εὑρίσκω	I find εὑρήσω, εὗρον, εὕρηκα, -, εὑρέθην
ἔχω	I have ἕξω, ἔσχον, ἔσχηκα, -, -
καταβαίνω	I go down καταβήσομαι, κατέβην, -, -, -
λαμβάνω	I take λήμψομαι, ἔλαβον, εἴληφα, εἴλημμαι, ἐλήμφθην
λέγω	I say ἐρῶ, εἶπον, εἴρηκα, εἴρημαι, ἐρρέθην
πίνω	I drink πίομαι, ἔπιον, πέπωκα, -, ἐπόθην
πίπτω	I fall πεσοῦμαι, ἔπεσον, πέπτωκα, -, -
προσέρχομαι	I come to προσελεύσομαι, προσῆλθον, προσελήλυθα, -, -
συνάγω	I gather together συνάξω, συνήγαγον, -, συνῆγμαι, συνήχθην
ὑπάγω	I depart ὑπάξω, ὑπήγαγον, -, ὑπῆγμαι, ὑπήχθην
φέρω	I carry οἴσω, ἤνεγκα, ἐνήνοχα, ἐνήνεκμαι, ἠνέχθην

Words Occurring Fifty Times and More in the New Testament (by frequency)

When you are done with this grammar, this list will be helpful for your vocabulary review. Start with the most frequently used words and work down.

Freq	Chpt	Word	Definition
19870	6	ὁ, ἡ, τό	the

9153	4	καί	and, even, also, namely
5595	6	αὐτός, -ή, -ό	personal: he, she, it (him, her); they (them) reflexive: him/her/itself identical: same
2792	6	δέ	but, and
2752	6	ἐν	dat: in, on, among
2460	6	εἰμί	I am, exist, live, am present (ἤμην), ἔσομαι, -, -, -, -
2354	8	λέγω	I say, speak (ἔλεγον), ἐρῶ, εἶπον, εἴρηκα, εἴρημαι, ἐρρέθην
1840	11	ὑμεῖς	you (plural)
1768	7	εἰς	acc: into, in, among
1725	4	ἐγώ	I
1606	6	οὐ, οὐκ, οὐχ	not
1388	7	οὗτος, αὕτη, τοῦτο	singular: this; he, her, it plural: these
1365	14	ὅς, ἥ, ὅ	who, whom
1317	4	θεός -οῦ, -ὁ	God, god
1296	6	ὅτι	that, since, because
1244	10	πᾶς, πᾶσα, πᾶν	singular: each, every plural: all
1069	7	σύ	you
1042	7	μή	not, lest
1041	7	γάρ	for, then
917	7	Ἰησοῦς, -οῦ, ὁ	Jesus, Joshua
914	8	ἐκ, ἐξ	gen: from, out of
890	11	ἐπί (ἐπ᾽, ἐφ᾽)	gen: on, over, when dat: on the basis of, at acc: on, to, against
864	11	ἡμεῖς	we
717	7	κύριος -ου,-ὁ	Lord, lord, master, sir
708	16	ἔχω	I have, hold (εἶχον), ἕξω, ἔσχον, ἔσχηκα, -, -
700	8	πρός	acc: to, towards, with
669	22	γίνομαι	I become, am, exist, am born, am created (ἐγινόμην), γενήσομαι, ἐγενόμην, γέγονα, γεγένημαι, ἐγενήθην
667	8	διά	gen: through acc: on account of
663	8	ἵνα	in order that, that

646	8	ἀπό (ἀπ᾽, ἀφ᾽)	gen: (away) from
638	8	ἀλλά	but, yet, except
634	18	ἔρχομαι	I come, go (ἠρχόμην), ἐλεύσομαι, ἦλθον or ἦλθα, ἐλήλυθα, -, -
568	17	ποιέω	I do, make (ἐποίουν), ποιήσω, ἐποίησα, πεποίηκα, πεποίημαι, -
555	10	τίς, τί	who? what? which? why?
550	4	ἄνθρωπος, -ου, ὁ	man, mankind, person, people, human kind, human being
529	4	Χριστός, -οῦ, ὁ	Christ, Messiah, Anointed One
525	10	τις, τι	someone/thing, certain one/thing, anyone/thing
504	18	ὡς	as, like, when, that, how, about
503	10	εἰ	if
499	12	οὖν	therefore, then, accordingly
473	14	κατά	gen: down from, against acc: according to, throughout, during
469	8	μετά	gen: with acc: after
454	20	ὁράω	I see, notice, experience ὄψομαι, εἶδον, ἑώρακα, -, ὤφθην
428	16	ἀκούω	I hear, learn, obey, understand (ἤκουον), ἀκούσω, ἤκουσα, ἀκήκοα, -, ἠκούσθην
416	13	πολύς, πολλή, πολύ	singular: much plural: many adverb: often
415	34	δίδωμι	I give (out), entrust, give back, put (ἐδίδουν), δώσω, ἔδωκα, δέδωκα, δέδομαι, ἐδόθην
413	10	πατήρ, πατρός, ὁ	father
389	8	ἡμέρα, -ας, ἡ	day
379	4	πνεῦμα, -ματος, τό	spirit, Spirit, wind, breath, inner life
377	7	υἱός, -οῦ, ὁ	son, descendant
351	9	ἐάν	if, when
344	10	εἷς, μία, ἕν	one
343	11	ἀδελφός, -οῦ, ὁ	brother
343	13	ἤ	or

333	10	περί	gen: concerning, about acc: around
330	4	λόγος, -ου, ὁ	word, Word, statement, message
319	13	ἑαυτοῦ, -ῆς	singular: of himself/herself/itself plural: of themselves
318	17	οἶδα	I know, understand εἰδήσω, ᾔδειν, -, -, -
296	17	λαλέω	I speak, say (ἐλάλουν), λαλήσω, ἐλάλησα, λελάληκα, λελάλημαι, ἐλαλήθην
273	7	οὐρανός, -οῦ, ὁ	heaven, sky
265	13	ἐκεῖνος, -η, -ο	singular: that (man/woman/thing) plural: those (men/women, things)
261	12	μαθητής, -οῦ, ὁ	disciple
258	22	λαμβάνω	I take, receive (ἐλάμβανον), λήμψομαι, ἔλαβον, εἴληφα, -, ἐλήμφθην
250	22	γῆ, γῆς, ἡ	earth, land, region, humanity
243	13	μέγας, μεγάλη, μέγα	large, great
241	16	πιστεύω	I believe, I have faith (in), trust (ἐπίστευον), πιστεύσω, ἐπίστευσα, πεπίστευκα, πεπίστευμαι, ἐπιστεύθην
243	10	πίστις, -εως, ἡ	faith, belief
234	11	οὐδείς, οὐδεμία, οὐδέν	no one, none, nothing
233	10	ἅγιος, -ια, -ιον	adjective: holy plural noun: saints
231	18	ἀποκρίνομαι	I answer -, ἀπεκρινάμην, -, -, ἀπεκρίθην
231	10	ὄνομα, -ματος, τό	name, reputation
222	20	γινώσκω	I know, come to know, realize, learn (ἐγίνωσκον), γνώσομαι, ἔγνων, ἔγνωκα, ἔγνωσμαι, ἐγνώσθην
220	8	ὑπό	gen: by (preposition) acc: under
218	22	ἐξέρχομαι	I go out (ἐξηρχόμην), ἐξελεύσομαι, ἐξῆλθον, ἐξελήλυθα, -, -
216	10	ἀνήρ, ἀνδρός, ὁ	man, male, husband
215	13	γυνή, γυναικός, ἡ	woman, wife
215	14	τε	and (so), so

210	18	δύναμαι	I am able, am powerful (ἐδυνάμην or ἠδυνάμην), δυνήσομαι, -, -, -, ἠδυνήθην
208	21	θέλω	I will, wish, desire, enjoy (ἤθελον), θελήσω, ἠθέλησα, -, -, ἐθελήθην
208	14	οὕτως	thus, so, in this manner
200	11	ἰδού	See! Behold!
195	19	Ἰουδαῖος, -αία, -αῖον	adjective: Jewish noun: Jew
194	22	εἰσέρχομαι	I come in(to), go in(to), enter εἰσελεύσομαι, εἰσῆλθον, εἰσελήλυθα, -, -
194	16	νόμος, -ου, ὁ	law, principle
194	8	παρά	gen: from dat: beside, in the presence of acc: alongside of
191	23	γράφω	I write (ἔγραφον), γράψω, ἔγραψα, γέγραφα, γέγραπμαι or γέγραμμαι, ἐγράφην
186	4	κόσμος, ου, ὁ	world, universe, humankind
182	9	καθώς	as, even as
179	12	μέν	on the one hand, indeed
177	14	χείρ, χειρός, ἡ	hand, arm, finger
176	22	εὑρίσκω	I find (εὕρισκον or ηὕρισκον), εὑρήσω, εὗρον, εὕρηκα, -, εὑρέθην
175	4	ἄγγελος, -ου, ὁ	messenger, angel
175	8	ὄχλος	crowd, multitude
175	30	ὀψία, -ας, ἡ	evening
173	7	ἁμαρτία, -ας, ἡ	sin
169	6	ἔργον, -ου, τό	work, deed, action
167	11	ἄν	an untranslatable, uninflected word, used to make a definite statement contingent upon something
166	4	δόξα, -ης, ἡ	glory, majesty, fame
162	6	βασιλεία, -ας, ἡ	kingdom
162	34	ἔθνος, -ους, τό	nation plural: Gentiles
162	13	πόλις, -εως, ἡ	city
160	16	τότε	then, thereafter

158	29	ἐσθίω	I eat (ἤσθιον), φάγομαι, ἔφαγον, -, -, -
158	4	Παῦλος, -ου, ὁ	Paul
156	4	καρδία, -ας, ἡ	heart, inner self
156	4	Πέτρος, -ου, ὁ	Peter
156	9	πρῶτος, -η, -ον	first, earlier
155	6	ἄλλος, -η, -ο	other, another
155	10	χάρις, -ιτος, ἡ	grace, favor, kindness
154	35	ἵστημι	intransitive: I stand transitive: I cause to stand (ἵστην), στήσω, ἔστησα, ἕστηκα, ἕσταμαι, ἐστάθην
153	18	ὅστις, ἥτις, ὅτι	whoever, whichever, whatever
153	18	πορεύομαι	I go, proceed, live (ἐπορευόμην), πορεύσομαι, -, -, πεπόρευμαι, ἐπορεύθην
150	12	ὑπέρ	gen: in behalf of acc: above
148	17	καλέω	I call, name, invite (ἐκάλουν), καλέσω, ἐκάλεσα, κέκληκα, κέκλημαι, ἐκλήθην
147	6	νῦν	now, the present
147	10	σάρξ, σαρκός, ἡ	flesh, body
146	12	ἕως	conj: until prep (gen): as far as
144	20	ἐγείρω	I raise up, wake ἐγερῶ, ἤγειρα, -, ἐγήγερμαι, ἠγέρθην
144	4	προφήτης, -ου, ὁ	prophet
143	17	ἀγαπάω	I love, cherish ἀγαπήσω, ἠγάπησα, ἠγάπηκα, ἠγάπημαι, ἠγαπήθην
143	35	ἀφίημι	I let go, leave, permit (ἤφιον), ἀφήσω, ἀφῆκα, -, ἀφέωμαι, ἀφέθην
143	11	οὐδέ	and not, not even, neither, nor
142	20	λαός, -οῦ, ὁ	people, crowd
142	10	σῶμα, -ατος, τό	body
141	12	πάλιν	again
140	19	ζάω	I live (ἔζων), ζήσω, ἔζησα, -, -, -
139	4	φωνή, -ῆς, ἡ	sound, noise, voice

135	27	δύο	two
135	4	ζωή, -ῆς, ἡ	life
135	8	Ἰωάννης, -ου, ὁ	John
133	16	βλέπω	I see, look at (ἔβλεπον),βλέψω, ἔβλεψα, -, -, -
132	20	ἀποστέλλω	I send (away) ἀποστελῶ, ἀπέστειλα, ἀπέσταλκα, ἀπέσταλμαι, ἀπεστάλην
129	4	ἀμήν	verily, truly, amen, so let it be
128	9	νεκρός, -ά, -όν	adjective: dead noun: dead body, corpse
128	10	σύν	dat: with
124	9	δοῦλος, -ου, ὁ	slave, servant
123	17	ὅταν	whenever
122	12	αἰών, -ῶνος, ὁ	age, eternity
122	27	ἀρχιερεύς, -έως, ὁ	chief priest, high priest
122	22	βάλλω	I throw (ἔβαλλον), βαλῶ, ἔβαλον, βέβληκα, βέβλημαι, ἐβλήθην
120	8	θάνατος, -ου, ὁ	death
119	23	δύναμις, -εως, ἡ	power, miracle
119	34	παραδίδωμι	I entrust, hand over, betray (παρεδίδουν), παραδώσω, παρέδωκα or παρέδοσα, παραδέδωκα, παραδέδομαι, παρεδόθην
118	20	μένω	I remain, live (ἔμενον), μενῶ, ἔμεινα, μεμένηκα, -, -
117	23	ἀπέρχομαι	I depart ἀπελεύσομαι, ἀπῆλθον, ἀπελήλυθα, -, -
117	17	ζητέω	I seek, desire, try to obtain (ἐζήτουν), ζητήσω, ἐζήτησα, -, -, ἐζητήθην
116	6	ἀγάπη, -ης, ἡ	love
115	19	βασιλεύς, -έως, ὁ	king
114	11	ἐκκλησία, -ας, ἡ	a church, (the) Church, assembly, congregation
114	35	ἴδιος, -α, -ον	one's own (e.g., people, home)
114	20	κρίνω	I judge, decide, prefer (ἐκρινόμην), κρινῶ, ἔκρινα, κέκρικα, κέκριμαι, ἐκρίθην
114	12	μόνος, -η, -ον	alone, only

114	8	οἶκος, -ου, ὁ	house, home
111	22	ἀποθνῄσκω	I die, am about to die, am freed from (ἀπέθνῃσκον), ἀποθανοῦμαι, ἀπέθανον, -, -, -
110	12	ὅσος, -η, -ον	as great as, as many as
109	14	ἀλήθεια, -ας, ἡ	truth
109	32	μέλλω	I am about to (ἔμελλον or ἤμελλον), μελλήσω, -, -, -, -
109	19	ὅλος, -η, -ον	adj: whole, complete adverb: entirely
109	27	παρακαλέω	I call, urge, exhort, comfort (παρεκάλουν), -, παρεκάλεσα, -, παρακέκλημαι, παρεκλήθην
108	35	ἀνίστημι	intransitive: I rise, get up transitive: I raise ἀναστήσω, ἀνέστησα, -, -, -
106	20	σῴζω	I save, deliver, rescue (ἐσῳζόμην), σώσω, ἔσωσα, σέσωκα, σέσωσμαι, ἐσώθην
106	6	ὥρα, -ας, ἡ	hour, occasion, moment
105	20	ἐκεῖ	there, in that place
103	14	ὅτε	when
103	13	πῶς	how?
103	14	ψυχή, -ῆς, ἡ	soul, life, self
102	9	ἀγαθός, -ή, -όν	good, useful
102	7	ἐξουσία, -ας, ἡ	authority, power
101	20	αἴρω	I raise, take up, take away ἀρῶ, ἦρα, ἦρκα, ἦρμαι, ἤρθην
101	18	δεῖ	it is necessary
101	14	ὁδός, -οῦ, ἡ	way, road, journey, conduct
100	9	ἀλλήλων	one another
100	12	ὀφθαλμός, -οῦ, ὁ	eye, sight
100	11	καλός, -ή, -όν	beautiful, good
100	35	τίθημι	I put, place (ἐτίθουν), θήσω, ἔθηκα, τέθεικα, τέθειμαι, ἐτέθην
99	27	ἕτερος, -α, -ον	other, another, different
99	10	τέκνον, -ου, τό	child, descendant
98	21	Φαρισαῖος, -ου, ὁ	Pharisee
97	24	αἷμα, -ματος, τό	blood
97	22	ἄρτος, -ου, ὁ	bread, loaf, food

97	19	γεννάω	I beget, give birth to, produce γεννήσω, ἐγέννησα, γεγέννηκα, γεγέννημαι, ἐγεννήθην
97	21	διδάσκω	I teach (ἐδίδασκον), διδάξω, ἐδίδαξα, -, -, ἐδιδάχθην
95	21	περιπατέω	I walk (around), live (περιεπάτουν), περιπατήσω, περιεπάτησα, -, -, -
95	24	φοβέομαι	I fear (ἐφοβούμην), -, -, -, -, ἐφοβήθην
94	14	ἐνώπιον	gen: before
94	18	τόπος, -ου, ὁ	place, location
93	22	ἔτι	still, yet, even
93	8	οἰκία, -ας, ἡ	house, home
93	12	πούς, ποδός, ὁ	foot
92	13	δικαιοσύνη, -ης, ἡ	righteousness
92	14	εἰρήνη, -ης, ἡ	peace
91	8	θάλασσα, -ης, ἡ	sea, lake
91	27	κάθημαι	I sit (down), live (ἐκαθήμην), καθήσομαι, -, -, -, -
90	21	ἀκολουθέω	I follow, accompany (ἠκολούθουν), ἀκολουθήσω, ἠκολούθησα, ἠκολούθηκα, -, -
90	33	ἀπόλλυμι	active: I destroy, kill middle: I perish, die (ἀπώλλυον), ἀπολέσω or ἀπολῶ, ἀπώλεσα, -, -, -
90	12	μηδείς, μηδεμία, μηδέν	no one/thing
90	34	πίπτω	I fall (ἔπιπτον), πεσοῦμαι, ἔπεσον or ἔπεσα, πέπτωκα, -, -
88	14	ἑπτά	seven
87	22	οὔτε	and not, neither, nor
86	23	ἄρχω	active: I rule middle: I begin ἄρξομαι, ἠρξάμην, -, -, -
86	17	πληρόω	I fill, complete, fulfill (ἐπλήρουν), πληρώσω, ἐπλήρωσα, πεπλήρωκα, πεπλήρωμαι, ἐπληρώθην

86	22	προσέρχομαι	I come/go to (προσηρχόμην), -, προσῆλθον, προσελήλυθα, -, -
85	6	καιρός, -οῦ, ὁ	(appointed) time, season
85	22	προσεύχομαι	I pray (προσηυχόμην), προσεύξομαι, προσηυξάμην, -, -, -
84	13	κἀγώ	and I, but I
83	11	μήτηρ, μητρός, ἡ	mother
83	7	ὥστε	therefore, so that
82	27	ἀναβαίνω	I go up, come up (ἀνέβαινον), ἀναβήσομαι, ἀνέβην, ἀναβέβηκα, -, -
82	24	ἕκαστος, -η, -ον	each, every
82	16	ὅπου	where
81	20	ἐκβάλλω	I cast out, send out (ἐξέβαλλον), -, ἐξέβαλον, -, -, ἐξεβλήθην
81	27	καταβαίνω	I go down, come down (κατέβαινον), καταβήσομαι, κατέβην, καταβέβηκα, -, -
81	25	μᾶλλον	more, rather
80	4	ἀπόστολος, -ου, ὁ	apostle, envoy, messenger
80	34	Μωϋσῆς, -έως, ὁ	Moses
79	32	δίκαιος, -αία, -αιον	right, just, righteous
79	29	πέμπω	I send πέμψω, ἔπεμψα, -, -, ἐπέμφθην
79	24	ὑπάγω	I depart (ὑπῆγον), -, -, -, -, -
78	9	πονηρός, -ά, -όν	evil, bad
78	20	στόμα, -ατος, τό	mouth
77	35	ἀνοίγω	I open ἀνοίξω, ἠνέῳξα or ἀνέῳξα, ἀνέῳγα, ἀγέῳγμαι or ἠνέῳγμαι, ἠνεῴχθην or ἠνοίχθην
77	20	βαπτίζω	I baptize, dip, immerse (ἐβάπτιζον), βαπτίσω, ἐβάπτισα, -, βεβάπτισμαι, ἐβαπτίσθην
77	14	Ἰερουσαλήμ, ἡ	Jerusalem
77	13	σημεῖον, -ου, τό	sign, miracle
76	9	ἐμός, ἐμή, ἐμόν	my, mine
76	7	εὐαγγέλιον, -ου, τό	good news, Gospel

76	25	μαρτυρέω	I bear witness, testify (ἐμαρτύρουν), μαρτυρήσω, ἐμαρτύρησα, μεμαρτύρηκα, μεμαρτύρημαι, ἐμαρτυρήθην
76	16	πρόσωπον, -ου, τό	face, appearance
76	10	ὕδωρ, ὕδατος, τό	water
75	13	δώδεκα	twelve
75	14	κεφαλή, -ῆς, ἡ	head
75	4	Σίμων, -ωνος, ὁ	Simon
74	20	ἀποκτείνω	I kill ἀποκτενῶ, ἀπέκτεινα, -, -, ἀπεκτάνθην
74	24	χαίρω	I rejoice (ἔχαιρον), χαρήσομαι, -, -, -, ἐχάρην
73	4	Ἀβραάμ, ὁ	Abraham
73	23	πίνω	I drink (ἔπινον), πίομαι, ἔπιον, πέπωκα, -, -επόθην
73	22	πῦρ, πυρός, τό	fire
73	10	φῶς, φωτός, τό	light
71	9	αἰώνιος, -ον	eternal
71	28	ἱερόν, -οῦ, τό	temple
70	25	αἰτέω	I ask, demand (ᾔτουν), αἰτήσω, ᾔτησα, ᾔτηκα, -, -
70	17	τηρέω	I keep, guard, observe (ἐτήρουν), τηρήσω, ἐτήρησα, τετήρηκα, τετήρημαι, ἐτηρήθην
68	19	Ἰσραήλ, ὁ	Israel
68	14	πλοῖον, -ου, τό	ship, boat
68	14	ῥῆμα, -ματος, τό	word, saying
68	4	σάββατον, -ου, τό	Sabbath, week
68	27	τρεῖς, τρία	three
67	24	ἄγω	I lead, bring, arrest (ἦγον), ἄξω, ἤγαγον, -, -, ἤχθην
67	9	ἐντολή, -ῆς, ἡ	commandment
67	9	πιστός, -ή, -όν	faithful, believing
66	33	ἀπολύω	I release (ἀπέλυον), ἀπολύσω, ἀπέλυσα, -, ἀπολέλυμαι, ἀπελύθην
66	19	καρπός, -οῦ, ὁ	fruit, crop, result
66	30	πρεσβύτερος, -α, -ον	elder

66	29	φέρω	I carry, bear, produce (ἔφερον), οἴσω, ἤνεγκα, ἐνήνοχα, ἐνήνεγμαι, ἠνέχθην
66	35	φημί	I say, affirm (ἔφη), -, ἔφη, -, -, -
65	33	εἴτε	if, whether
63	28	γραμματεύς, -έως, ὁ	scribe
63	17	δαιμόνιον, -ου, τό	demon
63	21	ἐρωτάω	I ask, request, entreat (ἠρώτων), ἐρωτήσω, ἠρώτησα, -, -, ἠρωτήθην
63	11	ἔξω	adverb: without prep (gen): outside
63	24	ὄρος, ὄρους, τό	mountain, hill
62	34	δοκέω	I think, seem (ἐδόκουν), δόξω, ἔδοξα, -, -, -
62	11	θέλημα, -ματος, τό	will, desire
62	14	θρόνος, -ου, ὁ	throne
62	27	Ἱερόσολυμα, τά or ἡ	Jerusalem
61	9	ἀγαπητός, -ή, -όν	beloved
61	4	Γαλιλαία, -ας, ἡ	Galilee
61	23	δοξάζω	I praise, honor, glorify (ἐδόξαζον), δοξάσω, ἐδόξασα, -, δεδόξασμαι, ἐδοξάσθην
61	10	ἤδη	now, already
61	23	κηρύσσω	I proclaim, preach (ἐκήρυσσον), κηρύξω, ἐκήρυξα, -, -, ἐκηρύχθην
61	18	νύξ, νυκτός, ἡ	night
61	11	ὧδε	here
60	24	ἱμάτιον, -ου, τό	garment, cloak
60	19	προσκυνέω	I worship (προσεκύνουν), προσκυνήσω, προσεκύνησα, -, -, -
60	34	ὑπάρχω	I am, exist (ὑπῆρχον), -, -, -, -, - τά ὑπάρχοντα: one's belongings
59	28	ἀσπάζομαι	I greet, salute (ἠσπαζόμην), -, ἠσπασάμην, -, -, -
59	4	Δαυίδ, ὁ	David
59	12	διδάσκαλος, -ου, ὁ	teacher

59	31	λίθος, -ου, ὁ	stone
59	18	συνάγω	I gather together, invite συνάξω, συνήγαγον, -, συνῆγμαι, συνήχθην
59	16	χαρά, -ᾶς, ἡ	joy, delight
58	27	θεωρέω	I look at, behold -, ἐθεώρησα, -, -, -
58	35	μέσος, -η, -ον	middle, in the midst
57	31	τοιοῦτος, -αύτη, -οῦτον	such, of such a kind
56	29	δέχομαι	I take, receive δέξομαι, ἐδεξάμην, -, δέδεγμαι, ἐδέχθην
56	21	ἐπερωτάω	I ask (for), question, demand of (ἐπηρώτων), ἐπερωτήσω, ἐπηρώτησα, -, -, ἐπηρωτήθην
56	28	κράζω	I cry out, call out (ἔκραζον), κράξω, ἔκραξα, κέκραγα, -, -
56	30	μηδέ	but not, nor, not even
56	21	συναγωγή, -ῆς, ἡ	synagogue, meeting
56	9	τρίτος, -η, -ον	third
55	7	ἀρχή, -ῆς, ἡ	beginning, ruler
55	34	λοιπός, -ή, -όν	adjective: remaining noun: (the) rest adverb: for the rest, henceforth
55	4	Πιλᾶτος, -ου, ὁ	Pilate
55	17	πλείων, πλεῖον	larger, more
54	27	δεξιός, -ιά, -ιόν	right
54	27	εὐαγγελίζω	I bring good news, preach (εὐηγγέλιζον), -, εὐηγγέλισα, -, εὐηγγέλισμαι, εὐηγγελίσθην
54	27	οὗ	where
54	28	οὐχί	not
54	21	χρόνος, -ου, ὁ	time
53	23	διό	therefore, for this reason
53	13	ἐλπίς, -ίδος, ἡ	hope, expectation
53	12	ὅπως	how, that, in order that
52	14	ἐπαγγελία, -ας, ἡ	promise
52	4	ἔσχατος, -η, -ον	last
52	28	παιδίον, -ου, τό	child, infant
52	27	πείθω	I persuade (ἔπειθον), πείσω, ἔπεισα, πέποιθα, πέπεισμαι, ἐπείσθην

52	28	σπείρω	I sow
			-, ἔσπειρα, -, ἔσπαρμαι, -
51	12	εὐθύς	immediately
51	20	σοφία, -ας, ἡ	wisdom
50	20	γλῶσσα, -ης, ἡ	tongue, language
50	4	γραφή, -ῆς, ἡ	writing, Scripture
50	9	κακός, -ή, -όν	bad, evil
50	13	μακάριος, -α, -ον	blessed, happy
50	8	παραβολή, -ῆς, ἡ	parable
50	16	τυφλός, -ή, -όν	blind
48	22	μείζων, -ον	greater
43	19	Ἰουδαία, -ας, ἡ	Judea
42	16	λύω	I loose, untie, destroy
			(ἔλυον), λύσω, ἔλυσα, -, λέλυμαι, ἐλύθην
33	35	δείκνυμι	I show, explain
			δείξω, ἔδειξα, δέδειχα, -, ἐδείχθην
11	34	ἴδε	See! Behold!

Lexicon

The definitions in this lexicon are derived from Prof. Bruce Metzger's *Lexical Aids* and Warren Trenchard's *Complete Vocabulary Guide* (both used with permission). It includes all the words that occur ten times or more in the Greek Testament, including proper names. The number in the far left column is the chapter in which the vocabulary term is learned. The definition is followed by its frequency in the New Testament and its category in *MBG*. Following is a quick summary of the nomenclature.

"n-" means the word is a noun.

  n-1 is first declension.

  n-2 is second declension.

  n-3 is third declension.

"a-" means the word is an adjective.

  a-1 are adjectives with three endings where the masculine and neuter are second declension and the feminine is first declension (ἅγιος, -ία, -ιον).

  a-2 are adjectives with three endings where the masculine and neuter are third declension and the feminine is first declension (πᾶς, πᾶσα, πᾶν).

  a-3 are adjectives with two endings where the masculine and feminine are the same ending (second declension) and the neuter has a separate ending (second declension; ἁμαρτωλός, όν).

  a-4 are adjectives with two endings where the masculine and feminine are the same ending (third declension) and the neuter has a separate ending (third declension; ἀληθής, ές).

  a-5 are irregular adjectives.

"v-" means that the word is a verb. The verbs in this list are broken down into v-1 through v-8. Since these categories are somewhat complicated, detailed comment is deferred to *MBG*. Following are a few simple categories.

  v-1 Apparently regular verbs (λύω, ἀγαπάω).

  v-2 Present tense has a consonantal iota that is not used in the other tenses (*βαπτιδ + ι ‣ βαπτίζω ‣ βαπτίσω).

  v-3 Present tense has a nu that is lost in the other tenses (*πι ‣ πίνω ‣ ἔπιον).

  v-4 Present tense has a tau that is lost in the other tenses (*κρυπ ‣ κρύπτω ‣ ἔκρυψα).

v-5   Present tense has (ι)σκ that are lost in the other tenses (*αρε ‣ ἀρέσκω
        ‣ ἤρεσα).

The following three categories are words that fall into the first five categories, but have also been included in these three categories.

v-6   The μι verbs (δίδωμι).

v-7   Verbs that undergo ablaut (ἀκούω ‣ ἀκήκοα).

v-8   Verbs that use different verbal roots in the formation of their vari-
        ous tense stems (λέγω, ἐρῶ, εἶπον).

"cv-" means the word is a compound verb.

The tense stems are listed in the normal order of future active, aorist active, perfect active, perfect middle/passive, aorist passive (from which is derived the future passive). Unlike other listing, we have also included the imperfect in
parentheses before the future if it occurs in the New Testament.

ἄλφα

4	Ἀβραάμ, ὁ	Abraham (73, n-3g[2])
9	ἀγαθός, -ή, -όν	good, useful (102, a-1a[2a])
	ἀγαλλιάω	I exult (11, v-1d[1b]) -, ἠγαλλίασα, -, -, ἠγαλλιάθην
17	ἀγαπάω	I love, cherish (143, v-1d[1a]) ἀγαπήσω, ἠγάπησα, ἠγάπηκα, ἠγάπημαι, ἠγαπήθην
6	ἀγάπη, -ης, ἡ	love (116, n-1b)
9	ἀγαπητός, -ή, -όν	beloved (61, a-1a[2a])
4	ἄγγελος, -ου, ὁ	messenger, angel (175, n-2a)
	ἁγιάζω	I sanctify (28, v-2a[1]) -, ἡγίασα, -, ἡγίασμαι, ἡγιάσθην
	ἁγιασμός, -οῦ, ὁ	sanctification (10, n-2a)
10	ἅγιος, -ία, -ιον	holy (233, a-1a[1]) plural noun: saints
	ἀγνοέω	I do not know (22, v-1d[2a]) (ἠγνόουν), -, -, -, -, -
	ἀγορά, -ᾶς, ἡ	marketplace (11, n-1a)
	ἀγοράζω	I buy (30, v-2a[1]) (ἠγόραζον), -, ἠγόρασα, -, ἠγόρασμαι, ἠγοράσθην
	Ἀγρίππας, -α, ὁ	Agrippa (11, n-1e)
	ἀγρός, -οῦ, ὁ	field (37, n-2a)
24	ἄγω	I lead, bring, arrest (67, v-1b[2]) (ἦγον), ἄξω, ἤγαγον, -, -, ἤχθην

	ἀδελφή, -ῆς, ἡ	sister (26, n-1b)
11	ἀδελφός, -οῦ, ὁ	brother (343, n-2a)
	ᾅδης, -ου, ὁ	Hades (10, n-1f)
	ἀδικέω	I wrong, do wrong (28, v-1d[2a]) ἀδικήσω, ἠδίκησα, ἠδίκηκα, -, ἠδικήθην
	ἀδικία, -ας, ἡ	unrighteousness (25, n-1a)
	ἄδικος, -ον	unjust (12, a-3a)
	ἀδύνατος, -ον	incapable, impossible (10, a-3a)
	ἀθετέω	I reject (16, v-1d[2a]) ἀθετήσω, ἠθέτησα, -, -, -
	Αἴγυπτος, -ου, ἡ	Egypt (25, n-2b)
24	αἷμα, -ματος, τό	blood (97, n-3c[4])
20	αἴρω	I raise, take up, take away (101, v-2d[2]) ἀρῶ, ἦρα, ἦρκα, ἦρμαι, ἤρθην
25	αἰτέω	I ask, demand (70, v-1d[2a]) (ἤτουν), αἰτήσω, ᾔτησα, ᾔτηκα, -, -
	αἰτία, -ας, ἡ	cause, accusation (20, n-1a)
12	αἰών, -ῶνος, ὁ	age, eternity (122, n-3f[1a])
9	αἰώνιος, -ον	eternal (71, a-3b[1])
	ἀκαθαρσία, -ας, ἡ	uncleanness (10, n-1a)
	ἀκάθαρτος, -ον	unclean (32, a-3a)
	ἄκανθα, -ης, ἡ	thorn bush (14, n-1c)
	ἀκοή, -ῆς, ἡ	hearing, report (24, n-1b)
21	ἀκολουθέω	I follow, accompany (90, v-1d[2a]) (ἠκολούθουν), ἀκολουθήσω, ἠκολούθησα, ἠκολούθηκα, -, -
16	ἀκούω	I hear, learn, obey, understand (428, v-1a[8]) (ἤκουον), ἀκούσω, ἤκουσα, ἀκήκοα, -, ἠκούσθην
	ἀκροβυστία, -ας, ἡ	uncircumcision (20, n-1a)
	ἀλέκτωρ, -ορος, ὁ	cock (12, n-3f[2b])
14	ἀλήθεια, -ας, ἡ	truth (109, n-1a)
	ἀληθής, -ές	true (26, a-4a)
	ἀληθινός, -ή, -όν	true (28, a-1a[2a])
	ἀληθῶς	truly (18, adverb)
8	ἀλλά	but, yet, except (638, particle)
9	ἀλλήλων	one another (100, a-1a[2b])
6	ἄλλος, -η, -ο	other, another (155, a-1a[2b])
	ἀλλότριος, -α, -ον	another's, strange (14, a-1a[1])
	ἅλυσις, -εως, ἡ	chain (11, n-3e[5b])

	ἅμα	adverb: at the same time (10, adverb) dat: together with
	ἁμαρτάνω	I sin (43, v-3a[2a]) ἁμαρτήσω, ἥμαρτον or ἡμάρτησα, ἡμάρτηκα, -, -
7	ἁμαρτία, -ας, ἡ	sin (173, n-1a)
	ἁμαρτωλός, -όν	adj: sinful (47, a-3a) noun: sinner
4	ἀμήν	verily, truly, amen, so let it be (129, particle)
	ἀμπελών, -ῶνος, ὁ	vineyard (23, n-3f[1a])
	ἀμφότεροι, -αι, -α	both (14, a-1a[1])
11	ἄν	an untranslatable, uninflected word, used to make a definite statement contingent upon something (167)
	ἀνά	acc: upwards, up (13, preposition) (with numerals) each
27	ἀναβαίνω	I go up, come up (82, cv-2d[7]) (ἀνέβαινον), ἀναβήσομαι, ἀνέβην, ἀναβέβηκα, -, -
	ἀναβλέπω	I look up, receive sight (25, cv-1b[1]) -, ἀνέβλεψα, -, -, -
	ἀναγγέλλω	I announce, report (14, cv-2d[1]) (ἀνήγγελλον), ἀναγγελῶ, ἀνήγγειλα, -, -, ἀνηγγέλην
	ἀναγινώσκω	I read (32, cv-5a) (ἀνεγίνωσκον), -, ἀνέγνων, -, -, ἀνεγνώσθην
	ἀνάγκη, -ης, ἡ	necessity (18, n-1b)
	ἀνάγω	I lead up (23, cv-1b[2]) (middle) I put to sea, set sail -, ἀνήγαγον, -, -, ἀνήχθην
	ἀναιρέω	I take up, kill (24, cv-1d[2a]) ἀνελῶ, ἀνεῖλα, -, -, ἀνῃρέθην
	ἀνάκειμαι	I recline (at meals) (14, cv-6b) (ἀνεκείμην), -, -, -, -, -
	ἀνακρίνω	I examine (16, cv-2d[6]) -, ἀνέκρινα, -, -, ἀνεκρίθην
	ἀναλαμβάνω	I take up (13, cv-3a[2b]) -, ἀνέλαβον, -, -, ἀνελήμφθην
	Ἀνανίας, -ου, ὁ	Ananias (11, n-1d)
	ἀναπαύω	I refresh (12, cv-1a[5]) (middle) I take rest ἀναπαύσω, ἀνέπαυσα, -, ἀναπέπαυμαι, -

	ἀναπίπτω	I recline (12, cv-1b[3]) -, ἀνέπεσα, -, -, -
	ἀνάστασις, -εως, ἡ	resurrection (42, n-3e[5b])
	ἀναστρέφω	I return, live (11, cv-1b[1]) ἀναστρέψω, ἀνέστρεψα, -, -, ἀνεσράφην
	ἀναστροφή, -ῆς, ἡ	conduct (13, n-1b)
	ἀνατολή, -ῆς, ἡ	east, dawn (11, n-1b)
	ἀναφέρω	I bring up, offer (10, cv-1c[1]) (ἀνεφερόμην), -, ἀνήνεγκα or ἀνήνεκον, -, -, -
	ἀναχωρέω	I depart (14, cv-1d[2a]) -, ἀνεχώρησα, -, -, -
	Ἀνδρέας, -ου, ὁ	Andrew (13, n-1d)
	ἄνεμος, -ου, ὁ	wind (31, n-2a)
	ἀνέχομαι	I endure (15, cv-1b[2]) ἀνέξομαι, ἀνεσχόμην -, -, -
10	ἀνήρ, ἀνδρός, ὁ	man, male, husband (216, n-3f[2c])
	ἀνθίστημι	I resist (14, cv-6a) (ἀνθιστόμην), -, ἀντέστην, ἀνθέστηκα, -, -
4	ἄνθρωπος, -ου, ὁ	man, mankind, person, people, humankind, human being (550, n-2a)
35	ἀνίστημι	intransitive: I rise, get up (108, cv-6a) transitive: I raise ἀναστήσω, ἀνέστησα, -, -, -
35	ἀνοίγω	I open (77, v-1b[2]) ἀνοίξω, ἤνέῳξα or ἀνέῳξα, ἀνέῳγα, ἀγέῳγμαι or ἠνέῳγμαι, ἠνεῴχθην or ἠνοίχθην
	ἀνομία, -ας, ἡ	lawlessness (15, n-1a)
	ἄνομος, -ον	lawless, without law (10, a-3a)
	ἀντί	gen: instead of, for (22, preposition)
	Ἀντιόχεια, -ας, ἡ	Antioch (18, n-1a)
	ἄνωθεν	from above, again (13, adverb)
	ἄξιος, -α, -ον	worthy (41, a-1a[1])
	ἀπαγγέλλω	I announce, report (45, cv-2d[1]) (ἀπήγγελλον), ἀπαγγελῶ, ἀπήγγειλα, -, -, ἀπηγγέλην
	ἀπάγω	I lead away (16, cv-1b[2]) -, ἀπήγαγον, -, -, ἀπήχθην
	ἅπαξ	once, once for all (14, adverb)
	ἀπαρνέομαι	I deny (11, cv-1d[2a]) ἀπαρνήσομαι, ἀπήρνησα, -, -, ἀπαρνηθήσομαι

	ἅπας, -ασα, -αν	all (34, a-2a)
	ἀπειθέω	I disbelieve, disobey (14, v-1d[2a]) (ἠπείθουν), -, ἠπείθησα, -, -, -
23	ἀπέρχομαι	I depart (117, cv-1b[2]) ἀπελεύσομαι, ἀπῆλθον, ἀπελήλυθα, -, -
	ἀπέχω	I have received, am distant (19, cv-1b[2]) (ἀπεῖχον), -, -, -, -, -
	ἀπιστία, -ας, ἡ	unbelief (11, n-1a)
	ἄπιστος, -ον	unbelieving, faithless (23, a-3a)
8	ἀπό	gen: (away) from (646, preposition)
	ἀποδίδωμι	I give back, pay (48, cv-6a) (middle) I sell (ἀπεδίδουν), ἀποδώσω, ἀπέδωκα, -, -, ἀπεδόθην
22	ἀποθνῄσκω	I die, am about to die, am freed from (111, cv-5a) (ἀπέθνῃσκον), ἀποθανοῦμαι, ἀπέθανον, -, -, -
	ἀποκαλύπτω	I reveal (26, cv-4) ἀποκαλύψω, ἀπεκάλυψα, -, -, ἀπεκαλύφθην
	ἀποκάλυψις, -εως, ἡ	revelation (18, n-3e[5b])
18	ἀποκρίνομαι	I answer (231, cv-2d[6]) -, ἀπεκρινάμην, -, -, ἀπεκρίθην
20	ἀποκτείνω	I kill (74, cv-2d[5]) ἀποκτενῶ, ἀπέκτεινα, -, -, ἀπεκτάνθην
	ἀπολαμβάνω	I take aside (10, cv-3a[2b])* ἀπολήμψομαι, ἀπέλαβον, -, -, -
33	ἀπόλλυμι	active: I destroy, kill (90, cv-3c[2]) middle: I perish, die (ἀπώλλυον), ἀπολέσω or ἀπολῶ, ἀπώλεσα, -, -, -
	Ἀπολλῶς, -ῶ, ὁ	Apollos (10, n-2e)
	ἀπολογέομαι	I defend myself (10, cv-1d[2a]) ἀπολογήσω, -, -, -, ἀπελογήθην
	ἀπολύτρωσις, -εως, ἡ	redemption (10, n-3e[5b])
33	ἀπολύω	I release (66, cv-1a[4]) (ἀπέλυον), ἀπολύσω, ἀπέλυσα, -, ἀπολέλυμαι, ἀπελύθην
20	ἀποστέλλω	I send (away) (132, cv-2d[1]) ἀποστελῶ, ἀπέστειλα, ἀπέσταλκα, ἀπέσταλμαι, ἀπεστάλην
4	ἀπόστολος, -ου, ὁ	apostle, envoy, messenger (80, n-2a)
	ἅπτομαι or ἅπτω	I touch (39, v-4) -, ἧψα, -, -, -
	ἀπώλεια, -ας, ἡ	destruction (18, n-1a)

	ἄρα	then, therefore (49, n-1a)
	ἀργύριον, -ου, τό	silver (20, n-2c)
	ἀρέσκω	I please (17, v-5a)
		(ἤρεσκον), ἀρέσω, ἤρεσα, -, -, -
	ἀριθμός, -οῦ, ὁ	number (18, n-2a)
	ἀρνέομαι	I deny (33, v-1d[2a])
		(ἠρνούμην), ἀρνήσομαι, ἠρνησάμην, -, ἤρνημαι, -
	ἀρνίον, -ου, τό	lamb (30, n-2c)
	ἁρπάζω	I seize (14, v-2a[2])
		ἁρπάσω, ἥρπασα, -, -, ἡρπάσθην or ἡρπάγην
	ἄρτι	now, just now (36, adverb)
22	ἄρτος, -ου, ὁ	bread, loaf, food (97, n-2a)
	ἀρχαῖος, -αία, -αῖον	old, ancient (11, a-1a[1])
7	ἀρχή, -ῆς, ἡ	beginning, ruler (55, n-1b)
27	ἀρχιερεύς, -έως, ὁ	chief priest, high priest (122, n-3e[3])
23	ἄρχω	active: I rule (86, v-1b[2])
		middle: I begin
		ἄρξομαι, ἠρξάμην, -, -, -
	ἄρχων, -οντος, ὁ	ruler (37, n-3c[5b])
	ἀσέλγεια, -ας, ἡ	licentiousness, debauchery, sensuality (10, n-1a)
	ἀσθένεια, -ας, ἡ	weakness (24, n-1a)
	ἀσθενέω	I am weak (33, v-1d[2a])
		(ἠσθενοῦν), -, ἠσθένησα, ἠσθένηκα, -, -
	ἀσθενής, -ές	weak (26, a-4a)
	Ἀσία, -ας, ἡ	Asia (18, n-1a)
	ἀσκός, -οῦ, ὁ	(leather) bottle, wine-skin (12, n-2a)
28	ἀσπάζομαι	I greet, salute (59, v-2a[1])
		(ἠσπαζόμην), -, ἠσπασάμην, -, -, -
	ἀσπασμός, -οῦ, ὁ	greeting (10, n-2a)
	ἀστήρ, -έρος, ὁ	star (24, n-3f[2b])
	ἀτενίζω	I look intently, gaze upon intently (14, v-2a[1])
		-, ἠτένισα, -, -, -
	αὐλή, -ῆς, ἡ	court (12, n-1b)
	αὐξάνω	I cause to grow, increase (23, v-3a[1])
		(ηὔξανον), αὐξήσω, ηὔξησα, -, -, ηὐξήθην
	αὔριον	tomorrow (14, adverb)
6	αὐτός, -ή, -ό	he, she, it (5595, a-1a[2b])
		him/her/itself
		same
	αὐτοῦ, -ῆς	there (17, adverb)

	ἀφαιρέω	I take away (10, cv-1d[2a]) ἀφελῶ, ἀφεῖλον, -, -, ἀφαιρεθήσομαι
	ἄφεσις, -εως, ἡ	sending away, remission (17, n-3e[5b])
35	ἀφίημι	I let go, leave, permit (143, cv-6a) (ἤφιον), ἀφήσω, ἀφῆκα, -, ἀφέωμαι, ἀφέθην
	ἀφίστημι	I withdraw, depart (14, cv-6a) (ἀφιστόμην), ἀποστήσομαι, ἀπέστησα, -, -, -
	ἀφορίζω	I separate (10, cv-2a[1]) (ἀφώριζον), ἀφοριῶ or ἀφορίσω, ἀφώρισα, -, ἀφώρισμαι, -
	ἄφρων, -ον	foolish (11, a-4b[1])
	Ἀχαΐα, -ας, ἡ	Achaia (10, n-1a)
	ἄχρι, ἄχρις	gen: as far as, up to (49, preposition) conj: until

βῆτα

	Βαβυλών, -ῶνος, ἡ	Babylon (12, n-3f[1a])
22	βάλλω	I throw (122, v-2d[1]) (ἔβαλλον), βαλῶ, ἔβαλον, βέβληκα, βέβλημαι, ἐβλήθην
20	βαπτίζω	I baptize (77, v-2a[1]) (ἐβάπτιζον), βαπτίσω, ἐβάπτισα, -, βεβάπτισμαι, ἐβαπτίσθην
	βάπτισμα, -ατος, τό	baptism (19, n-3c[4])
	βαπτιστής, -οῦ, ὁ	baptist (12, n-1f)
	Βαραββᾶς, -ᾶ, ὁ	Barabbas (11, n-1e)
	Βαρναβᾶς, -ᾶ, ὁ	Barnabas (28, n-1e)
	βασανίζω	I torment (12, v-2a[1]) (ἐβασάνιζον), -, ἐβασάνισα, -, -, βασανισθήσομαι
6	βασιλεία, -ας, ἡ	kingdom (162, n-1a)
19	βασιλεύς, -έως, ὁ	king (115, n-3e[3])
	βασιλεύω	I reign (21, v-1a[6]) βασιλεύσω, ἐβασίλευσα, -, -, -
	βαστάζω	I bear, carry (27, v-2a[1]) (ἐβάσταζον), βαστάσω, ἐβάστασα, -, -, -
	Βηθανία, -ας, ἡ	Bethany (12, n-1a)
	βῆμα, -ατος, τό	judgment seat (12, n-3c[4])
	βιβλίον, -ου, τό	book (34, n-2c)
	βίβλος, -ου, ἡ	book (10, n-2b)
	βίος, -ου, ὁ	life (10, n-2a)

	βλασφημέω	I blaspheme, revile (34, v-1d[2a]) (ἐβλασφήμουν), -, ἐβλασφήμησα, -, -, βλασφημηθήσομαι
	βλασφημία, -ας, ἡ	blasphemy, reproach (18, n-1a)
16	βλέπω	I see, look at (133, v-1b[1]) (ἔβλεπον),βλέψω, ἔβλεψα, -, -, -
	βοάω	I cry aloud (12, v-1d[1a]) βοήσω, ἐβόησα, -, -, -
	βουλή, -ῆς, ἡ	counsel, purpose (12, n-1b)
	βούλομαι	I wish, determine (37, v-1d[2c]) (ἐβουλόμην), -, -, -, -, ἐβουλήθην
	βροντή, -ῆς, ἡ	thunder (12, n-1b)
	βρῶμα, -ατος, τό	food (17, n-3c[4])
	βρῶσις, -εως, ἡ	eating, food, rust (11, n-3e[5b])

γάμμα

4	Γαλιλαία, -ας, ἡ	Galilee (61, n-1a)
	Γαλιλαῖος, -α, -ον	Galilean (11, a-1a[1])
	γαμέω	I marry (28, v-1d[2a]) (ἐγάμουν), -, ἔγμηα or ἐγάμησα, γεγάμηκα, -, ἐγαμήθην
	γάμος, -ου, ὁ	marriage, wedding (16, n-2a)
7	γάρ	for, then (1042, conjunction)
	γε	indeed, at least, really, even (28, particle)
	γέεννα, -ης, ἡ	gehenna (12, n-1c)
	γέμω	I fill (11, v-1c[2])
	γενεά, -ᾶς, ἡ	generation (43, n-1a)
19	γεννάω	I beget, give birth to, produce (97, v-1d[1a]) γεννήσω, ἐγέννησα, γεγέννηκα, γεγέννημαι, ἐγεννήθην
	γένος, -ους, τό	race, kind (21, n-3d[2b])
	γεύομαι	I taste (15, v-1a[6]) γεύσομαι, ἐγευσάμην, -, -, -
	γεωργός, -οῦ, ὁ	farmer (19, n-2a)
22	γῆ, γῆς, ἡ	earth, land, region, humanity (250, n-1h)
22	γίνομαι	I become, am, exist, am born, created (669, v-1c[2]) (ἐγινόμην), γενήσομαι, ἐγενόμην, γέγονα, γεγένημαι, ἐγενήθην

20	γινώσκω	I know, come to know, realize, learn (222, v-5a) (ἐγίνωσκον), γνώσομαι, ἔγνων, ἔγνωκα, ἔγνωσμαι, ἐγνώσθην
20	γλῶσσα, -ης, ἡ	tongue, language (50, n-1c)
	γνωρίζω	I make known (25, v-2a[1]) γνωρίσω, ἐγνώρισα, -, -, ἐγνωρίσθην
	γνῶσις, -εως, ἡ	knowledge (29, n-3e[5b])
	γνωστός, -ή, -όν	known (15, a-1a[2a])
	γονεύς, -έως, ὁ	parent (20, n-3e[3])
	γόνυ, -ατος, τό	knee (12, n-3c[6d])
	γράμμα, -ατος, τό	letter (14, n-3c[4])
28	γραμματεύς, -έως, ὁ	scribe (63, n-3e[3])
4	γραφή, -ῆς, ἡ	writing, Scripture (51, n-1b)
23	γράφω	I write (191, v-1b[1]) (ἔγραφον), γράψω, ἔγραψα, γέγραφα, γέγραπμαι or γέγραμμαι, ἐγράφην
	γρηγορέω	I watch (22, v-1d[2a]) -, ἐγρηγόρησα, -, -, -
	γυμνός, -ή, -όν	naked (15, a-1a[2a])
13	γυνή, γυναικός, ἡ	woman, wife (215, n-3b[1])

δέλτα

	δαιμονίζομαι	I am demon possessed (13, v-2a[1]) -, -, -, -, ἐδαιμονίσθην
17	δαιμόνιον, -ου, τό	demon (63, n-2c)
	δάκρυον, -ου, τό	tear (10, n-2c)
	Δαμασκός, -οῦ, ὁ	Damascus (15, n-2b)
4	Δαυίδ, ὁ	David (59, n-3g[2])
6	δέ	but, and (2792, particle)
	δέησις, -εως, ἡ	entreaty (18, n-3e[5b])
18	δεῖ	it is necessary (101, v-1d[2c])
35	δείκνυμι	I show, explain (33, v-3c[2]) δείξω, ἔδειξα, δέδειχα, -, ἐδείχθην
	δεῖπνον, -ου, τό	supper (16, n-2c)
	δέκα	ten (24, n-3g[2])
	δένδρον, -ου, τό	tree (25, n-2c)
27	δεξιός, -ιά, -ιόν	right (54, a-1a[1])
	δέομαι	I beseech (22, v-1d[2c]) (ἐδούμην), -, -, -, -, ἐδεήθην

	δέρω	I beat (15, v-1c[1])
		-, ἔδειρα, -, -, δαρήσομαι,
	δέσμιος, -ου, ὁ	prisoner (16, n-2a)
	δεσμός, -οῦ, ὁ	bond, fetter (18, n-2a)
	δεσπότης, -ου, ὁ	master, lord (10, n-1f)
	δεῦτε	come! (12, adverb)
	δεύτερος, -α, -ον	second (43, a-1a[1])
29	δέχομαι	I take, receive (56, v-1b[2])
		δέξομαι, ἐδεξάμην, -, δέδεγμαι, ἐδέχθην
	δέω	I bind (43, v-1d[2b])
		-, ἔδησα, δέδεκα, δέδεμαι, ἐδέθην
	δηνάριον, -ου, τό	denarius (16, n-2c)
8	διά	gen: through (667, preposition)
		acc: on account of
	διάβολος, -ον	adj: slanderous, accusing falsely (37, a-3a)
		noun: Accuser, Devil
	διαθήκη, -ης, ἡ	covenant (33, n-1b)
	διακονέω	I serve, minister, wait upon (37, v-1d[2a])
		(διηκόνουν), διακονήσω, διηκόνησα, -, -,
		διηκονήθην
	διακονία, -ας, ἡ	service, ministry, waiting at table (34, n-1a)
	διάκονος, -ου, ὁ, ἡ	servant, administrator, deacon (29, n-2a)
	διακρίνω	I judge, discriminate (19, cv-1c[2])
		(middle) I doubt
		(διεκρινόμην), -, διεκρίνα, -, -, διεκρίθην
	διαλέγομαι	I dispute (13, cv-1b[2])
		(διελεγόμην), -, διελεξάμην, -, -, διελέχθην
	διαλογίζομαι	I debate (16, cv-2a[1])
		(διελογιζόμην), -, -, -, -, -
	διαλογισμός, -οῦ, ὁ	reasoning, questioning (14, n-2a)
	διαμαρτύρομαι	I testify solemnly (15, cv-1c[1])
		(διεμαρτυρόμην), -, διεμαρτυράμην, -, -, -
	διαμερίζω	I divide, distribute (11, cv-2a[1])
		(διεμέριζον), -, διεμερισάμην, -, διαμεμέρισμαι,
		διεμερίσθην
	διάνοια, -ας, ἡ	the mind, understanding, a thought (12, n-1a)
	διατάσσω	I command (16, cv-2b)
		διατάξομαι, διέταξα, διατέταχα, διατέταγμαι,
		διετάχθην
	διατρίβω	I continue (10, cv-1b[1])
		(διέτριβον), -, διετρίψα, -, -, -

	διαφέρω	I differ (13, cv-1c[1]) (διεφερόμην), -, διήνεγκα, -, -, -
	διδασκαλία, -ας, ἡ	teaching (21, n-1a)
12	διδάσκαλος, -ου, ὁ	teacher (59, n-2a)
21	διδάσκω	I teach (97, v-5a) (ἐδίδασκον), διδάξω, ἐδίδαξα, -, -, ἐδιδάχθην
	διδαχή, -ῆς, ἡ	teaching (30, n-1b)
34	δίδωμι	I give (out), entrust, give back, put (415, v-6a) (ἐδίδουν), δώσω, ἔδωκα, δέδωκα, δέδομαι, ἐδόθην
	διέρχομαι	I pass through (43, cv-1b[2]) (διηρχόμην), διελεύσομαι, διῆλθον, διελήλυθα, -, -
32	δίκαιος, -αία, -αιον	right, just, righteous (79, a-1a[1])
13	δικαιοσύνη, -ης, ἡ	righteousness (92, n-1b)
	δικαιόω	I justify, pronounce righteous (39, v-1d[3]) δικαιώσω, ἐδικαίωσα, -, δεδικαίωμαι, ἐδικαιώθην
	δικαίωμα, -ατος, τό	regulation, righteous deed (10, n-3c[4])
	δίκτυον, -ου, τό	net (12, n-2c)
23	διό	therefore, for this reason (53, conjunction)
	διότι	because (23, conjunction)
	διψάω	I thirst (16, v-1d[1a]) διψήσω, ἐδίψησα, -, -, -
	διωγμός, -οῦ, ὁ	persecution (10, n-2a)
	διώκω	I pursue, persecute (45, v-1b[2]) (ἐδίωκον), διώξω, ἐδίωξα, -, δεδίωγμαι, διωχθήσομαι
29	δοκέω	I think, seem (62, v-1b[4]) (ἐδόκουν), δόξω, ἔδοξα, -, -, -
	δοκιμάζω	I prove, approve (22, v-2a[1]) δοκιμάσω, ἐδοκίμασα, -, δεδοκίμασμαι, -
	δόλος, -ου, ὁ	guile (11, n-2a)
4	δόξα, -ης, ἡ	glory, majesty, fame (166, n-1c)
23	δοξάζω	I glorify, praise, honor (61, v-2a[1]) (ἐδόξαζον), δοξάσω, ἐδόξασα, -, δεδόξασμαι, ἐδοξάσθην
	δουλεύω	I serve (25, v-1a[6]) δουλεύσω, ἐδούλευσα, δεδούλευκα, -, -
9	δοῦλος, -ου, ὁ	slave, servant (124, a-1a[2a])
	δράκων, -οντος, ὁ	dragon (13, n-3c[5b])
18	δύναμαι	I am powerful, am able (210, v-6b) (ἐδυνάμην or ἠδυνάμην), δυνήσομαι, -, -, -, ἠδυνήθην

23	δύναμις, -εως, ἡ	power, miracle (119, n-3e[5b])
	δυνατός, -ή, -όν	powerful, possible (32, a-1a[2a])
27	δύο	two (135, a-5)
13	δώδεκα	twelve (75, n-3g[2])
	δωρεά, -ᾶς, ἡ	gift (11, n-1a)
	δῶρον, -ου, τό	gift (19, n-2c)

ἒ ψιλόν

9	ἐάν	if, when (351, conjunction)
13	ἑαυτοῦ, -ῆς	singular: of himself/herself/itself (319, a-1a[2b])
		plural: of themselves
	ἐάω	I permit (11, v-1d[1b])
		(εἴων), ἐάσω, εἴασα, -, -, -
	ἐγγίζω	I come near (42, v-2a[1])
		(ἤγγιζον), ἐγγιῶ, ἤγγισα, ἤγγικα, -, -
	ἐγγύς	near (31, adverb)
20	ἐγείρω	I raise up, wake (144, v-2d[3])
		ἐγερῶ, ἤγειρα, -, ἐγήγερμαι, ἠγέρθην
	ἐγκαταλείπω	I leave behind, forsake, abandon (10, cv-1b[1])
		ἐγκαταλείψω, ἐγκατέλιπον, -, -, ἐγκατελείφθην
4	ἐγώ	I (1775, a-5)
34	ἔθνος, -ους, τό	nation (162, n-3d[2b])
		plural: Gentiles
	ἔθος, -ους, τό	custom (12, n-3d[2b])
10	εἰ	if (503, particle)
	εἴδωλον, -ου, τό	image, idol (11, n-2c)
	εἴκοσι	twenty (10, n-3g[2])
	εἰκών, -όνος, ἡ	image (23, n-3f[1b])
6	εἰμί	I am, exist, live, am present (2460, v-6b)
		(ἔμεν or ἤμεν), ἔσομαι, -, -, -, -
14	εἰρήνη, -ης, ἡ	peace (92, n-1b)
7	εἰς	acc: into, in, among (1768, preposition)
10	εἷς, μία, ἕν	one (344, a-4b[2])
	εἰσάγω	I lead in (11, cv-1b[2])
		-, εἰσήγαγον, -, -, -
22	εἰσέρχομαι	I come in(to), go in(to), enter (194, cv-1b[2])
		εἰσελεύσομαι, εἰσῆλθον, εἰσελήλυθα, -, -
	εἰσπορεύομαι	I enter (18, cv-1a[6])
		(εἰσεπορευόμην), -, -, -, -, -

	εἶτα	then (15, adverb)
33	εἴτε	if, whether (65, particle)
8	ἐκ, ἐξ	gen: from, out of (914, preposition)
24	ἕκαστος, -η, -ον	each, every (82, a-1a[2a])
	ἑκατόν	one hundred (11, n-3g[2])
	ἑκατοντάρχης, -ου, ὁ	centurion (16, n-1f)
20	ἐκβάλλω	I cast out, send out (81, cv-2d[1]) (ἐξέβαλλον), ἐκβαλῶ, ἐξέβαλον, -, -, ἐξεβλήθην
20	ἐκεῖ	there (105, adverb)
	ἐκεῖθεν	from that place, thence (37, adverb)
13	ἐκεῖνος, -η, -ο	sing: that (man/woman/thing) (265, a-1a[2b]) plural: those (men/women/things)
11	ἐκκλησία, -ας, ἡ	a church, (the) Church, assembly, congregation (114, n-1a)
	ἐκκόπτω	I cut out, cut off (10, cv-4) ἐκκόψω, -, -, -, ἐξεκόπην
	ἐκλέγομαι	I pick out, choose (22, cv-1b[2]) (ἐξελεγόμην), -, ἐξελεξάμην, -, ἐκλέλεγμαι, -
	ἐκλεκτός, -ή, -όν	chosen, elect (22, a-1a[2a])
	ἐκπίπτω	I fall away (10, cv-1b[3]) -, ἐξέπεσα, ἐκπέπτωκα, -, -
	ἐκπλήσσομαι	I am astonished, amazed (13, cv-2b) (ἐξεπλησσόμην), -, -, -, -, ἐξεπλάγην
	ἐκπορεύομαι	I go out (34, cv-1a[6]) (ἐξεπορευόμην), ἐκπορεύσομαι, -, -, -, -
	ἐκτείνω	I stretch forth (16, cv-2d[5]) ἐκτενῶ, ἐξέτεινα, -, -, -
	ἕκτος, -η, -ον	sixth (14, a-1a[2a])
	ἐκχέω	I pour out (16, cv-1a[7]) ἐκχεῶ, ἐξέχεα, -, -, -
	ἐκχύννομαι	I pour out (11, cv-3a[1]) (ἐξεχυνόμην), -, -, ἐκκέχυμαι, -
	ἐλαία, -ας, ἡ	olive tree (13, n-1a)
	ἔλαιον, -ου, τό	olive-oil (11, n-2c)
	ἐλάχιστος, -η, -ον	least (14, a-1a[2a])
	ἐλέγχω	I convict, reprove (17, v-1b[2]) ἐλέγξω, ἤλεγξα, -, -, ἠλέγχθην
	ἐλεέω	I have mercy (29, v-1d[2a]) ἐλεήσω, ἠλέησα, -, ἠλέημαι, ἠλεήθην
	ἐλεημοσύνη, -ης, ἡ	alms (13, n-1b)

	ἔλεος, -ους, τό	pity, mercy (27, n-3d[2b])
	ἐλευθερία, -ας, ἡ	liberty (11, n-1a)
	ἐλεύθερος, -α, -ον	free (23, a-1a[1])
	Ἕλλην, -ηνος, ὁ	Greek (25, n-3f[1a])
	ἐλπίζω	I hope (31, v-2a[1])
		(ἤλπιζον), ἐλπιῶ, ἤλπισα, ἤλπικα, -, -
13	ἐλπίς, -ίδος, ἡ	hope, expectation (53, n-3c[2])
	ἐμαυτου, -ῆς	of myself (37, a-1a[2a])
	ἐμβαίνω	I embark (17, cv-2d[7])
		-, ἐνέβην, -, -, -
	ἐμβλέπω	I look at (12, cv-1b[1])
		(ἐνέβλεπον), -, ἐνέβλεψα, -, -, -
9	ἐμός, ἐμή, ἐμόν	my, mine (76, a-1a[2a])
	ἐμπαίζω	I mock (13, cv-2a[2])
		(ἐνέπαιζον), ἐμπαίξω, ἐνέπαιξα, -, -, ἐνεπαίχθην
	ἔμπροσθεν	gen: in front of, before (48, adverb)
	ἐμφανίζω	I manifest (10, cv-2a[1])
		ἐμφανίσω,, ἐνεφάνισα, -, -, ἐνεφανίσθην
6	ἐν	dat: in, on, among (2752, preposition)
	ἔνατος, -η, -ον	ninth (10, a-1a[2a])
	ἐνδείκνυμι	I show forth (11, cv-3c[2])
		-, ἐνεδειξάμην, -, -, -
	ἐνδύω	I put on, clothe (27, v-1a[4])
		-, ἐνέδυσα, -, ἐνδέδυμαι, -
	ἕνεκα or ἕνεκεν	gen: on account of (19, preposition)
	ἐνεργέω	I work, effect (21, cv-1d[2a])
		(ἐνηργούμην), -, ἐνήργησα, -, -, -
	ἐνιαυτός, -οῦ, ὁ	year (14, n-2a)
	ἔνοχος, -ον	involved in, liable, guilty (10, a-3a)
	ἐντέλλομαι	I command (15, cv-2d[1])
		ἐντελοῦμαι, ἐνετειλάμην, -, ἐντέταλμαι, -
9	ἐντολή, -ῆς, ἡ	commandment (67, n-1b)
14	ἐνώπιον	gen: before (94, preposition)
	ἕξ	six (10, n-3g[2])
	ἐξάγω	I lead out (12, cv-1b[2])
		-, ἐξήγαγον, -, -, -
	ἐξαποστέλλω	I send forth (13, cv-2d[1])
		ἐξαποστελῶ, ἐξαπέστειλα, -, -, ἐξαπεστάλην
22	ἐξέρχομαι	I go out (218, cv-1b[2])
		(ἐξηρχόμην), ἐξελεύσομαι, ἐξῆλθον, ἐξελήλυθα, -, -

	ἔξεστι	it is lawful (32, cv-6b)
	ἐξίστημι	I amaze, am amazed (17, cv-6a) (ἐξιστάμην), -, ἐξέστησα, ἐξέστακα, -, -
	ἐξομολογέομαι	I confess, profess (10, cv-1d[2a]) ἐξομολογήσομαι, ἐξωμολόγησα, -, -, -
	ἐξουθενέω	I despise (11, v-1d[2a]) -, ἐξουθένησα, -, ἐξουθένημαι, ἐξουθενήθην
7	ἐξουσία, -ας, ἡ	authority, power (102, n-1a)
11	ἔξω	adverb: without (63) prep (gen): outside
	ἔξωθεν	gen: from without (13, adverb)
	ἑορτή, -ῆς, ἡ	feast (26, n-1b)
14	ἐπαγγελία, -ας, ἡ	promise (52, n-1a)
	ἐπαγγέλλομαι	I promise (15, cv-2d[1]) -, ἐπηγγειλάμην, -, ἐπήγγελμαι, -
	ἔπαινος, -ου, ὁ	praise (11, n-2a)
	ἐπαίρω	I lift up (19, cv-2d[2]) -, ἐπῆρα, -, -, ἐπήρθην
	ἐπαισχύνομαι	I am ashamed (11, cv-1c[2]) -, -, -, -, ἐπαισχυνθήσομαι
	ἐπάνω	adverb: above (19) gen: over
	ἐπαύριον	on the morrow (17, adverb)
	ἐπεί	when, since (26, conjunction)
	ἐπειδή	since, because (10, conjunction)
	ἔπειτα	then (16, adverb)
21	ἐπερωτάω	I ask (for), question, demand of (56, cv-1d[1a]) (ἐπηρώτων), ἐπερωτήσω, ἐπηρώτησα, -, -, ἐπηρωτήθην
11	ἐπί (ἐπ᾽, ἐφ᾽)	gen: on, over, when (890, preposition) dat: on the basis of, at acc: on, to, against
	ἐπιβάλλω	I lay upon (18, cv-2d[1]) (ἐπέβαλλον), ἐπιβαλῶ, ἐπέβαλον, -, -, -
	ἐπιγινώσκω	I come to know, recognize (44, cv-5a) (ἐπεγίνωσκον), ἐπιγινώσομαι, ἐπέγνων, ἐπέγνωκα, -, ἐπεγνώσθην
	ἐπίγνωσις, -εως, ἡ	knowledge (20, n-3e[5b])
	ἐπιζητέω	I seek for (13, cv-1d[2a]) (ἐπεζήτουν), -, ἐπεζήτησα, -, -, -

	ἐπιθυμέω	I desire (16, cv-1d[2a]) (ἐπεθύμουν), ἐπιθυμήσω, ἐπεθύμησα, -, -, -
	ἐπιθυμία, -ας, ἡ	eager desire, passion (38, n-1a)
	ἐπικαλέω	I call, name (30, cv-1d[2b]) (middle) I invoke, appeal to -, ἐπεκάλεσα, -, ἐπικέκλημαι, ἐπεκλήθην
	ἐπιλαμβάνομαι	I take hold of (19, cv-3a[2b]) -, ἐπελαβόμην, -, -, -
	ἐπιμένω	I continue (17, cv-1c[2]) (ἐπέμενον), ἐπιμενῶ, ἐπέμεινα, -, -, -
	ἐπιπίπτω	I fall upon (11, cv-1b[3]) -, ἐπέπεσον, ἐπιπέπτωκα, -, -
	ἐπισκέπτομαι	I visit, have a care for (11, cv-4) -, ἐπεσκεψάμην, -, -, -
	ἐπίσταμαι	I understand (14, cv-6b)
	ἐπιστολή, -ῆς, ἡ	letter (24, n-1b)
	ἐπιστρέφω	I turn to, return (36, cv-1b[1]) ἐπιστρέψω, ἐπέστρεψα, -, -, ἐπεστράφην
	ἐπιτάσσω	I command (10, cv-2b) -, ἐπέταξα, -, -, -
	ἐπιτελέω	I complete, perform (10, cv-1d[2]) ἐπιτελέσω, ἐπετέλεσα, -, -, -
	ἐπιτίθημι	I lay upon (39, cv-6a) (ἐπετίθουν), ἐπιθήσω, ἐπέθηκα, -, -, -
	ἐπιτιμάω	I rebuke, warn (29, cv-1d[1a]) (ἐπετίμων), -, ἐπετίμησα, -, -, -
	ἐπιτρέπω	I permit (18, cv-1b[1]) -, ἐπέτρεψα, -, -, ἐπετράπην
	ἐπουράνιος, -ον	heavenly (19, a-3a)
14	ἑπτά	seven (88, n-3g[2])
	ἐργάζομαι	I work (41, v-2a[1]) (ἠργαζόμην), -, ἠργασάμην, -, -, -
	ἐργάτης, -ου, ὁ	workperson (16, n-1f)
6	ἔργον, -ου, τό	work, deed, action (169, n-2c)
	ἔρημος, -ον	adj: solitary, deserted (48, a-3a) noun: desert, wilderness (n-2b)
18	ἔρχομαι	I come, go (636, v-1b[2]) (ἠρχόμην), ἐλεύσομαι, ἦλθον or ἦλθα, ἐλήλυθα, -, -
21	ἐρωτάω	I ask (for), request, entreat (63, v-1d[1a]) (ἠρώτων), ἐρωτήσω, ἠρώτησα, -, -, ἠρωτήθην

29	ἐσθίω	I eat (158, v-1b[3]) (ἤσθιον), φάγομαι, ἔφαγον, -, -, -
4	ἔσχατος, -η, -ον	last (52, a-1a[2a])
	ἔσωθεν	from within, within (12, adverb)
27	ἕτερος, -α, -ον	other, another, different (99, a-1a[1])
22	ἔτι	still, yet, even (93, adverb)
	ἑτοιμάζω	I prepare (40, v-2a[1]) ἑτοιμάσω, ἡτοίμασα, ἡτοίμακα, ἡτοίμασμαι, ἡτοιμάσθην
	ἕτοιμος, -η, -ον	ready, prepared (17, a-3b[2])
	ἔτος, -ους, τό	year (49, n-3d[2b])
27	εὐαγγελίζω	I bring good news, preach (54, v-2a[1]) (εὐηγγέλιζον), -, εὐηγγέλισα, -, εὐηγγέλισμαι, εὐηγγελίσθην
7	εὐαγγέλιον, -ου, τό	good news, Gospel (76, n-2c)
	εὐδοκέω	I think it good, am well pleased with (21, v-1d[2a]) -, εὐδόκησα, -, -, -
	εὐθέως	immediately (33, adverb)
12	εὐθύς	immediately (54, adverb)
	εὐλογέω	I bless (42, v-1d[2a]) εὐλογήσω, εὐλόγησα, εὐλόγηκα, εὐλόγημαι, εὐλογηθήσομαι
	εὐλογία, -ας, ἡ	blessing (16, n-1a)
22	εὑρίσκω	I find (176, v-5b) (εὕρισκον or ηὕρισκον), εὑρήσω, εὗρον, εὕρηκα, -, εὑρέθην
	εὐσέβεια, -ας, ἡ	piety, godliness (15, n-1a)
	εὐφραίνω	I rejoice (14, v-2d[4]) (εὐφραινόμην), -, -, -, -, ηὐφράνθην
	εὐχαριστέω	I give thanks (38, v-1d[2a]) -, εὐχαρίστησα or ηὐχαρίστησα, -, -, εὐχαριστήθην
	εὐχαριστία, -ας, ἡ	thanksgiving (15, n-1a)
	Ἔφεσος, -ου, ἡ	Ephesus (16, n-2b)
	ἐφίστημι	I stand over, come upon (21, cv-6a) -, ἐπέστην, ἐφέστηκα, -, -
	ἐχθρός, -ά, -όν	hating (32, a-1a[1]) (as a noun) an enemy
16	ἔχω	I have, hold (708, v-1b[2]) (εἶχον), ἕξω, ἔσχον, ἔσχηκα, -, -

12	ἕως	conj: until (146) gen: as far as

ζῆτα

	Ζαχαρίας, -ου ὁ	Zechariah (11, n-1d)*
19	ζάω	I live (140, v-1d[1a]) (ἔζων), ζήσω, ἔζησα, -, -, -
	Ζεβεδαῖος, -ου, ὁ	Zebedee (12, n-2a)
	ζῆλος, -ου, ὁ	zeal, jealousy (16, n-2a)
	ζηλόω	I am zealous (11, v-1d[3]) -, ἐζήλωσα, -, -, -
17	ζητέω	I seek, desire, try to obtain (117, v-1d[2a]) (ἐζήτουν), ζητήσω, ἐζήτησα, -, -, ἐζητήθην
	ζύμη, -ης, ἡ	leaven (13, n-1b)
4	ζωή, -ῆς, ἡ	life (135, n-1b)
	ζῷον, -ου, τό	living creature, an animal (23, n-2c)
	ζῳοποιέω	I make alive (11, cv-1d[2a]) ζῳοποιήσω, ζῳοποιησα, -, -, ζῳοποιήθην

ἦτα

13	ἤ	or, than (343, particle)
	ἡγεμών, -όνος, ὁ	leader, a governor (20, n-3f[1b])
	ἡγέομαι	I am chief, think, regard (28, v-1d[2a]) -, ἡγησάμην, -, ἥγημαι, -
10	ἤδη	now, already (61, adverb)
	ἥκω	I have come (26, v-1b[2]) ἥξω, ἦξα, ἥκα, -, -
	Ἠλίας, -ου, ὁ	Elijah (29, n-1d)
	ἥλιος, -ου, ὁ	the sun (32, n-2a)
11	ἡμεῖς	we (864, a-5a)
8	ἡμέρα, -ας, ἡ	day (389, n-1a)
	Ἡρῴδης, -ου, ὁ	Herod (43, n-1f)
	Ἠσαΐας, -ου ὁ	Isaiah (22, n-1d)

θῆτα

8	θάλασσα, -ης, ἡ	sea, lake (91, n-1c)
8	θάνατος, -ου, ὁ	death (120, n-2a)

	θανατόω	I put to death (11, v-1d[3]) θανατώσω, ἐθανάτωσα, -, -, ἐθανατώθην
	θάπτω	I bury (11, v-4) -, ἔθαψα, -, -, ἐτάφην
	θαυμάζω	I marvel, wonder at (43, v-2a[1]) (ἐθαύμαζον), -, ἐθαύμασα, -, -, ἐθαυμάσθην
	θεάομαι	I behold (22, v-1d[1b]) -, ἐθεασάμην, -, τεθέαμαι, ἐθεάθην
11	θέλημα, -ματος, τό	will, desire (62, n-3c[4])
21	θέλω	I will, wish, desire, enjoy (208, v-1d[2c]) (ἤθελον), θελήσω, ἠθέλησα, -, -, ἠθελήθην
	θεμέλιον, -ου, τό	foundation, basis (11, n-2c)
	θεμέλιος, -ου, ὁ	foundation (15, n-2a)
4	θεός -οῦ, -ὁ	God, god (1317, n-2a)
	θεραπεύω	I heal (43, v-1a[6]) θεραπεύσω, ἐθεράπευσα, -, τεθεράπευμαι, ἐθεραπεύθην
	θερίζω	I reap (21, v-2a[1]) θερίσω, ἐθέρισα, -, -, ἐθερίσθην
	θερισμός, -οῦ, ὁ	harvest (13, n-2a)
27	θεωρέω	I look at, behold (58, v-1d[2a]) -, ἐθεώρησα, -, -, -
	θηρίον, -ου, τό	wild beast (46, n-2c)
	θησαυρός. -οῦ, ὁ	storehouse, treasure (17, n-2a)
	θλίβω	I press, oppress (10, v-1b[1]) -, -, -, τέθλιμμαι, ἐθλίβην
	θλῖψις, -εως, ἡ	tribulation (45, n-3e[5b])
	θρίξ, τριχός, ἡ	hair (15, n-3b[3])
14	θρόνος, -ου, ὁ	throne (62, n-2a)
	θυγάτηρ, -τρος, ἡ	daughter (28, n-3f[2c])
	θυμός, -οῦ, ὁ	wrath (18, n-2a)
	θύρα, -ας, ἡ	door (39, n-1a)
	θυσία, -ας, ἡ	sacrifice (28, n-1a)
	θυσιαστήριον, -ου, τό	altar (23, n-2c)
	θύω	I sacrifice, kill (14, v-1a[4]) (ἔθυον), -, ἔθυσα, -, τέθυμαι, ἐτύθην
	Θωμᾶς, -ᾶ, ἡ	Thomas (11, n-1e)

ἰῶτα

	Ἰακώβ, ὁ	Jacob (27, n-3g[2])
	Ἰάκωβος, -ου, ὁ	James (42, n-2a)*
	ἰάομαι	I heal (26, v-1d[1b]) (ἰώμην), ἰάσομαι, ἰασάμην, -, ἴαμαι, ἰάθην
11	ἴδε	See! Behold! (34)
35	ἴδιος, -α, -ον	one's own (e.g., people, home; 114, a-1a[1])
11	ἰδού	See! Behold! (200, particle)
	ἱερεύς, -έως, ὁ	priest (31, n-3e[3])
28	ἱερόν, -οῦ, τό	temple (71, n-2c)
27	Ἱεροσόλυμα, τά or ἡ	Jerusalem (62, n-1a or n-2c)
14	Ἱερουσαλήμ, ἡ	Jerusalem (77, n-3g[2])
7	Ἰησοῦς, -οῦ, ὁ	Jesus, Joshua (919, n-3g[1])
	ἱκανός, -ή, -όν	sufficient, able, considerable (39, a-1a[2a])
24	ἱμάτιον, -ου, τό	garment (60, n-2c)
8	ἵνα	in order that, that (663, conjunction)
	Ἰόππη, -ης, ἡ	Joppa (10, n-1b)
	Ἰορδάνης, -ου, ὁ	Jordon (15, n-1f)
19	Ἰουδαία, -ας, ἡ	Judea (43, n-1a)
19	Ἰουδαῖος, -αία, -αον	adjective: Jewish (195, a-1a[1]) noun: Jew
	Ἰούδας, -α, ὁ	Judas (43, n-1e)
	ἵππος, -ου, ὁ	horse (17, n-2a)
	Ἰσαάκ, ὁ	Isaac (20, n-3g[2])
19	Ἰσραήλ, ὁ	Israel (68, n-3g[2])
35	ἵστημι	intransitive: I stand (154, v-6a) transitive: I cause to stand (ἵστην), στήσω, ἔστησα or ἔστην, ἔστηκα, ἔσταμαι, ἐστάθην
	ἰσχυρός, -ά, -όν	strong (29, a-1a[1])
	ἰσχύς, -ύος, ἡ	strength (28, n-3e[1])
	ἰσχύω	I am strong, able (10, v-1a[4]) (ἴσχυον), ἰσχύσω, ἴσχυσα, -, -, -
	ἰχθύς, -ύος, ὁ	fish (20, n-3e[1])
8	Ἰωάννης, -ου, ὁ	John (135, n-1f)
	Ἰωσήφ, ὁ	Joseph (35, n-3g[2])

κάππα

13	κἀγώ	and I, but I (84, a-5)
	καθάπερ	even as, as (13, adverb; conjunction)
	καθαρίζω	I cleanse (31, v-2a[1]) καθαριῶ, ἐκαθάρισα, -, κεκαθάρισμαι, ἐκαθαρίσθην
	καθαρός, -ά, -όν	clean (27, a-1a[1])
	καθεύδω	I sleep (22, v-1b[3]) (ἐκάθευδον), -, -, -, -, -
27	κάθημαι	I sit (down), live (91, v-6b) (ἐκαθήμην), καθήσομαι, -, -, -, -
	καθίζω	I seat, sit (46, v-2a[1]) καθίσω, ἐκάθισα, κεκάθικα, -, -
	καθίστημι	I set, constitute (21, cv-6a) καταστήσω, κατέστησα, -, -, κατεστάθην
9	καθώς	as, even as (182, adverb)
4	καί	and, even, also, namely (9153, conjunction)
	καινός, -ή, -όν	new (42, a-1a[2a])
6	καιρός, -οῦ, ὁ	(appointed) time, season (85, n-2a)
	Καῖσαρ, -ος, ὁ	Caesar (29, n-3f[2a])
	Καισάρεια, -ας, ἡ	Caesarea (17, n-1a)
	καίω	I burn (12, v-2c) καύσω, ἔκαυσα, -, κέκαυμαι, ἐκαύθην
	κἀκεῖ	and there (10, adverb)
	κἀκεῖθεν	and from there, and then (10, adverb)
	κἀκεῖνος	and that one (22, a-1a[2b])
	κακία, -ας, ἡ	malice, evil (11, n-1a)
9	κακός, -ή, -όν	bad, evil (50, a-1a[2a])
	κακῶς	badly (16, adverb)
	κάλαμος, -ου, ὁ	reed (12, n-2a)
17	καλέω	I call, name, invite (148, v-1d[2b]) (ἐκάλουν), καλέσω, ἐκάλεσα, κέκληκα, κέκλημαι, ἐκλήθην
11	καλός, -ή, -όν	beautiful, good (100, a-1a[2a])
	καλῶς	well (37, adverb)
	κἄν	and if (17, particle)
	καπνός, -οῦ, ὁ	smoke (13, n-2a)
4	καρδία, -ας, ἡ	heart (156, n-1a)
19	καρπός, -οῦ, ὁ	fruit, crop, result (66, n-2a)

14	κατά	gen: down from, against (473, preposition) acc: according to, throughout, during
27	καταβαίνω	I go down, come down (81, cv-2d[7]) (κατέβαινον), καταβήσομαι, κατέβην, καταβέβηκα, -, -
	καταβολή, -ῆς, ἡ	foundation (11, n-1b)
	καταγγέλλω	I proclaim (18, cv-2d[1]) (κατήγγελλον), -, κατήγγειλα, -, -, -
	καταισχύνω	I put to shame (13, cv-1c[2]) (κατησχυνόμην), -, -, -, -, κατῃσχύνθην
	κατακαίω	I burn up (12, cv-2c) (κατέκαινον), κατακαύσω, κατέκαυσα, -, -, κατεκάην
	κατάκειμαι	I lie down, lie sick, recline (12, cv-6b) (κατεκείμην), -, -, -, -, -
	κατακρίνω	I condemn (18, cv-2d[6]) -, κατέκρινα, -, κατακέκριμαι, κατεκρίθην
	καταλαμβάνω	I overtake, apprehend (15, cv-3a[2b]) -, κατέλαβον, -, κατείλημμαι, κατελήμφθην
	καταλείπω	I leave (24, cv-1b[1]) καταλείψω, κατέλειψα or κατέλιπον, -, καταλέλειμαι, κατελείφθην
	καταλύω	I destroy, lodge (17, cv-1a[4]) καταλύσω, κατέλυσα, -, -, κατελύθην
	κατανοέω	I observe (14, cv-1d[2a]) (κατενόουν), -, κατενόησα, -, -, -
	καταντάω	I come to (13, cv-1d[1a]) καταντήσω, κατήντησα, κατήντηκα, -, -
	καταργέω	I abolish, bring to naught (27, cv-1d[2a]) καταργήσω, κατήργησα, κατήργηκα, κατήργημαι, κατηργήθην
	καταρτίζω	I mend, fit, perfect (13, cv-2a[1]) καταρτίσω, κατήρτισα, -, κατήρτισμαι, -
	κατασκευάζω	I prepare (11, cv-2a[1]) κατασκευάσω, κατεσκεύασα, -, κατεσκεύασμαι, κατεσκευάσθην
	κατεργάζομαι	I work out (22, cv-2a[1]) -, κατειργασάμην, -, -, κατειργάσθην
	κατέρχομαι	I come down, go down (16, cv-1b[2]) -, κατῆλθον, -, -, -
	κατεσθίω	I eat up, devour (15, cv-1b[3]) -, κατέφαγον, -, -, -

	κατέχω	I hold back, hold fast (18, cv-1b[2]) (κατεῖχον), -, κατέσχον, -, -, -
	κατηγορέω	I accuse (23, v-1d[2a]) (κατηγόρουν), κατηγορήσω, κατηγόρησα, -, -, -
	κατοικέω	I inhabit, dwell (44, cv-1d[2a]) -, κατῴκησα, -, -, -
	κάτω	down, below (11, adverb)
	καυχάομαι	I boast (37, v-1d[1a]) καυχήσομαι, ἐκαυχησάμην, -, κεκαύχημαι, -
	καύχημα, -ατος, τό	boasting, ground of boasting (11, n-3c[4])
	καύχησις, -εως, ἡ	boasting (11, n-3e[5b])
	Καφαρναούμ, ἡ	Capernaum (16, n-3g[2])
	κεῖμαι	I lie, am laid (24, v-6b) (ἐκειόμην), -, -, -, -, -
	κελεύω	I order (26, v-1a[6]) (ἐκέλευον), -, ἐκέλευσα, -, -, -
	κενός, -ή, -όν	empty, vain (18, a-1a[2a])
	κέρας, -ατος, τό	horn (11, n-3c[6a])
	κερδαίνω	I gain (17, v-2d[7]) κερδήσω, ἐκέρδησα, -, -, κερδηθήσομαι
14	κεφαλή, -ῆς, ἡ	head (75, n-1b)
23	κηρύσσω	I proclaim, preach (61, v-2b) (ἐκήρυσσον), κηρύξω, ἐκήρυξα, -, -, ἐκηρύχθην
	κλάδος, -ου, ὁ	branch (11, n-2a)
	κλαίω	I weep (40, v-2c) (ἔκλαιον), κλαύσω, ἔκλαυσα, -, -, -
	κλάω	I break (14, v-1d[1b]) -, ἔκλασα, -, -, -
	κλείω	I shut (16, v-1a[3]) κλείσω, ἔκλεισα, -, κέκλεισμαι, ἐκλείσθην
	κλέπτης, -ου, ὁ	thief (16, n-1f)
	κλέπτω	I steal (13, v-4) κλέψω, ἔκλεψα, -, -, -
	κληρονομέω	I inherit (18, v-1d[2a]) κληρονομήσω, ἐκληρονόμησα, κεκληρονόμηκα, -, -
	κληρονομία, -ας, ἡ	inheritance (14, n-1a)
	κληρονόμος, -ου, ὁ	heir (15, n-2a)
	κλῆρος, -ου, ὁ	lot, a portion (11, n-2a)
	κλῆσις, -εως, ἡ	call, invitation, summons (11, n-3e[5b])
	κλητός, -ή, -όν	called (10, a-1a[2a])

	κοιλία, -ας, ἡ	the belly, womb (22, n-1a)
	κοιμάομαι	I sleep, fall asleep (18, v-1d[1a]) -, -, -, κεκοίμημαι, ἐκοιμήθην
	κοινός, -ή, -όν	common, unclean (14, a-1a[2a])
	κοινόω	I make common, defile (14, v-1d[3]) -, ἐκοίνωσα, κεκοίνωκα, κεκοίνωμαι, -
	κοινωνία, -ας, ἡ	fellowship, contribution (19, n-1a)
	κοινωνός, -οῦ, ὁ	partner, sharer (10, n-2a)
	κολλάομαι	I join, cleave to (12, v-1d[1a]) -, -, -, -, ἐκολλήθην
	κομίζω	I receive (10, v-2a[1]) κομίσομαι, ἐκομισάμην, -, -, -
	κοπιάω	I toil (23, v-1d[1b]) -, ἐκοπίασα, κεκοπίακα, -, -
	κόπος, -ου, ὁ	labor, trouble (18, n-2a)
	κοσμέω	I adorn (10, v-1d[2a]) (ἐκόσμουν), -, ἐκόσμησα, -, κεκόσμημαι, -
4	κόσμος, ου, ὁ	world, universe, humankind (186, n-2a)
	κράβαττος, -ου, ὁ	mattress, pallet, bed (of a poor person) (11, n-2a)
28	κράζω	I cry out, call out (56, v-2a[2]) (ἔκραζον), κράξω, ἔκραξα, κέκραγα, -, -
	κρατέω	I grasp (47, v-1d[2a]) (ἐκράτουν), κρατήσω, ἐκράτησα, κεκράτηκα, κεκράτημαι, -
	κράτος, -ους, τό	power, dominion (12, n-3d[2b])
	κρείσσων,-ονος	better (19, a-4b[1]) also spelled κρείττων
	κρίμα, -ατος, τό	judgment (28, n-3c[4])
20	κρίνω	I judge, decide, prefer (114, v-2d[6]) (ἐκρινόμην), κρινῶ, ἔκρινα, κέκρικα, κέκριμαι, ἐκρίθην
	κρίσις, -εως, ἡ	judgment (47, n-3e[5b])
	κριτής, -οῦ, ὁ	judge (19, n-1f)
	κρυπτός, -ή, -όν	hidden (17, a-1a[2a])
	κρύπτω	I conceal (19, v-4) -, ἔκρυψα, -, κέκρυμμαι, ἐκρύβην
	κτίζω	I create (15, v-2a[1]) -, ἔκτισα, -, ἔκτισμαι, ἐκτίσθην
	κτίσις, -εως, ἡ	creation, creature (19, n-3e[5b])
7	κύριος -ου,-ὁ	Lord, lord, master, sir (717, n-2a)

	κωλύω	I forbid, hinder (23, v-1a[4]) (ἐκώλυον), -, ἐκώλυσα, -, -, ἐκωλύθην
	κώμη, -ης, ἡ	village (27, n-1b)
	κωφός, -ή, -όν	deaf, dumb (14, a-1a[2a])

λάμβδα

	Λάζαρος, -ου, ὁ	Lazarus (15, n-2a)
17	λαλέω	I speak, say (296, v-1d[2a]) (ἐλάλουν), λαλήσω, ἐλάλησα, λελάληκα, λελάλημαι, ἐλαλήθην
22	λαμβάνω	I take, receive (260, v-3a[2b]) (ἐλάμβανον), λήμψομαι, ἔλαβον, εἴληφα, -, ἐλήμφθην
20	λαός, -οῦ, ὁ	people, crowd (142, n-2a)
	λατρεύω	I serve, worship (21, v-1a[6]) λατρεύσω, ἐλάτρευσα, -, -, -
8	λέγω	I say, speak (2354, v-1b[2]) (ἔλεγον), ἐρῶ, εἶπον, εἴρηκα, εἴρημαι, ἐρρέθην
	λευκός, -ή, -όν	white (25, a-1a[2a])
	λῃστής, -οῦ, ὁ	robber (15, n-1f)
	λίαν	greatly (12, adverb)
31	λίθος, -ου, ὁ	stone (59, n-2a)
	λίμνη, -ης, ἡ	lake (11, n-1b)
	λιμός, -οῦ, ὁ	hunger, famine (12, n-2a)
	λογίζομαι	I account, reckon (41, v-2a[1]) (ἐλογιζόμην), -, ἐλογισάμην -, -, ἐλογίσθην
4	λόγος, -ου, ὁ	word, Word, statement, message (330, n-2a)
34	λοιπός, -ή, -όν	adj: remaining (55, a-1a[2a]) noun: (the) rest adverb: for the rest, henceforth
	λυπέω	I grieve (26, v-1d[2a]) -, ἐλύπησα, λελύπηκα, -, ἐλυπήθην
	λύπη, -ης, ἡ	pain, grief (16, n-1b)
	λυχνία, -ας, ἡ	lampstand (12, n-1a)
	λύχνος, -ου, ὁ	lamp (14, n-2a)
16	λύω	I loose (42, v-1a[4]) (ἔλυον), λύσω, ἔλυσα, -, λέλυμαι, ἐλύθην

μῦ

	Μαγδαληνη, -ῆς, ἡ	Magdalene (12, n-1b)
12	μαθητής, -οῦ, ὁ	disciple (261, n-1f)
13	μακάριος, -ια, -ιον	blessed, happy (50, a-1a[1])
	Μακεδονία, -ας, ἡ	Macedonia (22, n-1a)
	μακράν	far away (10, adverb)
	μακρόθεν	from afar, afar (14, adverb)
	μακροθυμέω	I am patient (10, v-1d[2a]) -, ἐμακροθύμησα, -, -, -
	μακροθυμία, -ας, ἡ	long-suffering, patience, forbearance (14, n-1a)
	μάλιστα	especially (12, adverb)
25	μᾶλλον	more, rather (81, adverb)
	μανθάνω	I learn (25, v-3a[2b]) -, ἔμαθον, μεμάθηκα, -, -
	Μάρθα, -ας, ἡ	Martha (13, n-1a)
	Μαρία, -ας, ἡ	Mary (27, n-1a)
	Μαριάμ, ἡ	Miriam (27, n-3g[2])
25	μαρτυρέω	I bear witness, testify (76, v-1d[2a]) (ἐμαρτύρουν), μαρτυρήσω, ἐμαρτύρησα, μεμαρτύρηκα, μεμαρτύρημαι, ἐμαρτυρήθην
	μαρτυρία, -ας, ἡ	testimony, evidence (37, n-1a)
	μαρτύριον, -ίου, τό	testimony, witness, proof (19, n-2c)
	μάρτυς, -υρος, ὁ	witness (35, n-3f[2a])
	μάχαιρα, -ης, ἡ	sword (29, n-1c)
13	μέγας, μεγάλη, μέγα	large, great (243, a-1a[2a])
19	μείζων, ον	greater (48, a-4b[1])
	μέλει	it is a care (10, v-1d[2c]) (ἔμελεν), -, -, -, -, -
32	μέλλω	I am about to (109, v-1d[2c]) (ἔμελλον or ἤμελλον), μελλήσω, -, -, -, -
	μέλος, -ους, τό	member (34, n-3d[2b])
12	μέν	on the one hand, indeed (179, particle)
20	μένω	I remain, live (118, v-1c[2]) (ἔμενον), μενῶ, ἔμεινα, μεμένηκα, -, -
	μερίζω	I divide (14, v-2a[1]) -, ἐμέρισα, -, μεμέρισμαι, ἐμερίσθην
	μεριμνάω	I am anxious, distracted (19, v-1d[1a]) μεριμνήσω, ἐμερίμνησα, -, -, -

	μέρος, -ους, τό	part (42, n-3d[2b])
35	μέσος, -η, -ον	middle, in the midst (58, a-1a[2a])
8	μετά	gen: with (469, preposition) acc: after
	μεταβαίνω	I depart (12, cv-2d[6]) μεταβήσομαι, μετέβην, μεταβέβηκα, -, -
	μετανοέω	I repent (34, cv-1d[2a]) -, μετενόησα, -, -, -
	μετάνοια, -ας, ἡ	repentance (22, n-1a)
	μέτρον, -ου, τό	measure (14, n-2c)
	μέχρι or μέχρις	conj: until (17) gen: as far as
7	μή	not, lest (1042, particle)
30	μηδέ	but not, nor, not even (56, particle)
12	μηδείς, μηδεμία, μηδέν	no one/thing (90, a-4b[2])
	μηκέτι	no longer (22, adverb)
	μήν, μηνός, ὁ	month (18, particle)
	μήποτε	lest perchance (25, particle)
	μήτε	neither, nor (34, conjunction)
11	μήτηρ, μητρός, ἡ	mother (83, n-3f[2c])
	μήτι	interrogative particle in questions (18, particle) expecting a negative answer
	μικρός, -ά, -όν	small, little (46, a-1a[1])
	μιμνήσκομαι	I remember (23, v-5a) -, -, -, μέμνημαι, ἐμνήσθην
	μισέω	I hate (40, v-1d[2a]) (ἐμίσουν), μισήσω, ἐμίσησα, μεμίσηκα, μεμίσημαι, -
	μισθός, -οῦ, ὁ	wages, reward (29, n-2a)
	μνῆμα, -ατος, τό	grave, tomb (10, n-3c[4])
	μνημεῖον, -ου, τό	tomb, monument (40, n-2c)
	μνημονεύω	I remember (21, v-1a[6]) (ἐμνημόνευον), -, ἐμνημόνευσα, -, -, -
	μοιχεύω	I commit adultery (15, v-1a[6]) μοιχεύσω, ἐμοίχευσα, -, -, ἐμοιχεύθην
12	μόνος, -η, -ον	alone, only (114, a-1a[2a])
	μύρον, -ου, τό	ointment (14, n-2c)
	μυστήριον, -ου, τό	mystery (28, n-2c)
	μωρός, -ά, -όν	foolish (12, a-1a[1])
34	Μωϋσῆς, -έως, ὁ	Moses (80, n-3g[1])

νῦ

	Ναζωραῖος, -ου, ὁ	Nazarene (13, n-2a)
	ναί	yes, truly, yea (33, particle)
	ναός, -οῦ, ὁ	temple (45, n-2a)
	νεανίσκος, -ου, ὁ	youth (11, n-2a)
9	νεκρός, -ά, -όν	adj: dead (128, a-1a[1])
		noun:dead body, corpse
	νέος, -α, -ον	new, young (24, a-1a[1])
	νεφέλη, -ης, ἡ	cloud (25, n-1b)
	νήπιος, -ίου, ὁ	infant, child (15, a-1a[1])
	νηστεύω	I fast (20, v-1a[6])
		νηστεύσω, ἐνήστευσα, -, -, -
	νικάω	I conquer (28, v-1d[1a])
		νικήσω, ἐνίκησα, νενίκηκα, -, ἐνικήθην
	νίπτω	I wash (17, v-4)
		-, ἔνιψα, -, -, -
	νοέω	I understand (14, v-1d[2a])
		νοήσω, ἐνόησα, νενόηκα, -, -
	νομίζω	I suppose (15, v-2a[1])
		(ἐνόμιζον), -, ἐνόμισα, -, -, -
	νομικός, -ή, -όν	adj: pertaining to the law (10, a-1a[2a])
		noun: lawyer, one skilled in the Mosaic law
16	νόμος, -ου, ὁ	law, principle (194, n-2a)
	νόσος, -ου, ἡ	disease (11, n-2b)
	νοῦς, νοός, ὁ	mind (24, n-3e[4])
	νυμφίος, -ου, ὁ	bridegroom (16, n-2a)
6	νῦν	adverb: now (147)
		noun: (the) present
	νυνί	now (20, adverb)
18	νύξ, νυκτός, ἡ	night (61, n-3c[1])

ξῖ

ξενίζω	I entertain (a stranger) (10, v-2a[1])
	I startle, bewilder
	-, ἐξένισα, -, -, ἐξενίσθην
ξένος, -η, -ον	strange (14, a-1a[2a])
	(as a noun) a stranger, host
ξηραίνω	I dry up (15, v-2d[4])
	-, ἐξήρανα, -, ἐξήραμμαι, ἐξηράνθην

	ξύλον, -ου, τό	wood, tree (20, n-2c)

ὃ μικρόν

6	ὁ, ἡ, τό	the (19870, a-1a[2b])
	ὅδε, ἥδε, τόδε	this (here) (10, a-1a[2b])
14	ὁδός, -οῦ, ἡ	way, road, journey, conduct (101, n-2b)
	ὀδούς, -όντος, ὁ	tooth (12, n-3c[5a])
	ὅθεν	whence, wherefore (15, adverb)
17	οἶδα	I know, understand (318, v-1b[3]) εἰδήσω, ᾔδειν, -, -, -
8	οἰκία, -ας, ἡ	house, home (93, n-1a)
	οἰκοδεσπότης, -ου, ὁ	householder (12, n-1f)
	οἰκοδομέω	I build, edify (40, v-1d[2a]) (ᾠκοδόμουν), οἰκοδομήσω, ᾠκοδόμησα, -, -, οἰκοδομήθην
	οἰκοδομή, -ῆς, ἡ	building, edification (18, n-1b)
	οἰκονόμος, -ου, ὁ	steward (10, n-2a)
8	οἶκος, -ου, ὁ	house, home (114, n-2a)
	οἰκουμένη, -ης, ἡ	the (inhabited) world (15, n-1b)
	οἶνος, -ου, ὁ	wine (34, n-2a)
	οἷος, -α, -ον	such as (15, a-1a[1])
	ὀλίγος, -η, -ον	little, few (41, a-1a[2a])
19	ὅλος, -η, -ον	adjective: whole, complete (109, a-1a[2a]) adverb: entirely
	ὀμνύω or ὄμνυμι	I swear, take an oath (26, v-3c[2]) -, ὤμοσα, -, -, -
	ὁμοθυμαδόν	with one accord (11, adverb)
	ὅμοιος, -οία, -οιον	like (45, a-1a[1])
	ὁμοιόω	I make like, liken (15, v-1d[3]) ὁμοιώσω, ὡμοίωσα, -, -, ὡμοιώθην
	ὁμοίως	likewise (30, adverb)
	ὁμολογέω	I confess, profess (26, v-1d[2a]) (ὡμολόγουν), ὁμολογήσω, ὡμολόγησα, -, -, -
	ὀνειδίζω	I reproach (11, v-2a[1]) (ὠνείδιζον), -, ὠνείδισα, -, -, -
10	ὄνομα, -ματος, τό	name, reputation (231, n-3c[4])
	ὀνομάζω	I name (10, v-2a[1]) -, ὠνόμασα, -, -, ὠνομάσθην
	ὄντως	really (10, adverb)

	ὀπίσω	gen: behind, after (35, preposition, adverb)
16	ὅπου	where (82, particle)
12	ὅπως	how, that, in order that (53, conjunction, adverb)
	ὅραμα, -ατος, τό	vision (12, n-3c[4])
20	ὁράω	I see, notice, experience (454, v-1d[1a])
		ὄψομαι, εἶδον, ἑώρακα, -, ὤφθην
	ὀργή, -ῆς, ἡ	anger (36, n-1b)
	ὅρια, -ων, τά	boundaries (12, n-2c)
		(plural of ὅριον)
	ὅρκος, -ου, ὁ	oath (10, n-2a)
24	ὄρος, ὄρους, τό	mountain, hill (63, n-3d[2b])
14	ὅς, ἥ, ὅ	who, whom (1365, a-1a[2b])
12	ὅσος, -η, -ον	as great as, as many as (110, a-1a[2a])
18	ὅστις, ἥτις, ὅτι	whoever, whichever, whatever (153, a-1a[2b])
17	ὅταν	whenever (123, particle)
14	ὅτε	when (103, particle)
6	ὅτι	that, since, because (1296, conjunction)
27	οὗ	where (54, adverb)
6	οὐ, οὐκ, οὐχ	not (1606, adverb)
	οὐαί	woe! alas! (47, interjection)
11	οὐδέ	and not, not even, neither, nor (143, conjunction)
11	οὐδείς, οὐδεμία, οὐδέν	no one, none, nothing (234, a-2a)
	οὐδέποτε	never (16, adverb)
	οὐκέτι	no longer (47, adverb)
12	οὖν	therefore, then, accordingly (499, particle)
	οὔπω	not yet (26, adverb)
7	οὐρανός, -οῦ, ὁ	heaven, sky (273, n-2a)
	οὖς, ὠτός, τό	ear (37, n-3c[6c])
22	οὔτε	and not, neither, nor (87, adverb)
7	οὗτος, αὕτη, τοῦτο	singular: this; he, she, it (1388, a-1a[2b])
		plural: these; they
14	οὕτως	thus, so, in this manner (208, adverb)
28	οὐχί	not (54, adverb)
	ὀφείλω	I owe, ought (35, v-2d[1])
		(ὤφειλον), -, -, -, -, -
12	ὀφθαλμός, -οῦ, ὁ	eye, sight (100, n-2a)
	ὄφις, -εως, ὁ	serpent (14, n-3e[5b])
8	ὄχλος, -ου, ὁ	crowd, multitude (175, n-2a)

| 30 | ὀψία, -ας, ἡ | evening (175, a-1a[1]) |

πῖ

	πάθημα, -ατος, τό	suffering (16, n-3c[4])
	παιδεύω	I teach, chastise (13, v-1a[6]) (ἐπαίδευον), -, ἐπαίδευσα, -, πεπαίδευμαι, ἐπαιδεύθην
28	παιδίον, -ου, τό	child, infant (52, n-2c)
	παιδίσκη, -ης, ἡ	maid servant (13, n-1b)
	παῖς, παιδός, ὁ or ἡ	boy, girl, child, servant (24, n-3c[2])
	παλαιός, -ά, -όν	old (19, a-1a[1])
12	πάλιν	again (141, adverb)
	παντοκράτωρ, -ορος, ὁ	ruler of all, the Almighty (10, n-3f[2b])
	πάντοτε	always (41, adverb)
8	παρά	gen: from (194, preposition) dat: beside, in the presence of acc: alongside of
8	παραβολή, -ῆς, ἡ	parable (50, n-1b)
	παραγγέλλω	I command, charge (32, cv-2d[1]) (παρήγγελλον), -, παρήγγειλα, -, παρήγγελμαι, -
	παραγίνομαι	I come, arrive (37, cv-1c[2]) (παρεγινόμην), -, παρεγενόμην, -, -, -
	παράγω	I pass by (10, cv-1b[2])
34	παραδίδωμι	I entrust, hand over, betray (119, cv-6a) (παρεδίδουν), παραδώσω, παρέδωκα, παραδέδωκα, παραδέδομαι, παρεδόθην
	παράδοσις, -εως, ἡ	tradition (13, n-3e[5b])
	παραιτέομαι	I make excuse, refuse (12, cv-1d[2a]) (παρῃτούμην), -, παρῃτησάμην, -, παρῄτημαι, -
27	παρακαλέω	I call, urge, exhort, comfort (109, cv-1d[2b]) (παρεκάλουν), -, παρεκάλεσα, -, παρακέκλημαι, παρεκλήθην
	παράκλησις, -εως, ἡ	exhortation, consolation (29, n-3e[5b])
	παραλαμβάνω	I receive (49, cv-3a[2b]) παραλήμψομαι, παρέλαβον, -, -, παραλημφθήσομαι
	παραλυτικός, -οῦ, ὁ	paralytic (10, n-2a)
	παράπτωμα, -ατος, τό	trespass (20, n-3c[4])
	παρατίθημι	I set before (19, cv-6a) (middle) I entrust παραθήσω, παρέθηκα, -, -, -

	παραχρῆμα	immediately (18, adverb)
	πάρειμι	I am present, have arrived (24, cv-6b) (παρήμην), παρέσομαι, -, -, -, -
	παρεμβολή, -ῆς, ἡ	camp, army, fortress (10, n-1b)
	παρέρχομαι	I pass by, pass away, arrive (30, cv-1b[2]) παρελεύσομαι, παρῆλθον, παρελήλυθα, -, -
	παρέχω	I offer, afford (16, cv-1b[2]) (παρεῖχον), -, παρέσχον, -, -, -
	παρθένος, -ου, ἡ	virgin (15, n-2a)
	παρίστημι	I am present, stand by (41, cv-6a) παραστήσω, παρέστησα, παρέστηκα, -, παρεστάθην
	παρουσία, -ας, ἡ	presence, coming (24, n-1a)
	παρρησία, -ας, ἡ	boldness, confidence (31, n-1a)
10	πᾶς, πᾶσα, πᾶν	singular: each, every (1244, a-2a) plural: all
	πάσχα, τό	(indeclinable) a passover (29, n-3g[2])
	πάσχω	I suffer (42, v-5a) -, ἔπαθον, πέπονθα, -, -
	πατάσσω	I smite (10, v-2b) πατάξω, ἐπάταξα, -, -, -
10	πατήρ, πατρός, ὁ	father (413, n-3f[2c])
4	Παῦλος, -ου, ὁ	Paul (158, n-2a)
	παύομαι	I cease (15, v-1a[5]) (ἐπαυόμην), παύσομαι, ἐπαυσάμην, -, πέπαυμαι, ἐπαύθην
27	πείθω	I persuade (52, v-1b[3]) (ἔπειθον), πείσω, ἔπεισα, πέποιθα, πέπεισμαι, ἐπείσθην
	πεινάω	I hunger (23, v-1d[1b]) πεινάσω, ἐπείνασα, -, -, -
	πειράζω	I test, tempt, attempt (38, v-2a[1]) (ἐπείραζον), -, ἐπείρασα, -, πεπείρασμαι, ἐπειράσθην
	πειρασμός, -οῦ, ὁ	temptation (21, n-2a)
29	πέμπω	I send (79, v-1b[1]) πέμψω, ἔπεμψα, -, -, ἐπέμφθην
	πενθέω	I mourn (10, v-1d[2a]) πενθήσω, ἐπένθησα, -, -, -
	πέντε	five (36, n-3g[2])
	πέραν	gen: beyond (23, adverb)

10	περί	gen: concerning, about (333, preposition) acc: around
	περιβάλλω	I put around, clothe (23, cv-2d[1]) -, περιέβαλον, -, περιβέβλημαι, -
21	περιπατέω	I walk (around), live (95, cv-1d[2a]) (περιεπάτουν), περιπατήσω, περιεπάτησα, -, -, -
	περισσεύω	I abound, am rich (39, v-1a[6]) (ἐπερίσσευον), -, ἐπερίσσευσα, -, -, περισσευθήσομαι
	περισσότερος, -τέρα, -ον	greater, more (17, a-1a[1])
	περισσοτέρως	more abundantly (12, adverb)
	περιστερά, -ᾶς, ἡ	dove (10, n-1a)
	περιτέμνω	I circumcise (17, cv-3a[1]) -, περιέτεμον, -, περιτέτμημαι, περιετμήθην
	περιτομή, -ῆς, ἡ	circumcision (36, n-1b)
	πετεινόν, -οῦ, τό	bird (14, n-2c)
	πέτρα, -ας, ἡ	rock (15, n-1a)
4	Πέτρος, -ου, ὁ	Peter (156, n-2a)
	πηγή, -ῆς, ἡ	spring, fountain (11, n-1b)
	πιάζω	I take (12, v-2a[1]) -, ἐπίασα, -, -, ἐπιάσθην
4	Πιλᾶτος, -ου, ὁ	Pilate (55, n-2a)
	πίμπλημι	I fill (24, v-6a) -, ἔπλησα, -, πέπλησμαι, ἐπλήσθην
23	πίνω	I drink (73, v-3a[1]) (ἔπινον), πίομαι, ἔπιον, πέπωκα, -, ἐπόθην
34	πίπτω	I fall (90, v-1b[3]) (ἔπιπτον), πεσοῦμαι, ἔπεσον or ἔπεσα, πέπτωκα, -, -
16	πιστεύω	I believe, have faith (in), trust (241, v-1a[6]) (ἐπίστευον), πιστεύσω, ἐπίστευσα, πεπίστευκα, πεπίστευμαι, ἐπιστεύθην
10	πίστις, πίστεως, ἡ	faith, belief (243, n-3e[5b])
9	πιστός, -ή, -όν	faithful, believing (67, a-1a[2a])
	πλανάω	I lead astray (39, v-1d[1a]) πλανήσω, ἐπλάνησα, -, πεπλάνημαι, ἐπλανήθην
	πλάνη, -ης, ἡ	wandering, an error (10, n-1b)
	πλατεῖα, -ας, ἡ	street (place) (10, n-1a)
17	πλείων, πλεῖον	larger, more (55, a-4b[1])
	πλεονεξία, -ας, ἡ	covetousness (10, n-1a)
	πληγή, -ῆς, ἡ	plague, blow, wound (22, n-1b)

	πλῆθος, -ους, τό	multitude (31, n-3d[2b])
	πληθύνω	I multiply (12, v-1c[2]) (ἐπληθυνόμην), πληθυνῶ, ἐπλήθυνα, -, -, ἐπληθύνθην
	πλήν	adverb: however, but, only (31, adverb) gen: except
	πλήρης, -ες	full (16, a-4a)
17	πληρόω	I fill, complete, fulfill (86, v-1d[3]) (ἐπλήρουν), πληρώσω, ἐπλήρωσα, πεπλήρωκα, πεπλήρωμαι, ἐπληρώθην
	πλήρωμα, -ατος, τό	fullness (17, n-3c[4])
	πλησίον	adverb: near (17) noun: neighbor
14	πλοῖον, -ου, τό	ship, boat (68, n-2c)
	πλούσιος, -α, -ον	rich (28, a-1a[1])
	πλουτέω	I am rich (12, v-1d[2a]) -, ἐπλούτησα, πεπλούτηκα, -, -
	πλοῦτος, -ου, ὁ	wealth (22, n-2a)
4	πνεῦμα, -ατος, τό	spirit, Spirit, wind, breath, inner life (379, n-3c[4])
	πνευματικός, -ή, -όν	spiritual (26, a-1a[2a])
	πόθεν	from where? (29, adverb)
17	ποιέω	I do, make (568, v-1d[2a]) (ἐποίουν), ποιήσω, ἐποίησα, πεποίηκα, πεποίημαι, -
	ποικίλος, -η, -ον	varied, manifold (10, a-1a[2a])
	ποιμαίνω	I shepherd, rule (11, v-2d[4]) ποιμανῶ, ἐποίμανα, -, -, -
	ποιμήν, -ένος, ὁ	shepherd (18, n-3f[1b])
	ποῖος, -α, -ον	what sort of? what? (33, a-1a[1])
	πόλεμος, -ου, ὁ	war (18, n-2a)
13	πόλις, -εως, ἡ	city (162, n-3e[5b])
	πολλάκις	often (18, adverb)
13	πολύς, πολλή, πολύ	singular: much (416, a-1a[2a]) plural: many adverb: often
9	πονηρός, -ά, -όν	evil, bad (78, a-1a[1])
18	πορεύομαι	I go, proceed, live (154, v-1a[6]) (ἐπορευόμην), πορεύσομαι, -, -, πεπόρευμαι, ἐπορεύθην
	πορνεία, -ας, ἡ	fornication (25, n-1a)

	πόρνη, -ης, ἡ	prostitute (12, n-1b)
	πόρνος, -ου, ὁ	fornicator (10, n-2a)
	πόσος, -η, -ον	how great? how much? (27, a-1a[2a])
	ποταμός, -οῦ, ὁ	river (17, n-2a)
	ποτέ	at some time, once, ever (19, particle)
	πότε	when? (29, adverb)
	ποτήριον, -ου, τό	cup (31, n-2c)
	ποτίζω	I give drink to (15, v-2a[1]) (ἐπότιζον), -, ἐπότισα, πεπότικα, -, ἐποτίσθην
	ποῦ	where? whither? (48, adverb)
12	πούς, ποδός, ὁ	foot (93, n-3c[2])
	πρᾶγμα, -ατος, τό	deed, matter, thing (11, n-3c[4])
	πράσσω	I do, perform (39, v-2b) πράξω, ἔπραξα, πέπραχα, πέπραγμαι, -
	πραΰτης, -ῆτος, ἡ	gentleness, humility, courtesy (11, n-3c[1])
30	πρεσβύτερος, -α, -ον	elder (66, a-1a[1])
	πρίν	before (13, conjunction or preposition)
	πρό	gen: before (47, preposition)
	προάγω	I lead forth, go before (20, cv-1b[2]) (προῆγον), προάξω, προήγαγον, -, -, -
	πρόβατον, -ου, τό	sheep (39, n-2c)
	προέρχομαι	I go in front, precede (10, cv-1b[2]) (προηρχόμην), προελεύσομαι, προῆλθον, -, -, -
	πρόθεσις, -εως, ἡ	setting forth, a purpose (12, n-3e[5b])
8	πρός	acc: to, towards, with (700, preposition)
	προσδέχομαι	I receive, wait for (14, cv-1b[2]) (προσεδεχόμην), -, προσεδεξάμην, -, -, -
	προσδοκάω	I wait for (16, cv-1d[1a]) (προσεδόκων), -, -, -, -, -
22	προσέρχομαι	I come/go to (86, cv-1b[2]) (προσηρχόμην), -, προσῆλθον, προσελήλυθα, -, -
	προσευχή, -ῆς, ἡ	prayer (37, n-1b)
22	προσεύχομαι	I pray (85, cv-1b[2]) (προσηυχόμην), προσεύξομαι, προσηυξάμην, -, -, -
	προσέχω	I attend to, give heed to (24, cv-1b[2]) (προσεῖχον), -, -, προσέσχηκα, -, -
	προσκαλέομαι	I summon (29, cv-1d[2a]) -, προσεκαλεσάμην, -, προσκέκλημαι, -
	προσκαρτερέω	I continue in/with (10, cv-1d[2a]) προσκαρτερήσω, -, -, -, -

19	προσκυνέω	I worship (60, cv-3b])
		(προσεκύνουν), προσκυνήσω, προσεκύνησα, -, -, -
	προσλαμβάνω	I receive (12, cv-3a[2b])
		-, προσελαβόμην, -, -, -
	προστίθημι	I add, add to (18, cv-6a)
		(προσετίθουν), -, προσέθηκα, -, -, προσετέθην
	προσφέρω	I bring to, offer (47, cv-1c[1])
		(προσέφερον), -, προσήνεγκον or προσήνεγκα, προσενήνοχα, -, προσηνέχθην
16	πρόσωπον, -ου, τό	face, appearance (76, n-2c)
	πρότερος, -α, -ον	former (11, a-1a[1])
		(as an adverb) before
	προφητεία, -ας, ἡ	prophecy (19, n-1a)
	προφητεύω	I prophesy (28, v-1a[6])
		(ἐπροφήτευον), προφητεύσω, ἐπροφήτευσα or προεφήτευσα, -, -, -
4	προφήτης, -ου, ὁ	prophet (144, n-1f)
	πρωΐ	in the morning, early (12, adverb)
9	πρῶτος, -η, -ον	first, earlier (155, a-1a[2a])
	πτωχός, -ή, -όν	poor (34, a-1a[2a])
		(as a noun) a poor person
	πύλη, -ης, ἡ	gate, porch (10, n-1b)
	πυλών, -ῶνος, ὁ	gateway, vestibule (18, n-3f[1a])
	πυνθάνομαι	I inquire (12, v-3a[2b])
		(ἐπυνθανόμην), -, ἐπυθόμην, -, -, -
22	πῦρ, πυρός, τό	fire (71, n-3f[2a])
	πωλέω	I sell (22, v-1d[2a])
		(ἐπώλουν), -, ἐπώλησα, -, -, -
	πῶλος, -ου, ὁ	colt (12, n-2a)
13	πῶς	how? (103, particle)
	πώς	at all, somehow, in any way (15, particle)

ῥῶ

	ῥαββί, ὁ	(undeclinable) master (15, n-3g[2])
	ῥάβδος, -ου, ἡ	staff, rod (12, n-2b)
14	ῥῆμα, -ατος, τό	word, saying (68, n-3c[4])
	ῥίζα, -ης, ἡ	root (17, n-1c)
	ῥύομαι	I rescue, deliver (17, v-1a[4])
		ῥύσομαι, ἐρρυσάμην, -, -, ἐρρύσθην

Ῥωμαῖος, -α, -ον   Roman (12, a-1a[1])

σίγμα

4   σάββατον, -ου, τό   Sabbath, week (68, n-2c)

Σαδδουκαῖος, -ου, ὁ   Sadducee (14, n-2a)

σαλεύω   I shake (15, v-1a[6])
                       -, ἐσάλευσα, -, σεσάλευμαι, ἐσαλεύθην

σάλπιγξ, -ιγγος, ἡ   trumpet (11, n-3b[2])

σαλπίζω   I sound a trumpet (12, v-2a[1])
                       σαλπίσω, ἐσάλπισα, -, -, -

Σαμάρεια, -ας, ἡ   Samaria (11, n-1a)

10   σάρξ, σαρκός, ἡ   flesh, body (147, n-3b[1])

σατανᾶς, -ᾶ, ὁ   satan (36, n-1e)

Σαῦλος, -ου, ὁ   Saul (15, n-2a)

σεαυτοῦ, -ῆς   of thyself (43, a-1a[2b])

σέβομαι   I reverence, worship (10, v-1b[1])

σεισμός, -οῦ, ὁ   earthquake (14, n-2a)

13   σημεῖον, -ου, τό   sign, miracle (77, n-2c)

σήμερον   today (41, adverb)

σιγάω   I am silent, become silent (10, v-1d[1a])
                       -, ἐσίγησα, -, σεσίγημαι, -

Σίλας, -ᾶ, ὁ   Silas (13, n-1e)

4   Σίμων, -ωνος, ὁ   Simon (75, n-3f[1a])

σῖτος, -ου, ὁ   wheat (14, n-2a)

σιωπάω   I am silent (10, v-1d[1a])
                       (ἐσιώπων), σιωπήσω, ἐσιώπησα, -, -, -

σκανδαλίζω   I cause to stumble (29, v-2a[1])
                       (ἐσκανδαλιζόμην), -, ἐσκανδάλισα, -, -,
                       ἐσκανδαλίσθην

σκάνδαλον, -ου, τό   cause of stumbling (15, n-2c)

σκεῦος, -ους, τό   vessel (23, n-3d[2b])
                       (plural) goods

σκηνή, -ῆς, ἡ   tent, tabernacle (20, n-1b)

σκοτία, -ας, ἡ   darkness (16, n-1a)

σκότος, -ους, τό   darkness (31, n-3d[2b])

Σολομῶν, -ῶντος   Solomon (12, n-3c[5b])

σός, σή, σόν   thy, thine (27, a-1a[2a])

20   σοφία, -ας, ἡ   wisdom (51, n-1a)

	σοφός, -ή, -όν	wise (20, a-1a[2a])
28	σπείρω	I sow (52, v-2d[3]) -, ἔσπειρα, -, ἔσπαρμαι, -
	σπέρμα, -ατος, τό	seed (43, n-3c[4])
	σπλάγχνα, -ων, τά	bowels, heart, tender mercies, compassion (11, n-2c)
	σπλαγχνίζομαι	I have compassion (12, v-2a[1]) -, -, -, -, ἐσπλαγχνίσθην
	σπουδάζω	I hasten, am eager (11, v-2a[1]) σπουδάσω, ἐσπούδασα, -, -, -
	σπουδή, -ῆς, ἡ	haste, diligence (12, n-1b)
	σταυρός, -οῦ, ὁ	cross (27, n-2a)
	σταυρόω	I crucify (46, v-1d[3]) σταυρώσω, ἐσταύρωσα, -, ἐσταύρωμαι, ἐσταυρώθην
	στέφανος, -ου, ὁ	crown (18, n-1e)
	στήκω	I stand, stand fast (10, v-1b[2]) (ἔστηκεν), -, -, -, -, -, -
	στηρίζω	I establish (14, v-2a[2]) στηρίξω, ἐστήριξα or ἐστήρισα, -, ἐστήριγμαι, ἐστηρίχθην
20	στόμα, -ατος, τό	mouth (78, n-3c[4])
	στρατηγός, -οῦ, ὁ	commander (10, n-2a)
	στρατιώτης, -ου, ὁ	soldier (26, n-1f)
	στρέφω	I turn (21, v-1b[1]) -, ἔστρεψα, -, -, ἐστράφην
7	σύ	you (singular) (1069, a-5a)
	συγγενής, -ές	adj: kindred (10, a-4a) noun: relative, kinsperson
	συζητέω	I discuss, dispute (10, cv-1d[2a]) (συνεζήτουν), -, -, -, -, -
	συκῆ, -ῆς, ἡ	fig tree (16, n-1h)
	συλλαμβάνω	I take, conceive (16, cv-3a[2b]) συλλήμψομαι, συνέλαβον, συνείληφα, -, συνελήμφθην
	συμφέρω	I bring together (15, cv-1c[1]) (impersonally) it is profitable -, συνήνεγκα, -, -, -
10	σύν	dat: with (128, preposition)
18	συνάγω	I gather together, invite (59, cv-1b[2]) συνάξω, συνήγαγον, -, συνῆγμαι, συνήχθην
21	συναγωγή, -ῆς, ἡ	synagogue, meeting (56, n-1b)

σύνδουλος, -ου, ὁ	fellow slave (10, n-2a)
συνέδριον, -ου, τό	the Sanhedrin, a council (22, n-2c)
συνείδησις, -εως, ἡ	conscience (30, n-3e(5b)
συνεργός, -οῦ, ὁ	fellow worker (13, n-2a)
συνέρχομαι	I come together (30, cv-1b[2]) (συνηρχόμην), -, συνῆλθον, συνελήλυθα, -, -
συνέχω	I hold fast, oppress (12, cv-1b[2]) (συνειχόμην), συνέξω, συνέσχον, -, -, -
συνίημι	I understand (26, cv-6a) συνήσω, συνῆκα, -, -, -
συνίστημι	(transitive) I commend (16, cv-6a) (intransitive) I stand with, consist -, συνέστησα, συνέστηκα, -, - also formed as a regular verb, συνιστάνω
σφάζω	I slay (10, v-2a[2]) σφάξω, ἔσφαξα, -, ἔσφαγμαι, ἐσφάγην
σφόδρα	exceedingly (11, adverb)
σφραγίζω	I seal (15, v-2a[1]) -, ἐσφράγισα, -, ἐσφράγισμαι, ἐσφραγίσθην
σφραγίς, -ῖδος, ἡ	seal (16, n-3c[2])
σχίζω	I split (11, v-2a[1]) σχίσω, ἔσχισα, -, -, ἐσχίσθην
20 σῴζω	I save, deliver, rescue (106, v-2a[1]) (ἔσῳζον), σώσω, ἔσωσα, σέσωκα, σέσῳσμαι, ἐσώθην
10 σῶμα, -ματος, τό	body (142, n-3c[4])
σωτήρ, -ῆρος, ὁ	Savior (24, n-3f[2a])
σωτηρία, -ας, ἡ	salvation (45, n-1a)

ταῦ

τάλαντον, -ου, τό	talent (14, n-2c)
ταπεινόω	I humble (14, v-1d[3]) ταπεινώσω, ἐταπείνωσα, -, -, ἐταπεινώθην
ταράσσω	I trouble (18, v-2b) (ἐτάρασσον), -, ἐτάραξα, -, τετάραγμαι, ἐταράχθην
τάσσω	I arrange, appoint, order (10, v-2b) -, ἔταξα, -, τέταγμαι, -
ταχέως	quickly (15, adverb)
ταχύ	quickly (18, a-2a)
ταχύς, -εῖα, -ύ	quick, swift (13, a-2a)

14	τε	and (so), so (215, particle)
10	τέκνον, -ου, τό	child, descendant (99, n-2c)
	τέλειος, -α, -ον	complete, perfect, mature (19, a-1a[1])
	τελειόω	I fulfill, make perfect (23, v-1d[3]) -, ἐτελείωσα, τετελείωκα, τετελείωμαι, ἐτελειώθην
	τελευτάω	I die (13, v-1d[1a]) -, ἐτελεύτησα, τετελεύτηκα, -, -
	τελέω	I finish, fulfill (28, v-1d[2b]) τελέσω, ἐτέλεσα, τετέλεκα, τετέλεσμαι, ἐτελέσθην
	τέλος, -ους, τό	end (40, n-3d[2b])
	τελώνης, -ου, ὁ	taxgatherer (21, n-1f)
	τέρας, -ατος, τό	wonder (16, n-3c[6a])
	τεσσαράκοντα	forty (15, n-3g[2], indeclinable)
	τέσσαρες, -ων	four (30, a-4b[2])
	τέταρτος, -η, -ον	fourth (10, a-1a[2a])
17	τηρέω	I keep, guard, observe (70, v-1d[2a]) (ἐτήρουν), τηρήσω, ἐτήρησα, τετήρηκα, τετήρημαι, ἐτηρήθην
35	τίθημι	I put, place (100, v-6a) (ἐτίθην), θήσω, ἔθηκα, τέθεικα, τέθειμαι, ἐτέθην
	τίκτω	I give birth to (18, v-1b[2]) τέξομαι, ἔτεκον, -, -, ἐτέχθην
	τιμάω	I honor (21, v-1d[1a]) τιμήσω, ἐτίμησα, -, τετίμημαι, -
	τιμή, -ῆς, ἡ	honor, price (41, n-1b)
	τίμιος, -α, -ον	precious, honorable (13, a-1a[1])
	Τιμόθεος, -ου, ὁ	Timothy (24, n-2a)
10	τις, τι	someone, something, a certain one, a certain thing, anyone, anything (526, a-4b[2])
10	τίς, τί	who? what? which? why? (555, a-4b[2])
	Τίτος, -ου, ὁ	Titus (13, n-2a)
31	τοιοῦτος, -αύτη, -οῦτον	such, of such a kind (57, a-1a[2b])
	τολμάω	I dare (16, v-1d[1a]) (ἐτόλμων), τολμήσω, ἐτόλμησα, -, -, -
18	τόπος, -ου, ὁ	place, location (94, n-2a)
	τοσοῦτος, -αύτη, -οῦτον	singular: so great, so much (20, a-1a[2b]) plural: so many
16	τότε	then, thereafter (160, adverb)
	τράπεζα, -ης, ἡ	table (15, n-1c)
27	τρεῖς, τρία	three (68, a-4a)

	τρέχω	I run (20, v-1b[2]) (ἔτρεχον), -, ἔδραμον, -, -, -
	τριάκοντα	thirty (11, n-3g[2])
	τρίς	thrice (12, adverb)
9	τρίτος, -η, -ον	third (56, a-1a[2a])
	τρόπος, -ου, ὁ	manner, way (13, n-2a)
	τροφή, -ῆς, ἡ	food (16, n-1b)
	τυγχάνω	I obtain, happen (12, v-3a[2b]) -, ἔτυχον, τέτευχα, -, -
	τύπος, -ου, ὁ	mark, example (15, n-2a)
	τύπτω	I smite or strike (13, v-4) (ἔτυπτον), -, -, -, -, -
	Τύρος, -ου, ὁ	Tyre (11, n-2b)
16	τυφλός, -ή, -όν	blind (50, a-1a[2a])

ὖ ψιλόν

	ὑγιαίνω	I am in good health (12, v-2d[4])
	ὑγιής, -ές	whole, healthy (12, a-4a)
10	ὕδωρ, ὕδατος, τό	water (76, n-3c[6b])
7	υἱός, -οῦ, ὁ	son, descendant (377, n-2a)
11	ὑμεῖς	you (1840, a-5a)
	ὑμέτερος, -α, -ον	your (11, a-1a[1])
24	ὑπάγω	I depart (79, cv-1b[2]) (ὑπῆγον), -, -, -, -, -
	ὑπακοή, -ῆς, ἡ	obedience (15, n-1b)
	ὑπακούω	I obey (21, cv-1a[8]) (ὑπήκουον), -, ὑπήκουσα, -, -, -
	ὑπαντάω	I meet, go to meet (10, cv-1d[1a]) (ὑπήντων), -, -, -, -, -
34	ὑπάρχω	I am, exist (60, cv-1b[2]) (ὑπῆρχον), -, -, -, -, - τά ὑπάρχοντα: one's belongings
12	ὑπέρ	gen: in behalf of (150, preposition) acc: above
	ὑπηρέτης, -ου, ὁ	servant, assistant (20, n-1f)
8	ὑπό	gen: by (220, preposition) acc: under
	ὑπόδημα, -ατος, τό	sandal, shoe (10, n-3c[4])
	ὑποκάτω	under, below, down at (11, adverb)

ὑποκριτής, -οῦ, ὁ	hypocrite (18, n-1f)
ὑπομένω	I tarry, endure (17, cv-1c[2]) -, ὑπέμεινα, ὑπομεμένηκα, -, -
ὑπομονή, -ῆς, ἡ	steadfast endurance (32, n-1b)
ὑποστρέφω	I return (35, cv-1b[1]) (ὑπέστρεφον), ὑποστρέψω, ὑπέστρεψα, -, -, -
ὑποτάσσω	I subject, put in subjection (38, cv-2b) -, ὑπέταξα, -, ὑποτέταγμαι, ὑπετάγην
ὑστερέω	I lack (16, v-1d[2a]) -, ὑστέρησα, ὑστέρηκα, ὑστέρημαι, ὑστερήθην
ὕστερον	later, afterwards (11, adverb)
ὕστερος	latter, finally (12, a-1a[1])
ὑψηλός, -ή, -όν	high (11, a-1a[2a])
ὕψιστος, -η, -ον	highest (13, a-1a[2a])
ὑψόω	I lift up, exalt (20, v-1d[3]) ὑψώσω, ὕψωσα, -, -, ὑψώθην

φῖ

	φαίνω	I shine, appear (31, v-2d[4]) φανήσομαι, ἔφανα, -, -, ἐφάνην
	φανερός, -ά, όν	manifest (18, a-1a[1])
	φανερόω	I make manifest (49, v-1d[3]) φανερώσω, ἐφανέρωσα, -, πεφανέρωμαι, ἐφανερώθην
21	Φαρισαῖος, -ου, ὁ	Pharisee (98, n-2a)
	φείδομαι	I spare (10, v-1b[3]) φείσομαι, ἐφεισάμην, -, -, -
29	φέρω	I carry, bear, lead (66, v-1c[1]) (ἔφερον), οἴσω, ἤνεγκα, ἐνήνοχα, ἐνήνεγμαι, ἠνέχθην
	φεύγω	I flee (29, v-1b[2]) φεύξομαι, ἔφυγον, πέφευγα, -, -
35	φημί	I say, affirm (66, v-6b) (ἔφη), -, ἔφη, -, -, -
	φιάλη, -ης, ἡ	cup, bowl (12, n-1b)
	φιλέω	I love (25, v-1d[2a]) (ἐφίλουν), -, ἐφίλησα, πεφίληκα, -, -
	Φίλιππος, -ου, ὁ	Philip (36, n-2a)
	φίλος, -η, -ον	loving (29, a-1a[2a]) (as a noun) a friend

24	φοβέομαι	I fear (95, v-1d[2a]) (ἐφοβούμην), -, -, -, -, ἐφοβήθην
	φόβος, -ου, ὁ	fear, terror (48, n-2a)
	φονεύω	I kill, murder (12, v-1a[6]) φονεύσω, ἐφόνευσα, -, -, -
	φρονέω	I think (26, v-1d[2a]) (ἐφρονούμην), φρονήσω, -, -, -, -
	φρόνιμος, -η, -ον	prudent (14, a-3a)
	φυλακή, -ῆς, ἡ	guard, a prison, a watch (47, n-1b)
	φυλάσσω	I guard (31, v-2b) φυλάξω, ἐφύλαξα, -, -, -
	φυλή, -ῆς, ἡ	tribe (31, n-1b)
	φύσις, -εως, ἡ	nature (14, n-3e[5b])
	φυτεύω	I plant (11, v-1a[6]) (ἐφύτευον), -, ἐφύτευσα, -, πεφύτευμαι, ἐφυτεύθην
	φωνέω	I call (43, v-1d[2a]) (ἐφώνουν), φωνήσω, ἐφώνησα, -, -, ἐφωνήθην
4	φωνή, -ῆς, ἡ	sound, noise, voice (139, n-1b)
10	φῶς, φωτός, τό	light (73, n-3c[6c])
	φωτίζω	I give light, enlighten (11, v-2a[1]) φωτίσω, ἐφώτισα, -, πεφώτισμαι, ἐφωτίσθην

χῖ

24	χαίρω	I rejoice (74, v-2d[2]) (ἔχαιρον), χαρήσομαι, -, -, -, ἐχάρην
16	χαρά, -ᾶς, ἡ	joy, delight (59, n-1a)
	χαρίζομαι	I give freely, forgive (23, v-2a[1]) χαρίσομαι, ἐχαρισάμην, -, κεχάρισμαι, ἐχαρίσθην
10	χάρις, -ιτος, ἡ	grace, favor, kindness (155, n-3c[1])
	χάρισμα, -ατος, τό	gift (17, n-3c[4])
14	χείρ, χειρός, ἡ	hand, arm, finger (177, n-3f[2a])
	χείρων, -ον	worse, more severe (11, a-4b[1])
	χήρα, -ας, ἡ	window (27, n-1a)
	χιλίαρχος, -ου, ὁ	captain, military tribune (22, n-2a)
	χιλιάς, -άδος, ἡ	thousand (23, n-3c[2])
	χίλιοι, -αι, -α	thousand (10, a-1a[1])
	χιτών, -ῶνος, ὁ	tunic (11, n-3f[1a])
	χοῖρος, -ου, ὁ	pig (12, n-2a)

	χορτάζω	I eat to the full, am satisfied, am filled (16, v-2a[1]) -, ἐχόρτασα, -, -, ἐχορτάσθην
	χόρτος, -ου, ὁ	grass, hay (15, n-2a)
	χράομαι	I use (11, v-1d[1a]) (ἐχρώμην), -, ἐχρησάμην, -, κέχρημαι, -
	χρεία, -ας, ἡ	need (49, n-1a)
	χρηστότης, -ητος, ἡ	goodness, kindness (10, n-3c[1])
4	Χριστός, -οῦ, ὁ	Christ, Messiah, Anointed One (529, n-2a)
21	χρόνος, -ου, ὁ	time (54, n-2a)
	χρύσεος, -α, -ον	golden (18, a-1b)
	χρυσίον, -ου, τό	gold (12, n-2c)
	χρυσός, -οῦ, ὁ	gold (10, n-2a)
	χωλός, -ή, -όν	lame (14, a-1a[2a])
	χώρα, -ας, ἡ	country (28, n-1a)
	χωρέω	I make room, give way (10, v-1d[2a])* χωρήσω, ἐχώρησα, κεχώρηκα, -, -
	χωρίζω	I separate, depart (13, v-2a[1]) χωρίσω, ἐχώρισα, -, κεχώρισμαι, ἐχωρίσθην
	χωρίον, -ου, τό	place, field (10, n-2c)
	χωρίς	without, apart from (41, adverb or improper prep. with the genitive)

ψῖ

	ψεύδομαι	I lie (12, v-1b[3]) ψεύσομαι, ἐψευσάμην, -, -, -
	ψευδοπροφήτης, -ου, ὁ	false prophet (11, n-1f)
	ψεῦδος, -ους, τό	lie (10, n-3d[2b])
	ψεύστης, -ου, ὁ	liar (10, n-1f)
14	ψυχή, -ῆς, ἡ	soul, life, self (103, n-1b)

ὦ μέγα

	ὦ	O! (17, n-3g[2])
11	ὧδε	here (61, adverb)
6	ὥρα, -ας, ἡ	hour, occasion, moment (106, n-1a)
18	ὡς	as, like, when, that, how, about (504, adverb)
	ὡσαύτως	likewise (17, adverb)

	ὡσεί	as, like, about (21, particle)
	ὥσπερ	just as, even as (36, particle)
7	ὥστε	therefore, so that (83, particle)
	ὠφελέω	I profit (15, v-1d[2a])
		ὠφελήσω, ὠφέλησα, -, -, ὠφελήθην

Index

This index was included in the fourth printing of the textbook. It is available as a separate document at the Internet web site mentioned on page xvii.

Alternate Paradigms

While most have responded positively to viewing the final stem vowel of a first or second declension noun as being separate from the case ending, some have preferred the "normal" method. Therefore, in the fourth printing we have added the following paradigms. They parallel paradigms in the text, but they separate the stem vowel from the stem. If you prefer this method, then your students can reference these pages.

We have also included a few verb paradigms that are more traditional in orientation.

Summary to Chapter 6

	2 *masc*	1 *fem*	2 *neut*
nom sg	ος	α / η	ον
acc sg	ον	αν / ην	ον
nom pl	οι	αι	α
acc pl	ους	ας	α

	2 *masc*	1 *fem*	2 *neut*
nom sg	ὁ λόγος	ἡ γραφή ἡ ὥρα	τὸ ἔργον
acc sg	τὸν λόγον	τὴν γραφήν τὴν ὥραν	τὸ ἔργον
nom pl	οἱ λογοί	αἱ γραφαί αἱ ὧραι	τὰ ἔργα
acc pl	τοὺς λόγους	τὰς γραφάς τὰς ὥρας	τὰ ἔργα

7.6   All four case endings

	2 *masc*	1 *fem*	2 *neut*
nom sg	ος	α / η	ον
gen sg	ου	ας / ης	ου
dat sg[1]	ῳ	ᾳ / ῃ	ῳ
acc sg	ον	αν / ην	ον
nom pl	οι	αι	α
gen pl	ων	ων	ων
dat pl	οις	αις	οις
acc pl	ους	ας	α

---

1   In the singular (first and second declensions), the iota will always subscript. This is the only place in the noun system where the iota subscripts.

10.10   Master case ending chart

	first/second declension			*third declension*	
	masc	*fem*	*neut*	*masc/ fem*	*neut*
nom sg	ος	α η	ον	ς -	_ª
gen sg	ου	ας ης	ου	ος	ος
dat sg	ῳ	ᾳ ῃ	ῳ	ιᵇ	ι
acc sg	ον	αν ην	ον	α/νᶜ	-
nom pl	οι	αι	α	ες	αᵈ
gen pl	ων	ων	ων	ων	ων
dat pl	οις	αις	οις	σι(ν)ᵉ	σι(ν)
acc pl	ους	ας	α	αςᶠ	α

a. Be prepared for the final stem letter to undergo changes (rule 8).

b. Because third declension stems end in a consonant, the iota cannot subscript as iota does in the first and second declensions; so it remains on the line.

c. The case ending alternates between alpha and nu.

d. As opposed to the first and second declensions, this alpha is an actual case ending and not a changed stem vowel. This is also true of the accusative plural.

e. The nu is a movable nu. Notice that the ending σι is a flipped version of ις found in the first and second declensions.

f. As opposed to the first declension (e.g., ὥρα), the alpha here is part of the case ending.

21.14   Four main verbal paradigms

	primary tenses		secondary tenses	
active voice	λύ ω	(ω)	ἔλυον	(ον)
	λύ εις	(εις)	ἔλυες	(ες)
	λύ ει	(ει)	ἔλυε(ν)	(ε)
	λύ ομεν	(ομεν)	ἐλύομεν	(ομεν)
	λύ ετε	(ετε)	ἐλύετε	(ετε)
	λύ ουσι(ν)	(ουσι)	ἔλυον	(ον)
middle/passive voice	λύ ομαι	(ομαι)	ἐλυόμην	(ομην)
	λύ ῃ	(ῃ)	ἐλύου	(ου)
	λύ εται	(εται)	ἐλύετο	(ετο)
	λυ όμεθα	(ομεθα)	ἐλυόμεθα	(ομεθα)
	λύ εσθε	(εσθε)	ἐλύεσθε	(εσθε)
	λύ ονται	(ονται)	ἐλύοντο	(οντο)

CD-ROM Instructions

Contents

Following are the items you will find on the enclosed CD-ROM. Please watch Teknia's web site for updates, at www.teknia.com.

1. *Learning the Basics of Biblical Greek.* This program pronounces the vocabulary words and suggests mnemonic devices to aid your memory (Macintosh and Windows 95/98). Some of these devices are revolutionary, such as using hymns, and we are constantly working on more. It also includes a greeting from Bill Mounce.

2. *Teknia Language Tools* (Windows 3.1 and Windows 95/98). *TLT* combines *FlashWorks* and *ParseWorks* to drill your vocabulary and parsing. See their description on page xvi.

   The two versions of *TLT* are roughly equivalent, although we have stopped development of the 3.1 version. *TLT* for Windows 95/98 will continue to be upgraded. In the "Teknia/Flash15" subdirectory there is an earlier version of the FlashWorks installer (Windows 3.1) that can still fit on a floppy.

   The CD-ROM contains earlier versions of *FlashWorks* and *ParseWorks* for the Macintosh. We are working on a Mac version of *TLT;* watch Teknia's web site for progress.

3. A demo version of Zondervan's Bible reference software is on this CD-ROM. Other resources such as the *Expositor's Bible Commentary* can be purchased from this CD-ROM by calling JLS Direct, an authorized Zondervan software dealer, at 1-800-332-0601.

Installation: Windows

When you insert the CD-ROM into a Windows machine, the "Browser" will load automatically. (If it does not, double click on the file "Launch.exe.") From the screen that appears you have several choices:

1. "Launch Learning the Basics of Biblical Greek" starts the vocabulary program. This can also be started by double clicking on "Learning/ Lbbg.exe" from the Windows Explorer window. (Windows 95 only.)

   Please see the help information by clicking the "HELP" button in the lower right corner of the screen. It will show you how to move around the program.

2. "Install Teknia Language Tools" launches the appropriate installer. (Windows 95/98 users should choose the Windows 95 option.) From that point, please follow the on-screen instructions. You can also run the installers by

double clicking on "Teknia/Win95/Setup.exe" (Windows 95/98) or "Teknia /Win31/Setup.exe" (Windows 3.1).

Notice #1 for Windows 95 Users: If you have a previous copy of *TLT* installed on your Windows 95 computer, you should save the database ("Flashwrk.mdb") if you wish (since it may contain your specific information, such as word difficulties), remove the current version of *TLT* using "Start > Settings > Control Panel > Add/Remove Programs," reboot your computer, and install the new version. If you saved your previous database, then delete the newly installed database ("Flashworks.mdb"), copy your old database into the new directory, and run *TLT*. It will recognize what you have done and update the file for you.

Notice #2 for Windows 3.1 Users: The installer does not load the Greek font into your system. You must do this yourself *before* starting *TLT*. Please see your Windows instructions if you do not know how to install fonts.

3. "Zondervan Reference Software" allows you to install a demo version of *The NIV Study Bible Basic Library*." You can also double click on "Zrs-demo /Setup.exe." Double clicking on "Unlock/Setup.exe" allows you to purchase locked databases such as the *Expositor's Bible Commentary*.

4. "Register your product" allows you to register your software if you have an internet connection.

5. "Who to contact" gives you support information if you need help on any of the software.

6. Clicking on the "Professor" takes you to Teknia's web site (if you have an internet connection). Keep watch there for updates and other language tools.

Installation: Macintosh

Inside the CD-ROM there are four folders.

1. Inside "Learning the Basics" is the single file "LEARNING.BBG." Double click it to start the vocabulary program.

   Please see the help information by clicking the "HELP" button in the lower right corner of the screen. It will show you how to move around the program.

2. The "FlashWorks" directory can be dragged to your hard disk or a floppy. Install the Greek font ("Mounce") and run the program.

3. The "ParseWorks" directory can be dragged to your hard disk or a floppy. Install the Greek font ("Mounce") and run the program.

4. "Accordance Catalog" gives you information on a great Bible search program for the Macintosh, which now includes Zondervan reference material.

System Requirements

Learning the Basics of Biblical Greek

Windows 95: Intel Pentium processor or compatible; Windows 95, Windows 98, Windows NT 4 or later; 12 MB of available RAM; Windows-compatible sound card; VGA 640x480 or higher-resolution screen supported by Microsoft Windows; CD-ROM.

LBBG requires that the file "msvcrt.dll" be installed with Windows. If your system does not have it, run the file "MSVCRT.EXE" found in the "Learning" subdirectory to install it.

Macintosh: PowerPC; System 7.5.3 or later; 12 MB of available RAM; 256 color 640 x 480 or higher-resolution screen; CD-ROM.

Teknia Language Tools

Windows 95: Pentium 90 MHz or higher microprocessor; VGA 640x480 or higher-resolution screen supported by Microsoft Windows; 24MB of available RAM; 4MB hard disk space; CD-ROM.

Windows 3.1: 80386 or higher processor; VGA 640x480 or higher-resolution screen supported by Microsoft Windows; 4-6 MB of available RAM; 4MB hard disk space; CD-ROM.

Macintosh: System 7.

Technical Support

Zondervan's friendly, full-time technical support staff will be glad to help you with any *Zondervan Reference Software*-related problems. If you have trouble installing the program, please give our support team a call at (800) 925-0316, fax in at (616) 698-3221, or e-mail our staff at ztech@zph.com.

Zondervan's technicians are available from 8:00 a.m. to 5:00 p.m., Monday through Friday, Eastern Standard time. If you are using *The Basics of Biblical Greek* CD-ROM and run into difficulties, please follow these steps *before* calling. Our support personnel will be able to help you more quickly and accurately if you follow these steps.

1. Write down *exactly* what you are trying to do and what the program's responses are. Sometimes doing this will help you catch your mistake.

2. If any error messages have appeared, please write them down, word-for-word.

3. The most important step is to call from a phone near your computer. Usually our support team can solve your problem in a few minutes. It's a lot more difficult for them to help you if you are not able to talk on the phone and run the program at the same time.

For additional textbooks on New Testament Greek look for these outstanding titles.

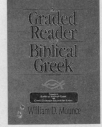